Main Street

Main Street

WINDSOR TO QUEBEC CITY

MAURICE YEATES

Published by
The Macmillan Company of Canada Limited
Toronto, Ontario, in association with the
Ministry of State for Urban Affairs
and Information Canada,
Ottawa, Canada,
1975.

ISBN 0-7705-1304-2 cloth
    0-7705-1305-0 paper
To be published in French under the title
La grand' rue: Québec à Windsor
ISBN 0-7705-1450-6

Printed in Canada

FOREWORD

More than half the population of Canada lives along the lower Great Lakes and the St. Lawrence between Windsor and Quebec City. Therefore, for the majority of Canadians this book is about where they live.

My own roots are in this area and I am very much conscious of its problems and opportunities. In this area, we face the problems of growth and its management. We also face questions associated with multi-culturalism, highlighted by the fact that more than one-third of the area's population is francophone. But these characteristics are challenges and opportunities for the axis itself and also for Confederation. The problems of growth are the problems of prosperity, and this prosperity makes it easier for us to attempt to make a better living place. Similarly, the richness of our cultural heritage affords us not only the opportunity of creating a more diversified society offering a wider range of opportunities for individual expression, advancement and self-fulfilment, but also the potential for enhancing the bi-cultural character of our nation.

For the rest of the country, what is the interest in this book? This "Main Street" has had both failures and triumphs. It is, therefore, an area from which others can learn and benefit. It is geographically and economically related to the northeastern United States, one of the largest markets for Canada's exports. It is also the service centre, the industrial centre and the central market of the nation. In these capacities the area benefits all Canadians. Finally, whether this area is home or faraway "Central Canada", we must all question the extent to which it should continue to grow and the extent to which it should be allowed to become dominant in terms of its concentration of people and economic activity. This is an issue of overwhelming importance for all Canadians.

This book helps me to address all these questions and I am sure others will benefit from Professor Yeates' insights into so many of the major issues facing the nation.

Barney Danson,
Minister of State for Urban Affairs,
Ottawa, 1975

This book is dedicated to my wife
Marilynn
and my children
Maurine and Harry.

CONTENTS

Acknowledgements xi
Preface xiii
1 The Form of the Axis 1
2 Growth, Expansion and Convergence 37
3 The Use of the Land 79
4 Housing 114
5 The Economic Structure of the Area 146
6 Interaction 191
7 Channels of Interaction 228
8 Structure and Finance 262
9 The Axis in the Year 2001 303
10 Summary and Conclusion 341
References 363
Appendices A 376
         B 428
         C 430

ACKNOWLEDGEMENTS

This book could not have been produced without the assistance and advice of many people. In Ottawa, Dr. C.I. Jackson, Director of the Planning and Evaluation Division at the Ministry of State for Urban Affairs, was an efficient yet sympathetic liaison person. In Kingston, my secretary, Edithe Béchard, was an ideal coordinator who kept the group cheerful and the work up-to-date. Jim Oeppen prepared the material for two chapters and provided the necessary computer programming skills. Mike Williams compiled the material for one chapter and organized the land-use survey, and Geoff Bannister prepared the population projection. The illustrations were prepared under the direction of Dr. H. Castner by Ross Hough and Elizabeth Goodson in the Queen's University Cartographic Laboratory. A host of students assisted with other facets of the data collection and organization; they included: Mary Malcolm, Chris Maziarski, Tim Reynolds, David Ducette, Jean Cooper, Brian Crawford, Donna Hackett, Nick Hally, Vena Jules, Fred J. Munn, Jean Munn, John Zakos.

Apart from the individuals named above, many others assisted by either "opening doors" or providing material. These people usually remain anonymous, but in this case they should be mentioned; without their support the task would have been quite impossible. The list of names is long and is presented in alphabetical order:

Mr. P.L. Appleton, Consultant; Mr. R. Baxter, Chief, Labour Force Survey Division, Statistics Canada; Professeur M. Bélanger, Université de Montréal (now Université Laval); M.M. Bérard, Directeur, Service de la Géographie, Ministère de la Voirie; Mlle Thérèse Bienvenue, Service de l'Habitation et de l'Urbanisme, Montréal; Mr. S. Clasky, Director, Regional Development Branch, Ontario; Mr. H. Crown, ARDA, Toronto; Dr. N. Drummond, McGill University; M.A. Dumas,

Chef, Division de la Recherche, Ministère de l'Industrie et du Commerce, Québec; Mr. D. Gierman, Lands Directorate, Environment Canada; Mrs. Amy Kempster, Chief, Department of Social and Economic Statistics, Statistics Canada; Mr. J. Kirkland, CMHC, Ottawa; Mr. M. Klein, Head, Regional Statistics Unit, Primary and Manufacturing Industries Statistics Division, Statistics Canada; Dr. R.R. Krueger, University of Waterloo; Professeur A. Lajoie, Université de Montréal; M.J. Lefebvre, Chef, Service de la Géographie, Statistics Canada; M.J.-M. Lévesque, Labour Force Survey Division, Statistics Canada; M. André Lord, Géographe, Ministère des Affaires Municipales; Mr. D.E. McFarland, Head, Area Transportation System Office, Ministry of Transportation and Communications, Toronto; Mr. I.H. Midgley, Director, Economic Analysis Branch, Department of Regional Economic Expansion, Ottawa; Mme Quesnel-Ouellet, Université Laval; Professeur J. Raveneau, Université Laval; Dr. B. Robert, Directeur, Division de la Démographie, Bureau de la Statistique du Québec; Dr. L.H. Russwurm, University of Waterloo; Professor R.D. Seale, University of Windsor; Mr. K. Simpson, Geography Division, Statistics Canada; Mrs. L. Sing, Data Dissemination Section, Statistics Canada; Mr. J.O. Spender, Coordinator, Special Projects, Regional Development Branch; Mr. Emrik Suiches, Intergovernmental Committee on Urban and Regional Research, Toronto; Mr. W.D. Winkworth, Ministry of Transport and Communications, Ontario; Mrs. Jeanne Wolfe, SATRA, Montréal.

Maurice Yeates
Kingston, March 1974

PREFACE

A book such as this takes many years of effort, and the published version is never the final version. This particular work was commissioned by the Ministry of State for Urban Affairs, and as a consequence, there was a definite time limit for completion of the project. The research commenced on September 1, 1972, and the final submission was due by March 31, 1974. The work schedule was originally designed to incorporate a large body of material from the 1971 Census of Canada, which should have been released during 1972 and 1973. Unfortunately, there were delays in the release of the census material, with the result that many parts of the work could not be undertaken as originally planned. In particular, 1971 data concerning the socio-economic characteristics of the population, journey-to-work information, and inter-county migration flows, have not been included within the research design, as was originally planned.

The result is that much time and effort have been spent circumventing the data difficulties by using other sources of information, such as the Province of Québec fiscal migration tables and the federal labour force survey estimates. These other sources are not, however, nearly as satisfactory as the census information would have been, so the work is something less than I had planned. But it was an interesting exercise for an academic, who had other responsibilities for much of the time, to meet a deadline in an information-world that was less perfect than expected. Of course, social-scientists always expect the worst as far as information quality is concerned, but I had hoped that the delays would not have been as severe as they have been.

A second prefatory note concerns the time period covered by the study. All of the comments relate to changes in the 1961–71 period, with the latter date referred to in the text as if it were yesterday. The result is that some of the statements may now appear outdated, for events since 1971 could well lead to alterations and modifications. Again, this situation is to be expected and must be accepted by the reader as a controlling parameter. In fact, it may be instructive to observe the number of statements and observations that need to be modified in the light of the experience of the first half of the 1970s, since one of the more remarkable gifts of man is his ability to accept rapid change as the expected norm.

A final prefatory note relates to the geographic scale at which this study is undertaken, for the scale determines the kind of statements which are made. In this context scale refers to the level of aggregation at which the research is conducted. Stated in another way, it is the distance from which a viewer perceives a subject, because the distance influences what a person actually sees. For example, if a jar is examined from a short distance it may be possible to see the variations in the colours and the intricacies of the design, but viewed from a greater distance all that can be seen is the outline of the jar and the general hue of the colours. In geographic analyses, an urban area can be studied in fine microscopic detail, with each house differentiated; at a neighbourhood scale, where variations between neighbourhoods are examined; or at a scale embracing entire urban areas or regions. In this volume, the analysis is undertaken at the macro, or larger scale; we are not interested in patterns of change that have occurred within specific urban areas, but in general changes that have occurred throughout the large Windsor to Québec City urban region. The analysis is structured to be at the macro level by the choice of census subdivisions as the recording unit for much of the information-base. There are occasions where within metropolitan areas variations are used to illustrate a particular concept, but these examples are few in number.

Though these cautionary prefatory comments must be made, they should not be interpreted as suggestive of despair by the author. In fact, I have been greatly exhilarated by the task, and though I might think long and hard before doing it again, I am nevertheless grateful to those who sponsored the study. The project was both an opportunity and an education, and, as such, it was a pleasant personal experience.

Maurice Yeates
Kingston
March 1974

1 THE FORM OF THE AXIS

Domination, or who owns what, appears to be one of the central issues in Canada. In Toronto and Montréal there is much discussion of the degree to which the multinational corporations, predominantly U.S.-owned, control the Canadian economy. In the west and the Atlantic provinces this discussion is subtly different, for it embraces not only a concern for the extent of U.S. control, but also concern for the degree of influence exerted by Toronto and Montréal. This concern is manifest in the suspicion of westerners and Maritimers who contend that even if the influence of foreign-owned corporations is reduced, it will only be replaced by increased influence of firms based in southern Ontario or the Montréal region. Of course, the main difference between the two forms of domination is that the former (existent) is foreign domination whereas the latter is domestic.

Our concern is not with the problems of the multinational corporation, but with domination, for the very essence of urbanism in Canada (and most of the world for that matter) revolves around a hierarchy of influence. This hierarchy is derived naturally from our adherence to an economic system that is, in effect, supportive of a stratified society. The fact that Canadian society is stratified has been well documented by Porter (1965) but the direct impact of the prevailing economic system on the urban system has not been so clearly demonstrated. The rationale for this inter-relationship is expressed very well by Harvey, when he states that "Cities, as historians of the phenomena are never tired of emphasizing, are founded upon the extraction of a surplus product" (Harvey, 1972, p. 6).

The means of achieving this surplus is specialization. Farmers do not try to produce all their physical needs from the land, they concentrate their production on a few crops which can be grown as efficiently as possible. These are then sold to wholesalers living in urban areas, who market the commodity and provide the farmers with the money to purchase the rest of their needs. In theory, if too much is produced the price of the commodity falls, and if too little is produced the price rises. These price changes are allowed to occur only within a limited range; price support and farm subsidy programs limit the amount below which prices are allowed to fall. Thus, the collecting and market organizing places, the urban areas, obtain the surplus, redistribute this surplus, and also keep the farmers in business if the natural market price appears to be falling below the minimal level considered desirable.

In a similar fashion our natural resources are used to generate a surplus which can be appropriated by urban areas. For example, petroleum and natural gas are extracted using capital and equipment generated in urban areas. The product is then either used for further production within urban areas, or consumed, or exported. If part of the product is exported, the foreign capital earned can be used to import goods to be purchased by the inhabitants of the exporting country. They are able to pay for these goods through the income they receive from organizing the exploitation of the natural resource, processing, and marketing the product. The problem with the petroleum industry (and agriculture) is that so few people are required to produce such a high value product that very little employment is created through the production process. Thus, in a society in which a person is required to work to receive income, the lack of employment opportunities can cause grave economic (and psychological) hardships.

Fortunately, urban areas have developed a series of mechanisms to generate employment, most of which, to one degree or another, are needed. Machinery and equipment have to be manufactured to provide the surplus generating activities with the facilities that contribute toward making them so efficient. The marketing, redistribution, processing and financial investment institutions have to be organized to facilitate the necessary exchanges. Government has to be organized to look after the internal and external needs of society. An educational system is needed to provide the necessary array of specialist skills for future production and organization. These, and many other institutions are located within urban areas because of the need for proximity. For example, a manager's secretary has to be located in the manager's office or close to it if they are to work together with any degree of efficiency. This desire for proximity in the redistributive, processing and organizational aspects of society gives rise to urban areas, and those urban areas which can appropriate the greatest share of these activities will become the largest.

There is competition, therefore, among urban areas for the redistributive, processing, and organizational functions of society, and cities use a variety of techniques to achieve dominance in this competitive situation. The most important techniques in a country the size of ours relate to communication, which, in this particular context, is regarded as ranging from highways, railroads, air traffic and telephone to the media in general. The existence of a highway and railroad network system constructed to focus on a particular urban area means that that city will have greater accessibility to the surrounding area than any other city. A more concrete example is the limited-access highway system which focuses on Toronto: the Macdonald-Cartier Freeway connects Toronto to Montréal but by-passes Ottawa. This limited-access highway, financed by public funds, in effect subsidizes truck haulage, and by reducing road time between the two cities to six and a half hours, emphasizes their dominance over the area between them. Institutions and services which may have been established in smaller urban areas to serve the local market will now locate either in Toronto or in Montréal, since the good road connections enable them to serve the metropolitan and smaller markets simultaneously. Similarly, an airline network focusing on Toronto and Montréal is indicative of the control that these urban areas exert over the rest of the nation.

The media (television, radio, newspapers, magazines, books, etc.) exert a more subtle, but probably more powerful, dominating force, because they are concerned with creating images. If these image-making forces cluster in one or two larger cities, and if they adopt the parochial attitudes, views, and values of the particular region in which they are located, then these images are "sold" to the country as a whole. Thus, by inference, the source of the image is also "sold", and the values of other parts of the country are negated or ignored. Therefore, it is not surprising that the image of Toronto as "the place to be" is oversold across the English-speaking parts of the nation, whereas that of Montréal remains confined largely to Québec. This may well have been the most potent underlying force behind the tremendous net migration from the rest of Canada to the Toronto region during the 1960s.

Dominance of one area over another is not to be feared as long as society recognizes its existence, agrees that it is necessary, and accepts as morally justifiable the methods by which it is achieved. It is the purpose of this monograph to document the extent of the domination of the urban areas between Windsor and Québec City over the Canadian economy, to examine variations in the extent of urbanism within this axis, to indicate ways in which these internal and external patterns of urban dominance are changing, and to comment upon possible future patterns which may be emerging.

THE AREA DEFINED

This study is concerned with the area between Windsor and Québec City which, because of its linearity and important supportive role to Canada, is described as an "axis". Ray (1971, p. 39) refers to the area anatomically as the "heartland" of Canada, Racine (1972, p. 108) notes that it contains the "centre of the country," Whebell (1969) analyses it as the archetypal "corridor" from which all innovations diffuse outwards, and Bourne and MacKinnon (1972) describe it quite categorically as "Central" Canada. The word "axis" is preferred, however, because it describes the shape of the area as well as its key position in Canadian economic, social, and cultural life. A similar argument is presented in the Report of the La Haye Commission (1968), in which the Montréal-Québec-Sherbrooke triangle is defined as an axis. The Windsor to Québec City area can also be considered an axis in the socio-political sense, for in its spatial transformation it becomes an area around which the two basic culture groups of Canada operate an economic and political *entente*.

The boundaries of the axis are shown in Figure 1.1. These boundaries contain an area of 67,567 square miles, which (quoting comparisons from our major cultural influences) is larger than the combined total areas of England and Wales, the same size as the state of Washington, and one-third the area of France. Its shape is that of a rectangle 650 to 750 miles long and 100 to 150 miles wide. The southern and western boundaries are very easy to define, for they correspond to the Georgian Bay, Lake Huron, Lake St. Clair, Lake Erie, Lake Ontario, the St. Lawrence River, and the Canada-U.S.A. border in Québec.

The northern and eastern boundaries do not have such a clear physical and political basis for their establishment. A number of

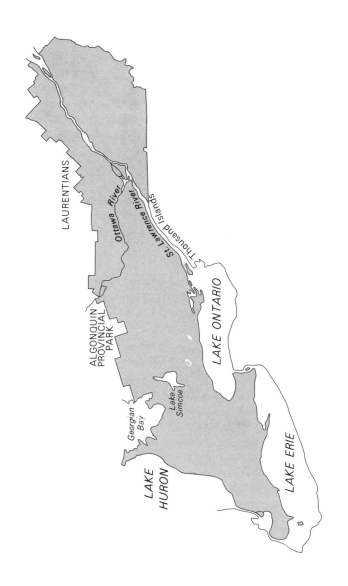

Figure 1.1: The boundaries of the axis

factors have been taken into consideration: population densities, physical constraints, functional regions (or spheres of influence), along with a strong dose of realism, meaning that, for statistical purposes, it is undoubtedly useful to have as many complete census divisions (counties) as possible. These various criteria are discussed individually in the following sections. The result of these series of qualitative judgments is that the eastern boundary is defined as the eastern limits of Montmagny and Montmorency No. 1 counties, which also coincide with the rather important eastern limits of the St. Lawrence Lowland area in Québec.

The northern boundary is also located as rationally as possible, but the reader will be excused if he dismisses the logic as another case of academic fast-penmanship. From Georgian Bay almost as far east as the Ottawa River, the boundary follows census division lines, with Algonquin Provincial Park acting as a buffer zone between northern and southern Ontario. This formal census line approximates closely the northern limits of the sphere of influence of Toronto, Peterborough, and Ottawa (Marshall, 1972, p. 80; Carol, 1969; Dean, 1969, Pl. 52). The county boundary lines are not followed from the southeastern corner of Algonquin Park to the Ottawa River because the northern prong of Renfrew County contains an area which is just as much within the sphere of influence of North Bay (outside the axis), as of Ottawa (inside the axis). Also, the boundary line crosses the river at a point which coincides rather closely with the sphere of influence of Hull as defined by the Ministère de l'Industrie et du Commerce (1967). Thus, in Renfrew County two census subdivisions (which in Ontario are usually referred to as townships) are excluded from the area included within the axis belt.

In the province of Québec the northern boundary of the axis follows, in general, the "Zone d'Influence des Centres Principaux" as defined by the Ministère de l'Industrie et du Commerce (1967). This boundary also coincides rather closely with the northern limit of the St. Lawrence Lowland physiographic region and that of relatively continuous human habitation. Unfortunately, this definition results in the partitioning of a number of census divisions (counties) north of the St. Lawrence River, because their elongated northwest-southwest parallel alignment (a relic of seigneurial land subdivision) lies at right angles to this zonal line. Thus, a portion of the area of most counties north of the Ottawa and St. Lawrence Rivers is excluded. A complete list of counties included, with the proportions of their 1971 populations that are excluded in parentheses, is attached as Table 1.1. This defined area contains the current population of the Windsor to Québec City axis, and will contain its future configuration.

POPULATION DENSITY IN 1971

Within this rather large area is found the greater part of the population of Canada. One of the more entertaining exercises of social-demographers is that of defining what is meant by urban population. The problem is quite straightforward in areas that can be clearly defined as urban, but is difficult to solve around the fringes of urban areas where families supported by urban and those supported by non-urban employment are intermingled. Fortunately, this dilemma can be avoided by using the definitions of rural, semi-rural, semi-urban, and urban developed by Russwurm (1970, p. 17–18) for the Toronto

Table 1.1: Census divisions (counties) included within the axis area

QUEBEC:
Argenteuil, Arthabaska, Bagot, Beauce, Beauharnois, Bellechasse, Berthier (10.23%), Brome, Chambly, Champlain (14.83%), Châteauguay, Compton, Deux-Montagnes, Dorchester, Drummond, Frontenac, Gatineau (31.45%), Hull, Huntingdon, Iberville, Joliette (0.04%), Laprairie, L'Assomption, Lévis, Lotbinière, Maskinongé (3%), Mégantic, Missisquoi, Montcalm (0.82%), Montmagny, Montmorency No. 1 (4.18%), Montmorency No. 2, Montréal et Ile Jésus, Napierville, Nicolet, Papineau, Pontiac (5.59%), Portneuf, Québec (0.22%), Richelieu, Richmond, Rouville, St-Hyacinthe, St-Jean, St-Maurice, Shefford, Sherbrooke, Soulanges, Stanstead, Terrebonne, Vaudreuil, Verchères, Wolfe, Yamaska.

ONTARIO:
Brant, Bruce, Dufferin, Dundas, Durham, Elgin, Essex, Frontenac, Grenville, Grey, Haldimand, Haliburton, Halton, Hastings, Huron, Kent, Lambton, Lanark, Leeds, Lennox and Addington, Metropolitan Toronto Area, Middlesex, Muskoka, Niagara, Norfolk, Northumberland, Ontario, Ottawa-Carleton, Oxford, Peel, Perth, Peterborough, Prescott, Prince Edward, Renfrew (10.24%), Russell, Simcoe, Stormont, Victoria, Waterloo, Wellington, Wentworth, York.

Note: Proportion of population of county excluded from axis area in parentheses.
Source: Statistics Canada.

to Stratford area. In this area, Russwurm notes that the farm population has remained fairly constant over a number of decades at around a mean of nineteen to twenty persons per square mile. Thus, he defines as *rural* an area that has a population of twenty-five persons per square mile or less. A second critical value is determined as forty-nine persons per square mile, for at this density an area changes from one in which the population is invariably at least half non-farm to one in which it is more than half non-farm. Thus the category range of twenty-five to forty-nine persons per square mile is defined as *semi-rural*.

The third critical value determined by Russwurm is extremely important for it portions these areas which could be defined generally as "urbanized" into semi-urban and urban. This value is calculated as one which distinguishes an area having more than twenty-five residence parcels per square mile concerned with urban activities from one which has less. Twenty-five urban residence parcels per square mile is approximately one urban residence parcel for every twenty-five acres; this density implies that the facilities of general urban servicing are required. Assuming four persons per residence, an urban population density of 100 persons per square mile can be derived, and to this must be added the mean rural density of nineteen to twenty persons per square mile. Consequently, the third critical value is 119 persons per square mile, and areas with a density between fifty and 119 persons per square mile are defined as *semi-urban*, and those with a density greater than 119 persons per square mile are defined as *urban*. Not surprisingly, Russwurm demonstrates that although many factors mixed in a variety of complex ways may be used to delimit the outer boundary of the urban fringe, a minimum population density of fifty persons per square mile appears to be the best single indicator.

Although these categories are accepted on the basis of Russwurm's persuasive argument and some more general evidence (Trotier, 1966, feuille 2; Thoman and Yeates, 1966, pp. 13–17), it is probably wise to reiterate that these are general definitions that pertain to areas. If accepted, they enable a researcher to make general statements about an area, and in dealing with density figures the area over which the figure applies is crucial. Density figures pertain to entire areas, and they suggest that the stated density applies to the whole area uniformly. Thus it is desirable to have the areas to which they pertain as homogeneous as possible with respect to the characteristic being examined and the purpose for which the information is to be used. Furthermore, as densities are vitally influenced by variation in size of area, the areas should be as close in size as possible. The ninety-eight counties (census divisions) and part counties are fairly useless data units because the areas to which they pertain are rarely homogeneous. For a study area of the size of the Windsor to Québec City axis, probably the most useful statistical unit is the census subdivision. Each census division is divided into a number of census subdivisions; in Ontario these subdivisions usually coincide with township boundaries, and in Québec, they invariably coincide with the boundaries of the rural cantons. Usually all and occasionally part of every village, town, and city can be assigned to the census subdivision in which they are located. When this is done there are 1,178 census subdivisions within the area, each containing all the rural and urban population located within the particular subdivision. Thus when the total population of a census subdivision is divided by the area of the census subdivision (Geography Section, 1971) the gross population density can be obtained. Alas! Life is not that simple. Not only is there a variation in size of census subdivision within the proportion of each province that is within the axis, there is also a vast difference in size between the census subdivisions in the province of Québec and those in Ontario. Those in Québec are a great deal smaller. Thus a greater variation in density in Québec than in Ontario would appear to exist if this discrepancy were not corrected.

As a consequence, the census subdivisions in Québec (cantons) have been aggregated so that the mean size of a census subdivision in Québec is similar to that in Ontario (93 square miles in Ontario and 91.9 square miles in Québec). The aggregation is achieved for the purpose of this study by locating the major urban centres in the canton and aggregating the immediate surrounding cantons to that nucleus, since they would be most likely to contain the fringe population. It is likely that completely rural cantons would also be grouped together. The grouping was not obtained through a computer-based normative process, because such a procedure would be totally unwarranted considering the existent variation in the Ontario set of census subdivisions. The census subdivisions and aggregations are listed in Appendix A, and the numerical locators refer to the base map in Appendix B. Following aggregation, the number of census subdivisions comprising the axis and used hereafter is 730.

The 1971 distribution

The 1971 distribution of population densities for the 730 census subdivisions is presented in choropleth map form in Figure 1.2, using Russwurm's categories. Even if we accept the fact that the map would be different if the census subdivisions were oriented in other directions or were of a different size, it is interesting to note that areas defined as urban or semi-urban (fringe) cover nearly the entire area between Windsor and Québec City. In some places the area "urbanized" is quite extensive, but in other parts of the map the area that is urbanized is discontinuous. For example, notable discontinuities occur between Chatham and London, and between Trois-Rivières and Portneuf, while the whole zone between Cobourg and the Québec border is a fragmented urban strip. The most concentrated areas of almost continuous urbanization occur around Windsor; between London, Hamilton, Toronto, Barrie, and Bowmanville; the Niagara Peninsula; around Ottawa and Hull; the Montréal area as far as Trois-Rivières; and the extended urban zone of Québec City. In total, 92.2 per cent of the total 1971 axis population of 11,917,655 resides within those census subdivisions that are generally defined as urban or semi-urban. Furthermore, 83 per cent of the total 1971 population resides within census subdivisions described as urban.

The dominance of the urban areas can be discerned even more clearly from the data exhibited in Table 1.2. The data have been calculated on the basis of census subdivisions that either are entirely or have the greatest part of their area within forty miles of Toronto and Montréal, and fifteen miles of Québec City and Ottawa. The data indicate that 11.3 per cent of the land surface of the axis contains 64 per cent of the population of the axis. In a more general Canadian context, the figures indicate that 35 per cent of the population of the country lies within easy access of one of the five major metropolises in the axis.

Basic influences on the distribution of people

One of the most important questions raised by the discussion of the distribution of population in 1971 is: why do this distribution and variation in density occur as shown in Table 1.2? The distribution of people and human activity at any one time is subject to a host of influences, among which those relating to the physical environment and historical antecedents are usually quite important. In Canada and in the axis the physical and historical influences are extremely important for they provide constraints to the human environment

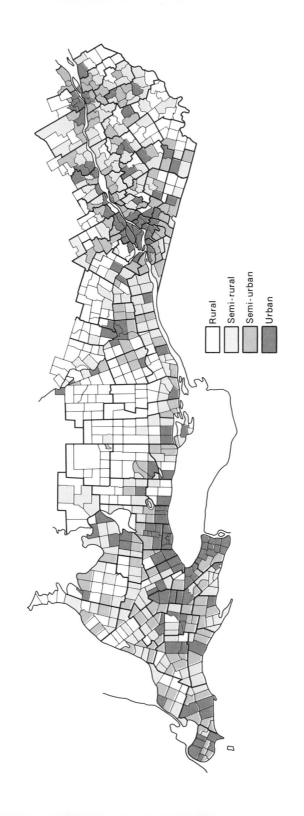

Figure 1.2: 1971 population densities

Rural

Semi-rural

Semi-urban

Urban

which are in effect today and will remain in effect in the future. It is impossible to attempt any detailed discussion of these influences in this monograph, so the discussion will focus on the basic elements of the geographic nature of the physical and historical constraints.

The physical environment

Although Canadians have learned to live with the realities of their physical environment with a sense of humour and a degree of *savoir-faire*, people living in other parts of the world (except the U.S.S.R.) view the situation with alarm, and occasionally with unmitigated horror. To them Canada appears a vast desolate open space with a horrific climate. The realities of the control of the physical and climatic environment on human habitation are quite apparent within the Windsor–Québec City axis. Though most geologists and physical geographers would probably cringe at the thought, the constraint framework of the physical environment can probably be expressed most clearly in terms of the regional physiography of the area. To the non-specialist, and undoubtedly clearer-thinking layman, the phrase "regional physiography" refers to the basic structure of the land.

Regional physiography

Although the occasional guru may choose to live on the top of a mountain, and the odd commune locates in a barren wilderness, most people like to live in more habitable areas where there are good, dry, building sites, a plentiful supply of drinking water, and where transportation is relatively easy. A glance at the highly generalized physiographic map indicates a number of features that would appear to, and have in fact, imposed constraints on the settlement of people in the axis. The large, deep lakes and fairly substantial rivers provide excellent sources of water and are good transport routes, except for occasional sections of rapids. The land area, which the Great Lakes bound and through which the St. Lawrence River flows, can be divided into four main physiographic regions.

The first of these, which is referred to as Interlake Ontario by Clibbon and Hamelin (1968), is basically the remnant of an old sea floor which has been sculpted by glacial erosion and refashioned with glacial deposits (Figure 1.3). Some of these deposits yield good soils along with little relief, such as in southwestern Ontario, but in

Table 1.2: The concentration of population in 1971 within the axis around four major cities

CITY	POPULATION	PERCENTAGE OF TOTAL	AREA	PERCENTAGE OF TOTAL
Montréal (40 miles)	3,173,097	26.63	4342.5	6.43
Toronto (40 miles)	3,396,505	28.50	2345.1	3.47
Ottawa (15 miles)	573,239	4.81	487.1	0.72
Québec (15 miles)	484,425	4.06	473.1	0.70
Total	7,627,266	64.00	7647.8	11.32
Axis	11,917,655		67,569.0	

other areas the surface debris is rather thin and sandy, yielding poor farmland. In many places hills of boulders, sand, and clay have been deposited on the surface by continental glaciation. The many little hills (known as drumlins) which result and the depressions between them are frequently interspersed with small lakes. This type of landscape is found most often east of a line joining Toronto to Lake Simcoe, and though poor for agricultural purposes, it provides excellent recreational facilities. Similarly, excellent recreational land is located on and around the Niagara scarp which runs in sinuous fashion from the Bruce Peninsula along the southern shore of Georgian Bay and south to the Niagara Peninsula. This resistant outcrop, with its steep easterly facing scarp, and shallow slope dipping gradually to the west, provides spectacular scenery, particularly where it is cut by the Niagara River to form the Niagara Falls.

In terms of human habitation, the least hospitable area is that portion of the Canadian Shield which is found within the axis. Its appearance is that of a much dissected plateau, varying in height from 3,100 feet at Mont-Tremblant to only a few hundred feet in eastern Ontario. Its joints, fault lines, and bands of weaker rock have been eroded by water and ice over the ages to form valleys and gorges. The occasional deposits of clay are useful for farming, but they are rarely extensive enough to provide a basis for profitable agriculture; throughout most of the area the rock has been scraped bare by abrasive glacial action. As a consequence the area of the Shield within the axis is basically inimical to settlement. The only exceptions are the occasional mining, lumbering, and pulp and paper towns which depend on the exploitation of natural resources, and the recreational centres, such as the skiing resorts found in the Laurentians and the vacation resorts located in the Thousand Islands region. The latter region is formed by the St. Lawrence River as it cuts through the southerly prong of the Shield that runs into the Adirondack Mountains.

This prong separates Interlake Ontario from the St. Lawrence Lowland. The two lowland areas are similar in appearance for both have been subjected to continental glaciation, though the incursion of an arm of the Atlantic during part of this period affected this area more than Interlake Ontario and has caused some differences. Pockets of sandy deposits are interspersed with broad areas of clay, such as those found on the broad and flat Montreal plain. This flat plain is relieved of its monotony by eleven hills, three of which are outliers of the Canadian Shield. The remaining eight are of harder rocks of volcanic

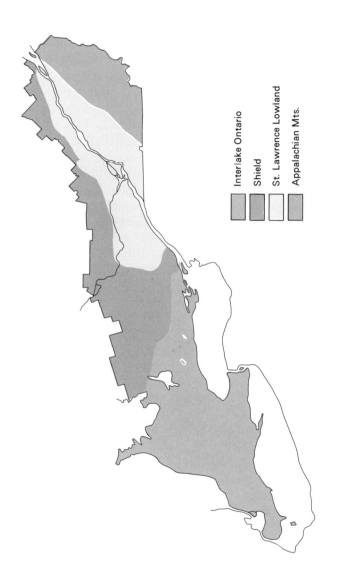

Interlake Ontario

Shield

St. Lawrence Lowland

Appalachian Mts.

Figure 1.3: *Physiographic regions of the axis*

origin; they have remained as hills following the erosion of the softer material surrounding them. These hills have become important for settlement purposes; for they are the sites of parks (Mount Royal) as well as private estates, and today many subdivisions are being located on their lower slopes. In fact, the location of parts of Westmount and Outremont on the slopes of Mount Royal gives credence to the physical analogy of the upper class highlands and lower class lowlands in the human habitation of central Montréal.

The fourth physiographic region, found in the Eastern Townships of Québec, consists of a part of the extensive Appalachian mountain system. In this northerly extension the mountains are not very high, most peaks being between 2,000 and 3,800 feet above sea level, since the surface has been eroded and disrupted through many ages of continuous abrasive and geologic action. The result is that all that remains are the rounded cores of the mountains, and a drainage pattern that has frequently been imposed upon them. Most of the upland areas are covered with forests or rough scrub, and the settlements are in the valleys along the rivers. There are some mining towns (Asbestos), but on the whole, the area does not encourage settlement because farming is uneconomic and transportation is difficult.

The settlement of the axis, therefore, has been very much influenced by the physiography of the area. The lowland areas contain nearly all the population and the only exceptions are in the valleys of the Appalachian zone and the occasional natural-resource-based town. Of course, within the lowland area there are considerable variations in density of settlement, and these variations are related to other influences. One of these is climate: few people really enjoy living in areas of continuous climatic extremes.

Climate

The climate of an area is the product of many features, such as rainfall, temperature, amount of sunlight, and so forth. More important, the variation in these characteristics throughout the day as well as throughout the seasons has a vital influence on agriculture and settlement in general. Watts (1968) has attempted to combine many of these features and variations in a map of climatic capability for Canada, and the portion of that map relevant to the axis area is indicated in Figure 1.4. It should be noted that this map pertains to agricultural capability, but as the present distribution of population

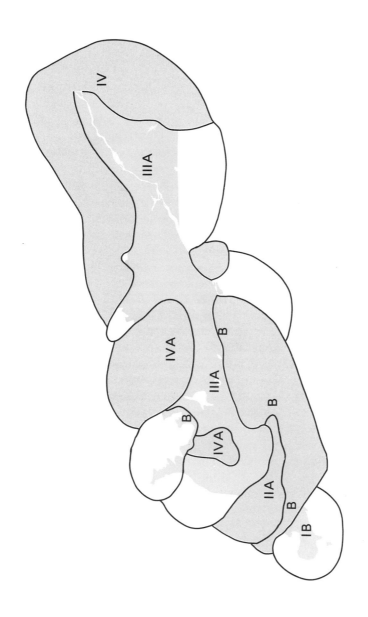

Figure 1.4: Climatic capability classes

has been determined (in part) by agricultural possibilities, the figure fulfils a double purpose. First, it delineates those areas of the axis, which, in terms of climate, are most useful for agricultural purposes. Second, since the original settlers tended to favour areas that were good for agricultural purposes, it also casts some light on the most desirable places for human habitation.

Figure 1.4 is a composite of two indices. The first index, arrayed in categories from numeral I to numeral VI is based on Thornwaite's index of thermal efficiency. It includes, in its calculation, a number of measurements (such as the length of the daylight period), and it can be interpreted fairly simply. The highest class is I, which is the category indicating the area with the greatest amount of heat accumulation for growing purposes. The lowest class is VI, and this category delineates zones which, in terms of thermal requirements, do not reach the necessary minimum heat accumulation for successful crop growth. Thus, as the numbers on the scale increase, corresponding general thermal conditions become gradually worse.

The second index, like the first, is a mixture of a number of climatic conditions, but this time these characteristics relate to summer moisture deficiency. Summer is used because it is taken for granted that only a certified optimist would attempt to grow anything out-of-doors anywhere in the axis in the winter. The alphabetic scale is arrayed from A to E, with A indicating a great deal of deficiency. Of course, any deficiency could be made up by irrigation, but the required amount of moisture would be somewhat excessive in zones D and E.

The composite of these two indices indicates the far more favourable position of southwestern Ontario over the rest of the axis in terms of climate. The lakes' littoral is the only area of moisture deficiency in the axis, but this deficiency is not great and can be compensated for by irrigation where necessary. The thermal conditions, however, are much more varied, with by far the warmest climate and greatest heat accumulation being in Essex County around Windsor, the Niagara Peninsula, and along the coastal margin of Lake Erie and Lake Ontario. The Ottawa Valley and the St. Lawrence Lowland have the worst climate in the axis for agriculture, but many would be quick to retort that they also have colder, crisper, snowier, and, therefore, more enjoyable winters. Whichever is preferable from the point of view of the individual, the climate for agriculture is definitely far better in southwestern Ontario. This fact, coupled with the more favourable topography and soil conditions of the area, results in a more varied and productive agricultural base and a less severe environment for human habitation.

THE PHASES OF SETTLEMENT

Now that all physical geographers and climatologists have been alienated by such a cursory glance at their domains, it is the turn of those with a more historical range of interests to be frustrated. The present distribution and density of population has occurred within the physical frame of the area through time. The first European settlers came from France and they entered a domain of scattered Indian tribes via the St. Lawrence River. The major locus of disembarkation and the nucleus from which the settlers colonized the surrounding country was Québec City, founded in 1608 (Biays, 1968). This early settlement of Canada was characterized by two main features. First, the colonizers used the only efficient means of transport available, the St. Lawrence River, and located along the river and the lower reaches of some of its tributaries, such as the St. Maurice and the Chaudière. They stayed as close as possible to the water, because it served as their major line of communication. The second feature was the mechanism of colonization through the seigneurial system, which attempted to superimpose the French hierarchical social structure through land ownership in the New World. Harris (1966) suggests, rather convincingly, that such a superimposition was impossible given the isolation of the habitants (or would-be peasants), the predilection of the seigneurs (or land-owning aristocracy) for an urban and French life style, and the relatively weak control exerted by the homeland on the colony. The remnants of the land tenure system are seen today in the elongated subdivision of the counties and farms throughout much of the area bordering the lower St. Lawrence.

The spread of French control in the developing colony of New France up the St. Lawrence River progressed fairly slowly through the seventeenth and early eighteenth centuries. Not only were there physical obstacles in terms of the rapids in the river as it traversed the north-south prong of the Shield, but also the Iroquois Indians resisted the slow but continuous incursion into their territory. Gradually, however, the hinterland was opened up for fur trading and small-scale agriculture, and the town of Montréal was established at the base of the last set of really severe rapids (the Lachine Rapids) in the upper St. Lawrence River. It was at this focus, connecting the navigable section of the river to the ocean and Europe with the rich natural resources of the Shield and Great Lakes area, that the greatest metropolis in the St. Lawrence Lowland developed. Thus Montréal came to dominate the trading throughout the Shield, Great Lakes, and St. Lawrence Lowland area, and by 1825–30 had surpassed Québec City in population.

The gradual opening up of that part of the axis now called Interlake Ontario was greatly accelerated by two events, which together changed the patterns of dominance. The first event was the replacement of French influence over the area by British influence during the early 1760s. The second event was the aristocrat-led leftist (in those days!) revolution in the Thirteen Colonies, known as the War of Independence, which caused a number of settlers to flee to the north and settle in the area that became the eastern townships of Québec. Some of the United Empire Loyalists, as they were called, also moved into the area bordering the upper St. Lawrence River and Lakes Erie and Ontario. Once again, the physical features of the countryside exerted a controlling influence over the spread of the population; a settler rarely located far from water transportation.

One of the first concerns of the new régime was the reinforcement of the military protective network that had been originally developed by the French. As in most cases of military (and political) conflict, where black can become white at a stroke of a pen, forts that were originally constructed as a protection against Indian and possible British incursions from the south now were re-enforced to protect the new British territory of Upper (Ontario) and Lower (Québec) Canada from possible invasion from the new revolutionary state. As a part of this plan a primitive road network was constructed, based in the old French fort site of Toronto, which was eventually chosen as the locus for government in the fledgeling province (Gentilcore, 1972).

During the middle decades of the nineteenth century, settlement continued, but the original pattern of development remained unchanged. The construction of railway systems accentuated the importance of Montréal and Toronto, and the dredging of the lower St. Lawrence River and canalization of parts of the upper St. Lawrence simply emphasized the increasing dominance of these centres over the rest of the territory.

The change of sovereignty in Lower Canada resulted in many cultural changes, since the French-speaking population was now cut off from its natural cultural source. In order to preserve its identity, the society became introverted, and the Roman Catholic Church assumed an important role in the preservation of the French cultural heritage. Thus the peculiar working arrangement between upper-class French society and the opportunist Scottish traders who controlled business in Montréal was not repeated beyond the city. In fact, over a period of time, the French population which, owing to its rapidly increasing numbers, desired more land, began to replace the loyalist English settlers in the eastern townships. This replacement was facilitated in large part by land purchases from the loyalist settlers made by the Church, which then redistributed the land to its parishioners.

The British North America Act of 1867 helped to re-enforce an urban situation which had already been developed within the axis. The old capital of New France (Québec City) was confirmed as the capital of the Province of Québec, Toronto became the capital of Ontario; and Ottawa, for militaristic-defensive reasons as much as any other, was selected as the capital of the new Confederation. Montréal, dominated by merchants and financiers of Scottish and English origin controlled the trade of most of the entire area. Developments over the ensuing century simply emphasized these patterns of urban dominance, though there have been considerable readjustments as the urban centres have changed in relative importance and other urban areas have grown (Spelt, 1955). The important feature, however, is that the distribution of people within the axis has, in large part, been constrained by these early developments, some of which were influenced by the physical environment, but others by changes in sovereignty and by political decisions.

MAJOR SPHERES OF INFLUENCE

One of the criteria that has been used to sketch the boundaries of the axis has been the spheres of influence of major urban centres. The delineation of spheres of influence is much more detailed and precise in the Québec portion of the axis than in the Ontario section. This is fortunate, because the northern boundary of the axis in Québec lacks the more compact and realistic census division boundaries that can be used in Ontario. Figure 1.5 is a composite of research undertaken in the two different provinces, and while the bases of the analysis are different, the end products illustrate similar characteristics of spatial organization. The sphere of influence of a city is the area which the city is considered to dominate with respect to specific services.

The Québec portion of Figure 1.5 is a generalized version of the detailed maps published by the Ministère de l'Industrie et du Commerce (1967). This study concerning poles of attraction and their spheres of influence used a detailed method of discerning the major urban centres and prescribing their hinterlands by asking a series of questions relating to where people went to work; where they went to purchase certain articles of clothing, electrical appliances, automobiles, and so forth; and where they went for various personal services, such as those provided by hospitals, lawyers, and centres of education. The questions were asked of a variety of administrative, financial, and religious persons residing in the many municipalities. The analysis of the replies from 3,000 questionnaires distributed in 1963 suggested the existence of six major work, shopping, and service centres around which much of the economic activity in the province is focused; they are: Hull, Montréal, Sherbrooke, Trois-Rivières, Québec, and Chicoutimi. The first four exhibit spheres of influence which are almost entirely within the axis, and, in fact, neatly approximate its northern boundary. Only the primary centres in Québec are used, because they are equivalent to the major centres defined for Ontario.

The Ontario portion of Figure 1.5 is extracted from Marshall's (1972, p. 80) revised version of the map of hinterlands of shopping centres presented by Dean (1969). The revision has taken into account not only retail sales volume but also the circulation records of daily newspapers, and the shopping behaviour of people throughout the area. This is not shopping behaviour for daily or even weekly needs, but trips for the occasional article or service unavailable in the more local towns and cities because of lack of demand. As a result of this compilation, the major centres in Ontario are considered to be: Windsor, London, Kitchener, Hamilton, St. Catharines, Toronto, Oshawa, Peterborough, Kingston, and Ottawa. Montréal's sphere of influence extends into Ontario, and Ottawa-Hull really exerts a joint influence over quite a large area.

The populations of these centres, the areas, and population that they serve are listed in Table 1.3. There are a number of aspects concerning Figure 1.5 and Table 1.3 that are worthy of comment, because they illustrate many facets of the human organization of space. The first is that the size of the city population is usually quite different from the population that it serves. Second, the areas served vary

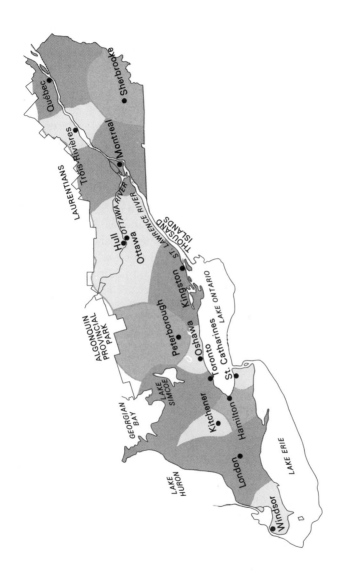

Figure 1.5: Major spheres of influence in the axis

Table 1.3: The principal centres and their spheres of influence in the axis: population, population served, area, population increase 1961–71

CENTRE	POPULATION OF CENTRE	POPULATION SERVED 1971	AREA	POPULATION INCREASE 1961–71 %
Québec City	186,088	762,530	7083.15	14.93
Trois-Rivières	55,869	372,277	3405.27	2.75
Sherbrooke	80,711	310,513	5209.71	6.13
Montréal	1,214,352	3,383,724	7891.71	21.96
Hull	63,580	201,586	3521.59	22.64
Ottawa	302,341	765,555	7797.95	19.12
Kingston	59,047	306,135	4530.66	11.6
Peterborough	58,111	179,505	6693.05	13.36
Oshawa	91,587	251,815	1254.33	37.29
Toronto	712,786	2,902,250	7103.12	40.29
Hamilton	309,173	671,325	1818.91	21.45
Kitchener	111,804	411,470	2166.18	34.58
St. Catharines	109,722	331,565	689.31	18.2
London	223,222	655,485	6558.71	15.52
Windsor	203,300	411,920	1843.11	18.0

Note: Populations are the city populations as defined for the 1971 census and reported in Statistics Canada 92-754-AP-3.

greatly in size; for where there are a large number of competing centres, the spheres of influence tend to be quite small. This is particularly noticeable for St. Catharines, Hamilton, Kitchener, and Oshawa. Third, the really large centres of Montréal and Toronto exert a dominant influence over sizeable urban centres which are quite close to them. For example, Montréal tends to dominate Laval, even though Laval has a population of 228,010. Fourth, some centres, remote from the larger agglomerations and frequently between them, dominate fairly large areas of the axis even though they are not large cities themselves. The most obvious examples are Trois-Rivières, Sherbrooke, and Kingston. Finally, these smaller centres exhibited the least increase in population within their spheres of influence between 1961 and 1971; the largest increases were in Toronto, Oshawa, and Kitchener, in south-central Ontario.

The last observation reveals an important limitation in the discussion, for the data and the map are static, fixed at a given point in time, whereas in the real world these spheres of influence fluctuate in size according to the relative competitive strengths of the centres. Furthermore, the criteria used for the delimitation of the centres in effect predetermines the type of centre that will be distinguished. For example, if the criteria had focused upon stock exchanges, head offices of companies, advertising and public relations companies, then it is quite likely that just Montréal and Toronto would have been included, and their spheres of influence would have not only divided the axis into two parts, but also included the rest of Canada. In the jargon of the geographer, the spheres of influence discerned in this section can be labelled those pertaining to "major regional centres," and Montréal and Toronto are not only major regional centres but national centres as well. Alternatively, if governmental activities are the sole criteria then Ottawa becomes the national centre, and Québec City and Toronto become provincial poles.

THE CONTEXT OF THE AXIS

Although it is possible to define the axis fairly clearly, it is well to remember that the axis is a part of a very large country. The degree to which it is a functioning entity linked to the rest of the nation is discussed in later sections, particularly those concerned with the economic structure of the area, interaction, and transport networks. While the scene is being set, however, it is instructive and provocative to glance at some indicators that suggest the relative importance of the axis in Canada. There are many indicators that could be used, and some, such as housing, are referred to in later chapters. In this section the importance of the axis with respect to people, money, jobs, and agriculture is demonstrated.

THE AXIS COMPARED WITH CANADA AS A WHOLE

The indicators are listed in Table 1.4 with comparable figures for 1971 and one other earlier time period in each case. The population of Canada is becoming increasingly concentrated in the axis: in the ten-year period between 1961 and 1971 there was a net comparative shift of over 400,000 people to the area. The fact that the population of the axis is comparatively wealthy is indicated by the estimate that 60.7 per cent of the total income of the nation is received by the inhabitants of the area. However, the proportion of total national income received by these inhabitants has not increased over the ten-year period in accordance with the increase in population. Thus it would appear that the axis, though still comparatively wealthy, is becoming less wealthy when compared with the country as a whole.

This decline in comparative wealth is perhaps related in part to the very slight comparative loss in manufacturing employment in the axis over a nine-year period. If manufacturing employment in the axis in 1970 had remained at the 1961 level of concentration (72.9 per cent) then manufacturing employment would have totalled 1,637,001 $\times$ 72.9 per cent = 1,193,373. As the 1970 figure was only 1,173,094, the actual increase of 186, 703 jobs was 20,279 less than it would have been if manufacturing employment had grown at the same rate as the nation as a whole. This arithmetic sleight-of-hand is significant because it indicates whether a gross increase or decrease is, in fact, a comparative increase or decrease. In this case, since the comparison is with Canada as a whole, the axis has incurred a comparative decrease of over twenty thousand jobs when the manufacturing situation is compared with that of the country as a whole. Even so, there is still a disproportionate concentration of manufacturing employment in the axis; it contains 55 per cent of the country's population, yet 71.7 per cent of the nation's manufacturing employment is located in the area.

The disproportionate contribution of the axis to the nation's wealth is probably most obvious with respect to the value added to a product through the various manufacturing processes. "Value added" is computed as the difference between the selling value of the output and the amount spent on materials and supplies purchased and the costs of fuel and electricity. The calculation does not take into account other costs incurred by the firm such as taxes, insurance, costs of communication, interests on capital borrowed, and so forth. An inter-

Table 1.4: Some indicators of the importance of the axis in Canada

INDICATORS	CANADA	AXIS	PER CENT
Population			
1961	18,328,247	9,730,950	53.1
1971	21,568,311	11,917,655	55.3
Total national income[1]			
1961 ($ in thousands)	21,479,544	12,987,050	60.5
1971 ($ in thousands)	50,825,409	30,858,380	60.7
Manufacturing employment[2]			
1961	1,352,605	986,391	72.9
1970	1,637,001	1,173,094	71.7
Value added[2]			
1961 ($ in thousands)	10,931,561	8,128,813	73.4
1971 ($ in thousands)	21,417,784	16,132,072	75.3
Farm cash receipts[3]			
1966 ($ in thousands)	4,280,033	1,533,490	35.8
1971 ($ in thousands)	4,513,147	1,747,281	38.7
Acres in farmland[3]			
1966	174,124,828	24,766,198	14.2
1971	169,668,614	22,114,901	13.0

Notes:

1 Estimates based on total income derived from an analysis of all taxable and non-taxable returns in *Taxation Statistics, 1972* and *Taxation Statistics, 1963* for census divisions. Income not reported or filed is obviously excluded.

2 Data obtained from Statistics Canada, *Manufacturing Industries: Series G* for 1964 and 1973, for census divisions. Data for the axis estimated by subtracting data for municipalities excluded.

3 Data and estimates for the axis obtained from Statistics Canada, *Number and Area of Census Farms, 1971: Advance Bulletin* and *Farm Cash Receipts, 1971.*

esting feature of the data calculated for the axis is that they suggest that the manufacturing establishments in the area produce a disproportionately large share of high value added products, and that this share has increased during the decade of the 1960s. This growth could also indicate that general productivity in manufacturing establishments in the area increased throughout the period at a greater rate than in the rest of the country.

The last two indicators relate to agriculture, for it is well to remember that though the axis contains the greatest concentration of urban development in Canada, it still has a very large and viable agricultural industry. To the ordinary urban dweller living within the axis (as defined) this fact might come as a surprise. The money indicator relates to farm cash receipts, which is not the same as farm income because it does not exclude the costs of equipment, supplies, insurance, interest, and so forth. At the outset it is useful to note that, in gross terms, farm cash receipts declined over the 1966–71 period because the rate of increase was less than the rate of inflation. The rate of inflation fluctuated, but if an average "ball-park" figure of 5 per cent is used, farm receipts in the axis would have been $1.957 billion, if they had merely remained at the 1966 level. This decrease in value of over $200 million is perhaps related to the loss of over 2.5 million acres of farmland in this same period in the axis; the reasons for this loss of land are discussed in later chapters. Notwithstanding this story of decline, the proportion of the total farm receipts received by the axis has increased, and currently 38.7 per cent of the value of farm receipts in Canada is derived from only 13 per cent of the farmland area in Canada. The implication is that the intensity of production is greater in the axis than in the area beyond, because the farms closer to the big urban markets can produce high value but more perishable crops.

TWO PROVINCES, TWO CULTURES

Although the axis is being viewed as a whole, there are a number of divisions contained within its boundaries. Most important, perhaps, it encompasses the two founding cultures of Canada, which are expressed and preserved most obviously in language. The French culture is particularly evident in the Québec portion; for as the inhabitants of the area began to feel isolated and surrounded by an alien and arrogant tongue they sought refuge and support in the preservatives of language and the church.

The odds, in the parlance of the race-track, have been stacked against the survival of French language and culture in North America, and, for that matter, the odds are still stacked against it. The problem is that English is the language of government and of money — indeed it is the language of money throughout much of the world. Furthermore, that friendly giant to the south, which can cause grave injury to the Canadian economy and society even in its most idle moments, tends to discourage diversity and to promote unity through melting pots, advertisements, and continentalism. The only way Canada can continue to preserve its varied society is through a continuous process of containment and re-enforcement within the country, and a sensitive appreciation by all of the importance of Canadian art, theatre, literature, history, films, political philosophy, varieties of cuisine, and so forth.

If Mephistopheles had been given the choice of two founding nations for a new country, there is little doubt that he would have chosen France and the United Kingdom, for there are few nations with greater pride, and frequently greater prejudice against others. The task has been, and will continue to be, to face up to these traits; this is particularly necessary in the two provinces of which the axis is comprised. The duality of the area is expressed most clearly in Figures 1.6a and 1.6b, which indicate the proportion of the population of each census subdivision which claims to have either French or English as its mother tongue in 1971. The only zone of communication is in the Ottawa valley, eastern Ontario between Cornwall and the Québec border, and in the few "loyalist" outliers of southwest Québec.

One way of achieving greater understanding in the future is for these zones of communication to increase in size. This would, hopefully, encourage greater integration of the two groups. Unfortunately, the gross pattern of changes between 1961 and 1971 for the two different portions of the axis suggests that this integration is not occurring (Table 1.5). The changes are slight but nevertheless ominous, for the degree of polarization is increasing. In Québec the proportion of the population whose mother tongue is English decreased between 1961 and 1971, and in Ontario a similar decrease can be observed for the proportion of the population whose mother tongue is French. Interestingly, the largest single minority in the Ontario portion of the axis now is comprised of those whose mother tongue is Italian.

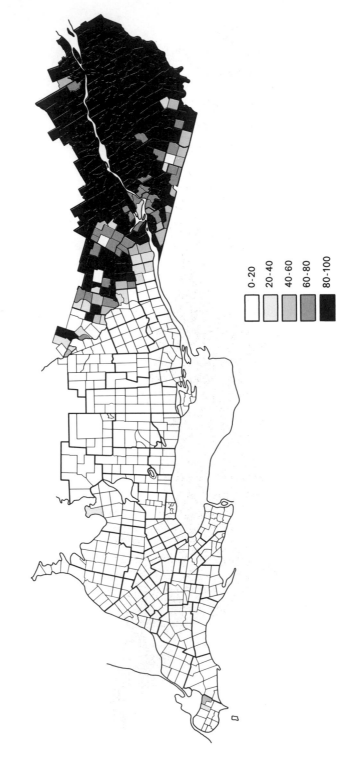

Figure 1.6: Percentage of total population by ethnic group, (a) per cent French;

0-20
20-40
40-60
60-80
80-100

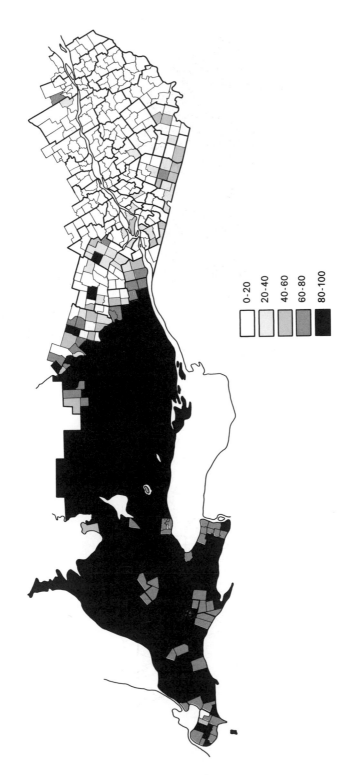

(b) per cent English;

In fact, the total Italian population in the axis has increased by over two-thirds during the decade, and this group now comprises nearly 4 per cent of the population of the axis. The Italian population is concentrated primarily in Ontario, and there has been very little change in this interprovincial distribution throughout the time period. One aspect of the distribution of Italians is extremely important, however, for they are concentrated primarily in the major metropolitan centres (Figure 1.6c). This is particularly evident in Québec, where the central and eastern parts of Ile de Montréal (particularly St-Léonard) contain over one-quarter of the Italian population in the axis. In Ontario, Metropolitan Toronto contains 46.6 per cent of all the Italians in the axis, and the bulk of the remainder are found in Hamilton, Windsor, and in various towns of the Niagara Peninsula. Recent immigrants from Europe — of which group Italians make up the largest number — have made immense contributions to urban life in the axis. Hockey and soccer can now flourish side by side in Metro Toronto!

THE AXIS COMPARED WITH OTHER ELONGATED URBAN AGGLOMERATIONS

Exploitation of a hinterland, a history intertwined with common threads, and transport developments — these are the themes that unite the axis and are the roots of future development as well as problems. These themes have been emphasized by Whebell (1969) in his five cumulative historical stages of the development of urban corridors:

Table 1.5: French-English ethnic (mother tongue) change in the axis, 1961–71

	1961		1971	
GROUP	ONTARIO	QUÉBEC	ONTARIO	QUÉBEC
English	4,386,413	651,359	5,449,014	745,539
percentage	80.00	15.30	79.12	14.82
French	263,218	3,319,802	308,539	3,939,990
percentage	4.80	77.98	4.48	78.32
Italian	182,052	87,700	318,869	133,814
percentage	3.32	2.06	4.53	2.66

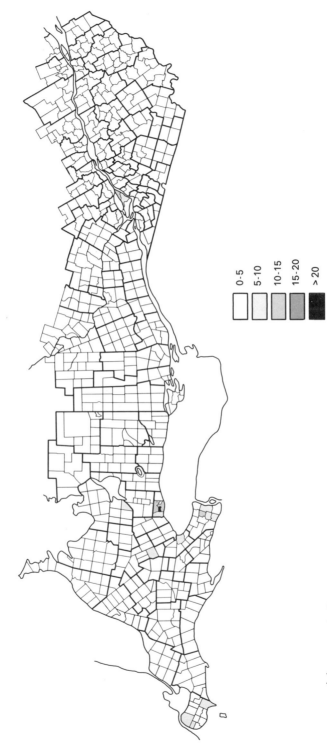

0-5
5-10
10-15
15-20
> 20

(c) per cent Italian

initial occupance; commercial agriculture; railway transport; motor transport; metropolitanism. The corridor acts as the agent which imports or generates innovations which then diffuse outward from the zone in a sequential pattern. These innovations enable the urban areas along the axis to gain increasing control over a larger and larger hinterland. This form of dominance-spreading has been well documented by Gottman (1961) for the northeast United States, an area that appears to be defined by a fringe population of fifty persons per square mile.

There are a number of elongated urban areas of this type in the world, and they are all characterized by urban growth along a linear mix of transport arteries. In some cases the urban areas have spread to such a degree that they are beginning to run into one another; overlapping of this kind can be avoided only by the strictest land-use controls. For example, in England the estimated population per linear mile for the London-Birmingham-Liverpool-Manchester-Leeds urban strip is similar to that for the Boston-New York-Philadelphia-Washington megalopolis (Table 1.6), but in England the preservation of rural and recreational areas between the cities has been far superior. Table 1.6, however, emphasizes that the Windsor to Québec City axis does not have as large a total population or as dense a population per linear mile as its Japanese, American, or British counterparts. This difference is emphasized in cartogram form in Figure 1.7, in which the circles represent the major urban centres and are proportionate to their population, and the black "worm" is a shortest path route that connects those centres.

Table 1.6: The axis compared with other elongated urban agglomerations

AGGLOMERATION	LENGTH (MILES)	ESTIMATED POPULATION (MILLIONS)	POPULATION PER LINEAR MILE
Windsor to Québec City	715	12	16,780
Boston to Washington	450	45	100,000
Tokyo to Osaka	370	35	94,590
London to Manchester	200	20	100,000

Source: CTCRB (1970), p. 1.

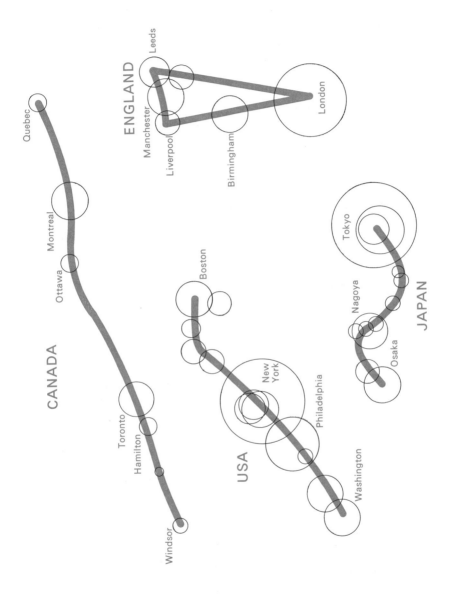

Figure 1.7: Comparisons between the Windsor to Québec City axis and other elongated urban agglomerations

Thus, there is an urban axis connecting southern Ontario and Québec, but it does not contain as large a population as, and has only one-sixth the population per linear mile of, three other major elongated urban agglomerations in the world. It is, in effect, a developing linear urban agglomeration that has a role which is totally disproportionate to its physical size in Canada. The axis is just as important, if not more so, as the other agglomerations are to their respective countries, and it is for this reason that the urban developments that occur have national repercussions. It is necessary, however, to realize that the basic problems arising from intensity of land use are not on the same scale as in the other countries mentioned, because there is more space available. As a consequence, the Canadian situation is similar to but not the same as these other situations and there are more opportunities available for avoiding the problems of congestion, pollution, overcrowding, lack of recreational opportunities, and so forth. Unfortunately, the growth and physical expansion of urban areas in some parts of the axis is greater than in others, and these are documented, projected, and discussed in the ensuing chapter.

2 GROWTH, EXPANSION, AND CONVERGENCE

Impressions, false or correct, create the images that set tones and, at times, affect policy. In an area in which six and a half million people live within forty miles of either Toronto or Montréal it is easy to gain an impression of massive expansion and dynamic growth. But impressions are made to be examined, and in this case such an examination has to be undertaken for the entire axis. If it is an independent entity, it should behave as a whole with respect to the growth and spread of the population. This is not to say that growth or decline should be uniform throughout the entire area, but that the areas of growth should have features in common and the areas of decline should also have features in common.

At the outset it is instructive to examine the gross changes in population that have occurred in the period between 1961 and 1971. These gross changes are summarized in Table 2.1, and even at this

Table 2.1: Population changes between 1961 and 1971 for the axis and Canada

PERIOD	AXIS %	CANADA %
1961–66		
Percentage increase	12.44	9.74
Rate of increase (annual)	2.3	1.9
1966–71		
Percentage increase	8.92	7.76
Rate of increase (annual)	1.7	1.5
1961–71		
Percentage increase	22.47	18.26
Rate of increase (annual)	2.0	1.7

level of aggregation the data emphasize the precarious nature of the population-forecasting business. The population of the axis increased by over one-fifth during the 1961 to 1971 period, and this increase was four percentage points greater than that for the nation as a whole. If the annual rate of growth of the population during the ten-year period were constant for the next few decades, the population of the axis would double every thirty-five years and the population of Canada would be forty-three million in forty years.

The dangers of this type of flamboyant statement can be perceived from an examination of the data for the two five-year periods. The data suggest the existence of two entirely different growth patterns. From 1961 to 1966 the population of the axis was increasing at the frightening rate of 2.3 per cent per annum. If this growth rate had carried on, the population of the axis in 1971 would have been 12.27 million, or nearly 360,000 more than it actually was. If the rate had continued through to 1996, the population would then have increased by the same amount in thirty years as it had over the preceding three centuries. Fortunately, the growth rate for the 1966 to 1971 period slowed down dramatically to 1.7 per cent per annum. If this rate continues, the population in the axis will be double the 1971 figure by the year 2011.

VARIATIONS IN THE GROWTH OF POPULATION WITHIN THE AXIS

Variations in growth within the axis can be examined in a number of ways, and for this portion of the study the primary concern is an analysis of urban growth rates. In the light of the earlier observation concerning the axis as an entity, however, it is most useful to determine whether there has been any great variation in growth between the two provincial portions of the axis. If differences do occur between these two portions, an argument can be made supporting the duality of the axis on cultural grounds on the basis of differential growth rates. On the other hand, if there is a difference in growth rates between the different portions of the axis but similarity in urban growth rates in the entire axis, it could be concluded that the cultural effect is existent but that there is a common pattern of urban growth.

The differences in rates of growth between the Québec and Ontario portions of the axis are indicated in Table 2.2. Whereas the average annual rates of population increase in the two portions of the axis were very similar between 1961 and 1966, they are dramatically different for the period between 1966 and 1971. In fact, the growth rate in the Ontario portion of the axis in the 1966 to 1971 period is very nearly twice that in the Québec portion. Thus the difference in axis growth rates for the two periods is directly attributable to the dramatic decline in the Québec growth rate, and the immediate question that comes to mind is: what has caused this decline?

THE DETERMINANTS OF POPULATION GROWTH OR DECLINE

The words "determine" and "cause" are very dangerous to use in any writing in the social sciences, because there are causes of causes and determinants of determinants, and in many cases the fundamental causes of things are very much open to speculation. In this instance, the word "cause" applies to the demographic components of growth or decline, and what causes changes in these demographic components could be argued continuously on a long walk from Windsor, Ontario, to Windsor, Québec. The main demographic components of growth or decline are related to change in the birth rate, death rate, net immigration, and internal migration. In this section the effect of the first three of these components on the population of the axis as a whole is examined; the fourth will be discussed later.

Table 2.2: Population changes between 1961 and 1971 for the Ontario and Québec portions of the axis

PERIOD	QUÉBEC %	ONTARIO %	AXIS %
1961–66			
Percentage increase	11.76	12.97	12.44
Rate of increase (annual)	2.25	2.46	2.3
1966–71			
Percentage increase	5.73	11.38	8.92
Rate of increase (annual)	1.12	2.15	1.7
1961–71			
Percentage increase	18.17	25.82	22.47
Rate of increase (annual)	1.69	2.31	2.0

Changing birth rates and death rates

The death rate, which is defined as the number deceased in any one year per thousand population, has been declining in Canada since the mid-1850s. In the middle of the nineteenth century mortality was high for all age groups; with increasing urbanization, improved sanitation and more sophisticated medical services, however, the rate dropped to one of the lowest in the western world. From the available data, which are for the whole of the provinces of Ontario and Québec (Table 2.3), it can be inferred that the rate changed very little in the axis during the 1961–71 period. The death rate in Québec is very low, and the figure for the province of Ontario is close to that of Québec. The rate is scarcely likely to change in the future, since infant mortality is extremely low, and humans are, after all, mortal.

Whereas the death rate has declined continuously over the last 100 years, the birth rate (live births per thousand population) has declined, but not as steadily. In Canada as a whole the rate declined from 45 per thousand people in the middle of the nineteenth century to 20.1 per thousand during the Depression years. In the late 1930s the birth rate increased along with general optimism, and following World War II it increased again, reaching a plateau of about 28 per thousand people. During the 1960s, there has, however, been a general decline, and this is quite marked in the Province of Québec (Table 2.4). In 1961 the birth rate was higher in Québec than in Ontario, but by 1971 it was 1.5 per thousand less. By inference, this situation prevailed in the two portions of the axis, and it helps to explain in part why the rate of increase in the Québec portion declined so drastically. This decline is illustrated even more dra-

Table 2.3: Changes in the death rate in the provinces of Ontario and Québec

DATE	ONTARIO	QUÉBEC
1961	8.2	7.0
1966	7.8	6.7
1971	7.5	6.7

Source: Statistics Canada, *Canada Yearbook*, various years.

matically by the gross reproduction rates that are also listed in Table 2.4. These rates indicate the extent to which the female population of child-bearing age (for statistical purposes defined as fifteen to fifty years old) is reproducing itself. A ratio of 1.0, if existent for a lengthy period, would suggest that each female was producing one other female, that is, just reproducing herself. By 1971 the Québec rate had almost reached unity, and the Ontario figure was not far behind.

In fact, the great drop in this rate occurred around 1965, and the reasons for it and the diminishing birth rate, have been discussed quite widely. There is little doubt that the birth rate, apart from the negative and positive psychological effects of the Depression years and post-war euphoria, has been declining over the last 100 years. A projection of the general trend would place the rate at around 17 to 18 per thousand people by 1971. This decline is the result of the desire for greater personal affluence and freedom and is facilitated through increased and widespread knowledge of birth control techniques. The rapid and widespread acceptance of new and improved methods of birth control in the 1960s, as reflected by the plunge in the reproduction ratio, merely accelerated this trend. Another interpretation is that the birth rate is now at about the level it would have been if the events of the 1930s and 1940s had not occurred.

Immigration

Thus, there are some long-standing demographic trends that help to

Table 2.4: Changes in the birth rate and gross reproduction rate in the provinces of Ontario and Québec

DATE	ONTARIO		QUÉBEC	
	BIRTH RATE	REPRODUCTION RATE	BIRTH RATE	REPRODUCTION RATE
1961	25.3	1.824	26.1	1.787
1966	19.0	1.361	19.0	1.284
1971	17.5	1.174	16.0	1.014

Source: Statistics Canada, *Canada Yearbook*, various years.

explain why the rate of population increase declined during the 1960s, and that also suggest why the rate in the Québec portion of the axis declined. The birth-rate figures do not, however, explain why the Québec rate has been so much lower than that of Ontario. This difference must be the result of other influences in addition to the declining birth rate, and of these, gross immigration into Canada is quite important. Gross immigration to Canada during the 1960s totalled 1,409,627 persons, but a vast number also left the country during the same period. Until the complete 1971 census is published it is only possible to guess at the loss through emigration. Statistics from the United States indicate that at least 413,310 entered the U.S.A. from Canada during the period, and a reasonably large number must have either returned to their country of origin or gone elsewhere. From these estimates and guesses it can be suggested that net immigration into Canada was probably of the order of 750,000, which implies that about one-fifth of the population increase in Canada between 1961 and 1971 was due to immigration. This estimate compares well wtih Kalbach's (1970) claim that net immigration accounted for 25.5 per cent of the 1951–61 Canadian population growth.

The question now arises: where did these people go? To obtain an answer to this question, data concerning intended province of destination of immigrants have to be used, and these data suggest that at least 50 per cent would have gone to the province of Ontario, and 20 per cent to the Province of Québec. As the axis portion of the two provinces is by far the most likely first destination of the vast majority of these immigrants, an estimate of 500,000 immigrants to the axis during the 1961–71 period is probably reasonable. Of these, around 150,000 have the Québec portion of the axis as their first destination, and 350,000 the Ontario part. Whether these people stayed where they first went is quite another story, but if they did, these figures represent quite a large proportion (23 per cent) of the absolute increase in the axis between 1961 and 1971. As these immigrants undoubtedly located in urban areas, they contributed, in effect, enough people in ten years to establish a city the size of Hamilton — without even taking the Canadian-born children of the immigrants into account.

The two provincial portions of the axis thus exhibit considerable differences in rates of population growth during the 1960s, differences which are the result of variations in birth rates and volume of immigration. In the last five years of the period the Québec birth rate was less than that for Ontario, and throughout the period five out of every ten immigrants to Canada went to Ontario, and only two out of ten to Québec. Since this immigration was extremely heavy during the middle years of the period, there is little doubt that it greatly influenced the different growth rates. As a consequence, the axis cannot be regarded as a unit with respect to population growth if its provincial portions are contrasted.

VARIATIONS IN URBAN AND RURAL GROWTH RATES

Having established the existence of differential growth patterns between the two provincial portions of the axis, it is now interesting to observe whether these differences also exist at the urban and rural levels. In Table 2.5 growth rates for the rural and semi-rural, semi-urban, and urban density categories are tabulated for the axis as a whole and for the two provincial portions. Based on the 1971 density figures, calculations of the growth rates for each classification have been made, and they suggest an important difference and some extremely interesting similarities in growth rates in the axis. First, the growth rates in the areas defined as urban in both portions of the

Table 2.5: Urban and rural growth rates, 1961–71, for the axis (in percentages)

DENSITY	QUÉBEC	ONTARIO	AXIS
Rural and semi-rural			
1961–66	−1.47	−1.33	−1.33
1966–71	0.29	−1.09	−0.51
1961–71	−0.59	−1.16	−0.92
Semi-urban			
1961–66	−0.78	0.20	−0.24
1966–71	−0.84	3.06	1.40
1961–71	−0.81	1.63	0.58
Urban			
1961–66	3.06	3.21	3.15
1966–71	1.42	2.38	1.97
1961–71	2.24	2.80	2.56

axis are reasonably similar. The rate of increase in the urban areas was extremely high in the 1961–66 period. A 3 per cent growth rate compounded annually implies a doubling of the population every fifteen years, a situation which has not proved to be easily manageable in a complex mixed economy (McLaughlin, 1972, p. 21). In the 1966–71 period the growth rate in both provinces decreased, but the decrease was greater in Québec than in Ontario. The general rate of growth for the ten-year period is reasonably similar, however.

The second observation is that the rural and semi-rural areas exhibit, in general, declining populations throughout the entire period, though the decreases have been comparatively greater in the Ontario portion than in Québec. Rural decline is not a new phenomena in Canada or in the axis, but an average rate of decline of about 1 per cent in rural areas is quite large when it is compared with a general overall rate of growth of 2 per cent for the ten-year period. In fact, the rural areas of the axis lost over 90,000 people during the ten-year period, and in this type of environment, losses of this magnitude have severe repercussions with respect to the availability of service facilities as well as deleterious effects on social welfare.

The third observation relates to the one single important feature distinguishing the Québec portion of the axis from the Ontario portion. In the Québec portion there has been a continuous decline in population in the semi-urban areas, that is, those areas where up to 50 per cent of the population is classified as rural non-farm. On the other hand, there has been a tremendous growth of semi-urban areas in the Ontario portion during the 1960s.

Thus, it is evident that although there are differences in the growth experiences of the two provincial portions of the axis, there are also certain characteristics of significant similarity. These similarities pertain to urban growth and rural decline, and they are of sufficient generality to embrace the entire axis. The growth experiences of the semi-rural areas typify the differences, for in the Ontario segment there has been a recent dramatic spread of direct urban development of more rural areas, whereas in Québec the spread is not noticeable in the aggregate.

URBAN EXPANSION

The sheer physical expansion of urban areas can be depicted in various media, but probably the most effective is the map. For this reason, a number of maps have been prepared to demonstrate the geographic variations in growth that occurred during the 1960s. The data units used in the maps are the census subdivisions and aggregated cantons described in the previous chapter. To ensure comparability of the data over time the 1966 and 1961 populations have been re-aggregated to conform with the 1971 boundaries. The number of changes in census subdivision boundaries over the ten-year period throughout the axis have been numerous (almost 300), and the task of re-aggregation was greatly facilitated by the work of Boucher (1969) and listings obtained from various provincial government sources. The major changes in the Ontario portion of the axis have resulted from the construction of new regional government areas, and the re-aggregations in the case of the regional municipalities of York and Niagara have been undertaken from maps of boundary changes.

The first set of maps relates to population density in the axis in 1961, 1966 and 1971 (Figure 2.1). Figure 2.1c is, of course, exactly the same map as Figure 1.2, and is reproduced here for comparative purposes. The major impression is that the census subdivisions classified as urban and semi-urban only are marginally more extensive in 1971 than in 1961. This impression is supported by the fact that the area occupied by densities of fifty persons per square mile or more has increased only by about 10 per cent during the ten-year period. The maps indicate, however, that the greatest extension of urbanization has been in the western part of the axis (west of a line of longitude passing through Peterborough) and in the areas around Montréal and Ottawa. There has been a perceptible extension of urbanization in a narrow strip bordering Lake Ontario from Oshawa eastwards. As a counterpoint to these areas of increasing population density, there are noticeable areas of decrease in the eastern part of the axis, particularly in the Cantons de l'Est south of Québec City.

These maps of population density do not indicate the overall range in density values found throughout the entire axis. If the axis is viewed as a whole, the average density has increased from 144 to 176 persons per square mile between 1961 and 1971. In 1971, however, the average population density of the census subdivisions defined as urban, which embrace 11,072 square miles, is 894 persons per square mile. The total extent of the area covered by these urban census subdivisions is only slightly less than the size of the Netherlands, and the population density is also about the same as in that country. By contrast, the average density in the area classified as semi-urban is

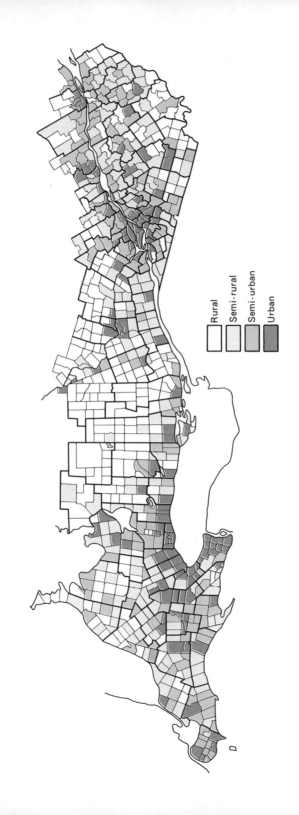

Rural

Semi-rural

Semi-urban

Urban

Figure 2.1: Population densities, (a) 1961;

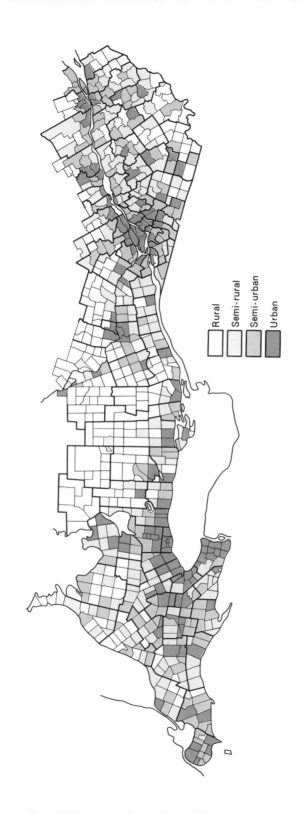

(b) 1966;

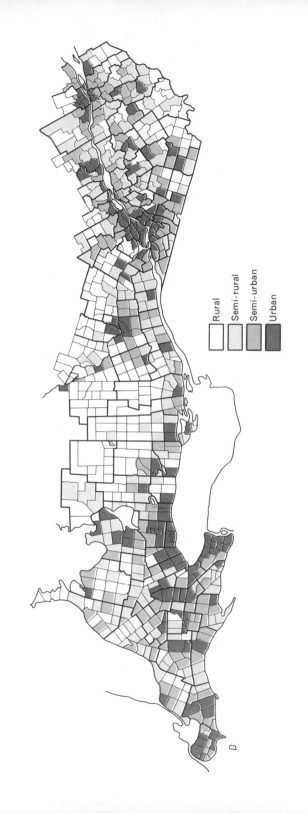

Rural

Semi-rural

Semi-urban

Urban

(c) 1971

seventy-three persons per square mile, and in the rural and semi-rural areas only twenty-three persons per square mile. The highest average densities are found in the census subdivisions containing the cities of Toronto and Montréal, and they are 19 and 17.6 thousand persons per square mile respectively. Even though these figures seem large, they are not particularly so for urban areas, since they imply densities of around thirty persons to the acre — well below the average densities of European cities and many U.S. urban areas.

GROWTH

Marginal changes of the kind illustrated by the population density maps are illustrated most clearly by the map indicating the spatial distribution of population growth rates by census subdivision for the period 1961 to 1971 (Figure 2.2). This map has been drawn according to two categories of growth and one of decline, based on two critical values. The decline/non-decline critical value is naturally an average annual rate of growth of 0 per cent. The second critical value is the average annual rate of growth in the axis during the 1961 to 1971 period, which was 2 per cent. These critical values distinguish three rather interesting areas, which can be labelled great growth, growth, and decline.

The areas of great growth are confined almost entirely to four urban regions within the axis, and these are all basically suburban in character. The largest contiguous area of great growth in the period has been around Montréal, though not central Montréal, which has lost population. A few municipalities on the south shore of the St. Lawrence River are included in this category, but most of the contiguous area is to the north of the city. A second large area involves the suburban townships around the city of Ottawa, south of the Ottawa River. The rapidity of urban growth in these townships led to a demand for the formation of a larger unit of local government in the late 1960s. Another, less contiguous zone of great growth, is around the city of Toronto, particularly to the west in Peel county. Finally, there is a small area of great suburban growth north of Québec City.

The more general areas of growth include and surround all the large cities in the axis. Growth has occurred in a cluster of census subdivisions surrounding Québec City, the Montréal region, Ottawa, and the Ottawa Valley, the townships bordering the St. Lawrence

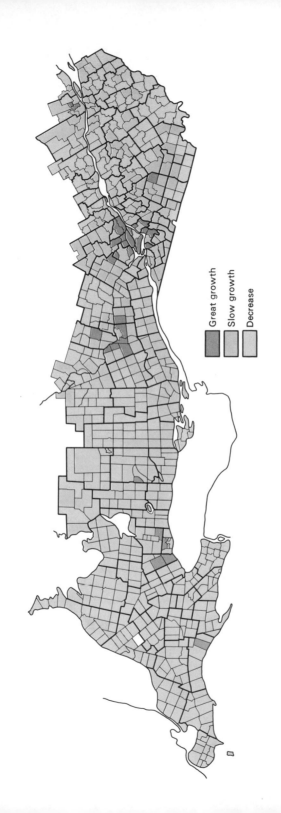

Figure 2.2: Population growth rates in the axis, 1961–71

Great growth

Slow growth

Decrease

River and eastern Lake Ontario, and the entire western one-third of the axis. These areas of growth are complemented by three very large areas of decline, which are located on the barren Shield region in the central part of the axis, in the Appalachian area of 'Est du Québec, and in the zone between Montréal and Québec City. The more favourable areas of settlement in southeastern Ontario are demarcated as zones of continuous and steady growth, though there are a few census subdivisions whose population is declining.

Comparative growth

Although the absolute growth rate data is quite interesting, there are certain problems that occur when the maps are used as a vehicle for the discussion of comparative shifts in population. Comparative shift information indicates whether a particular census subdivision has increased or decreased more than might be expected. The actual shift data details how much the census subdivision exceeds or falls short of the expected amount, and an index can be constructed from this to indicate the proportionate amount by which it exceeds or fails to meet the expected quantity. These indices can then be compared, and those census subdivisions with the greatest comparative shift can be distinguished from those with the least. The concept of comparative change was introduced in the preceding chapter, and here we shall extend the definition a little further.

The primary problem is to define the expected quantity for each census subdivision. If the analysis concerns comparative shift in population in census subdivisions within the axis for the period 1961–71, then one of the two values could be used to calculate the expected amount. Either the percentage increase in Canada between 1961 and 1971 (18.26 per cent) or the percentage increase in the axis (22.47 per cent), could be used. Use of the former would result in the calculation of expected values for census subdivisions based on the national growth situation; use of the latter would result in the calculation of values based on the axis growth, which has been much greater than that for the nation as a whole. In this case, since the discussion is concerned with the axis as a semantic entity, the axis growth performance will be used.

To illustrate the procedure, data will be used for the aggregated census subdivision of the cantons of St. Etienne, St. Nicholas, and Bernières, and the village of St. Rédempteur in Lévis County. The population of this aggregation in 1961 was 4,287 and in 1971 it was 5,979. Thus there had been a large percentage increase of 39.47 per cent, but the question arises as to whether this increase is more or less than would be expected if the census area had grown at the rate of the axis as a whole. The expected population in 1971, if it had grown at the axis rate (1 + 0.2247) would have been 4,287 × 1.2247 = 5,250. Thus the actual population exceeded the expected population by 5,970 − 5,250 = 729. This difference can be presented as a comparative index in this particular case by expressing it as a percentage of the predicted 1971 value. The comparative growth (or decline) index for this aggregation in Lévis County therefore, is 729/5250 = 13.88 per cent. In other words, the population of the census subdivision increased 13.88 per cent more than would have been predicted on the basis of the axis growth rate. Areas with positive values have, in effect, experienced a relative gain in population over and above what would be expected, while areas of negative values have failed to meet the overall performance of the axis.

The pattern of these positive and negative values for the period 1961–71 indicates that most of the area has experienced relative decline (Figure 2.3a). This is because a few areas with large populations have experienced substantial increases, and these sections include a broad area surrounding central Toronto extending from Lake Ontario north to Lake Simcoe and west to Kitchener-Waterloo; a large area surrounding central Ottawa; quite an extensive zone encircling but not including central Montréal; and a smaller area north of Québec City. Other isolated areas of comparative growth include Sherbrooke, Cowansville, London, and suburban Windsor. Thus, in general, there has been a relative convergence of population to the major urban centres over the ten-year period.

This process cannot be regarded as continuous throughout the 1960s, however; the change in the growth rate between the early and later parts of the period are reflected in two different patterns of shift. The 1961–66 pattern (Figure 2.3b) is based on the 12.44 per cent increase in total axis population over the five-year period. During this early period the areas of relative increase are more confined than those displayed in Figure 2.3a. Comparative increases are still associated with the same few urban nuclei mentioned above, but the areas affected are not nearly as extensive. This situation contrasts sharply with the 1966–71 pattern (Figure 2.3c), which is based on the 8.92 per cent increase observed over the second five-year period. In this

Figure 2.3: Comparative shift in population, (a) 1961–71;

> 20

0-20

-0.--20

< --20

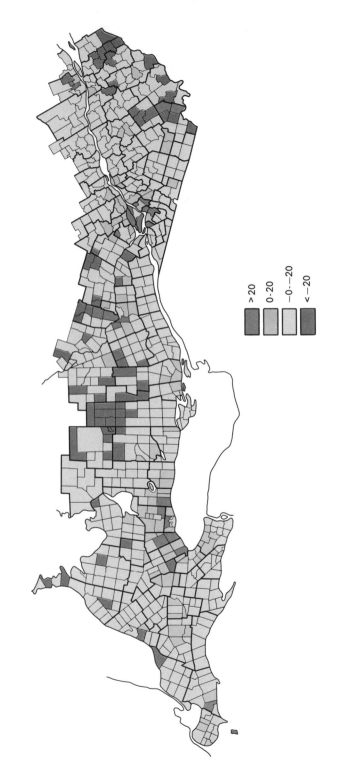

> 20

0-20

— 0·—20

< —20

(b) 1961–66;

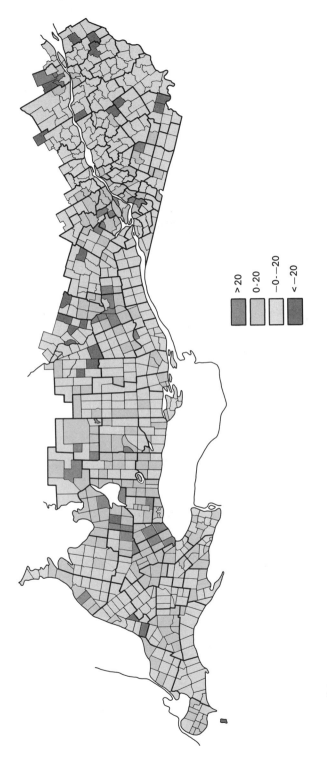

> 20

0-20

−0-−20

< −20

(c) 1966–71

period the parts of the map exhibiting relative increases are more extensive around Montréal and Québec City, and are dramatically extensive in the western one-third of the axis. During the first part of the period, therefore, when the population of the axis increased by 1,210,358, the bulk of this increase was located in a very small part of the area. In the second half of the period, however, when the population increased by 976,347, the bulk of the increase was spread over a more extensive portion of the axis. Thus, the early part of the period is characterized by concentration, and the second part by expansion.

POPULATION MOVEMENTS TO AND WITHIN THE AXIS

The apparent shifts in population detailed in the previous section could have occurred for a variety of reasons including differential death rates, differential birth rates, differential location of immigrants, and internal migration of people. The first two of these characteristics can be summarized by an index known as "natural increase", which is the difference between births and deaths expressed as a ratio per thousand people. If this natural increase index is examined for incorporated urban centres of 10,000 population or over within the axis, the general conclusion has to be that the relative shift of population to the vicinities of the largest urban agglomerations is not the result of significantly higher rates of natural increase in areas of comparative gain than in the areas that have exhibited comparative decline. The evidence is somewhat confusing, because the rates vary enormously, depending upon whether the incorporated centre is a recent suburban-type development, an older central city, or a clearly identifiable urban unit in a rural environment. The corollary to the observation, therefore, is that the areas of comparative decline exhibit rates of natural increase similar to those found in the areas that have exceeded the growth performance of the axis.

If the apparent shift in population is not really the result of differences in birth and death rates, is it the result of the differential location of immigrants and internal migration? The immigration evidence is rather inferential, but nevertheless fairly conclusive. With an estimated 20 per cent of the total increase in population in the axis being attributable to immigration, any concentration of destinations on one or more parts of the axis is quite important. The previous discussion has already indicated that at least 50 per cent of all immigrants to Canada between 1961 and 1971 probably went to Ontario, and about 20 per cent to Québec. These estimates compare well with those of Kalbach (1970, p.124) who suggests that 55.3 per cent of immigrants between 1945 and 1961 had Ontario as their destination, and 16.4 per cent Québec. More specifically, Kalbach identifies the western one-third of the axis as the major location of immigrants, with the major concentration extending from Toronto to Hamilton. In Québec, the only real destination for post-war immigrants has been Ile de Montréal.

With these distinct locational trends in mind, it is not too difficult to accept the argument that most of the 1961–71 immigrants to the axis settled in the same general area as the 1945–61 immigrants (Richmond, 1967). For example, if the primary focus defined by Kalbach is analysed separately, it can be estimated that the area between Toronto and Hamilton has 493,421 more people than it would have if it had grown at the axis growth rate for the 1961–71 period. Furthermore, if there was, in fact, a net immigration of some 350,000 people to the Ontario portion of the axis during the 1961–71 period, it is not at all unlikely that at least 200,000 of these immigrants settled in this primary zone. In that case about 40 per cent of the comparative shift of population to the Toronto-Hamilton area can be accounted for by immigration. Thus, it would appear that the differential location of immigrants has contributed significantly to the comparative shift of population to the positive areas in Figure 2.3a. This conclusion is based partly on general post-war evidence, and partly on "educated guesstimates."

MIGRATION WITHIN CANADA

Although the differential location of immigrants helps to explain part of the comparative increase in population in certain urban-centred regions, it would appear that the bulk of the changes are the result of internal migration within Canada. This is because internal migration streams are, on the whole, much larger than those to and from the country (Stone, 1969). Until the complete 1971 Census is published it is difficult to determine exactly how large these internal migration streams are compared with the volume of net immigration from beyond the country. Using various estimates from Stone (1969) and Wolfe (in Weir, 1968, Fig. 6.14) for the period 1956–61 it is possible to reconstruct some comparative "ball park" estimates. At the outset, it would appear that migration streams within Canada are about thirty-five times greater in volume than net immigration is. Most of these migration streams involve short-distance moves, however, so it is necessary to distinguish between moves made within the axis, and those made between the axis and the rest of Canada.

Unfortunately, it is not possible to define migration with respect to the axis as clearly as would be desirable, but by fitting together various sources of information (DBS 98-509, 98-510; Anderson, 1966; Stone, 1965, pp. 34–47; Weir, 1968) it is possible to develop a series of probability models that illustrate what is happening. As the axis cannot be distinguished from the provinces in this instance, the migration data for Ontario and Québec will be used as surrogates for specific axis information. This is not an unreasonable procedure, since 86.8 per cent of the total population of Québec and Ontario was located in the axis in 1971, and the most attractive possible locations for potential migrants are also located within the area.

Most migrations are of short distance, and the great bulk of these occur within the same municipality. In the aggregate, it can be estimated that if a person located somewhere in the axis is going to move his place of residence, there is a 97.8 per cent chance that he will stay within the axis (Table 2.6). In other words, out of every 1000 people who change residence in the axis, 978 relocate within the axis and 22 move outside to another province in Canada. Four of these twenty-two would move to British Columbia, nine to the prairie provinces, and nine to the Maritimes. Scanning down the diagonal of the data in Table 2.6 it is possible to discern the proba-

Table 2.6: The likelihood of a migrant moving within provinces or between provinces, based on 1956–61 data

| | | TO | | |
FROM	AXIS	BRITISH COLUMBIA	PRAIRIE PROVINCES	MARITIMES
Axis	.978	.004	.009	.009
British Columbia	.033	.885	.074	.008
Prairie provinces	.073	.075	.845	.007
Maritimes	.159	.011	.011	.819

bility of a migrant staying within the general geographic region of his origin. There is an 88.5 per cent chance that a migrant located in British Columbia will remain in British Columbia, and 84.5 per cent chance that a migrant in the prairie provinces will remain in the prairie provinces, and an 81.9 per cent chance that a person located in the Maritimes will remain in the Maritimes. It will be noted that the axis area has by far the highest probability of retention of a migrant, and the maritime provinces the least.

One of the drawbacks of Table 2.6 is that it does not include in and out migrations from outside Canada. It is, therefore, constructed as if Canada were a closed system, but as it has already been estimated that net immigration accounted for about one-fifth of the increase between 1961 and 1971, a more general model should take this factor into account. A method of including it does exist, however, and it will be noted in the subsequent section concerning the prediction of population distributions.

Migration and future patterns

Table 2.6 can be used to illustrate the impact of migration on the distribution of population, though in its present form it cannot be used for prediction. If it can be assumed that the migration probabilities listed in the table represent a situation that exists over a number of decades (Farrar, 1962), then they can be regarded as descriptive of the most probable 1961–71 pattern and that of subsequent decades. A test of adequacy of this table would, in effect, be whether it can be used to forecast the 1971 distribution of population. But first, it is necessary to illustrate what would happen if the data are used, as they are, for forecasting purposes.

Consider a situation in which Canada is divided into four regions: the axis, British Columbia, the Prairie provinces and Shield, and the Maritime provinces and Newfoundland. The population in the non-axis portions of Ontario and Québec is cast into the vast Prairie province and Shield area. In 1961 the populations of these regions were:

axis	9,730,950
British Columbia	1,629,082
Prairie provinces and Shield	4,943,234
Maritime provinces and Newfoundland	1,897,425

What would be the distribution of this population if the entire population of 18,200,691 moved once in each of five ten-year periods? The probabilities in Table 2.6 indicate that many people would remain where they were or in the same province, but some would move. The forecasted distributions can be obtained by matrix multiplication procedures (Yeates, 1974) and are listed in Table 2.7.

Forecasting using matrix multiplication in a simple model of this kind usually results in a convergence of the projections after six periods. In this example the convergence becomes noticeable after five iterations, at which time 63.8 per cent of the population of the country is located in the axis, as compared with 53.1 per cent in 1961. British Columbia increases its share of the total population as well, while the Prairie provinces and Shield, and the mysterious east incur net out-migration. Thus , in this type of artificial closed, non-growth situation most of the population of Canada would eventually live in the axis if the 1956–61 migration pattern is applicable now and in the future.

Growth and migration

One simple method of building growth into the migration model presented in Table 2.6 is to add to the numbers on the diagonal of the table indices of natural growth for the respective regions. The problem is in the selection of the growth indices (Rogers and Miller, 1967). To illustrate the nature of the problem and the procedures an example will be used to forecast the 1971 and subsequent population distributions based on the following assumptions: 1) the within Canada migration pattern will remain as described in Table 2.6 for the period of the forecast; 2) the rate of population growth in each of the regions will be the same as that exhibited by the 1961–71 performance.

A basic conceptual problem is that the growth index required is not the simple ratio between the 1971 and 1961 axis populations (which is $11,917,655/9,730,950 = 1.225$), because the 1971 population includes the net in-migration (from the rest of Canada) for that period. Net in-migration (positive or negative) for each region, therefore, has to be estimated and removed from the 1971 population. Estimates of net immigration can be obtained by calculating gross immigration using the off-diagonal column probabilities, and gross out-migration can be calculated using the appropriate off-diagonal row

Table 2.7: Forecast population distributions resulting from interprovincial migration in a non-growth environment

REGION	1961 (t)	t + 1	t + 2	t + 3	t + 4	t + 5
Axis	9,730,950	10,233,175	10,660,054	11,024,961	11,338,694	11,609,991
British Columbia	1,629,082	1,872,275	2,046,930	2,168,833	2,250,322	2,301,027
Prairie provinces and Shield	4,943,234	4,406,035	3,972,327	3,620,765	3,334,512	3,100,284
Maritime provinces and Newfoundland	1,897,425	1,689,204	1,521,377	1,386,130	1,277,161	1,189,387

probabilities in Table 2.6. For example, in the axis total in-migration
(from the rest of Canada) is:

$$(1,629,082) \ (.033) + (4,943,234) \ (.073) + (1,897,425)$$
$$(.159) = 716,306$$

and out-migration is:

$$9,730,950 \ (.004 + .009 + .009) = 214,081$$

which yields a net in-migration of 502,225. This figure suggests that
migration to the axis from the rest of Canada probably accounted for
a proportion of the total increase in population in the axis between
1961 and 1971 similar to that of immigration from beyond the country.
When net in-migration is subtracted from the 1971 axis population
the growth index is:

$$11,415,430/9,730,950 = 1.1731.$$

When this growth index (minus one) is added to the probability
of a person in the axis staying in the axis $(.978 + .1731 = 1.1511)$
the growth performance of the 1961–71 period is built into the model.
It should be noted that net immigration from outside Canada is, in
effect, subsumed within the growth index as additional "births."

The procedure outlined above is used to calculate probabilities including "natural" growth for the other three regions, and the data are
listed in Table 2.8. As the diagonal values have been modified by

Table 2.8: A growth and allocational model for the population of Canada
based on the 1956–61 migration performance and 1961–71
growth rates

FROM	AXIS	BRITISH COLUMBIA	PRAIRIE PROVINCES AND SHIELD	MARITIME PROVINCES AND NEW-FOUNDLAND
Axis	1.151	0.004	0.009	0.009
British Columbia	0.033	1.077	0.074	0.008
Prairie provinces and Shield	0.073	0.075	1.0371	0.007
Maritime provinces and Newfoundland	0.159	0.011	0.011	1.013

using 1961–71 "natural" growth indices, projections based on these data must involve decennial iterations. If the 1961 regional distribution of population is used as a starting date, the 1971 projection should be the same as the actual distribution at that time, for the growth and allocation table has been constructed in part on the basis of the 1971 data. The forecasts, detailed in Table 2.9, indicate that there is a slight error of ±50 persons in each case for 1971, and these deviations can be attributed to rounding errors. The important point, however, is that trivial rounding errors of this kind compound, because the forecasts of each succeeding year are based on the forecast of that preceding.

The rough-and-ready forecasts in Table 2.9 are extremely interesting because they indicate the likely impact on the axis of population growth through natural increase and immigration as well as internal migration. If natural growth and immigration continue at the same rate as that experienced during the 1961–71 period, and internal migration streams remain similar to those for the 1956–61 period, then the population of the axis in the year 2001 will be practically equal to that for the whole of Canada in 1971, and by the year 2011 nearly 61 per cent of the population of the country will be located in the area. But both rough-and-ready and sophisticated techniques are just as likely to yield erroneous forecasts in the population projection business as they do at the race track on a fair summer afternoon. This word of caution will not deter the addicted but an observer or potential user should be warned.

For example, it has been established that the growth in population in the axis was much greater in the 1961–66 period than in the 1966–71 period. In fact, the pattern of the first five-year period was a continuation of the dramatic growth of the immediate post-war period. The growth pattern of the second part of the decade is probably not an aberration, but a sign of the growth performance to be expected in the future. Thus it would be judicious to examine the nature of the forecasts based on the 1966–71 estimated "natural" growth for each region. The estimated new diagonal elements are 1.0203, 0.9236, 0.0935, and 0.966, and the five-year period to which they pertain dictates that the forecasts should be calculated in five-year periods. The predictions, which use the 1966 distribution as the starting date, are listed in Table 2.10, and they indicate not only more conservative projections, but also a slightly lower concentration of population in the axis (58.7 per cent) than is suggested by the data in Table 2.9.

Table 2.9: Forecasts of the distribution of population in Canada to the year 2011 based on the growth and allocational model detailed in Table 2.8

REGION	1961	1971 (ACTUAL)	1971 (PREDICTED)	1981	1991	2001	2011
Axis	9,730,950	11,917,655	11,917,603	14,508,516	17,577,854	21,213,244	25,518,203
British Columbia	1,629,082	2,184,620	2,184,571	2,824,100	3,561,892	4,414,593	5,401,693
Prairie provinces and Shield	4,943,234	5,355,570	5,355,630	5,845,871	6,427,022	7,114,411	7,926,021
Maritime provinces and Newfoundland	1,897,425	2,057,265	2,057,305	2,246,275	2,469,567	2,733,356	3,044,927
Total*	18,200,691	21,515,110	21,515,109	25,424,762	30,036,335	35,475,604	41,890,843

* The 1961 and 1971 figures are a few thousand less than the actual population of Canada because the Yukon and Northwest Territories have been excluded.

Table 2.10: Forecasts of the distribution of population in Canada to the year 2011, based on the 1966–71 growth experience and 1956–61 migration

REGION	1961	1971 (ACTUAL)	1971 (PREDICTED)	1981	1991	2001	2011
Axis	10,941,308	11,917,655	11,917,522	14,042,204	16,428,741	19,119,317	22,160,941
British Columbia	1,873,674	2,184,620	2,184,664	2,791,831	3,398,273	4,204,202	4,687,791
Prairie provinces and Shield	5,182,020	5,355,570	5,355,363	5,791,268	6,345,331	7,020,139	7,821,934
Maritime provinces and Newfoundland	1,974,758	2,057,265	2,057,352	2,251,911	2,488,230	2,769,745	3,101,368
Total	18,200,691	21,515,110	21,514,901	24,877,213	28,660,475	32,933,403	37,772,034

The aggregate predictions compared

The question that confronts all race-goers must now be faced: which forecast should be selected? The easy answers are "none", "pick another", "change the method of forecasting". But eventually a forecast has to be selected, even if it is only for planning purposes, and it must be continually updated. A useful evaluation procedure is to examine the forecasts of others, such as those made by Systems Research Group (1970). The projections made by SRG are more conservative than those made by other forecasters (Brown, 1965; Illing, 1967) in Canada who used the very high 1951–61 growth performance of the nation.

The SRG projections are made on the basis of a cohort survival method by calculating estimates of births, deaths, and net migration for the population, partitioned into discrete age groups by sex. Different assumptions for each of these determinants will result in varying projections, and SRG produces a "preferred" projection based on natural growth and migration estimates which are lower than those achieved during the 1951–66 period. As a consequence, the "preferred" projection of SRG compares well with the simple projection based on the 1966–71 growth performance of the individual regions and the 1956–61 migration pattern. The curves in Figure 2.4 suggest that the preferred SRG projection overstates the "most likely" forecast, but is less than the crude forecast based on the 1961–71 growth performance. The forecast based on the 1966–71 growth performance is considered "most likely" because it assumes an *average birth rate* for the 1966–71 period which, on the basis of past trends, is considered most probable in the future. The SRG forecast overpredicts the 1971 actual total for Canada (less the Yukon and Northwest Territories) by 140,000 people, and, if the "most likely" forecast is correct, overpredicts the population of Canada in the year 2001 by more than 800,000 people.

As the "most likely" total population forecast is derived from projections for the individual regions, it is instructive to compare the SRG forecast with the "most likely" regional estimates. SRG gazed into the crystal ball for the various provinces for the years 1981 and 2001. The growth rates from these provincial projections can be used to derive equivalent estimates for the regions used in this report, and these estimates are compared with the "most likely" estimates in Table 2.11. One of the more interesting aberrations is that the "most likely" estimates suggest a much greater future growth for the Maritimes

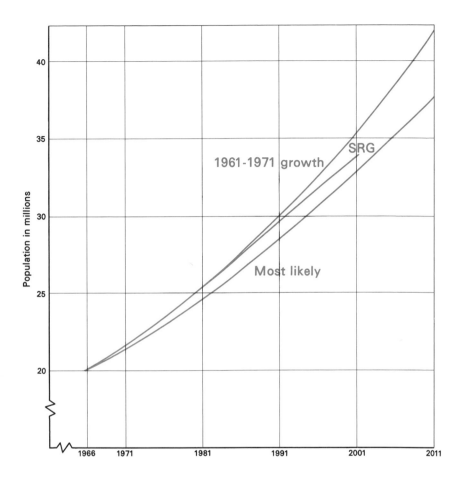

Figure 2.4: Comparison between the SRG preferred projection and the
1961–71 and 1966–71 based growth performances (SRG
axis figures estimated from provincial totals)

than was predicted by SRG. Interestingly, by 1971, the population of the Maritimes had almost achieved the SRG-predicted total for 1981. This development suggests that the out-migration parameters for the 1951–61 period used by SRG may not be applicable to the post-1966 period, and that the rate of out-migration from this area is decreasing. Concomitantly, SRG appears to overstate the potential in-migration to British Columbia by the year 2001. The prediction for the axis also appears to overstate the potential rate of growth as well as in-migration.

Nevertheless, even with these differences it is encouraging to conclude that the simple growth and migration model postulated and calibrated in this section yields projections that are quite similar to those provided by the more complex SRG procedure. There are times when simplicity is a virtue, and this would appear to be a possible example. The assumptions of the simple model can be discerned easily and remembered, and so the ephemeral basis of the "most likely"

Table 2.11: Comparison between the SRG regional population predictions (in thousands) and the most likely estimates for 1981 and 2001

AREA	1981	2001
Axis		
SRG	14,483	20,072
Most likely	14,042	19,119
British Columbia		
SRG	2,813	4,777
Most likely	2,792	4,204
Prairie provinces and Shield		
SRG	5,980	6,891
Most likely	5,791	7,020
Maritime provinces and Newfoundland		
SRG	2,086	2,061
Most likely	2,252	2,770
Total		
SRG	25,362	33,801
Most likely	24,877	32,993

estimates are apparent to all. Thus, the "most likely" estimates of the axis population will be used in any ensuing excursion into "futuristics".

MIGRATION WITHIN THE AXIS

Having noted the effect of immigration from beyond Canada and in-migration within Canada on the growth of population in the axis, it is now necessary to isolate the effect of internal migration within the axis on the population shifts previously documented. It has already been indicated that most of these external immigrants and in-migrants locate in Montréal and the major urban areas of southeastern Ontario. Furthermore, it has already been suggested that the shift in population is not attributable to higher natural increases (births minus deaths) in the urbanized parts of the axis; for the evidence in this respect is flimsy and, if anything, points in the direction of higher natural increases in rural areas (SRG, p. 64). Therefore, most of the comparative losses and a good proportion of the comparative gains must have been derived from internal movements of people within the axis. This is not surprising if there is a 97.8 per cent chance of a mover located in the axis staying in the axis.

Migration patterns within Québec

Complete data concerning migration within the axis cannot be obtained at this time, but information concerning migration in the province of Québec is available. These data have been prepared by Robert (1971), and they pertain to the proportion of the population of Québec paying taxes on earned income in the 1965 fiscal year. Thus the migration pattern relates to a one-year period between the 1965–66 fiscal period. Furthermore, the data relate only to that proportion of the population paying taxes, so a very large element of the migratory population is excluded. Specifically, most young persons who have never had a job but who are seeking employment for the first time are excluded. Therefore, the pattern of migration flows may well be a biased sample. The principles that emerge from the analysis are quite useful, however, because they document and help to forecast the nature of future trends.

The basic flow data for the population of Québec that submitted federal income tax returns in the 1965–66 period have been obtained from estimates tabulated by Robert (1972). These estimates relate to the ten administrative regions of the province of Québec, but for the purpose of this discussion, Côte-Nord and Nouveau-Québec have been combined to form one region. Most of the regions have at least one major urban area as their focus, and these urban areas usually account for a large proportion of the total population of each region (Table 2.12). Thus, although the discussion relates to the regions, the concentration of the population within the regions to urban areas implies that the bulk of the data really relates to inter-urban movements, and this comment applies particularly to those regions juxtaposed along the axis. In this context, Stone (1969) notes that the most significant (in terms of volume) internal migration streams in Canada during the 1956–61 period were inter-urban. This situation persisted and intensified during the 1960s.

The pattern of flows between each of the administrative subregions is summarized in probability form in Table 2.13. The off-diagonal elements have been derived from data tabulated by Robert (1972), while the elements on the diagonal have been calculated as a residual from estimates of the total fiscal population of each region. Thus, the data in the first row indicate that out of 10,000 potential movers (all the fiscal population are potential movers), 9,678 stayed in Bas-St-Laurent-Gaspésie, 7 moved to Saguenay-Lac-St-Jean, 48 went to Québec, 5 moved to Trois-Rivières, 2 to Cantons de l'Est, 167 migrated to Montréal, 3 to Outaouais, 8 to Nord-Ouest, and 82 to Côte-Nord, Nouveau-Québec. It is noticeable that the propensity to stay in the same region is extremely high but that out-migration to and in-migration from the largest population centres (Québec and Montréal) and the closest regions are also significant in each case. These are, in fact, general concepts which underlay most migration streams, for most streams are largest to and from the closer places, and diminish with distance, and they are also proportionate to the size of the receiving and sending places. Furthermore, the general pattern of flows suggested in Table 2.13 appears to have been existent for some decades (Robert, 1973).

Growth can be built into this model in exactly the same way as in the previous case discussed for Canada as a whole. Unfortunately, the axis proportion of the Québec population cannot be distinguished separately, but since the combined population of the five administrative regions marked with an asterisk in Table 2.13 exceeded the actual population of the axis in 1971 by only 4.4 per cent these areas

Table 2.12: Administrative regions used in the analysis of migration within the province of Quebéc, including the proportion of the population in each region located in major urban areas, 1971

ADMINISTRATIVE REGION	MAJOR URBAN AREAS	PER CENT OF POPULATION
Bas-St-Laurent, Gaspésie	Rimouski	11.6
Saguenay, Lac-St-Jean	Chicoutimi-Jonquière CMA	47.6
*Québec	Québec, Lévis CMA	52.8
*Trois-Rivières, Bois-Franc	Trois-Rivières, Cap de la Madeleine	40.2
*Cantons de l'Est	Shawinigan, Drummondville, Victoriaville, Sherbrooke, Magog	41.9
*Montréal	Montréal CMA, St-Hyancinthe, Valleyfield, Sorel, Granby	83.3
*Outaouais	Hull CMA	26.1
Nord-Ouest	Rouyn-Noranda, Val d'Or	28.7
Côte-Nord, Nouveau-Québec	Sept-Iles, Baie Comeau	31.7

* Administrative regions co-existent with the axis.

Table 2.13: The likelihood of a potential mover staying within the same administrative region, or moving between administrative regions, based on 1965–66 data

FROM	TO								
	(1)	(2)	(3)	(4)	(5)	(6)	(7)	(8)	(9)
(1) Bas-St-Laurent, Gaspésie	.9678	.0007	.0048	.0005	.0002	.0167	.0003	.0008	.0082
(2) Saguenay, Lac-St-Jean	.0005	.9785	.0050	.0008	.0003	.0103	.0001	.0021	.0024
(3) *Québec	.0010	.0011	.9827	.0015	.0009	.0110	.0002	.0005	.0011
(4) *Trois-Rivières, Bois Franc	.0002	.0004	.0032	.9760	.0013	.0175	.0004	.0005	.0005
(5) *Cantons de l'Est	.0001	.0002	.0041	.0023	.9746	.0177	.0002	.0006	.0002
(6) *Montréal	.0008	.0006	.0022	.0012	.0008	.9933	.0004	.0005	.0002
(7) *Outaouais	.0000	.0002	.0004	.0001	.0002	.0065	.9919	.0005	.0002
(8) Nord-Ouest	.0006	.0020	.0040	.0010	.0008	.0159	.0017	.9735	.0005
(9) Côte-Nord, Nouveau-Québec	.0095	.0054	.0098	.0027	.0009	.0162	.0002	.0027	.9526

* Administrative regions co-existent with the axis.

can be regarded as equivalent to the axis. Growth is included for the 1966–71 period for this has been the most recent period of significant change in population in the province. Net inmigration (positive or negative) is calculated for each region, and these figures are used to modify the 1971 region totals. Noticeably, Montréal is by far the largest area of positive net in-migration, with slight positive balances in Outaouais and Côte-Nord, Nouveau-Québec (including Baie James). The other regions all incurred net out-migration, particularly Québec and Bas-St-Laurent, Gaspésie.

Once the growth factors for each region have been calculated, the indices (less one) are added to the diagonal elements in Table 2.13, and the future population of the different regions can be forecast using regular matrix multiplication procedures. It should be noted that these growth factors in effect subsume migration to or from areas beyond the province as either "births", or "deaths" depending upon whether the balance is positive or negative. Thus the overall forecasts assume not only that the distributory mechanism detailed for the 1965–66 period and the 1966–71 average growth pattern will be applicable in the future, but also that the balance of migration to and from the province will hold constant. These assumptions are worth re-emphasizing, for though a certain horse should win on a hard track, it might rain!

The forecasts tabulated in Table 2.14 are quite interesting. The projection begins with the 1966 distribution, and continues through to the year 2011, with the 1971 prediction calculated for comparative purposes. It should be noted that the model tends to overpredict the Montréal region and underpredict a number of others, including the Québec and Trois-Rivières regions. Even though these deviations tend to compound in successive forecasts, they cannot be regarded as excessive, given the assumptions involved in the forecast model, and they do not detract from the major implications of the results. A very important implication is that if present trends continue the proportion of the axis population located in Québec is going to continue to decrease. The total axis population in the year 2001 is likely to be 21.21 million, and of this 6.98 million will probably be located in the Québec portion. In other words, the Québec share will have decreased from 42.2 per cent in 1971 to one-third by the year 2001. Activities which tend to be market-oriented may, therefore, be more likely to locate in the western part of the axis than in the eastern.

A second implication can be observed from an examination of the

Table 2.14: Forecasts of the distribution of population in Québec to the year 2011, based on the 1966–71 growth experience and 1965–66 fiscal migration

REGION	1966	1971 (ACTUAL)	1971 (PREDICTED)	1981	1991	2001	2011
Bas St-Laurent, Gaspésie	239,772	232,598	230,749	214,994	202,093	191,845	184,082
Saguenay, Lac-St-Jean	280,687	279,879	278,778	275,601	273,337	272,058	271,845
*Québec	907,415	941,488	940,258	1,009,406	1,083,619	1,163,480	1,249,623
*Trois-Rivières, Bois-Franc	424,168	420,694	418,532	408,720	400,892	395,111	391,452
*Cantons de l'Est	219,498	224,184	223,449	231,910	241,199	251,431	262,731
*Montréal	3,217,193	3,423,458	3,430,620	3,894,518	4,413,021	4,993,009	5,642,160
*Outaouais	224,257	243,352	243,512	286,769	337,247	396,164	464,936
Nord-Ouest	160,125	147,223	146,801	124,628	107,481	94,432	84,951
Côte-Nord, Nouveau-Québec	107,730	114,884	114,711	129,125	114,247	160,208	177,148
Total	5,780,845	6,027,760	6,027,415	6,575,675	7,203,139	7,917,741	8,728,732

* Administrative regions co-existent with the axis.

data pertaining to the two regions in which large urban areas contain the greatest proportion of the total population of the areas. If the regions of Montréal and Québec are combined, the share of these two, large, urban-dominated regions of the Québec total population will likely increase from 72.4 per cent in 1971 to 77.8 per cent in the year 2001. Robert (1972) also isolates these two areas as being the focus of the migratory network in the province, with the migration streams between the two regions being the largest, and the relative magnitudes of the other flows that focus upon them being the largest as well. Furthermore, he indicates that Montréal also acts as a provincial "clearing house" for external migration streams. It is likely that the rather large interprovincial migration between Québec and Ontario is, in essence, between Montréal and the urban areas of southwestern Ontario (particularly Toronto).

Thus, the growth of population and the pattern of migration in the province of Québec will probably result in an increasing proportion of the province's total population being located in the axis area (from 83.5 per cent in 1971 to 88 per cent in 2001). Furthermore, this population will be concentrated primarily in the urban region of Montréal (Bélanger *et al.*, 1972) and secondarily in the region of Québec. Those parts of the axis in Québec beyond the influence of these growth poles will show a relative decline in population, and Trois-Rivières, Bois-Franc, which is located in between these two poles, will likely suffer a gross decline.

Migration patterns within Ontario.

Data are not available at this time to perform a similar analysis of the effects of migration for the western two-thirds of the axis that is located in Ontario. Studies prepared by Whebell (1971), Hill (1971), and Hughes (1971), however, provide some evidence with which certain comparisons can be made. Whebell calculates the expected 1966 population of each census division in Ontario on the basis of a survivor ratio for age cohorts. He then subtracts the actual population of the county in 1966 from this figure and thus obtains a difference that is attributed to net immigration (positive or negative). There is, therefore, no distinction made according to the source of the migrants, and there are no flows. The data are useful, however, in that the pattern of positive and negative values indicates whether the same urban influence experienced in Québec is repeated in Ontario.

Whebell demonstrates that the whole zone around Toronto as far as Kitchener-Waterloo and St. Catharines, Ottawa, and Windsor-London has been an area of net immigration, whereas the rest of the axis area in the province is an area of out-migration. This pattern is confirmed in one area by Hill (1971) in a study which analyses in-migration and out-migration from Toronto. He demonstrates that there is a considerable area of southern Ontario over which Toronto exerts an influence in terms of migration. Hughes (1971) focuses upon an area of net out-migration in eastern Ontario in which he traces the movements of a sample of graduates from grade 10 in 1961 in Frontenac County. This study reveals a massive out-migration of young people form the rural districts and smaller urban areas of the county, which is directed primarily towards the Toronto and southwestern part of the province.

It is possible, therefore, to envisage a pattern of flows similar to that in Québec. As there are more urban areas of intermediate size in Ontario than in Québec, there are more poles of in-migration. The primary poles are Toronto and Ottawa, but Hamilton, London, Windsor, Kitchener-Waterloo, and St. Catharines are also important. The areas of out-migration are the rural districts and smaller urban centres of central and eastern Ontario, and a triangular area bounded by Lake Huron and the southern shore of Georgian Bay. The largest migration streams are, as in the Québec case, inter-urban. The implication of the Québec data is that by the year 2001 the Ontario portion of the axis will contain very nearly 14,000,000 people, with the vast bulk of this population located in urban areas in the western one-third of the axis.

CONCLUSION

Thus, it would appear that much of the population increase in the major urban regions of the axis during the 1960s was due to natural increase, immigration from outside the country, and in-migration from other urban areas from within and beyond the axis area. Examination of the migration probabilities indicates that even a small change in the probabilities of movements between areas will result in very large changes in the net growth of the different regions. Thus, if the rate of immigration from overseas and the probability of movement between different areas can be influenced even marginally by public policy, the gross size of these largest urban areas will be greatly affected. If current trends continue in the axis and in the country as a whole, the result will be that the largest urban areas will grow larger at the expense of the smaller urban centres. This growth pattern will accelerate if the rate of natural increase continues to decline, because growth will increasingly become a product of inter-urban population shifts. In addition, as these movements include a high proportion of the younger age groups with the highest fertility rates the growth prospects of the larger cities are compounded while those of the smaller centres are further diminished.

A major issue facing those responsible for national and provincial urban policy is the degree to which the three or four largest urban areas should be permitted to dominate the rest of the nation. Is there anything wrong with letting the chips fall where they may? In the axis such a policy (no policy at all is, in fact, a policy) has resulted in very high rates of growth in two large urban regions. In these areas the rates of growth have been so excessive that it has been difficult for the local and provincial governments to cope with the accelerating demands for services, transport facilities, and people-responsive administration, while financial institutions and the construction industry have found it nearly impossible to keep pace with the demand for low-priced single-family housing. Meanwhile, the very necessary concentration of governmental and construction efforts in these regions has meant that the equally serious problems of slow growth or decline in other parts of the axis have been neglected.

This is not to imply that concentrated growth in a few areas is wrong; for it is quite likely that large urban areas are a more efficient form of human organization. They certainly become extremely efficient in production, exchange, and general management owing to sheer population size, a large skilled-labour force, and the greater possibilities for personal interaction. There are disadvantages for the axis and the nation as a whole, however, and at least one of them cannot be ignored. Rapid growth in a few areas results in a distortion of the image of an entire nation; for growth has an aura which seems to outweigh all other values. To the businessman and manufacturer growth seems to imply the assurance of success; as a result, he will naturally choose to expand or locate in the growing area even though there are other areas in which the business may be just as successful. Certainly there are many activities which require location within large markets in order to survive, but equally there are a large number of activities to which size of market *per se* does not really matter.

Unfortunately, it seems that the image of large urban areas is so compelling that the locators of these activities are blinkered against alternatives.

To the potential migrant, large, high-growth urban areas are alluring places where employment and high wages are assured. Certainly to young people, the few large metropolitan areas in the axis and the country appear to be the only areas of opportunity. Indeed they frequently are, because this is what they have been allowed to become. In a later chapter the way in which these areas have become the depository of most new jobs in the axis and the nation will be documented and discussed. But at the same time, it will be demonstrated that this situation exists only because the problem has been tackled in the wrong way. Alonso (1972) points out that large net out-migration from certain areas may be necessary and that it is, perhaps, counter-productive to develop programs to retain the people there. Instead, it would be more efficient to use the developed infrastructure by creating large streams of in-migration of new and different kinds of people to regenerate and change the image and productive base of the area. Mechanisms for undertaking such a redirection of flows other than through manufacturing employment are available, and a discussion at this juncture is premature and would not sustain the drama. The next task is to indicate the effects of the past and future population increase and redistribution on land and housing.

3   THE USE OF THE LAND

For those who have driven along the Macdonald-Cartier Freeway (Highway 401) and Route 20 (Québec), the designation of the axis as an area of developing continuous urbanization may appear as illusory as a feat performed by Houdini. The traveller is confronted with miles and miles of open countryside, farmland, wooded areas, and occasional rough-looking scrub. This is so because the roads are built away from urban areas, the only exceptions being in the Oshawa-Toronto and Montréal regions. Signs indicating that Kitchener is so many miles away, or that Drummondville is somewhere to the south, are the only real indicators of the existence of urban areas. Nevertheless, the villages, towns, and cities are there, and in total they do contain most of the people and economic activity of Canada.

URBAN LAND IN THE AXIS

One of the reasons why urban areas do not appear to be a dominant feature of the traveller's landscape is that they occupy a small proportion of land. A good estimate of the amount of land in the axis occupied by continuous urban uses is 2,146.2 square miles. This estimate has been obtained from a detailed analysis of maps of predominant land use in the development regions of Ontario in 1971, prepared by the Regional Development Branch of the Ministry of Treasury, Economics, and Intergovernmental Affairs at a scale of one inch to four miles (1:253440); and from maps prepared by the Canada Land Inventory for Québec and aggregated to a scale of 1:250000. The basic survey work for the Canada Land Inventory in Québec was undertaken between 1965 and 1967 on a map base of 1:50000, and the detail for the Regional Development Branch maps was obtained from similar land-use surveys updated by direct field survey and analysis of pertinent aerial photographs. Many difficulties were encountered in comparing the different classification schemes, and these problems are discussed in detail in Appendix c.

Regardless of interpretative difficulties, the estimation procedures and basic information sources yield fairly good results when the figure of 2,146.2 square miles is compared against the population of the axis and other areas of similar size. If all the population of the axis in 1971 were concentrated in the estimated urbanized area, the density would be only 8.7 persons to the acre. A more reasonable supposition would relate to the population that has been classified as urban on the basis of density by census subdivisions. In this case 83 per cent of the population of the axis would be classified as urban, and if the population were concentrated in the estimated urban area, the density would be 7.2 persons to the acre. This is not a very high density, though it must be remembered that the land estimated as "urbanized" includes not only residential and commercial areas, but industrial and transport land uses as well as parks within and conterminous with urban areas.

What do these densities imply? Imagine yourself, as the owner of a football team, sitting in the best seats overlooking the fifty-yard line on a bright Fall afternoon. A football field, including the end zones, usually measures in area about 2.3 acres. If we assume four persons to a family, and that each family lives in one detached house, then the field would contain at most four houses according to the densities implied by this estimate of land urbanized. As this density figure includes non-residential uses, part of the land would not be occupied by houses, and these other uses usually comprise about 44.4 per cent of the urban land occupied in many axis cities (Maher and Bourne, 1969).

The essential point is that the estimate of 2,146.2 square miles urbanized is definitely not an underestimate. Neither is it an overestimate; for not only does the figure represent a wide variety of residential and non-residential uses, it also compares well with estimates calculated in other countries. For example, the area of the axis is roughly similar to that of England and Wales combined. To be precise, it is fifteen per cent larger. Notwithstanding this difference, it is instructive to compare the proportions of land used in three major categories in England and Wales in 1965 with those used in the axis in the 1970 period. These dates are, of course, general dates, and each item of data must be regarded as a reasonable estimate for the period to which it pertains.

The proportions listed in Table 3.1 must be interpreted with respect to two observations. First, it is generally believed that urban densities tend to be higher in Europe than in North America because of the greater pressure of population on land. Thus, it is not surprising to find that the density in England and Wales would be 11.2 persons per acre compared with 8.7 persons per acre for the axis, if the entire population of each area were regarded as urban. Consequently, the estimate that 3.2 per cent of the axis is defined as urban is encouragingly comparable. Secondly, the definitions "urban" and "agriculture" vary between the surveys undertaken in the axis and those in England and Wales. The estimate of agricultural land in the axis in 1970 is, in fact, farmland acreage interpolated from the Census farm data (see footnotes to Table 1.4). The higher proportion for England and Wales can, again, be explained in the light of the far greater pressure on land for domestic food production as well as the generally more favourable environment (physical and climatological) for agriculture. In the latter context, it is interesting to note that the part of the axis defined as Shield and Appalachian in Figure 1.3 comprises 40.2 per cent of the axis. There are areas of farmland within these zones, although they are declining in acreage and being transferred to forest cover. Likewise there are extensive areas of woodland and forest cover in the Interlake Ontario and St. Lawrence Lowland

Table 3.1: *The major uses of land in the axis in 1970, compared with those in England and Wales*

	AXIS 1970	ENGLAND AND WALES 1965
Urban land	3.2	11.5
Agriculture (farmland)	52.4	78.6
The rest (forest, woods, etc.)	44.4	9.9
Population (in thousands)	11,918	47,953

Sources: Data for England and Wales in Edwards and Wibberley (1971), p. 83; estimates for the axis compiled by the author.

zones that offset the Shield and Appalachian agricultural areas.

Thus, it would appear that the general land-use estimates for 1970 are reasonably correct given the general problem of defining what is marginally urban or marginally rural. The conclusion has to be that the urban population of the axis occupies a very small proportion of the area, even though its influence dominates the entire region and much of the rest of Canada as well. Even if the boundaries of the axis were limited to the physiographic regions of Interlake Ontario and the St. Lawrence Lowland, the proportion of the area actually urbanized would be only 5.3 per cent. While these proportions are reasonably small they should not be disregarded, because if urban land is concentrated in a few areas and is consuming agricultural land at an increasing rate, then a number of problems may emerge.

VARIATIONS IN URBAN LAND USE WITHIN THE AXIS

The general features of variations in urban land use within the axis are depicted in Figure 3.1. This map indicates the proporton of total land area in a census subdivision that is defined as minimum urban land in Appendix C; it is this classification that is most nearly similar for the two provincial portions of the axis. The categories of intensities have not, in this particular case, been selected according to any logical conceptual framework, but have been selected geometrically. The highest category delimits those census subdivisions that contain 40 per cent or more of the land surface in urban use. Just as with the maps of densities, Figure 3.1 is greatly affected by the physical size of the census subdivisions, since relatively small urban areas in large townships or cantons tend to be overlooked. Thus, urban concentrations along the St. Lawrence River, Est du Québec, and in the far western portion of the axis, tend to be under-represented.

Nevertheless, the general pattern exhibited in Figure 3.1 gives a fair impression of the variation in concentration of urban land use throughout the axis. This impression will, of course, depend upon the manner in which the map is interpreted, for maps, if "read" incorrectly, can be as misleading as some advertising. A correct impression of the actual extent of urbanism can be gained by concentrating on the distribution of those twenty-seven census subdivisions with 20 per cent or more of their land in urban use, for these represent only a little more than 3.2 per cent of the axis area. A false general impres-

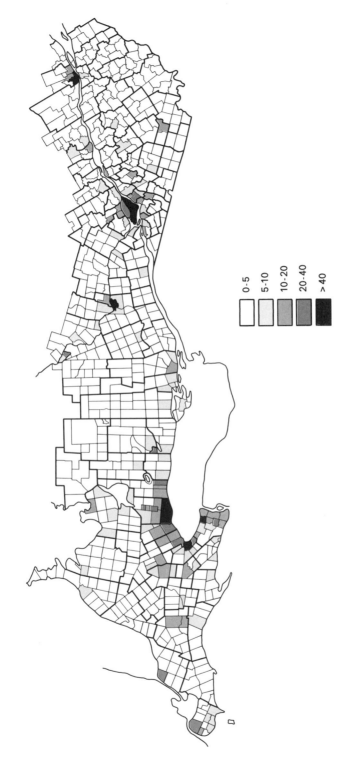

Figure 3.1: Urban land in the axis as a per cent of total land in census subdivisions, 1971

0-5
5-10
10-20
20-40
> 40

sion is received if the interpreter concentrates on all those areas where more than 5 per cent of the area is in urban use, since on the map these areas comprise 17.7 per cent of the total axis area. On this note of caution about impressions it is now possible to proceed!

As would be expected, the land within the axis is fairly heavily urbanized only in the areas of greatest population density. In particular, urban land use is extremely heavy in the area between Whitby and the Niagara Peninsula and in the Montréal region. A swift calculation reveals that these two urban regions together contain well over one-third (37.1 per cent) of all the urban land in the axis. Other reasonably extensive concentrations of urban land are found in conjunction with Québec City, Trois-Rivières, Sherbrooke, Ottawa-Hull, Kingston, Kitchener-Waterloo-Guelph, London, Sarnia, and Windsor. Beyond these areas, there is little extensive continuous urbanization, as most of the towns are small, with clearly prescribed limits and well defined local hinterlands.

Urban land use and urban land users

At the risk of boring the inquisitive layman, it is probably useful at this juncture to indicate the basic problem of classification and why all the land-use maps and the Canada Land Inventory may be a waste of time. The problem with the classification of urban land as defined within this chapter is that the designation depends on the *appearance* of the land *use*. It does not focus on the purpose of the actual land *user* or owner who occupies the land. This point is made in academic style by Found and Morley (1972) in a series of studies of rural areas within the Metropolitan Toronto Region.

For example, Found and Morley (1972, p. 32) propose a classification of rural parcels of land based on ten classes of land users. These are:

1) prestige rural estate (urban-based owner)
2) short-term rural treatment (urban dweller)
3) social and/or ethnic group property (urban-based or resident)
4) rural residence (commuter)
5) retirement property (non-farmer, intended or actual retirement)
6) property of semi-retired farmer
7) rural recreational enterprise (owner-operator)
8) commercial farm property (includes part-time farmer)
9) speculative land holding (non-resident)

10) public conservation recreation area.

It is immediately apparent from even a cursory glance at this suggested classification that its application to all parcels of land in the axis would result in an entirely different estimate of land uses from those calculated. Although the estimate of urban land contained in this chapter includes conservation or recreational areas attached directly to continuous zones of urban land, it does not include categories 1, 2, 3, 4, 5, 7, and 9, which inevitably involve urban-based users. The contention is, therefore, that there are parts of the axis in which the inhabitants of the cities have consumed much of their rural surroundings without a rural to urban change in land *use* being physically apparent. Thus the real extent of urban ownership is undoubtedly understated.

THE EXPANSION OF URBAN LAND USE

The volume of land used for urban purposes is related to the total population involved and the amount of land consumed by each person. The population of the axis has increased quite dramatically over the past few decades, and all the evidence points toward a further concentration of a growing Canadian population in this area. Thus it would be expected that the amount of urban land being used within the axis will increase, but the amount by which it will increase is extraordinarily difficult to estimate. This is because the amount of land consumed by each individual is changing over time, and the consumption of land for urban purposes takes place at the periphery of urban areas. The latter observation may be regarded as trivial, but it is most important, because the periphery is sensitive, not only to an increasing total population, but to a changing distribution of population within the urban area.

THE SENSITIVITY OF THE PERIPHERY

To illustrate this sensitivity, examples can be used of the changing distribution of population in the three largest cities plotted for a variety of annular rings which have been centred over the theoretical centre of each urban area, which is usually located within the Central Business District. In the case of Montréal the central point is defined as the intersection of Craig and McGill streets (Service d'Urbanisme, 1964), for Metro Toronto, it is Queen and Yonge streets (Latham,

1968), and in Ottawa, it is Sparks and Bank streets (Oeppen, 1973). In each urban area the annular rings include all the land area within an eleven-mile radius of these central points, and they are the same width, except in Toronto where different radii are used for the rings within three miles of the centre. Thus the densities are "gross densities", since the measurements relate to the entire area of a ring, not just to the residential area.

In Figure 3.2 these densities (per acre) are plotted against the halfway distance of each ring. Note that the resultant curves for Toronto and Montreal are similar in shape, whereas those for Ottawa are less complex. The traditional view is that population densities are greatest close to the centre of urban areas, and that they decrease with distance away from these locations at a decreasing rate. This view is based on the assumption that the area within and adjacent to the Central Business District (CBD) of large urban areas contains the greatest concentration and variety of employment opportunities within the urban area, as well as being the focus of shopping, entertainment, and other socio-economic activities. The net result is that a large number of people wish to locate as close as possible to these diverse activities, thus causing high densities. Proximity may be considered desirable for a number of reasons, among which the most commonly touted are minimization of transport costs and/or time spent travelling, the magnetic attraction of the bright lights, and the availability of a variety of rental accommodation, which ranges widely in price and quality.

In all urban areas the very centre of the CBD is usually devoid of any significant residential population as most of the buildings are devoted to non-residential uses. In small urban areas this central zone of low density may consist of no more than the equivalent of one block, but in large urban areas this non-residential zone may extend over many blocks. As a consequence, in large urban areas, rings of a half-mile, or even one mile in radius may include comparatively few people, but in smaller urban areas rings of this width may include a large number of people. This is probably the major reason for the difference between the Montréal and Toronto curves and those for Ottawa within the inner four-mile zone.

Apart from the inverted lemon squeezer appearance of the two big-city graphs, the rest of the curves within each illustration are remarkably similar. Population densities decrease with distance away from the centre of the city, since the space occupied by each individual

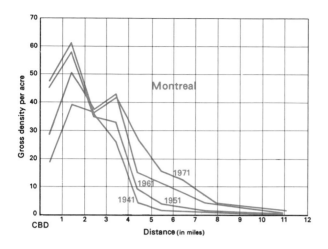

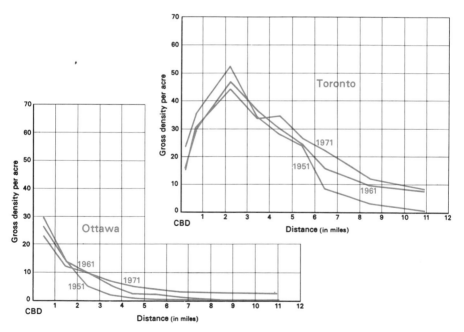

Figure 3.2: Population density (persons per acre) by anular rings, for Montréal, 1941–71; Toronto, 1951–71; and Ottawa 1951–71

increases as lot sizes increase owing to the greater availability of cheaper land. Also, open spaces, parks, industrial estates, and expansive shopping centres tend to proliferate in the outermost zones of urban regions; such uses consume a great deal of land and contribute to the apparent decline in population densities. The interesting feature of these curves is that they all indicate that population densities in the central part of the urban area are decreasing over time, but that in the outermost zones they are increasing. In Montréal and Toronto the central section of decreasing densities appears to extend outwards for a distance of about four miles, whereas in the smaller city of Ottawa the "tipping" distance seems to be approximately two miles. The predicted end result of these changes is a more even distribution of population throughout the entire urban area.

The reason for these fundamental changes in the distribution of population has been discussed in detail elsewhere (Yeates and Garner, 1971; Newling, 1969), for they are just a few examples of a situation that is general across the whole of North America, and in many European countries as well. Although the central part of the city may (in Canada and the axis) be an exciting location and the focus of a variety of employment opportunities, it is not a necessary residential location for a vast majority of the population. Transport and communication improvements within urban areas have made it possible for many manufacturing firms and businesses to locate just about anywhere in the urban region. Furthermore, even if a family wanted to locate "downtown" it might not be able to afford to do so; its requirements for living space, comforts, and standard of housing have now increased to such a high level that it is probably impossible for it to purchase the expensive land and rebuild or renovate the old housing. These costs of renovation are made to appear even more expensive by the limited availability of mortgage funds for older housing compared with the greater availability of money to finance new housing, which inevitably requires "new" urban land. The paradox of Canadian life is that although real incomes may have risen substantially over the past few decades, the structural changes within urban areas and the social changes in society have accelerated at an even greater rate, with the result that there are still rather large discrepancies between the residential and locational aspirations of people and the actual situations that they can afford.

The implications of this general flattening in the population density curve are extremely important in any future estimate of the amount of land that may be absorbed into direct contiguous urban use. Not only are the populations of large urban areas going to increase in the future, but it would appear that the population will spread outward from these urban cores at an even faster rate. The repercussions of this situation are illustrated in graph form in Figure 3.3. The two sets of graphs depict the same situation, but Figure 3.3a is in semi-logarithmic form, and Figure 3.3b is in arithmetic form. It will be noted that the general form of the curves is similar to those for Ottawa in Figure 3.2, and that in the semi-logarithmic case the curve becomes a straight line. This transformation, therefore, is useful for analytic purposes. If the curves are rotated around 360 degrees, the areas beneath the cones equal the total population of the urban area. As the area defined by cone t contains two million people, the urban region in this hypothetical example will be referred to as "Torontreal," which is translated colloquially in the eastern portion of the axis as "Montronto."

The theoretical real limit of the urban area at time t is 7.7 miles from the centre of the city (the focus of the CBD). This limit is, for the sake of logical consistency, based upon the threshold value of "urban" population density of 119 persons per square mile, or 0.186 persons per acre, discussed previously. Therefore, at 7.7 miles from the centre of the city, Torontreal merges into a semi-urban zone of scattered housing along the major roads and occasional small subdivisions. If the total population of Torontreal remains at two million, but the slope of the population density curve decreases, the limit of the urban area moves farther away from the centre of the city. An example of this type of occurrence is given by curve $t+0$, where the decrease in slope has been accomplished by lowering the central density from forty persons per square mile to thirty persons per square mile. Even though the population of the urban area at $t+0$ is the same as at time t, the limit at $t+0$ has moved outward to 8.14 miles. All locations within approximately four miles of the centre of the city will have a lower population density than at time t, and all locations farther than four miles will have experienced an increase. The area of Torontreal would thus have increased from 119,040 acres to 133,120 acres. Even if the population of Torontreal stays the same, the trend for decreasing central densities and a concomitant flattening of the population density curve would have resulted in an additional consumption of 14,080 acres of land for urban uses.

But it is predicted that the population of Torontreal will increase tremendously by the year 2001; if this increase is only at the predicted rate for the axis as a whole, the population of the metropolis will be about 3.2 million by the end of the century. If the central density remains at thirty persons per square mile but the area under the cone is expanded to contain 3.2 million people, the slope of the density curve will again decrease, as is illustrated by curve $t+1$, and the theoretical limit of the metropolis would be almost twice the distance from the centre of the city than it was at time t. The population density curve declines to 0.186 persons per square mile at a distance of 13.02 miles from the centre of the city, and the metropolis at time $t+1$ would occupy 341,120 acres. Thus, a tendency for declining central densities, a 1.6 per cent per annum population growth rate, and a general decrease in slope of the population density curve, would result, in a span of thirty years, in a tripling in size of the urban area while the urban population would increase by only 60 per cent.

Thus, the periphery of an urban area is very sensitive to increases in population as well as changes in family space preferences. It is vital that in this zone where people and jobs are being translated into new urban land that good and careful planning should be practised to maximize public benefits. Unfortunately, experience shows that this is not the case, for the theoretical real limits of an urban area such as Torontreal have in the past been located beyond the actual legal planning limits of the city. In fact, this zone of metamorphism of non-urban to urban land has invariably been located in agricultural areas in which the virtues of private land ownership and disposal have been extended to embrace the parochial interests of private subdevelopment. The absence of any prior experience and understanding of urban management has been unwittingly exploited to produce an urban sprawl that is invariably badly integrated with the socio-economic structure of the urban community, and frequently is within itself poorly served by basic services. These problems of the urban fringe have been detailed elsewhere (Russwurm, 1971) and are referred to frequently in later chapters.

LAND ABSORPTION COEFFICIENTS AND LAND CONSUMPTION RATES

I do not live in the ethereal clouds of academia on a permanent basis, and am well aware that urban areas are not circular, nor do they have a population density that conforms uniformly to the conical pattern

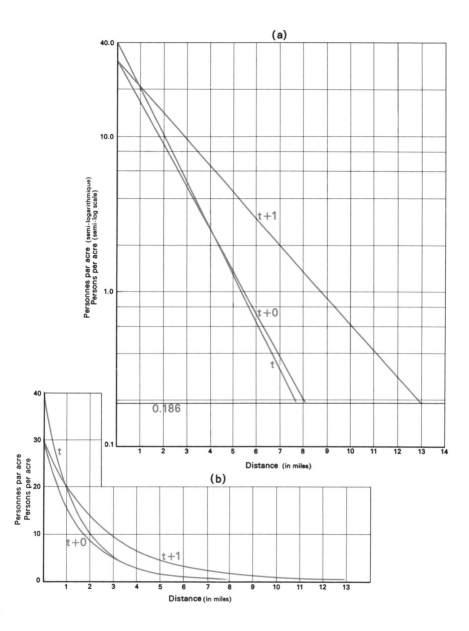

Figure 3.3: Persons per acre, (a) semi-logarithmic scale; (b) arithmetic scale

envisaged for Torontreal. Thus, it is usually impossible to calculate and predict urban growth on the basis of the graphical model outlined in the previous section. Instead, real-world empirical data, based on measured changes, has to be employed to arrive at some crude estimate of the rate of conversion of land from non-urban to urban uses. These measurements are usually expressed in the form of land consumption rates and land absorption coefficients.

Land consumption rates

One of the most useful reviews of the subject of estimating urban expansion in Canada is that compiled by Gad (1970), and it is the terminology of that research paper which is used in this volume. The land consumption rate is the amount of urban land actually used expressed as a ratio with respect to the urban population. Usually this ratio is defined in acres per thousand people, and it is, therefore, the reciprocal of population density. If central densities have been declining and the slope of the population density curve has been decreasing over time, then the land consumption rate should be increasing. For example, in the Torontreal example, the land consumption rate at time t is 119,040 (1000)/2,000,000 = 59.5 acres per thousand people. At time $t+1$ the ratio is 106.6 per thousand people. One method of estimating future demands for urban space, therefore, is to obtain some general land consumption rates for a series of time periods and to project these rates into the future. The assumption will be, of course, that past trends will continue into the future. Even if this assumption were tenable, the problems associated with obtaining comparable estimates of urban land consumption rates for the axis or even parts of the area for a long enough time period are horrendous. Most of the estimates that are available, or that can be calculated, relate to municipalities that have clearly defined boundaries. Since most municipalities are underbounded with respect to the real limits of the urban population, any estimate is likely to be misleading as well as difficult to compare against rates calculated for a number of time periods. Comparisons among urban areas are also likely to be impossible, because some municipalities are more underbounded than others.

These problems, as well as some general trends, can be observed quite clearly from the data presented in Table 3.2. In this table it will be noted that, on the whole, land consumption rates have increased

Table 3.2: *Estimates of land consumption rates for various years in selected axis urban areas*

	Lindsay[1]	Stratford[1]	Kingston[1]	London[1]	London CMA[1]	City of Toronto[2]	York[2]	Etobicoke[2]	Metro Toronto[2]	Ile de Montréal[3]	Québec CMA	Trois-Rivières CMA	Sherbrooke	Ottawa*
1951	190.9	106.0	92.0	102.0	77.3									32.2
1952										33.0				
1953														
1954														
1955										33.5				46.7
1956														
1957														
1958										34.6				
1959														
1960														
1961	175.0	120.0	106.0	97.0	94.0					37.8				57.7
1962														
1963						33.2	39.3	96.1	63.0					
1964										41.2				
1965														
1966						33.4	38.7	90.4	61.8					58.7
1967														
1968						33.3	38.7	87.9	60.7					
1969														
1970										41.7	72.7	79.2	61.5	55.0

Sources:
1 Hind-Smith (1962);   2 Gad (1970);   3 Feherdy (1971).

* Ottawa data refers to net residential land consumption.

during the twenty-year period, but that these increases are not the same for the different urban areas. In some cases it is quite obvious that changes in the limits of the area under study result not only in entirely different consumption rates, but also in reversals in apparent trends. For example, if the city of London is used as the area of study, the consumption rate for urban land declined between 1951 and 1961. But if the census metropolitan area (CMA) is used to define the boundaries, then the rate increased. Obviously, the difference in the two sets of data can be attributed to underbounding, although even if the CMA boundaries are used, there may well be areas of urban sprawl beyond this census artifact.

Thus, the data are so affected by boundary problems that they are useless. The rates are not only influenced by the size of the area being examined but also are themselves related to the size of the area; for when the area is almost completely transferred to urban land uses the rate is stable or appears to decrease. Such is the case in the various cities and boroughs of Metro Toronto. As an attempt to circumnavigate these various problems, a special study of Ottawa has been undertaken for the area within the "green belt". In this particular case the area actually used for residential purposes (plus roads) was determined from land-use maps and aerial photographs for the same years as the decennial and mid-decennial census of population. Thus, the indices are actually net residential land consumption rates, and they are as accurate as any could be for a twenty-year period. The tendency, as indicated by the figures in Table 3.2, is for the rates to increase through time, but unfortunately, in the latter part of the period the green belt itself appears to underbound the real limits of Ottawa, and the rate begins to decrease.

General trends in micro-level land consumption rates

Although it is evident that there are many problems associated with using land consumption rates generated at the micro-level (that is, from the basis of an individual urban area), it is possible to make certain general statements. Unfortunately, these statements relate only to one general time period (the last few years of the decade of the 1960s), and they pertain directly to municipalities. Information concerning the total area developed for urban purposes and the associated population has been obtained for seventy municipalities and metropolitan areas in the axis, which have a population of more than

4,000 people (Maher and Bourne, 1969; Raveneau et al., 1973). When the data are plotted on logarithmic paper the scatter of points appears to describe a fairly general relationship, which is that the amount of urban land use in a municipality is related to the size of that municipality (Maher and Bourne, 1969). The relationship is quite linear, and there is no significant difference between the data for the Québec portion of the axis and the data for Ontario.

The general trend suggested by this relationship is for urban land consumption rates to be lower for large urban areas than for smaller towns and cities. Consumption rates calculated for eight different city sizes from data read from the graph in Figure 3.4 are listed in Table 3.3. Although the graph pertains to a cross-section of munici-palities at a given era, the same graph can also be interpreted dynamically, if it is assumed that the same relationship for urban areas will hold in the future. If the relationship is used in this par-ticular way, the suggestion is that as the population of an urban area increases, the amount of urban land it will consume will increase in accordance with the trend of the graph. Thus, if a municipality in-creases in size from 25,000 to 50,000 people, the urban land that it would occupy would, on the average, increase from 2,255 acres to 4,300 acres.

The trouble with using this particular procedure for forecasting is not only that it requires an individual projection for each municipality, but also that it is based upon data already established as biased. Land within the legal limits of municipalities provides the only data used,

Table 3.3: Land consumption rates for eight different sizes of urban areas; data calculated from information contained in Figure 3.4

POPULATION SIZE OF URBAN AREA	ACRES PER 1000 PEOPLE
10,000	100
25,000	91
50,000	86
100,000	78
250,000	70
500,000	66
1,000,000	61
2,000,000	57

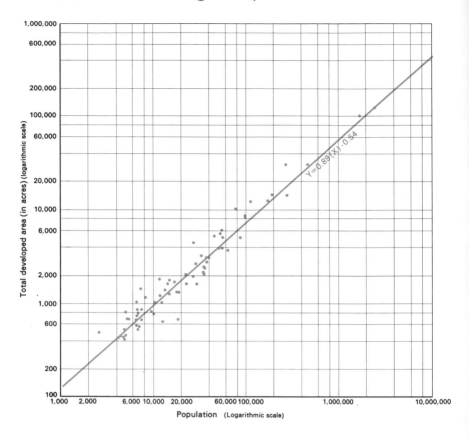

Figure 3.4: Relationship between total developed area in urban land-use and the total population of the municipalities concerned

and land beyond these areas is ignored. Thus, although planners may suggest that this method be used for forecasting the amount of land required for urban purposes (Ontario Department of Municipal Affairs, 1969), it cannot be suggested as anything more than a very general procedure. It is based on data that are greatly influenced by the limits of municipal boundaries and the location of green belts, rivers, lakes, and so forth. Furthermore, the dynamic aspect of the procedure is really based on cross-sectional data which do not inherently indicate change.

General trends in macro-level land consumption rates

Although the information on micro-level land consumption rates is fairly voluminous, the evidence suggests that data obtained for larger areas are probably more meaningful, because the boundary effect for particular urban areas can be circumvented. Unfortunately, there have been very few studies of urban land at the macro-geographical level, that is, for large units of territory that embrace a number of counties. The data obtained thus far permit the calculation of a land consumption rate for the axis as a whole; for if the total urban land is expressed as a ratio with respect to the population in 1971 residing in census subdivisions defined as urban, the rate is 139 acres per thousand people. This rate can be interpreted as a general "ball-park" figure which, if anything, is an overestimate, since villages, towns, and cities of any size are included. Nevertheless it is useful, because it provides a yardstick against which other estimates may be compared.

One fairly comprehensive study has been undertaken by Howard (1972), but as he bases his analysis on data aggregated from the municipalities, all the boundary problems discussed previously are inherent throughout the entire report. For example, the basic data used in the study (Howard, 1972, p. 3) imply that the land consumption rate in the western one-third of the axis has increased from 72 acres per thousand people in 1951 (a reasonable figure) to 220 acres per thousand people in 1961 (an exaggeration!). Nevertheless, the conclusions in the report are quite interesting and they are supported later in this chapter.

Another rather interesting source of information at the macro-level pertains to an area within thirty-five miles of Montréal that is referred to as the "Montréal Region" by Service d'Urbanisme (1969). In this report, land-use maps and air photographs have been used to estimate the total amount of land urbanized for the entire region in 1952 and 1961. When these figures are related to the estimated urban population for these time periods, rates of forty acres per thousand people and fifty-two acres per thousand people are calculated. These figures appear reasonable, and they become even more plausible when the 1971 estimates for exactly the same area are added to the series! The 1971 estimate is sixty-nine acres per thousand urban population. When these urban land consumption rates are plotted on semi-logarithmic paper the rate of increase is remarkably constant over the

twenty-year period (Figure 3.5). But three points for one macro-region
are merely encouraging, not persuasive.

The only other comparable series that can be calculated for a similar
large area pertains to the broad Toronto planning region, which
roughly embraces an area within thirty-five miles of Toronto. The
land consumption rate estimated for 1966 (Gad, 1970) is eighty-six
acres per thousand people, and this compares well with an estimate
of ninety-eight acres per thousand people which has been made for
the planning region in 1971. These rates are also plotted in Figure 3.5,
along with estimates made for the areas within fifteen miles of Ottawa
and Québec City. It should be noted that the Ottawa estimate for
1971 compares well with the general trend in residential land consumption rates which have been calculated for the area within the
green belt up to 1961 (Table 3.2).

The trends in land consumption rates plotted in Figure 3.5, and
the general weight of the evidence cited thus far, leads to a suggestion
of an urban land consumption rate of about 160 acres per thousand
people for the entire axis area by the year 2001. If, at that time, 90 per
cent of the axis population resides in census subdivisions that are
defined as urban, the total amount of land that will be used for direct

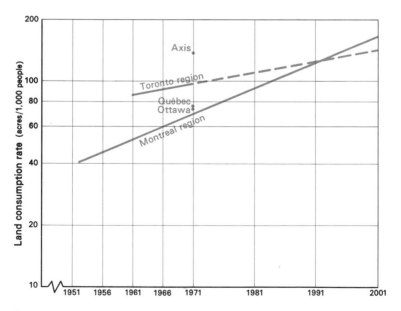

Figure 3.5: General trends in macro-level land consumption rates

urban purposes will be about 4,302 square miles, or about 6.4 per cent of the total axis area. This is not an extraordinarily large amount of land, but it does indicate that if past trends continue, the amount of land devoted to urban uses will double in the thirty-year period, and that 2,155 square miles of additional land will be urbanized. There is, of course, rather a large error range to this estimate, but on the basis of the evidence, it can be regarded as a reasonable trend figure.

Land absorption coefficients

The implications of the preceding forecast (based on past trends) of future urban land requirements can be discussed quite profitably within the context of land absorption coefficients. Land absorption coefficients indicate the amount of new urban land that is absorbed by each additional person to the urban area. For comparative purposes this coefficient is usually multiplied by 1,000, so that it is interpreted as the amount of land urbanized for each increment of 1,000 in the urban population. Torontreal (Montronto), for example, incurs an increase in population of 1.2 million between time periods t and $t+1$, and this increase is associated with an increase in area of 220,080 acres. The land absorption coefficient is, therefore, 0.183, or 183 new acres of urban land for every 1,000 increment in urban population. Obviously, if the general trend for the land consumption rate is to increase through time, then the trend will be for the land absorption coefficient to increase also.

Land absorption coefficients can be calculated for all urban areas listed in Table 3.2 and contained in Figure 3.5, but at this juncture such an activity would not be a fruitful exercise, for little would be added to the previous discussion. However, the land absorption rate implied by the forecast in the previous section is of great interest because it can be compared to other estimates made within the axis and in North America as a whole. The land absorption rate implied by the forecast of a requirement for 2,115 square miles of additional urban land by the year 2001 is 0.186. To be precise, this is the predicted average rate for the period 1971 to 2001. When this rate is compared to coefficients in the Montréal region of 0.083 for the 1951–61 period, and 0.145 for the 1961–71 period, it is apparent that the forecasted coefficient implies a slight decrease in the rate of increase of absorption of new land.

The forecasted coefficient compares reasonably well with the estimate made by Dill and Otte (1971) for rural land urbanized in ninety-six counties in twelve states in the northeastern United States. For the period 1950 to 1960 they estimated a land absorption coefficient of 0.22, or 220 acres for each increment of 1,000 people. Since many of the counties are on the fringe of this megalopolitan area, it is not surprising that the estimate is quite large. Furthermore, it has been the trend for many suburban subdivisions in the United States to be developed in half-acre lots, a tendency leading to the consumption of enormous quantities of land for urban purposes. Undoubtedly, land consumption coefficients of this magnitude result in large portions of urban areas which are difficult to service economically with sewers, public transport, storm drainage, public utilities, waste disposal systems, schools, and so forth.

In this context of "overconsumption" at low suburban densities, it must be re-emphasized that the forecasted coefficient based on past trends also yields very low densities. In fact, the average urban population density would decrease from 7.2 persons per acre in 1971 to 6.2 persons per acre in 2001, a figure which, though in accordance with past trends, would undoubtedly lead to severe servicing problems in the future. In fact, Blumenfeld (1967, p. 175) comments that for servicing and general community reasons it is ridiculous to continue developing new suburban areas at residential densities of 4.5 houses or less per acre. If this is regarded as a threshold figure, then based on assumptions of four persons to a house and of 55.6 per cent of urbanized land in the axis usually being devoted to residential uses, the maximum permissible average land absorption coefficient would be 0.100. This estimate is not very different from the actual coefficient of 0.091 calculated by Niedercorn and Hearle (1964) for twenty-two large U.S. cities using data pertaining to the decade of the 1950s. Acceptance of this maximum permissible figure would lead, by the year 2001, to a future land consumption for direct urban purposes of an additional 1,124 square miles. These estimates of future land consumption for urban purposes, of course, assume that land currently urbanized is not used at greater densities, and lead to the question: what figure should be used? Should the various governments responsible for planning in the axis permit and plan for the trend figure of 2,115 square miles of additional urban land by the year 2001, or the maximum of 1,124 square miles implied by the Blumenfeld comment?

PROBLEMS OF URBAN LAND
CONSUMPTION

Unfortunately, experience of the immediate past leads to the conclusion that it is difficult to change the course of a trend, let alone modify it. Such a position is awkward to justify when the logic of urban servicing points towards the necessity for higher average densities. Furthermore, as the Blumenfeld-based projection implies an average gross density of only 8.1 persons per square mile in the urbanized portion of the axis by the year 2001, an increment of 1,124 square miles of new urban land is not particularly spartan and restricting. The extent to which this preferred figure should be utilized depends upon the uses which are foregone by the transference of the land to urban activities, and it is impossible to estimate the impact of such a transference in the future without examining the effect of urban expansion in the immediate past.

The components of the rural to urban land conversion experience can be isolated as: 1) the absolute loss of farmland to urban land use; 2) the agricultural importance of land lost to urbanism; and 3) the indirect effects on farming of what can be loosely called sprawl. The ideal situation would be for each component to be measured precisely, but unfortunately, the information is simply not available to allow such a task to be undertaken for the entire axis. There is, however, enough information to gain a fairly good understanding of the relative importance of the first two components, but the third can be approached only inferentially.

THE LOSS OF FARMLAND TO URBAN LAND USE

Horrific stories are related in the dark corners of certain agricultural and environmentalist lobbies concerning the demands of growing urban areas for agricultural land. Quite obviously, with an expanding urban population, there are competing demands for a finite amount of space, so the question arises as to whether the demands are so massive that they are detrimental to future needs. The data presented by Crerar (1962) with respect to the six largest metropolitan areas in the western one-third of the axis suggested that in the 1941–66 period 148 acres of improved farmland were lost for every 1,000 increase in urban population. This figure is considerably less than the 375 acres of farmland lost per 1,000 people added to the population calculated by Russwurm (1970, p. 85) for the Toronto to Stratford area for the same time period. The fact that this figure may well be inflated is acknowledged by Russwurm for he notes that it is affected by land abandonment on the backslope of the Niagara escarpment, and his earlier study of the Hamilton to London area (Russwurm, 1967) estimated an absorption coefficient of only 0.192.

Over the axis as a whole, the area devoted to farmland (which includes improved and unimproved land, as well as areas within farms in woods) incurred a net decline of 4,148 square miles in the 1966–71 period. As has been previously noted, the decline within the axis was proportionately greater than the decline experienced by Canada as a whole. But it is quite obvious that only a small portion of this land could have been transferred to urban use, because by 1971 there were only 2,146.2 square miles in that category, and this total had been achieved incrementally from the French colonial period. It would appear that the greatest proportion of this net decrease occurred as a result of farm abandonment, afforestation, and the transfer of land to recreational purposes, particularly in the Shield and Appalachian areas. In fact, only 12.5 per cent of the decrease is associated with census subdivisions defined as urban in 1971, and this does not mean that the decrease in these areas is caused by urban growth.

The amount of decrease can be put into perspective only if it is possible to obtain the amount of land devoted to urban uses in the axis at some date prior to 1971. Unfortunately, there is no readily accessible source of information which can be analysed in a finite amount of time, and as time is man's only real finite resource it is probably best to use an estimating procedure based on the information already developed. The trends already calculated suggest a land consumption rate in 1961 of 130 acres per thousand urban persons, and in 1966, a figure of 134 acres per thousand urban persons would appear to be appropriate. If, on the basis of the evidence, these figures are accepted as reasonable, then the increase in urban land in the axis between 1966 and 1971 would have been about 266 square miles. This figure obviously represents only a very small proportion (6.4 per cent) of the total decrease in farmland. Thus, even though the estimates may be subject to error, the general conclusion is clear: urban growth during the 1960s was responsible for the direct consumption of only a small amount of the total farmland in the axis.

This conclusion is similar to that presented by Gray *et al.* (1972, p. 109) who suggest that much of the land lost to agriculture in the western one-third of the axis between 1951 and 1966 was unimproved land, and if improved land was lost, this loss was compensated for by a cultivation of formerly unimproved areas.

THE LOSS OF EXCELLENT AGRICULTURAL LAND

There is one area of concern, however, which, because of its unique-ness and economic implications, deserves special attention. This is the Niagara fruit belt, an almost continuous strip of agricultural activity in the Niagara peninsula bordering Lake Ontario, which depends for its existence on the mild climate (discussed in Chapter 1) and pockets of good sandy loam that are found in this area. Plants and trees that produce the tender fruits of the grape, peach, cherry, pear, and plum varieties are particularly sensitive to these two physical characteristics and, as a consequence, are produced in few other re-gions in the axis. The only other areas of production are in the milder climatic regions bordering Lake Erie and southern Georgian Bay. Furthermore, there is only one other part of Canada that produces tender fruit on any scale: British Columbia; the Niagara tender fruit output, however, is three times greater.

Therefore, the Niagara fruit belt is particularly important in an axis and Canadian context, and this importance is enhanced by its proximity to the bulk of the population in the axis. Unfortunately, the fruit belt lies in an area of average population growth and the areas of best soils lie athwart some of the possible paths of urban expansion (Figure 3.6). The impact of urban expansion on the acre-age devoted to tender fruits in the Niagara peninsula has been well documented by Kreuger (1959) and Gertler (1968), and the actual loss of fruit land has been estimated to average 518 acres per year for the 1951–66 period. Even though only 215 acres per year were lost to direct urban expansion, the real loss (as a result of sprawl and speculation) was probably about 430 acres per year (Kreuger, 1968). As there were only about 21,500 acres of land devoted to tree fruit and vineyards on the Niagara Peninsula in 1966, an annual loss of such magnitude is quite severe if projected thirty years hence.

The solution, suggested by Kreuger (1968), is to recognize that the land is unique for the production of Canadian-grown tender fruit, and to set aside 22,000 acres of land in the area for the specific use of this agricultural activity. Presumably, if the population of Canada is to increase by 60 per cent over the next thirty years, the logical continuance of this suggestion would be to set aside 35,200 acres. The problem with a land allocation solution of this type is that it incurs the opposition of farmers and some consumers. Farmers regard their land as their only real asset, and if it can be used for urban purposes it is usually many times more valuable per acre than land that can be used for even the highest-price agricultural production. In this context it is interesting to observe Martin's (1972) comment that $700 per acre is a steep price to pay for prime agricultural land, but that same land for future urban purposes may be worth many times that amount, depending on the size of the parcel of land. Thus, if a farmer regards his land prices as "money in the bank" — and the trend in land prices definitely proves this to be so — then the original owner should be compensated for his price foregone if the Kreuger plan is adopted. In effect, the community (state or province) would become the owner of the land.

But, does the community want this land to remain in tender fruit production? Theoretically, it would if there were neither an alternative supplier of tender fruit nor a cheaper alternative source, or if the community simply wanted to maintain some tender fruit production in Canada. The third alternative is quite tenable, because the country maintains production in many areas by means of high protective tariffs. The alternative supplier for tender fruit is the United States, and Chudleigh (1972) indicates that for some fruits, such as peaches, it is probably cheaper to import than to produce them domestically. Therefore, the issue is resolved to one of deciding the level to which the consumer (who is predominantly urban) is prepared to subsidize, through protective tariffs, the fruit-belt producer, as well as to pay the original farmer compensation if he wishes to sell his land.

Issues of this kind are invariably resolved through political trade-offs, but at this juncture, perhaps my preferences might be of interest. The visual environment, like the Canadian seasons, is delightful because of its diversity. Those features of the environment which are attractive and unique should be preserved, providing that the costs are not outrageous when they are compared with other national needs, such as defence requirements. Impressionistic measurements suggest that the value of preserving this unique feature of Canadian environmental diversity would be well worth the cost, providing that the farmers do not use the protective tariffs to cover for gross inefficiency.

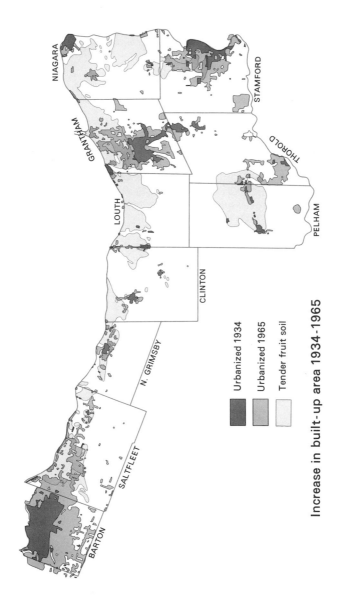

Increase in built-up area 1934-1965

Urbanized 1934

Urbanized 1965

Tender fruit soil

Figure 3.6: Increase in built-up area, 1934–65—tender fruit soil

Source: Gertler [1968].

If a farmer wishes to realize his land capital, the community should purchase the land at a fair price that has been predetermined. It may well be that at some time in the future, all the land will be owned by the public and the farms rented. In this case, the tender fruit area of the Niagara peninsula will become a public resource like the national and provincial parks.

URBAN INTRUSION EFFECTS

In this chapter estimates of coefficients and other values have, at times, flowed faster than meltwater in March. Two interesting figures in this flood are: 1) the calculation that the total acreage devoted to farmland in census subdivisions defined as urban has declined by 518 square miles between 1966 and 1971; and 2) the estimate, on the basis of perceived trends, that an additional 266 square miles has been consumed as a result of urban expansion between 1966 and 1971. These two figures are interesting, since the latter can be interpreted as direct urban consumption, and the difference between the two can be regarded as associated indirect urban consumption. Support for this interpretation can be found in Gertler and Hindsmith (1962) and Crerar (1962) who claim that the indirect urban sprawl effects are such that for every acre consumed by direct urban expansion about one acre is also ruined for agricultural use. To this must also be added the amount of land held by speculators and developers to cater for future urban growth, and this amount depends upon expected urban expansion as perceived from the growth performance of the region in the immediate past.

It is possible to distinguish two kinds of sprawl, one of which is conceptually simple (but practically quite difficult) to measure, and the second is very nearly impossible. The first type, general urban sprawl, can be directly measured, and it is included within the urban measurements calculated for the axis as a whole. General urban sprawl results from the piecemeal attempts of individuals, development companies, and governments to satisfy a perceived demand at the periphery of an urban area by a plugging-in process (McLaughlin, 1972). The result is continuous sprawl along highways and urban arterials where each parcel of land appears to be developed independently of any other. The second type of sprawl, technological sprawl, is really one component of the indirect effect of urban expansion, and it pertains to the indiscriminate lacing of highways and electrical power lines and the pockmarks of city dumps and auto-wreckers all over the countryside. Technological sprawl as a result of urban growth should be controlled just as much as direct urban sprawl, and since the axis is dominated by large urban areas, the planning for the entire area should be related to present and future urban pressures.

Probably one of the most detrimental effects of urban expansion is the effect of speculation on the rural landscape. Any person who owns land and keeps it in the hope that he may sell at a high price sometime in the future is a land speculator. Many owners of land are thus defined as speculators, but some people are worse speculators than others. Speculators exist because the rural-urban land conversion process in the type of economy existent in Canada results in vast increases in value per acre. For example, in the Montréal region it has been estimated that the maximum value of land for agricultural purposes is in the neighbourhood of $400 per acre, but prices up to five times this amount are paid if the land might at some time in the future be used for urban purposes (Service d'Urbanisme, 1969). As a city expands outwards, more and more land is available for speculative purposes, and it can be held in a variety of ways.

First, many farmers at the periphery of urban areas are, in fact, speculators. They stay in the business of farming until a buyer offering a high enough price comes along. This is not to suggest that all farmers are speculators; for there is reason to believe that many would prefer to stay in agriculture and many, in fact, do purchase another farm elsewhere. It is just that urban expansion seems inevitable, impossible to resist; so the farmer becomes resigned to an obvious course of action.

Large farms and large tracts of land may be purchased by development companies, and in the Toronto area it is estimated that six large companies own at least 22,500 acres (Spurr, 1971). Concentrated ownership of large areas in a few interrelated companies may result in a monopolistic control of prices and the rationed release of land to the public. The dangers inherent in a concentration of ownership of this type in private hands have been well documented and discussed by Lorrimer (1972), and Richardson (1972). There is little doubt that the private stockpiling of land raises land prices enormously. As the amount of speculative area increases due to urban expansion, it becomes necessary for companies in the business of speculation to hold large quantities of land in many locations in order to hedge their bets on predictions of the direction of further growth. These large land holdings incur heavy carrying costs, and these costs are retrieved when sales are made for final development purposes. Thus the individual purchaser of a home and lot ends up paying a portion of the immense carrying charges. Furthermore, since speculative companies have a vested interest in knowing where urban areas are going to grow — that is, where infrastructure purchased out of public funds may be located, or where development plans may be altered — they may try to influence these decisions by supporting sympathetic persons for public office. Hence, just as Prohibition in the United States had the indirect effect of escalating the hold of organized crime over society, so may the mercenary desires of land speculators have resulted in a moral corruption of the political process.

Land held for speculation may remain in farming, or it may be left abandoned. In the fringe area of Montréal it has been estimated that nearly 77,000 acres of land (fields and wood lots) are probably abandoned as they exhibit an uncared for appearance. In terms of the previous discussion of the value of the visual environment, abandoned land and broken-down farms and farmhouses cannot be regarded as pleasing. An appearance of rural decay is neither desirable nor productive, and if it has been caused by hopes for future urban profit, then the rural-urban land conversion process as it now exists may be not only morally corrupting to our political system, but environmentally corrupting as well. In essence, the rural to urban conversion process as it now operates, encourages greed, fosters moral corruption in government, permits decay in the visual environment, escalates the prices of new urban land, and creates more problems for urban development than it solves.

FUTURE URBAN LAND

The only way to reduce the number of problems which occur directly and indirectly as a result of the rural-urban land conversion process is to try to be more precise about future needs. Two gross figures have been suggested for the axis as a whole, a realistic but pessimistic trend forecast of 2,115 square miles, and a Blumenfeld-based preferred suggestion of 1,124 square miles. Both figures are estimates of direct urban land consumption by the year 2001 and should be regarded as absolute maximum forecasts with respect to the assumptions involved. As there is excellent evidence (just look around your own urban areas) to suggest that there are many thousands of acres of land remaining to be developed within the area already defined by the land use survey as urbanized (sixteen square miles in Montréal) the Blumenfeld-based suggestion would appear to be more than adequate. If this lower preferred figure were adopted and the entire 1,124 square miles consumed, the average density of the urban population would increase from 7.2 persons per acre in 1971 to only 8.1 persons per acre in 2001. But as the Blumenfeld-based suggestion involves a complete reversal of all past trends, the implications of both maxima will be examined.

The argument so far has been structured around a continued strengthening of the dominance of the major urban areas of the axis as measured by population and population shifts. The impact of differential growth and migration has been examined with respect to Canada and the axis as a whole, and the axis figures have been used to forecast future urban land consumption based on certain assumed absorption ratios. Within the axis, growth and migration have been used to allocate population by administrative region within the province, but this method has not been feasible for Ontario, though it has been demonstrated that exactly the same principles operate. Unfortunately, the argument used so far requires that similar allocations be prepared for the Ontario proportion of the axis if urban land-use allocations are to be forecast for sub-areas within the axis. In Table 3.4 allocations of population for the year 2001 have been made on the basis of the growth-migration data for Québec (Chapter 2), and 1966–71 growth rates for sub-areas in Ontario. The Québec data in four regions have been deflated by a constant proportion to take into account the areas that extend beyond the axis. The Ontario data pertain to large urban-centred units that have been constructed on the basis of development regions, spheres of influence, and common growth patterns (Figure 3.7). These units should not be regarded as anything more than a vehicle for examining the implications of future population growth for urban land requirements.

URBAN LAND ALLOCATIONS: 2001

The land allocations for the year 2001 have been calculated using the forecast population increase for each of nineteen sub-areas within the axis. Each of these allocations has assumed a constant land absorption coefficient for the 1971–2001 period for each sub-area. Furthermore, it has also been assumed that the non-urban population will not increase during the thirty-year period. Most of these assumptions are quite reasonable, though there is some evidence to suggest that land consumption rates in the more highly urbanized portions of the

Table 3.4: Population and urban land allocations for sub-areas in the year 2001

AREA	POPULATION, 1971 TOTAL (IN THOUSANDS)	% URBAN	POPULATION, 2001 TOTAL (IN THOUSANDS)	% URBAN	1971	URBAN AREA (IN SQ. MILES) TREND INCREASE	PREFERRED INCREASE
Windsor	522	79.5	722	85.2	145.4	58.13	30.87
London	483	67.5	746	80.0	103.4	76.43	40.59
Mid-west Ontario	479	68.7	884	83.3	111.9	118.28	62.83
Hamilton-Burlington	689	96.2	1119	97.7	148.7	124.97	66.38
Niagara	380	90.0	529	92.8	99.3	43.30	23.00
Toronto	2708	97.6	5623	98.8	396.0	847.17	449.97
Georgian Bay	114	14.0	161	39.1	46.9	13.66	7.25
Barrie-Orillia	154	61.0	399	85.0	63.9	71.20	37.83
Peterborough	168	55.4	230	67.4	53.6	18.02	9.57
Lake Ontario	96	39.6	126	54.0	45.0	8.72	4.63
Shield	178	30.3	213	38.7	73.7	10.17	5.40
Ottawa	488	89.1	977	94.6	65.7	142.16	75.49
Kingston	303	60.4	366	67.2	113.0	18.31	9.72
Cornwall	125	52.0	132	54.5	33.0	2.03	1.09
Outaouais	230	73.5	378	83.9	50.9	43.01	22.85
Montréal	3307	91.4	4773	94.1	365.7	426.06	226.30
Cantons de l'Est	244	55.3	251	57.0	42.8	2.33	1.24
Trois Rivières	457	69.1	378	83.6	75.0	0.0	0.0
Québec	792	70.6	1112	79.0	112.4	93.0	49.39
Total	11917	82.0	19119	89.2	2146.3	2116.95	1124.40

Note: Totals may differ slightly from those in the text owing to rounding errors.

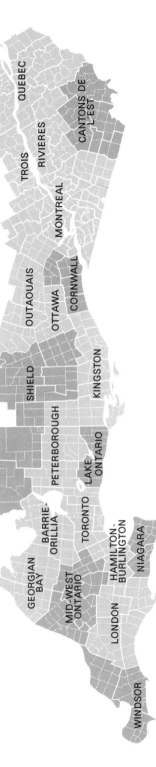

Figure 3.7: Sub-areas for 2001 population estimates

axis are lower than in the less urbanized areas. Variations of this kind have not been included in the allocations, so it may be useful to regard the estimates for the more urbanized areas as slight overestimates, and for the less urbanized areas as slight underestimates.

Nevertheless, the message contained in Table 3.4 is clear. The pressures are greatest in the Toronto area (roughly, the Toronto Centred Region), which is likely to consume 40 per cent of all new urban land over the next thirty years, and the Montréal region, which is likely to consume 20 per cent. How do these estimates compare with the amount of land already held under speculation as destined for urban use? Service d'Urbanisme (1969) estimates that in 1964, 137 square miles of land located within thirty-five miles of the centre of Montréal was already under obvious speculation. This same report also suggests that there is strong evidence to suppose that the amount of land really under speculation for future urban use is about 377 square miles (Service d'Urbanisme, 1969, p. 46). As some of this land has undoubtedly been used and even more bought under speculation since 1964, it is reasonable to assume that enough land is already held under speculation to satisfy the trend-based demand by the year 2001 — and more than enough to satisfy the preferred estimate — for the Montréal area. Of course, this does not mean that these particular lands should be used, but it does imply that more than enough future urban land has already been "stored" by a variety of speculators or by-passed during past growth.

In the Toronto portion of Figure 3.6 prices for "agricultural land" are now so high that it is difficult to believe that the entire area is not held by speculators hoping that it will be transferred to urban use some time in the future. For example, Martin (1972), in a study of recent (1968–71) selling prices of land in a 100-square-mile area covering parts of Pickering, Uxbridge, and Markham townships, determined that most farms had been sold for over $1,000 per acre, and a few for over $15,000 per acre. These prices have been escalating over the past ten years, because most landowners are convinced of the inevitability of impending urbanization. Under these price conditions the farming that does take place is quite ephemeral, for prices would have to drop below $700 per acre for agriculture to be an economically viable use of the land.

LAND BANKS

Obviously, some form of land management is required if the perceived and imagined influence of impending urbanization is to be prevented from overpricing land in many rural areas. The pressures are particularly heavy in the sub-areas of Toronto, Montréal, mid-west Ontario, Hamilton-Burlington, and Ottawa. In these areas at least, some clear statements should be made concerning the amount of land that will probably be urbanized by some future date (2001 or later), and the location of these lands. Then, a sufficient quantity of this land should be purchased by the appropriate government so that the government could influence significantly the price of lots when they are released to the urban market. The development process would require minimum densities for urban development (residential, industrial, parks, and so forth), because it is only through restrictions of this kind that urban areas can be serviced efficiently.

Many western European countries have, in fact, adopted similar policies for the purchase of substantial portions of future urban land requirements (Gibson, 1973). Ideally, these purchases should take place annually, with a considerable time lag before they are released for development purposes. The initial establishment of such a program thus costs an enormous amount of money, but it may not seem excessive when the costs are compared with other expenditures which already fall in the public domain. If the national community decides to adopt the sensible densities implied by the preferred urban land estimate and allocations, and if initial purchases are made in the areas of greatest predicted demand in the axis, and if 50 per cent of the future preferred requirements are purchased in these areas, and if the land is to be purchased on a thirty-year cycle, then about 562 square miles of land would need to be purchased within the axis to provide a sufficient degree of public influence over the future urban land prices. Finally, if these purchases are made at an average price of $2,000 per acre, then the cost of establishing an urban land bank would be about (at 1971 dollar values) $1,124 million. This land would be for use up to the year 2001, and annual purchases of about $35 million (at 1971 dollar values) would be required each year after establishment of the bank to add to the reserve for use after 2001. Similar costs for the trend data are $2.12 billion, and $70 million annually; these figures only serve to emphasize how excessively extravagant these low density trends can become if permitted to continue. Of course, these are not net expenditures, since most annual purchases will be financed through future sales.

The purchase of a house is, for the vast majority of Canadian families, the most important financial decision ever made by the decision-makers within the family. For example, if a family with an annual income of $12,000 in 1970 and expectation of an average of 7 per cent annual income increments to retirement in 35 years, purchases a house costing $35,000 with a $30,000 mortgage at 9.5 per cent interest spread out over twenty-five years, the total cost of the house is likely to be 8.79 per cent of the total income of the family during its working life. Unfortunately, these costs are disproportionately heavy for the first ten years, and are theoretically minimal (excluding repairs) for the last ten.

It is not surprising, therefore, that people become very sensitive if they perceive that the decision to purchase is unsound. One yardstick against which this decision can be measured is the cost of renting. If the family mentioned above were to rent a two- or three-bedroom unit for thirty-five years at a beginning price of $200 per month, with rents increasing at an average rate of 3 per cent per annum, the family would have spent 8.75 per cent of its total working life income. Though this proportion is about the same as that spent on purchasing, it has to be offset against the lack of home-ownership at the end of the twenty-five-year period which continues into retirement. If inflation continues at a high rate, it is quite likely that the rate of inflation may have offset or at least equalled the rate of depreciation, so that even though the family is not left with cash, it is at least left with some equity. Therefore, whether we like it or not, an economic system which appears unable to control the rate of inflation re-enforces the desire of people to own private property and to purchase land, because, for the bulk of the population, home ownership is their only real hedge against inflation. The corollary to this point is that once a given rate of inflation is accepted as useful to the bulk of homeowners, any real change in the economic system which is aimed at controlling house prices is severely resisted.

In many individual decisions the economic aspects of the personal investment may be less important than the house as home. It can be observed that people are spending considerable amounts of time within their houses, and demanding more comfortable homes, though it is recognized that standards of comfort vary among people. It is difficult to divorce these trends from the general increase in real family incomes, and the shorter working week. The result is that people are probably spending about 44 per cent of their time in some form of leisure activity in and around their home, and a little less than 30 per cent of their time in bed! The proportion of time spent in leisure activities will undoubtedly increase in the future, and with it the demands for greater comfort in personal living space.

With these changes it is likely that the home as symbol of self (Cooper, 1971) is likely to gain in importance. A rather carefree and completely debatable application of Jungian psychological theory to housing is that the house stands as a symbol of the family which resides within it. Carried further, the external façade represents the image that the family presents of itself to the outside world, whereas the interior is private space that reflects the image of the family within. Though most houses are built according to a "factory system", with the developer's notion of the market requirements, in time many houses do become symbols of this kind. This is particularly so of interior usage, for modifications to exterior façades are slightly more expensive. If this application of symbolism is in any way true, then goodness knows what the psychological effect of most public housing must be on families who have little choice but to inhabit them. Although older, run-down houses may appear to be decrepit and "slummy", they are frequently less impersonal than most recently constructed low-income rental units.

The importance of these images, symbols, and space requirements depends upon the type of family involved. Thus far the implication has been that any group involving one or more persons is a family. The housing requirements of a family change as its size fluctuates and the ages of its members alter. The type of house and location desired by the conventional husband and wife with two young children are quite different from those desired by an older couple with adolescents, or a commune of young adults. The discrepancy between space and location needs and the actual situation that results may be partly resolved by wise relocation decisions during the frequent moves that families have to make in our urban society. Unfortunately, many of these relocation decisions simply duplicate the previous situation, for little thought is given to the present and future needs of every member of the family. For example, many moves are made to areas of similar socio-economic structure, and very little consideration is given to the location *vis-à-vis* the possible array of social and cultural opportunities. This duplication of most residential location decisions results in the family not only living in similar locations within urban areas, but also occupying similar types and styles of housing.

THE SUPPLY OF AND DEMAND FOR DIFFERENT TYPES OF HOUSING

During the decade of the 1960s, housing became a topic of acute public awareness. Rising costs, inadequate housing for certain segments of society, redevelopment conflicts, and the very structure of the construction industry itself, these were all issues that drew attention to housing and housing policy. This interest manifested itself in several government and many individual reports, of which, perhaps, Hellyer's Task Force on Housing and Urban Development (1969) achieved the greatest publicity as it barnstormed around the country obtaining grass-roots information. The seriousness of the supply situation was underlined by the Economic Council of Canada (*Annual Report*, 1969) when they estimated that if housing starts did not average 200,000 per year there would be an impending crisis. Comments such as this were placed in perspective with the calm analysis of Lithwick (1969) who suggested that the country was going through a normal "re-adjustment" process where the supply would soon reach a new level of output which would satisfy the increasing demand.

THE DEMAND FOR HOUSING

In the aggregate, the demand for housing is determined by the number of existing household units, and the rate of formation of new households. Traditionally, household units have been characterized as either family or non-family, the former consisting of two or more related persons. In this chapter, the distinction between family and non-family household units will be ignored, and the terms "family" and "household unit" will be used synonymously.

At the outset it is necessary to distinguish between the "census" household unit and the real number of household units, for it is this distinction which is at the heart of the housing problem on the demand side. The 1961 and 1971 Census of Housing indicates that the number of household units in the axis increased from 2,475,759 in 1961 to 3,399,135 in 1971. This represents a rate of increase of 3.2 per cent per annum, which is well above the rate of increase in population for the axis as a whole. Unfortunately these census figures are not the real number of household units; for the figures are defined on the basis of a census which is taken with respect to dwelling units and their inhabitants. In other words, there were 2,475,759 dwelling units in the axis in 1961, and 3,399,135 dwelling units in the axis in 1971.

This census estimate of household units includes all the inhabitants of a dwelling unit, even though an individual dwelling may contain more than one family, or more than one potential family. Families which do not maintain their own dwelling unit are usually described as lodging families, and they may be either related or unrelated to the head of the dwelling unit. Furthermore, they may consist of non-family single persons, one-parent families, or husband-and-wife lodging families (Kirkland, 1971). Disregarding the perennial domestic comedy concerning the role of a working son or daughter as an economic or non-economic lodger, it is interesting to note that lodging is related to income, particularly in the case of husband-and-wife lodging families (Goracz, 1969). Of course, the relationship really means income relative to the cost of alternative comparable housing, though the degree of comparability of an acceptable alternative depends very much upon the equilibrium of the domestic arrangement.

Thus, while the number of census household units may be a good measure, in gross terms, of the number of families, it does not really measure the exact number of families. It could be suggested that a good measure of the "housing problem" would be the number of families forced to "double-up" in lodging-type accommodation compared with those who live in a non-lodging situation. This figure would, of course, be difficult to determine, because many lodging families prefer to live in that particular situation. Perhaps the fact that the rate of increase in census household units between 1961 and 1971 was 50 per cent greater than the increase in population in the axis is a good indicator of a significant degree of "undoubling". Not only has there been an actual increase of 923,376 census household units between 1961 and 1971, there has also been a comparative increase (based on 1961 population-household unit ratios) of 367,284 units. While much of this comparative increase may be attributable to demographic trends, a considerable proportion may also be attributed to "undoubling", particularly in the husband-and-wife lodging group.

Influences on household-unit formation

Undoubtedly the major influence on the gross formation of household units is the stage in the life cycle of the general population. During the past two decades the proportion of the population in the axis within the "potential" household-unit-forming group (twenty years of age and over) has been increasing, and this increase is particularly noticeable in the past ten years (Figure 4.1). Between 1961 and 1971 the "potential" household-forming group increased from 58.5 to 61.2 per cent of the total axis population, and in raw figures this represents an increase of 1,603,699 persons. This raw figure is 325,352 persons more than it would have been if the "potential" household-forming group represented the same proportion in 1971 as it had in 1961. To place these figures in perspective, assume that this increase in the potential household-forming group actually got married and set up house. This assumption would imply, in round figures, the provision of about 800,000 housing units during the ten-year period. Of this 800,000, about 160,000 housing units would be required simply to cater for the maturing of the population.

Thus, general demographic changes in the age distribution of the population have a tremendous impact on the demand for housing units. It must be recognized, however, that there is one important feature incorporated within these general demographic trends. The population by age profiles includes net immigration, and as most migrants are young people in the twenty- to thirty-year age group, the heavy immigration of the 1960s to the axis has undoubtedly swollen the proportion in the "potential" household-forming group. The important aspect of this development is the difference between total net immigration of persons twenty years of age or more to the axis in the 1960s from that of the 1950s, and a reasonable "ball-park" estimate for this would be about 100,000 people — a significant but not extraordinarily large figure. In fact, immigrants probably generated about 6–7 per cent of the total increase in demand for housing units between 1961 and 1971.

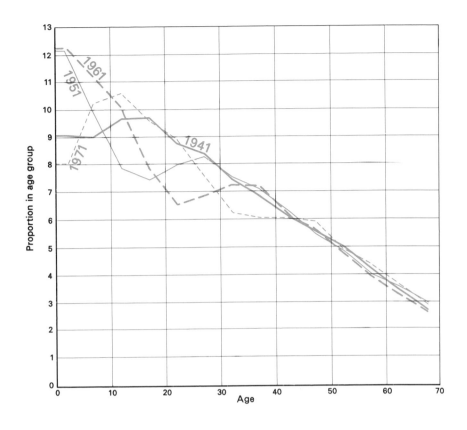

Figure 4.1: Changes in the distribution of the axis population by age, 1941–71

The life cycle

This gross division of the population into "potential" household-unit forming and the rest under the age of twenty is a good but crude method of illustrating the effect of the life cycle on the demand for housing units. A more detailed examination of the effects of life cycle on the demand for housing reveals that the type of housing unit required varies according to the actual age and responsibilities of the "potential" household forming group (Yeates, 1972). An individual passes through many stages in life, of which the most obvious are: infancy, early childhood, play age, school age, adolescence, young adulthood (marriage), adulthood (parents), late adulthood (children left home), and old age. The first five of these stages are characterized by dependency and are crammed into about twenty years. The last four stages feature independence (to a degree) and definitely a heavy dose of responsibility, and they cover about fifty years.

A cursory glance at these stages indicates quite clear categories of general housing requirements that are developing in the axis and the Canadian urban environment. These categories are becoming even more distinguishable as the size of families is decreasing, and they lead to a rather speculative life-cycle-based model of the demand for housing. In the young adulthood stage it is usual for both partners to work, and to live in a one- or two-bedroom rental unit in an apartment building which is accessible to employment opportunities and entertainment. The onset of children alters this idyllic post-marital bliss (if it has not already changed as a result of increased self-awareness!) as the couple perceive that their space requirements have now increased dramatically. Furthermore, the nagging suspicion that children need open, grassed play areas, as well as other playmates, causes the young parents to seek a dwelling unit that provides easy access to these needs.

The general consensus is that high-rise apartments are not the best environment for raising children, though there are many instances where this consensus has been proved palpably untrue. Low-rise walk-up apartment units are acceptable for family living in Québec, and somewhat less acceptable in Ontario cities. The most desired environment is undoubtedly a single-family house, or at least a townhouse (the resurrected modern version of a row house), and home-ownership appears to be preferred. Here again, there are differences between the Ontario and Québec portions of the axis, for the French Canadian would undoubtedly place greater emphasis on locating within the old family neighbourhood than would the English Canadian. This would mean that renting is a more acceptable alternative in Québec than in Ontario. Nevertheless, the general requirement for greater space is common at this stage in the life cycle, and this need is frequently manifested in the purchase of single-family homes, or the rental of townhouses or row houses. The costs of purchasing a home at this stage are, of course, disproportionately high. Using the example cited earlier, if this stage begins at age thirty, mortgage, interest, and property tax payments will consume 24.1 per cent of the total family income within the first ten years. If the same family rented, the terms of the previous example would imply a consumption of only 16.6 per cent of the total family income in the ten-year period.

At last, the typical family of the early 1970s, with its two children, progresses to a situation where the heads of the household attain the late adulthood stage which, for the sake of definition, can be presumed to commence around the age of fifty. The children leave home to set up household units of their own, and if the parents have been purchasing a home, the mortgage payments, residual interest, and property taxes consume very little of the total income. No longer does the household unit require much space, and there is a temptation to rent either part or all of the house, though usually the parents remain occupying the family home, out of habit or sentiment as much as anything else. The problem is that they do not require much personal space, and it is doubtful whether they really want the responsibility of the upkeep. Increasingly, persons in this stage of the life cycle are selling their homes and returning to apartment living. An examination of Figure 4.1 suggests the existence of a very large proportion of the axis population at this stage beginning around the year 2001, and it may well create a very disturbing situation. It is possible to envisage a glut of thirty- to forty-year-old single-family, duplex, and row or townhouses coming onto the housing market (given that new housing will continue to be built) as the wealthy "swinging fifties" return to carefree high-rise living!

Old age brings with it problems that are more severe than most Canadians are willing to contemplate. Golant's (1972) study of the position of the elderly in Metropolitan Toronto leads one to the conclusion that our society callously disregards the needs of senior citizens. In terms of housing it is apparent that the elderly require a limited but well defined quantity of personal space, but they do not and cannot perform much upkeep. The housing unit should be located with ready access to public transportation and lively features of the urban environment, and health care and alternative eating facilities should be close at hand. External and internal facilities of this kind can be well provided by single-bedroom apartments within urban areas. But to avoid the establishment of geriatric ghettos, the apartment buildings should be dispersed discreetly around urban areas. There is no harm in designating particular buildings for habitation for the elderly; in fact, this arrangement may well be preferred because of certain economies of organization.

Income

Though the major influence on the demand for housing is the general stage in life cycle of the population, there is little doubt that income is also important. This is because the general level of income also affects the amount of living space to be purchased and the quality of the dwelling unit. In Canada, income incorporates many other attributes of which mere purchasing power is but one. Closely associated with income is education, although it doesn't necessarily follow that education causes increases in income or even assures higher incomes: it just so happens that in general, the better educated segment of the population is usually able to obtain, and retain, the higher paying jobs. This association does not mean that only the better educated are wealthy, and only the worst educated poor, it is simply a statement of probability, based on past experience.

THE SUPPLY OF HOUSING

The axis area is fortunate in having a rather diverse supply of dwelling units available for renting or purchase, and it is possible to group the various housing types into five major categories according to structure. The topology suggested by the Central Mortgage and Housing Corporation (CMHC) is: single detached (one family); single attached (which includes duplexes and semi-detached dwellings); row (multiple family); apartments (multiple family); and mobile homes. Although this classification is useful from an occupancy point of view because it groups dwelling units neatly into family combinations (one, two, or multiple), it is less than useful for other purposes. For example, duplex and semi-detached dwellings are included within the same category, but duplex units are normally rented and frequently have little external private space, whereas semi-detached units are quite often owned and each resident usually has some private space. It is for this reason that Statistics Canada groups duplexes with apartments, and semi-detached dwellings with row houses, in the 1971 census. However, since inter-census information is available according to CMHC definitions only, the categories used in this section are all as defined by CMHC, and the 1971 census data have been converted to these groupings.

Housing types within the axis

In 1971, 56.3 per cent of all occupied dwelling units in Canada were located within the axis. This percentage is slightly in excess of the proportion of total Canadian population that is located within the axis (55.3 per cent), and it is also similar to the situation in 1961 when 54.5 per cent of all dwelling units were located within the axis as compared with 53.1 per cent of the population. In terms of type of house, the 1971 data indicate that 47.7 per cent of all single detached homes in Canada, 72.9 per cent of all single attached units, 74.8 per cent of all row houses, 67.9 per cent of all apartment units, and only 13.2 per cent of all mobile homes, were located within the axis area. These variations in concentration by type of dwelling unit are, of course, symptomatic of the more urbanized and densely populated areas which are found within the axis. In particular, it is interesting that less than one-half of all the single detached homes in Canada are located within the axis, but that almost three-quarters of the single attached units and row houses are found in the area.

Though less than one-half of all single detached homes in Canada are located within the axis, almost exactly one-half of all dwelling units in the axis are of this type (Table 4.1). This situation is very different from that existing in the rest of Canada, where nearly three-quarters of all dwelling units are of the single detached variety. The difference between the axis and the rest of Canada is also apparent with respect to apartment units: over one-quarter of all residential units in the axis are apartments, but in the rest of the country, less than one-sixth are of this type. On the other hand, mobile homes are very well represented in the rest of Canada, quite understandably, since there is little place for this kind of unit in well-established urban areas.

The changes that have taken place between 1961 and 1971 are quite dramatic. On the whole, the trends in these changes have been similar for both the axis and non-axis area of the country. It must be noted, at the outset, that the 1971 data have been corrected, since in the 1971 census many thousand apartments were incorrectly classified as row housing in Montréal and the rest of the province of Québec, and a few thousand in other parts of the axis. The corrections have been estimated on the basis of dwelling units completed in these urban areas, as listed annually by the Building Permits Division of Statistics Canada. With these corrections in mind, it is noticeable that the basic trend has been for a relative (not absolute) decline in the number of single family homes, and an increase in the number of apartment units. In fact, in parts of the country there has been a veritable apartment boom, and the nature of this boom with respect to the axis will be discussed in a later section.

In summary, the number of dwelling units in the axis increased by 923,376 between 1961 and 1971. The bulk of this increase was provided by apartment units (481,441) and single detached residences (354,663). The remainder of the increase in dwelling units was in the form of single attached housing (22,920) and row housing (62,752), with mobile homes being located in a few places (5,965). The single attached houses constructed in the period were commonly of the duplex variety which can be purchased by a prospective home-owner, whereas the increase in row housing was primarily in the form of townhouses, which are usually rented. The apartment units constructed were predominantly in high-rise developments, and it is these

Table 4.1: Comparison of housing types between the axis and the rest of Canada, 1961–71, by occupied dwellings

HOUSING TYPE	AXIS 1961	AXIS 1971	REST OF CANADA 1961	REST OF CANADA 1971
Single detached	54.9	50.4	77.9	71.3
Single attached	19.3	16.6	9.7	8.0
Row	3.2	4.2	2.4	3.0
Apartment	22.5	28.5	9.2	15.7
Mobile	0.1	0.3	0.8	2.0

Source: DBS, 1961, Cat. 93-523, Table 6; Statistics Canada, 1971, unpublished (HO-1 (0–D)).

structures which have done much to change the visual image of many axis cities.

The apartment boom

A little more than 42 per cent of all apartments in the axis in 1971 were created or constructed during the 1960s. This proportion is remarkably large when compared to single detached dwellings; fot only 20 per cent of all such units in 1971 were constructed or converted in the same period. The dimensions and nature of this boom are really quite simple. Eighty per cent of all apartments constructed during the decade are located in the eight major urban areas of Toronto, Montréal, Hamilton, Ottawa-Hull, Québec City, Windsor, London, and Kitchener. During the late 1950s and up to 1965, the urban areas in Québec had more apartment completions than those in Ontario. But during the latter half of the 1960s, the urban areas in Ontario experienced a tremendous acceleration in apartment construction, and in the peak year of 1969 when almost 100,000 apartment units were completed in Canada, 39,000 were completed in Ontario, and almost 30,000 in Québec. Since that time the rate of completion of apartment units has decreased, though it is still very high. In 1971, 35,000 apartment units were completed in the major urban areas of Ontario, and 25,000 in Quebec.

But not all apartments are similar, and that is why the 1971 census enumeration exhibits its confusion. There is no doubt that the continuous rows of three- or four-level walk-up apartments with external staircases that are found in Québec are very much different from the conventional low-rise and high-rise apartment blocks found in the western portion of the axis. This difference in style has been accentuated throughout the 1960s, for most of the large apartment buildings (defined as containing fifty-one or more units) constructed were located in Ontario. Between 1966 and 1971, 80 per cent of all apartment units completed within the axis were in large apartment buildings, and of these 82 per cent were in urban areas in the province of Ontario. There has been a tendency in recent years for an increasing number of large apartment buildings to be constructed in Québec, but the level is still well below that of Ontario.

With these facts in mind, it is interesting to pose questions such as why the apartment boom, and what are the implications of this tremendous addition to the apartment dwelling-unit stock for the future?

It is tempting to relate the apartment boom to demographic trends, for there is little doubt that the tremendous increase of population in the young adult group between 1961 and 1971 provided a large demand for residential units of this type. In fact, the rate of growth of population in the twenty- to twenty-nine-year age group between 1961 and 1971 was twice (4 per cent per annum) that of the growth in population of the axis as a whole. This increase obviously created a tremendous demand for apartments, for the majority of this age group could be well satisfied with apartments. Looking to the future, it is likely that the population in this age group will increase at a rate of only 2 per cent per annum to 1981, and thereafter the rate of increase in this group will decline. Thus if the apartment boom of the 1960s was really demand based, the rate of construction of new apartments should soon decline to a level which simply replaces depleted stocks.

But there is also some evidence to suggest that apartments are required because many people who prefer single detached homes cannot afford to purchase or rent them (Bourne, 1971). Trends in areas within the axis will be discussed in a later section, so at this juncture the only observations are that the "average" price of a new NHA-financed single detached home in the axis in 1971 was about $26,000 and that this home is barely purchasable by our "average" axis family of four with an income of $10,356 per year. In fact, the greatest concentration of apartment construction has been in those urban areas where the price of single detached homes is the highest, which tends to re-enforce the argument that it is not just demand related to the general stage in the life cycle of the population that has encouraged this apartment boom, but also the prohibitive cost of alternative forms of housing in some cities.

It is apparent from the buying versus renting example discussed previously that the economic advantage of owning a home is not all that great, except as a hedge against inflation. In fact, it can be demonstrated that wise investment of the money saved by renting in the first ten years could well yield a greater return after thirty-five years than the property asset. But many Canadians appear to have a definite preference for single-family detached homes. Hellyer's Task Force on housing indicates that 80 per cent of the people attending open meetings expressed a desire to live in single-family detached homes. In a more academic survey of the literature, Michelson (1970, p. 101) suggests that parents with young children overwhelmingly desire single-family housing. It is important, however, to distinguish the real preference from the sentiment. The Housing and Urban Development Association of Canada (HUDAC, 1971, p. 19), who have their own particular bias, suggests that home ownership is ". . . not as important as physical, social, and economic factors in determining housing situation, housing satisfaction and future living expectation." This particular study goes on to suggest that a greater proportion of apartment dwellers than home-owners is satisfied with their dwelling units.

TRENDS IN HOUSING WITHIN THE AXIS

Though there are differences between the axis as a whole and the rest of Canada, these differences are relatively minor when compared to the variations in housing trends within the axis. The variations within the axis are to be analysed on the basis of eight major census metropolitan areas over the 1961–71 time period. The 1971 data have been re-aggregated to the 1961 census metropolitan area boundaries, and the relative importance of these urban areas to the axis as a whole is suggested in cartographic form in Figure 4.2. In this diagram the size of the axis and of each census metropolitan area is directly proportional to the population of the axis and of each metropolitan unit. Thus, though the census metropolitan areas of Hamilton, Kitchener, London, Montréal, Ottawa-Hull, Québec City, Toronto, and Windsor comprise only 4.4 per cent of the total area of the axis, they contain 62.4 per cent of the total occupied dwelling units in 1971. Furthermore, three-quarters of the total increase in number of occupied dwelling units in the 1961–71 period were located in these eight areas. Therefore, the concentration of attention on these particular census areas is quite justifiable in terms of their dominant position in the axis.

It is necessary, however, to repeat at this stage in the discussion the difficulties that have already been acknowledged in the 1971 census in the classification of dwelling units by type. These difficulties are accentuated when the data is examined at the census metropolitan area level, and though there has been a real attempt made to correct the census material by using information on new constructions, the data cannot be regarded as more than indicative estimates. The errors were particularly noticeable with respect to Montréal and Hamilton; in the former case the problem was apartments and row houses, and in the latter case the difficulty was with single attached houses. But even after correcting the 1971 census data, the nagging suspicion remains that the 1961 enumerations may not have been particularly accurate either! Nevertheless, these doubts are not so important when the discussion focuses on variations in total dwelling-unit ratios and changes.

GROSS CHANGES IN HOUSING WITHIN THE AXIS 1961–71

If the density of occupancy of dwelling units is accepted as a rough indicator of housing standards, then it can be suggested that housing standards within the axis have improved between 1961 and 1971. The proposition that this may have occurred simply because dwelling units have increased in number, but decreased in size, will be examined later. In gross terms, the population per dwelling unit in the eight metropolitan census areas has decreased from 3.84 persons per dwelling unit in 1961 to 3.44 persons per dwelling unit in 1971. Each of the eight urban areas has experienced a decrease in density, and the variation in density among the urban areas is much less in 1971 than in 1961 (Table 4.2). For example, the occupancy density in 1961 in Québec City was well above the average for the eight urban areas as a whole, but by 1971, although Québec City was still above average, it was not very far from the mean. This diminution of the variation between urban areas in terms of occupancy density is extremely important, for it at least suggests some improvement in housing inequalities in the axis over the ten-year period.

The diminution in variation has, of course, been achieved by a very large increase in the number of occupied dwelling units compared with population increase for some urban areas. For example, the last column of Table 4.2 indicates the ratio between the proportionate increase in occupied dwelling units between 1961 and 1971, and the proportionate increase in population. It is apparent from this table that Québec City has had an extraordinary concentration of construction, and the density data suggest that this was really needed. The next largest ratio is for Montréal, which in 1961 had about an average density, but by 1971 had a slightly less than average density. The lowest ratio of all is for Hamilton, which began the period well below average in terms of density, and ended the period only a little below the average. Apart from these slight anomalies, the general trend is

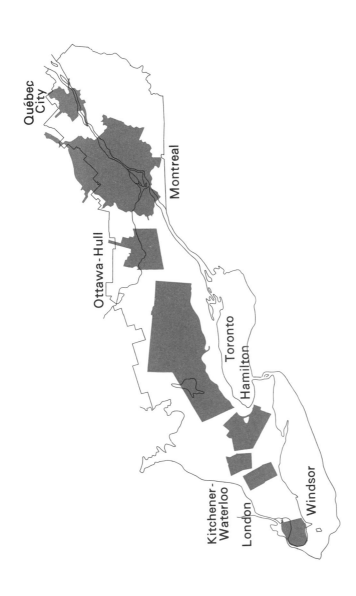

Figure 4.2: Cartogram showing the relative importance of census metropolitan areas (1961 delimitations) in the axis

Table 4.2: Dwelling unit density, absorption coefficients, and rate of increase for eight major metropolitan census units, 1961–71

	POPULATION PER DWELLING UNIT		DWELLING UNIT ABSORPTION COEFFICIENT *	PROPORTIONATE INCREASE IN OCCUPIED DWELLING UNITS 1961–71	PROPORTIONATE INCREASE IN POPULATION 1961–71	RATIO OF PROPORTIONS
	1961	1971				
Kitchener	3.67	3.41	34	57.3	46.4	1.23
Québec City	4.52	3.74	43	53.8	27.4	1.96
Toronto	3.78	3.37	39	51.1	34.8	1.47
Ottawa-Hull	4.00	3.51	41	46.4	28.6	1.62
London	3.59	3.25	40	43.7	30.1	1.45
Montréal	3.84	3.39	45	38.9	22.5	1.73
Hamilton	3.76	3.41	41	26.6	23.7	1.12
Windsor	3.63	3.46	37	23.5	17.6	1.33
Average	3.84	3.41	41	44.2	28.1	1.57
Axis	3.93	3.51	42	37.3	22.5	1.66

* Increase in dwelling units per increase of 100 people.

quite encouraging, although it must be remembered that the analysis assumes space homogeneity among dwelling units.

The dwelling unit absorption coefficients, which measure the increase in number of dwelling units for every 100 increase in population, can be used for projection purposes. The average for the eight urban areas is forty-one, and this is only slightly different from that recorded for the axis as a whole, which is forty-two dwelling units per 100 increase in population. There is, however, a considerable difference between the dwelling unit absorption coefficient for the axis for the 1961–71 period, and that for the 1951–61 period, when the coefficient was twenty-nine new dwelling units for every increase of 100 in population. This difference between the two periods reflects not only a general trend over time for a decrease in density of occupancy of dwelling units, but also the change in type of new dwelling units available. Apartments can house fewer people per unit than single detached or single attached residences, and the increased use of this kind of unit during the 1960s is reflected in the trend. But, the demographic structure of the Canadian population suggests that this may not be the preferred alternative for the next twenty years.

The implication of the trends

At this juncture it is interesting to speculate on the implication of these trends in housing, taking into account the forecasts of the previous chapters. On the basis of the estimate of the population located in urban areas, it is possible to suggest that in 1971 there were 2.02 residential units per urban acre in the axis. But, as the urban land use data suggest that only 55.6 per cent of all urban land is devoted to dwelling units, this density figure translates as being 3.64 residential units per residential urban acre, or eight residential units per football field.

The number of urban residential units within the axis in the year 2001 is related to the total urban population at that time and the predicted density of population per dwelling unit. The urban population can be obtained from Table 3.4 in which it is suggested that 89.2 per cent of the population of the axis in the year 2001 will be urban, yielding a figure of 17.054 million. The density of occupancy figure at this time can be estimated crudely using the axis figures for 1951, 1961, and 1971 in a statistical projection. This projection suggests that by the end of the century the average density of occupancy in the axis will be about three persons per dwelling unit. On the basis of the observation that the density of occupancy in the axis and the eight urban areas in 1971 are about the same, this figure can be used to calculate the number of residential units in the year 2001 within the axis. The estimate is 5.685 million, and it is, naturally, extremely sensitive to minute changes in the dwelling-unit density estimate.

The trend and preferred estimates of total urban land in the year 2001 can then be used to calculate future residential unit densities. If it is assumed that 55.6 per cent of urban land in the year 2001 will be in residential use, then the trend figure yields 3.74 residential units per residential acre, and the preferred urban land estimate 4.93 residential units per residential acre. Thus, the severe controls which are necessary to implement the preferred urban land estimate would result in a little less than ten residential units per football field, four in each half and one in each end-zone, if they were single-family detached dwelling units. But as these residential units will involve a mix of housing types likely to include an even greater proportion of apartments than in 1971, this density should not be too difficult to attain.

GENERAL TRENDS IN HOUSING BETWEEN METROPOLITAN AREAS

The aggregate view of axis trends conceals some interesting variations that occur within the axis. These variations can be analysed in terms of differences between major urban areas as a whole, and differences within the major urban areas. The general tenor of this study, which is to discuss urban issues at the macro-scale, implies that much of the analysis is to be presented with respect to urban areas as spaceless entities, though there is some attempt to discern spatial variations within urban areas. The basic conceptual problem is that housing and people should really be discussed at the local or neighbourhood level, which requires a number of detailed small area studies. Nevertheless, some interesting observations can be made concerning housing, even at this highly generalized level, and these observations relate to variations in type of dwelling unit, costs, quality, and age.

Variations in housing types

Basic information about the variation in housing types in the eight metropolitan areas within the axis in 1961 and 1971 is contained in Figure 4.3. Single detached units comprised the majority of dwelling

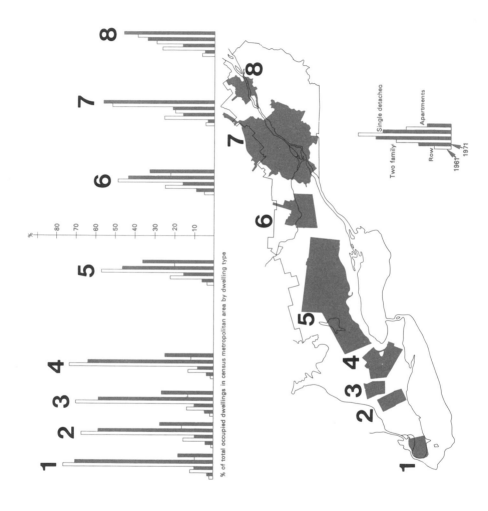

Figure 4.3: Variations in housing types in eight urban areas, 1961–71

units in all urban areas in Ontario in 1961 and 1971, but apartments comprised the bulk of dwelling units in Montréal and Québec City. This is an important difference, because apartment units can be regarded as rental units, whereas single detached houses are usually purchased by the inhabitant. This difference implies that problems of home-ownership may be permanent in the western portion of the axis, whereas rental problems and the lack of home-ownership are the prime housing problems in the eastern portion. It is, however, noticeable that the proportion of total dwelling units defined as single detached in each census metropolitan area in 1971 is less than in 1961 throughout the entire western portion of the axis, but that Montréal and Québec City in the east have incurred a relative increase in single detached units. Although the proportion of total units defined as single detached in these two urban areas has increased in the ten-year period, the figure is still very much less than in the Ontario cities.

In fact, the dominance of apartments in Montréal and Québec City has increased even more between 1961 and 1971, so that in Montréal nearly three-tenths and in Québec City approaching one-half of the dwelling units are apartments. This increase in relative importance of both apartments and single detached homes in the province of Québec has occurred at the expense of row housing and single attached homes, which exhibit a relative and absolute decline in these two cities. On the other hand, row houses in the western portion of the axis have gained in relative importance, particularly in London and Kitchener. Single attached homes have shown a relative decline in all eight metropolitan areas within the axis, and in all but Toronto, Kitchener, and Montréal this decline has been absolute as well.

The dominance of single detached houses and apartments as types of dwelling unit has accentuated during the 1961–71 period. In some urban areas, more than 95 per cent of all new dwelling units are in the form of single detached homes or apartments (Québec City, Montréal, Hamilton, and Windsor), and in the remainder more than 80 per cent of all new dwelling units are in the form of this combination. In all the metropolitan areas, apartments comprise over one-half of all dwelling units constructed — an indication of the particular metropolitan concentration of this form of habitation. This is emphasized by the observation that in Toronto and Montréal, over 65 per cent of all dwelling units created between 1961 and 1971 are apartments. On the other hand, more than 40 per cent of all new dwelling units in Windsor and Québec City are single detached homes. The only type of housing to make any small degree of impact on this combination is row housing (townhouses), and only in Ottawa-Hull and London has this type provided more than 10 per cent of all new dwelling units.

Variations in housing costs

There is an excellent discussion of housing costs in Canada and in some axis cities in Dennis and Fish (1972, pp. 73–124) and certain elements of their argument can be utilized at this juncture. The growth rates used in this section are all annual growth rates relating to the 1961–71 period. At the outset it is useful to realize that the per capita increase in income throughout the axis averaged 6.85 per cent per annum, which is the reason 7 per cent was used in the example of home-purchasing versus renting. The composite consumer price index for Canada as a whole increased about 3 per cent per annum for the same period, suggesting an increase in real income within the axis of about 3.85 per cent per annum. The cost of owning a home in Canada rose at a rate of 5.7 per cent per annum whereas the cost of renting rose 2.0 per cent per annum for the same period. There is reason to believe that both rates severely understate the rates of increase within the axis, and evidence for this belief will be presented later.

The components of the home ownership rate are property taxes, interest on mortgages, the price of new housing (including the land), and property insurance. Each of these components has increased by quite a large amount, with mortgage interest (7.1 per cent) and property insurance (7.0 per cent) leading the way. Property taxes have risen at a rate of 4.7 per cent per annum (hence the 5 per cent rate chosen in the home-purchase versus renting discussion), and the cost of new housing at a rate of 5.7 per cent per annum. Thus the costs of home-ownership have been rising at a rate two to three times greater than the composite price index, and some components of the cost of home-ownership have risen in Canada at a rate greater than the growth of per capita income in the axis, or almost the same as in Canada as a whole (7.2 per cent).

The cost of single detached houses

One of the greatest concerns is the cost of home-ownership, and, in particular, the cost of a single family house. For example, Derkowski (1972) indicates that in 1961 about 28 per cent of all income earners (not household units) could afford to purchase a new house, whereas in 1971 only 11 per cent could afford a new NHA-financed home and in Toronto only 4 per cent of all income earners could enter the home-ownership market. As an indication of the way in which the costs of single family units have risen over the ten-year period, Dennis and Fish (1972) detail the increase in costs of owning an NHA-financed new house, which, it must be remembered, invariably is part of an array of houses at the cheaper end of the cost spectrum. First, it is necessary to discount the effect of size on housing costs, for prices may well have risen as a natural result of new houses being larger. The discounting of this factor is quite simple, for the average, new, NHA-financed, single detached house has not increased at all in size between 1961 and 1971. To be precise, the evidence suggests an increase in size up to 1966 and a decrease thereafter, so that the average size was slightly less in 1971 than in 1961.

Thus, with size disregarded, the two main components of the costs of single family dwellings can be isolated as land and the construction costs of the building. Construction costs include the costs of materials (wood, bricks, electricals, and so forth), labour, and realty fees. Realty fees have stayed at a constant proportion throughout the time period. Labour costs, as represented by the hourly rates of construction workers, have risen at an average rate of 7.8 per cent per annum, and the costs of building materials at a rate of 3.8 per cent per annum. The result is that construction costs have risen at a rate of 4 per cent per annum per square foot in Canada between 1961 and 1971, and exhibit every sign of increasing at an even greater rate in the future.

Land costs have risen dramatically during this same period, and the best figure to use is for Canada as a whole, which cannot be that much different from the axis figure. The NHA land cost index indicates that the price of a lot for a single detached house rose at a rate of 5.9 per cent per annum between 1961 and 1971, although the acceleration has been much greater at the periphery of rapidly growing urban areas. As land costs usually contribute about 22 per cent of the total cost of a single detached home, the average price of a single-family house can be estimated as increasing at a rate of 4.4

per cent per annum between 1961 and 1971.

Furthermore, Dennis and Fish (1972, p. 79) suggest that the proportionate contribution of land to the total cost of a new house has remained fairly constant throughout most of the ten-year period, although it is evident that these costs vary between cities. For example, in Toronto they constitute about 30 per cent of the total cost of a new single detached dwelling, whereas in Montréal land constitutes only about 12 per cent of the total cost. There are signs over the past few years (1970–73) that these proportions are escalating, as serviced urban land becomes even more expensive.

Information for the eight metropolitan areas indicates that the prices of new NHA-financed detached houses have risen at varying rates throughout the axis (Table 4.3). In the Ontario portion, the growth rate of prices exceeds that for Canada as a whole (4.4 per cent), whereas in the Québec portion, the growth rate has been less than that for the entire country. This difference may be attributable to the different types of home that appear to be most preferred in the two portions of the axis, but it may also reflect the contrast in home-purchasing possibilities. In 1971, the per capita income of inhabitants in the western portion of the axis ($2,869) was 30 per cent greater than that of inhabitants in the eastern portion ($2,206), although the proportionate difference between the two is less than the proportionate difference in average house prices between the two areas.

Table 4.3: The average price of NHA-financed single detached houses in eight metropolitan areas within the axis

METROPOLITAN AREA	1961	1971	RATE OF INCREASE
Windsor	14,652	30,322	7.5
Toronto	17,368	32,567	6.5
Kitchener	13,648	25,122	6.3
Hamilton	15,637	28,429	6.1
Ottawa–Hull	15,772	27,775	5.9
London	14,706	25,344	5.6
Québec	13,241	18,449	3.4
Montréal	13,222	18,042	3.1

Source: CHS 1961 Table 83 (data for bungalows only); CHS 1971, Table 87 (data for all single-detached houses).

Thus, as the difference in average prices reflects more than the difference in per capita income, it can be argued that the varying rates of increase in value of single detached houses is related to the general variation in housing preferences between the two areas.

The price of a single detached house

One of the great difficulties in any analysis of prices of single detached houses is to obtain some picture of the overall effect of the different components of the price. Table 4.4 details the breakdown of the initial purchase price of an average NHA-financed house in Canada, Montréal and Toronto in 1971, and the final price in 1996 at completion of a twenty-five-year mortgage at 9.5 per cent interest. The most noticeable feature is the great difference between Montréal and Toronto in land costs as part of the price of a house. This discrepancy can be explained, in part, by the difference in servicing arrangements between the two provinces. Generally, though not always, the costs of servicing a lot in Ontario are borne by the developer and are included in the land cost component of the house price. In Québec, the usual situation is for the costs of servicing to be assumed by the municipality, which then seeks repayment from the homeowner in property taxes. Spurr (1972) claims that in Toronto in 1971 the cost of servicing a lot usually doubles the price of the lot. Thus, if the average cost of servicing is about $6,000 per lot, the implication is that variations in the price of raw land account for about $4,000 of the difference in average prices between Montréal and Toronto.

In other words, 28 per cent of the difference in house prices between Montréal and Toronto is related to the astronomical price of land in this portion of southern Ontario. To place these dollar values in perspective, consider the Blumenfeld reasonable density threshold of 4.5 houses per acre. If a suburban subdivision were developed at this density, and the unserviced lots sold at the Montréal average price of $2,000 per lot, the original owner of the land would be receiving $10,000 per acre, which is five times greater than the average price of farms quoted by Martin (1972). But, as the Toronto price appears to be around $6,000 for an unserviced lot in 1971, it follows that the original owner of the land would be receiving $27,000 per acre in the Toronto area. This sum is thirteen times greater than the average price of farms in Pickering township in 1971 quoted by Martin (1972). It is quite apparent that the price of these

Table 4.4: The price of a single detached house in Canada, Toronto, and Montréal, in 1971 and by 1996

COSTS	CANADA			TORONTO			MONTRÉAL		
	AT PURCHASE	1996	PRO-PORTION	AT PURCHASE	1996	PRO-PORTION	AT PURCHASE	1996	PRO-PORTION
Land cost	4,588	11,851	20.6	12,107	31,274	36.9	2,179	5,629	12.1
Construction	17,052	44,047	76.5	19,597	50,621	59.7	15,221	39,317	84.5
Mortgage insurance fee (MIF)	186	480	0.8	186	480	0.5	186	480	1.0
Other costs	457	1,172	2.0	943	2,436	2.9	434	1,121	2.4
Total	22,280	57,550		32,833	84,811		18,020	46,547	

Source: 1971 Costs from CHS 1972, Table 86; MIF from Table 85 (assumed constant across Canada).

lots has been escalated beyond all normal expectation of profit.

Unfortunately, the homeowner does not really own a house, he owns a mortgage. If this mortgage is at 9½ per cent interest amortized over a twenty-five-year period, then 61 per cent of the final cost of the house in 1996 is, in fact, interest payments. In Toronto, the original land cost plus interest in 1996 is almost equal to the original price of the house in 1971. Home-buyers rarely look at the price of their house in terms of the difference between original purchase cost and the purchase cost plus interest because the vast majority have no choice but to purchase with a mortgage.

The bulk of the costs, however, are construction costs. It has already been demonstrated that labour costs, in particular, have risen astronomically, and the costs of materials are not far behind. The only way of reducing these costs is to substitute less expensive building materials, and to increase the efficiency of labour. If housing components are produced in a factory system, it is possible to replace expensive skilled labour (at $10–12 per hour) with cheaper unskilled labour (at $2.50–3 per hour), and to achieve greater economies through production-line methods and strict quality control. From the point of view of employment and society in general, it may not be wise to encourage the replacement of the traditional labour-intensive construction industry by one less labour-intensive; for unemployment rates indicate that Canada requires more labour-intensive industries, not fewer. If this view is accepted, the essential corollary is that housing should be considered a national public concern, not an arena for the uncontrolled forces of private profit and ownership.

Variations in quality and age

One of the most difficult characteristics to analyse in any discussion of housing is quality. This is because quality consists of a variety of indicators, and it is doubtful whether they really measure quality in the wealthier countries of the world. The most used indicators are the proportion of dwelling units with flush toilets, and various measures of overcrowding. Using these measures, Canadians are about the best housed people in the world, and the inhabitants of the axis are, on the average, even better housed than the average Canadian family. But an average conceals an enormous amount of variation, and an important matter for concern is whether there are groups within the population which inhabit dwelling units of such inferior quality that they may be injurious to health (in the broadest sense).

The general trend has been for the quality of housing in Canada and within the axis to improve between 1961 and 1971. There are fewer homes without flush toilets, and fewer persons per dwelling unit! The improvement in standards has been particularly noticeable in the eastern portion of the axis, although housing quality (as measured by these indicators) in this area is still generally inferior to that enjoyed by the rest of the axis. But any examination of housing quality within urban areas reveals that the inner sections of central cities contain a disproportionately large component of low-quality homes (Kirkland, 1972). Some of these are of such bad quality, in terms of heat, insulation, ventilation and vermin, that they can be considered injurious to health. The inhabitants of these dwelling units are always the poor (Puxley, 1971) and frequently the elderly (Lithwick, 1970). Although this particular problem may be regarded as an income problem and treated as such, there has to be a concerted effort made to upgrade or eradicate low-quality dwellings and at the same time re-enforce the positive characteristics of the neighbourhood.

In many studies of housing, age is usually considered to be associated with quality. Older dwelling units are more likely than newer units to be of inferior quality and to lack basic facilities. Even more important, however, families with young children are more likely than any other type of family to live in newer residential units, be they single detached, attached, row or low-rise apartment. These newer units are invariably located at the edge of urban areas, for new units and new land are given preference in the established mortgage structure. It is noticeable that a large proportion of new apartment units constructed between 1961 and 1971 have also been located in suburban areas in Toronto (Bourne, 1971), although this is not true of Montréal. The general peripheral location of residential units constructed since 1961 is documented by the sketch maps of age of dwelling units within metropolitan areas in Figure 4.4. The 1961 isoline indicates those areas in which an average of 60 per cent or more of the residential units have been built since that date. The maps emphasize the concentric nature of urban growth within metropolitan areas in the axis, with clearly defined radials being the spearhead of outward expansion. Nevertheless, it should be noted that there are a few areas within the central parts of some cities in which the recent construction of high-rise apartments has resulted in that area containing a very large proportion of post-1961 residential units.

CONCLUSION

Just as the tributaries of a drainage basin eventually unite within the body of the main river, so do the facts and various implications of the housing scene in the axis and Canada combine to form a particular conclusion. It is clear that housing has to be life-cycle oriented and responsive to basic needs, be they physical or perceptual, of the individual families. It is apparent that although the general quality of housing within the axis has improved between 1961 and 1971, there are many parts of cities in which the residential units are of low

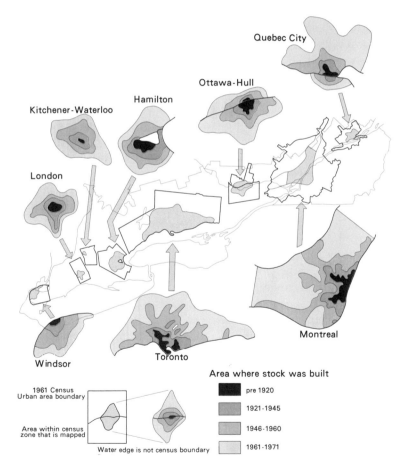

Figure 4.4: Maps of age of dwelling units within eight metropolitan areas

quality. These units must be replaced or upgraded, and the rebuilding or improvements must be managed in a way that preserves the positive features of the neighbourhood as perceived by the inhabitants of the area. During the 1960s there were virtually no federally financed schemes for the renovation or rebuilding of individual dwelling units in old neighbourhoods. The only schemes that were available were for new housing on empty urban land.

Furthermore, it is also clear that although many people feel it necessary to raise children in single family units, be they detached or attached, they have not been able to obtain such accommodation, owing to high prices. Note that the stumbling block is high prices, not lack of income; for it has been demonstrated that the prices of single detached homes, for example, have risen at an astronomical rate in some parts of the axis. The problem is not confined to the Toronto area, but the magnitude of the demand, as well as the prices, is greatest in this area. The result has been a tremendous reliance on the apartment form of dwelling unit, as witnessed by the dramatic concentration of apartment construction in the Toronto (and Montréal) area between 1961 and 1971.

This apartment construction was, in fact, partially demand responsive, for many young adults entered the housing market during the 1960s. This factor may well result in a future imbalance in the supply of dwelling units, for the young adult of yester-decade is the adult and prospective parent of this decade. As a consequence, the current intensive demand for single-family residential units of the detached and attached varieties is likely to continue apace. Many families are unable to afford the down payment and carrying charges of most new single detached homes, and they are forced to reside in dwelling units which they perceive as incongruous with their life-cycle situation. This is not to imply that rental units are cheap compared with income, although the average rents in the major urban areas have risen 1.5 per cent per annum in Montréal and 2.4 per cent per annum in Toronto. In 1969, shelter consumed 36 per cent of the poorest families' incomes and only 13 per cent of the richest families' incomes in major urban areas within the axis.

The conclusion has to be that housing should be life-cycle oriented, and that a family of a given size should live in a certain minimum number of rooms embracing a defined, minimum amount of space. If a family cannot afford the minimum space it requires (according to defined standards) then it should be permitted to obtain the necessary space via rental or income supplements. A rudimentary scheme of this type is already in partial operation in the provinces of Ontario and Québec, but for a good example of the scheme in operation it might be interesting to review housing policies in Denmark. There, once a family no longer requires the amount of space in which it resides then the income, or rent supplement, can be reduced.

Along with a scheme of income and rent supplement severe controls on housing prices should be effected. Such controls can be achieved in part by the land bank system proposed in the previous chapter. If the land bank scheme is really effective then the price of raw land could be held to as low as 10 per cent or 12 per cent of the value of a new home, and ideally as low as 5 per cent. Servicing costs could be held at the 1971 level or even reduced by careful planning which would avoid the promotion of subdivisions discontiguous from the chief direction of growth of the urban area. Furthermore, all basic services, such as water, and sewage, could be linked to large, efficient, purifying and filtration plants, thus eliminating many of the smaller pollution-creating systems already in existence. If it is decided to maintain the construction industry as labour intensive, then the renter or purchaser should receive a subsidy or tax rebate similar to the subsidies and tax holidays given manufacturers for locating in labour-surplus parts of the country.

If these schemes do not achieve significant reductions in housing costs, or at least a lowering of the rate of increase in house prices, then it may well be necessary for the federal government to enter not only the land bank business via the municipalities, but also the housing bank business as well. The federal government could establish a public corporation, financed with housing bonds, which would be charged with the task of purchasing and constructing a housing inventory of different types of dwelling units in a variety of locations within all the cities of the country. This housing stock would be rented according to life-cycle needs at rates that can be afforded by the individual families. The stock would not be sold, and the rents used to defray expenses, repairs, and increase the volume of stock owned. The result would be that in time the corporation would be able to own sufficient stock to influence significantly rental prices and home-ownership costs within different cities.

These proposals, which have been only briefly outlined, should be considered, because it is quite evident that the supply procedure already in operation does not meet the needs of urban Canada at reasonable cost. Furthermore, the procedure accentuates some of the worst features of the economic system, which are then borne by the family for much of its life. Shelter and food are essential to the existence of all Canadians, but the current system of providing dwelling units is responsive to the needs of only a small proportion of the total population. Future programs should be responsive to the needs of all income groups at whatever stage in the life cycle the family may be, and these programs should be coordinated centrally. The aim of these programs should be to reduce inequalities of standards of shelter among all income groups, and to ensure adequate space (internal and external) for all families, whether they consist of one or more persons. The latter objective requires careful neighbourhood planning as well as an understanding of the space requirements of families at different stages in the life cycle.

5   THE ECONOMIC STRUCTURE OF THE AREA

The distribution of the urban population and the consumption of land in the axis having been discussed, it is necessary now to examine its economic base and the distribution of those activities that are most important in providing employment for the inhabitants of the area. By 1971 there were over 4.75 million persons in the labour force within the axis, although that figure does not imply that all these persons were employed. However, it is probably safe to assume that, at that time, the vast majority were employed, although unemployment estimates ranged from 13.3 per cent of the labour force in St. George to less than 5 per cent in Toronto. In general, unemployment in the axis area (1971 average, 5.4 per cent) was, and is, less than in the rest of Canada, although any unemployment rates should be perused with a suspicious eye, since close inspection of the data frequently reveals variations in estimates of total employment for a given Canada Manpower Centre that exceed the calculated unemployment rates.

SOME GENERAL OBSERVATIONS

The magnitude of the labour force in the axis increased with great rapidity during the 1960s. Tentative estimates suggest that the labour force expanded at a rate of 3.0 per cent per annum between 1961 and 1971 (Table 5.1), a far greater increase than the population growth rate for the same period (2.0 per cent per annum). The growth rate of the labour force in the rest of Canada reflects this same pattern, although the increase (2.5 per cent per annum) is less than that for the axis area. It is tempting to relate this expanding labour force to the rate of increase of persons in the sixteen to sixty-five potential-employment age group, but in the axis area the growth rate of the labour force exceeds the rate of growth of the sixteen to sixty-five-year age group (2.4 per cent per annum). Thus the increase in the labour force is only partially attributable to the increase in numbers in the potential employment group, and it must, therefore, be related to the increased rate of female participation in the labour force. Though it is ludicrous to regard women at home taking care of children, husband and house as not participating in the labour force, this is exactly what the female participation concept implies. The increased rate of female participation in the labour force has had, and is having, tremendous repercussions not only on the economy of the country, but on society in general. The urban implications are also interesting, and will be commented upon in the final chapter.

The differences between the axis and the rest of Canada are marked in 1971, but not quite as accentuated as in 1961. The axis shows a very large proportion of its labour force concerned with manufacturing in both 1961 and 1971, whereas the rest of Canada shows a smaller proportion concerned with manufacturing and a much larger proportion concerned with agriculture and other primary industry. This difference illustrates one phase of McInnis's (1973) specialization argument with respect to the Canadian economy: that central Canada focuses on manufacturing, whereas the peripheral regions specialize in particular natural resources. This situation appears to prevail in 1971, though the total numbers concerned with agriculture and the primary industries have declined in absolute terms in both the axis and the rest of Canada between 1961 and 1971. It is interesting to note that this absolute decline has been counterbalanced in both parts of the country by rather large increases in employment in the commercial, business, and personal service sector of industry, and the implications of this trend with respect to the post-industrial age will be discussed in the concluding chapter.

The axis area itself exhibits some quite significant shifts in employment between the rather large industry divisions listed in Table 5.1. Although the total labour force increased at a rate of 3.0 per cent per annum between 1961 and 1971, employment in only two industry divisions increased at a greater rate. These embrace the financial and commercial group, which employed over 30 per cent of the total labour force in 1971. If employment in trade (wholesale and retail) and public administration, which increased at a rate only slightly less than the axis average, are included with these services, the four

Table 5.1: Axis and rest of Canada labour force, 1961 and 1971, and proportion of total labour force in each industry group

INDUSTRY GROUP	1961		1971		AXIS GROWTH RATE
	AXIS	REST OF CANADA	AXIS	REST OF CANADA	
Agriculture	7.3	13.8	4.5	9.3	−1.9
Other primary industries	0.9	8.4	0.5	6.6	−3.3
Manufacturing	29.0	13.5	27.8	13.9	2.6
Construction	6.9	6.8	6.4	6.9	2.2
Transport, commercial, and other utilities	8.5	10.9	7.6	9.9	1.8
Trade	15.6	15.9	15.1	16.6	2.7
Finance, insurance, and real estate	4.3	2.7	5.3	4.0	5.3
Commercial, business, personal service	20.2	19.7	25.8	25.9	5.5
Public administration	7.3	8.2	7.0	6.9	2.7
Total labour force (in thousands)	3,554	2,759	4,781	3,527	3.0

Sources: 1961 data obtained from 1961 Census of Canada, "Labour Force by Industry Group," 94–522; 1971 data estimated from the June 19, 1971 "The Labour Force" survey, by province.

industry groups contained well over half the total axis labour force in 1971. Furthermore, over 70 per cent of all the new jobs created within the axis between 1961 and 1971 are classified within these four groups. As a consequence, the distribution of these four industry groups, which are defined broadly as tertiary activities, within the axis are discussed in greater detail in a later section.

The sector of economic activity which most distinguishes the axis from the rest of the country is manufacturing. Even though the rate of growth of manufacturing employment in the rest of Canada was slightly ahead of that for the axis, southern Ontario and southern Québec are still the focus of manufacturing activity in the country. One of the means by which it maintains this dominance is discussed in the following chapter, but it cannot be denied that the proximity of the bulk of the Canadian capital and purchasing market, and the proximity of the U.S. market and all too frequently the parent firms (Ray, 1965), are major localizing factors. Despite the fact that the growth rate in manufacturing was less than that for the services, the labour force in manufacturing increased at a greater rate than the potential labour force, and also provided over 24 per cent of all the new jobs created in the axis between 1961 and 1971. The great importance of manufacturing dictates that it should be discussed separately along with the tertiary activities. But first, let us consider agriculture.

AGRICULTURE

Though agricultural activities occupy only 4.5 per cent of the axis labour force, this sector of activity cannot be ignored because farms within the axis receive over 38 per cent of all farm cash receipts in the country. Axis agriculture comprises a very important part of the Canadian agricultural scene, although its products and geographical distribution are becoming increasingly influenced by the axis urban environment. A number of these influences have been discussed previously, and are mentioned in this section only for the sake of completeness. There are places in the axis where the direct expansion of urban areas has absorbed or threatens agriculture. These places are particularly conducive to specialized agricultural activities. More important, in terms of gross acreage, are the associated urban effects of technological sprawl and the purchase of recreation facilities, whether in the form of summer cottages or "landed gentry" play-farms that may also be held for speculative purposes.

Most of the gross decline in farm acreage, however, is associated with farm abandonment, because many lands do not provide an adequate livelihood. This situation is particularly noticeable in the Appalachian zone of Québec and in eastern Ontario, and in many smaller sub-regions, such as the "mer bleue" along the shore of the St. Lawrence River between Drummondville and Québec City, and in the rougher rocky areas of parts of the Bruce Peninsula (Bélanger, 1972; Gray, *et al.*, 1972). The abandonment of these lands, though necessary in terms of the economic welfare of the inhabitants, is an indirect result of urbanization, since the market for agricultural products is in the rich cities. As urban dwellers have become wealthier, a smaller proportion of their personal income is being spent on agricultural goods, and the proportion that is spent is being devoted increasingly to luxury foods and a higher level of processing and packaging (McDonald, 1972).

The result of these changing urban demands is that farmers have had to become more productive, and productivity has been achieved through an even greater use of fertilizers, machinery, and improved feeds, a reduction in the amount of labour required, and increased specialization. These trends have meant that only the most productive farms on good quality lands can survive. From a social point of view, the trends have also resulted in the farmers becoming very market-conscious, with their production geared to a sales schedule that cannot be easily altered to suit variations in demand. Greater specialization has also meant that the farmer is extremely sensitive to price fluctuations as well as aberrations in the weather. Thus, the family farm as a way of life is rapidly disappearing within the axis, and it is being replaced by the farm as a business (Tremblay and Anderson, 1966). Consequently, the social distinction between rural and urban living hardly exists throughout much of the axis area.

Variations in agriculture within the axis

Details concerning the general distribution of agricultural regions and types of output in the axis area can be obtained from Reeds (1967), *The Quebec Atlas of Agriculture* (Ministère de l'Industrie et du Commerce, 1966), Thibodeau (1972), and Grégoire (1972). These sources, among others, indicate locations, but this particular section is concerned with examining the spatial variation in agricultural productivity. Figure 5.1 illustrates the variation in agricultural produc-

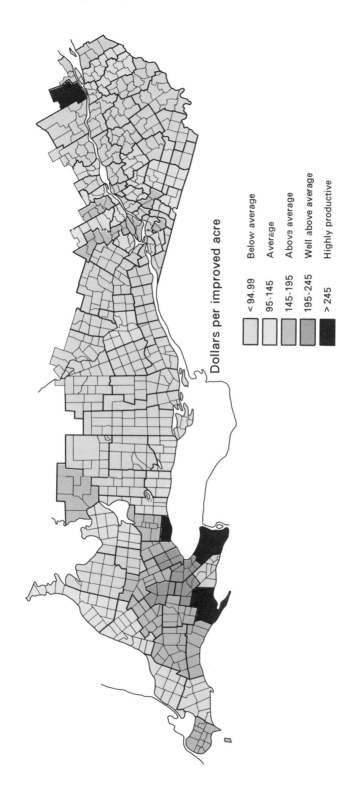

Dollars per improved acre

< 94.99	Below average
95-145	Average
145-195	Above average
195-245	Well above average
> 245	Highly productive

Figure 5.1: Total value of farm production by improved acre, by census divisions, 1971

tivity of census divisions within the axis as defined by the total value
of farm production sold per improved acre in 1971. The average value
of this indicator for the entire axis is $120 per improved acre, so the
$95–145 category delimits those counties that are about average.

It should be noted that the counties that are below average are located almost exactly where the conclusions from previous discussions
would predict. The Shield and Appalachian physiographic regions
and the swampy lowland area south of the St. Lawrence River contain
most of the least productive census divisions. The most productive
areas are located in areas of more suitable agricultural land and around
the larger urban centres. In fact nearly all of the above-average productive census divisions devote a substantial proportion of their improved land to vegetables, fruit, and other land-intensive crops. All
the average and above average counties also have a considerable
number of farms concerned with the dairy industry, with milk being
the major product around Montréal, and in the area between Toronto
and Kitchener. Milk products (butter, cheese, and so forth), are
produced farther afield in the broad area to the south of Montréal, and
in the census divisions bordering Lake Huron and Georgian Bay.

The highly productive areas feature certain very specialized types
of agricultural production. The Niagara Peninsula has been mentioned previously as an area of intensive fruit production, with peaches
and grapes being of primary importance. Norfolk county is the centre
of tobacco production in Ontario, and contains almost a half (41,000
acres) of all the acreage devoted to tobacco production in the province.
The other two areas of highly productive agriculture are statistical
deviates, based on their limited supply of improved farmland. The
census division of Toronto appears to have an extraordinarily large
number of egg-laying chickens per improved acre, while the census
division of Québec City contains a remarkable concentration of
turkeys! Thus it seems that not only do urban areas, good quality land,
and climate affect agricultural productivity, but centres of provincial
government exude a certain influence also.

THE ECONOMIC STRUCTURE OF URBAN AREAS

Before embarking upon a detailed discussion of manufacturing and
tertiary activities, it is perhaps well to emphasize that these activities
are located in urban areas. Current estimates suggest that at least 82
per cent of all manufacturing employment, and 81 per cent of all the

major growth tertiary activities (trade, finance, services, and public administration) are located in fifty-five metropolitan areas, cities and towns, that contain 71 per cent of the population of the axis. Thus, even if some of the ensuing discussion is involved with data concerning census divisions, it should be emphasized that the data really pertain to urban areas within the census division. Furthermore, it would be wise to acknowledge that many of the estimates should be viewed with a degree of suspicion, although the general conclusions are tenable. Although this may sound contradictory, it is not meant to imply that the data are inaccurate, but simply that the data are acceptable only within the terms of reference of their compilation.

For example, decennial census data concerning the manufacturing labour force for urban areas are usually different from the data on manufacturing employment compiled by the Primary and Manufacturing Industries Division of Statistics Canada. This is because the decennial census is based on an enumeration of a person's current or most recent employment by residence, whereas the data provided by the Primary and Manufacturing Industries Division are compiled on the basis of an annual survey of manufacturing plants, and the figures may refer to an average or particular month in the year. This comment may indicate why certain totals may differ, and also why care is taken to make sure that for any series the data are consistent with respect to source.

The distribution of occupations among urban areas within the axis

An employed person may be classified according to either occupation or industry. The occupational categories include such labels as machinists, miners, paper workers, managers, professors, clerical workers, labourers, service workers, and so forth. Thus, within any particular office or plant there are a variety of occupations, and it would be interesting to observe the way in which the proportion of the labour force concerned with particular occupations has changed during the past decade. The trend up to 1961 was for relative increase in the number of engineers, scientists, clerical workers, and service workers, and for a relative decrease in the number of miners, longshoremen, labourers, and so forth. Unfortunately, it is not possible to document these changes for the 1961–71 period, because the 1971 occupational classification is entirely different from that used in 1961. The tasks included within particular occupational categories have been altered, as have some of the labels themselves.

Britton (1972) has analysed the 1961 occupational data for urban areas in Ontario and Québec, and the axis portion of his analysis is presented in Figure 5.2. The technique used for the analysis is very complicated, but the results cast some light on the various concentrations of employment throughout the axis. The labels simply imply that in that particular town "machinists", "service workers", or "machinists and paper workers" predominate. Happily, most of the results are as expected. Thetford Mines and Asbestos appear to contain a large number of persons occupied as miners. Shawinigan, Cap-de-la-Madeleine, and Victoriaville contain many paper workers; Oshawa and St. Catharines are crowded with machinists; and spinners and weavers either dominate or are found in conjunction with other occupations in a number of towns in l'Est du Québec. Most of the centres have a preponderance of employment in the service occupations, and this feature is particularly noticeable among those defined as "principal centres" in Table 1.3.

The distribution of industrial employment among urban areas within the axis

The industrial classification groups employment according to the type of industry in which it is located. Thus, if a person is a machinist in a factory making televisions, he is classified as a worker in the "manufacturers of household radio and television receivers" group in the "electrical products industries" major group, of manufacturing industry. Likewise, if a person is a saleswoman in a women's clothing store she is classified as an employee in the "women's ready-to-wear stores" sub-group, of the "apparel and shoe stores" group, of the "retail trade" major group, of the trade industry. A detailed listing of the various industries, major groups, groups, and sub-groups can be found in a Statistics Canada *Standard Industrial Classification* manual. The advantage of using employment data by industry group (were it available) is that it is possible to compare the 1961 census classification with the 1971 census classification, because the changes in group content that have occurred have been relatively minor.

Most of the urban areas within the axis have an above-axis-average proportion of their total employment in one or both of the two broad sectors of industry which have provided most of the new jobs between 1961 and 1971. These two broad sectors, it will be recalled, are manu-

Figure 5.2: *Occupational data for urban areas in the axis, 1961*

Occupational type

Machinists & service

Machinists & paper workers

Service, Spinners & weavers

Service & paper workers

Spinners, weavers & paper workers

Machinists, service & paper workers

⊗ Machinists

⊛ Miners

✦ Service

▲ Spinners & weavers

● Paper workers

Source: **Britton [1972].**

facturing, which (it is estimated) occupied 27.8 per cent of the labour force in 1971; and the tertiary activities, which include trade, finance, insurance, and real estate, commercial, business, and personal service, and public administration, which occupied 53.2 per cent of the Labour Force. In Figure 5.3 these two proportions have been used as benchmarks to define those urban areas that have greater than these axis proportions of the labour force employed in these two sectors, and they are described appropriately, as "manufacturing" and "tertiary". Of the fifty-five metropolitan areas, cities, and towns included within the analysis, ten are classified as having disproportionately large manufacturing and tertiary employment components in 1971, twenty-six have a concentration of manufacturing employment, and seventeen have an extra large tertiary component. The latter can be regarded as fundamentally service centres. The mining towns of Asbestos and Thetford Mines are included in none of the groups, and it is interesting to note that the census subdivisions in which these towns are located have experienced an absolute decrease in population.

MANUFACTURING

Although in many urban areas a proportion of the total labour force is concerned with manufacturing, the bulk of the employment in this sector of industry is concentrated in the major metropolitan areas. The census metropolitan areas (1961 boundaries) of Montréal and Toronto contain slightly less than one-half of the 1971 employment in manufacturing in the axis, and the other metropolitan areas contain very small proportions. Hamilton contributes 6.0 per cent; Kitchener–Waterloo, Windsor, St. Catharines–Niagara Falls, London, Oshawa–Whitby, Québec City, and Ottawa–Hull between 2 and 3 per cent each; and Sherbrooke, Chatham, Shawinigan (including Grand'Mère and Shawinigan-Sud), and Sarnia, about 1 per cent. All the other urban areas contain only a minute proportion of the total employment in manufacturing within the axis. The two most famous manufacturing agglomerations in Canada, the "Golden Horseshoe", and Montréal and "la rive sud de Montréal", are located within the axis; the area between Oshawa and Niagara Falls provides over one-third of all jobs in manufacturing in the axis and the Montréal region an additional quarter.

Not only are there these definite geographic concentrations in employment, there are also some concentrations in various industry

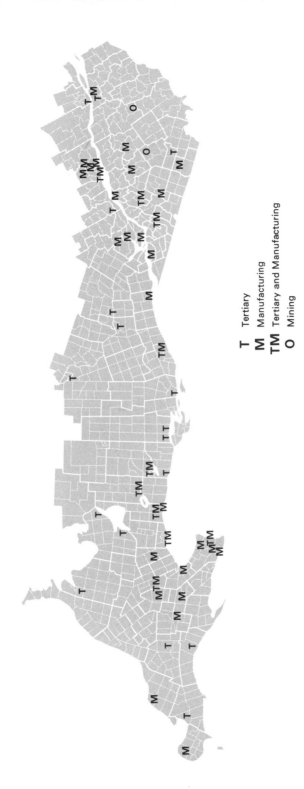

Figure 5.3: Dominant labour force concentration in fifty-five urban centres of more than 10,000 population

T Tertiary
M Manufacturing
TM Tertiary and Manufacturing
O Mining

groups. Probably the most noticeable is the metals and machinery industry (Table 5.2), which includes a wide variety of industry ranging from iron and steel mills to office machinery manufacturers. Nearly 20 per cent of the axis manufacturing labour force is devoted to this particular major group (which is actually a combination of two SIC major groups) and furthermore, many individual sub-groups of this manufacturing type are concentrated in particular locations within the axis. For example, three cities in Canada account for 90 per cent of all steel ingots and castings produced in the country; Hamilton produces 55 per cent, Sydney (Nova Scotia) 10 per cent, and Sault

Table 5.2: The distribution of employment among the major manufacturing groups within the axis, 1961

MAJOR GROUP	PROPORTION OF MANUFACTURING LABOUR FORCE 1961
Food	9.9
Beverages	2.1
Tobacco	0.9
Rubber	1.7
Leather	3.0
Primary textiles	4.2
Fabricated textiles	1.5
Knit goods	1.7
Clothing	8.3
Wood products	2.7
Furniture	2.8
Pulp and paper	6.1
Printing and publishing	6.2
Metals and machinery	17.5
Transport equipment	9.5
Electrical equipment	7.8
Non-metallics	2.9
Petroleum	0.9
Chemicals	5.9
Other manufactures	4.4

Source: Statistics Canada, Census of Manufactures, 1961.

Ste Marie 25 per cent (Kerr, 1967). This type of concentration can be noticed in a number of other major groups as well. Oshawa and St. Catharines are noted for production of transport equipment, and Drummondville, Granby, Sherbrooke, Valleyfield, and Victoriaville contain a number of textile firms.

The localization of many of these major industry groups in particular urban areas is emphasized in Figure 5.4, where the leading industry in each urban area is defined by a visual symbol. The seven leading industries are designated for the census metropolitan areas of Toronto and Montréal, because these two areas so dominate manufacturing within the axis. The three leading major groups are defined for Hamilton, and two for those cities containing more than 1 per cent of the axis manufacturing labour force that have a second industry of sufficient magnitude. This map confirms the observation of McInnis (1973) which is that since 1911, not only has manufacturing become more concentrated within the axis, but transfer of specialization between Ontario and Québec has occurred. For example, the net comparative shift in employment in clothing manufacture to Québec is almost exactly counterbalanced by a net comparative decline of similar magnitude to Ontario, while the comparative gain of employment in rubber manufacturing in Ontario is offset by a comparative loss of similar size in Québec.

The concentration of the bulk of manufacturing employment in a few areas and the emergence of a degree of industry specialization (Gilmour and Murricane, 1973) make it possible to define a few manufacturing regions within the two provinces, some of which are characterized by a particular type of manufacturing industry. In the Québec portion of the axis there are a number of manufacturing towns extending from Montreal to Québec City, and from Sherbrooke to Shawinigan. This portion, including Ottawa-Hull, will be referred to as the East Axis Manufacturing Area. In Ontario, there are a few minor manufacturing centres bordering Lake Ontario, but the real concentration is not only in the aforementioned crescent around the western end of Lake Ontario from Oshawa to Niagara Falls, but also in a broad belt between Toronto and Windsor. These two zones will be referred to as the West Axis Manufacturing Area.

THE EAST AXIS MANUFACTURING AREA

The East Axis Manufacturing Area, which extends from Ottawa–

Hull and Cornwall to Québec City, contains 43.12 per cent of the total 1971 axis employment in manufacturing. Though the labour force concerned with manufacturing in the East Axis area increased between 1961 and 1971 by around 100,000, the relative concentration of manufacturing employment in this area actually declined; for in 1961 it contained 45.34 per cent of the manufacturing labour force. The nature and reasons for this comparative decline will be discussed later, but at the outset it is necessary to understand the general structure of manufacturing in the area. In general, there are three major manufacturing areas. The most important is the Montréal census metropolitan area (Figure 5.4) which, for the purposes of this discussion includes the broad area along the south bank between Varennes and Sorel (la rive sud de Montréal). The second area is the area south and east of Montréal known as 'Est du Québec, and the region around Trois-Rivières. The Est du Québec and Trois-Rivières areas are characterized by a high degree of specialization. Finally, the peripheral manufacturing centres of Ottawa–Hull and Québec City are included for the sake of completeness.

The Montréal area

According to Manzagol (1972), Montréal is responsible for nearly 55 per cent of the output attributable to manufacturing in Québec, and about 16 per cent of that in Canada as a whole. Although there is a diversity of output (Figure 5.4) there are certain industries which are clearly specialized in the Montréal area. Probably the most obvious to any traveller is the petroleum refining industry which covers many bleak acres in the eastern portion of Ile de Montréal (Montréal Est). Montréal is the leading refining centre in Canada, producing 33 per cent of the total volume of petroleum refined within the country, but the refining plants employ very few people. This is true also of the few petro-chemical complexes located in the same area. In fact, the relative paucity of petro-chemical plants compared with the huge volume of output in the refining industry is interesting, for general knowledge concerning inter-industry linkages suggests that the opposite should be the case. In fact, Sarnia has almost twice as many petro-chemical plants as Montréal.

The leading industry in Montréal in terms of employment is the clothing industry, which, along with general textiles and knitting mills, provides employment for almost one-quarter of the Montréal

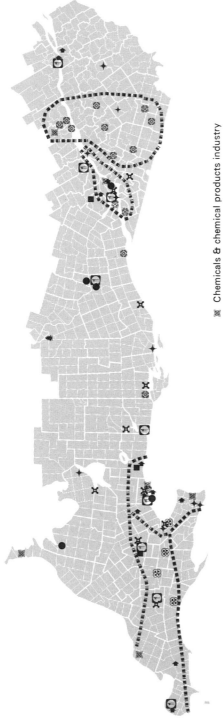

Figure 5.4: *Manufacturing industries within the axis*

Chemicals & chemical products industry

Electrical products industry

Food & beverage industry

Rubber

Textile and clothing

Wood

Paper and printing

Primary metal, metal fabric and non-metal industry

Machinery industry

Transportation industry

manufacturing labour force. Traditionally, the clothing industry has been concentrated in small- and medium-sized plants containing anywhere from ten to 200 employees, located in the St. Lawrence Boulevard–Bleury Street area. There has been some decentralization to the new industrial parks and the Metropolitan Boulevard strip in recent years, but the industry is still basically located in the traditional areas. The industry is characterized by its large labour requirements (particularly female labour), its low wages, and its demand-based pressure production. The smaller textile-producing firms in the Montréal region are closely linked with the clothing industry, and as a consequence, they too have to be prepared to respond to changing demands and tastes with some rapidity. The result, from the point of view of an employee, is not only low wages but a relatively high degree of job insecurity. The urban impact of this situation is that it helps to foster emotions of discontent among the lower-paid workers and their families in the urban area, and so, therefore, a low-wage and cyclical employment problem becomes an urban problem.

Any discussion of manufacturing in Montréal, however brief, cannot ignore the transportation, machinery, and food-processing industries, which together provide employment for another one-quarter of the manufacturing labour force. These industries are difficult to ignore also because many of the plants classified in these groups dominate much of the shoreline along the St. Lawrence River. Ship-repair yards, flour mills, sugar refineries, and so forth, are found interspersed along the waterfront, although very few are now dependent upon water transport either for raw materials or for the transport of finished products. Furthermore, these industries are declining in an axis and a Canadian context, in that they are non-competitive in the Montréal location and are part of an industry that is becoming less labour intensive. On the other hand, the electrical products industry is an expanding and generally high-wage industry which has increased employment in the Montréal area, particularly in the newer industrial parks, such as that found in Pointe-Claire.

One very important sub-region within and overlapping the census metropolitan area of Montréal is la rive sud de Montréal. This area consists, the name suggests, of those portions of the census divisions of Richelieu, Verchères, Chambly, Laprairie, Châteauguay, and Beauharnois that lie along the south bank of the St. Lawrence River. The area is important for three reasons. First, it contains a fairly large proportion (12 per cent) of the manufacturing employment in the

Montréal area. Secondly, the rate of increase in manufacturing employment in this sub-region has been much greater than that for the Montréal area in general. Thirdly, the area contains a large proportion of the "heavy industries" of Québec, which include iron and steel smelting and metal fabrication, the manufacture of machines and aircraft, as well as textile manufacturing and food processing (Lamonde, 1972). Much of the industrial activity is concentrated in the towns of Jacques Cartier and Longueuil, but the whole area between Varennes and Sorel has been described by Gagnon (1969) as an incipient "Ruhr du Québec".

Nevertheless, apart from one or two areas of growth, the general weakness of the manufacturing industry in the Montréal area, as far as employment is concerned, must be emphasized. Manufacturing employment in this area increased at the very most at a rate of 2 per cent per annum between 1961 and 1971. Furthermore, many of the dominant industries are either low wage and subject to cyclical fluctuations in employment, or old declining firms that are non-competitive in an axis and world context, or they do not require very much labour. Those industries which are concentrated in the area and do produce products required by other labour-intensive industries, such as the petroleum refining industry, do not seem to have generated these linked activities. The petro-chemical, general chemical, and pharmaceutical industries are not as prevalent in Montréal (or Québec) as would be expected from the quantity of by-products generated by the refining industries, and Manzagol (1972) claims that this situation is the result of the limited purchasing power of the relatively small Québec market, and the American takeovers of those firms which seem likely to succeed.

The textile and clothing industry of l'Est du Québec and Trois-Rivières

One of the industries noted by McInnis (1973) as having become increasingly specialized in Québec since 1911 is the textile and clothing industry. This development is, in fact, the result of a number of strong links which have been developed over the years between the clothing industry, which is primarily (though not exclusively) located in the towns within a 100-mile radius of Montréal. A fleeting glance at Figure 5.4 reveals that in nearly all the cities in this area the textile and clothing industries are the major sources of manufacturing employment, and this situation is repeated in many of the smaller towns as well (Polèse, 1972, pp. 99–102). In fact, information contained in Girard (1970) yields the estimate that 37 per cent of all the manufacturing labour force in this extensive area is concentrated in the textile and clothing industries.

It is wise, however, to place the magnitude of the industry in this area in perspective with respect to the axis as a whole. L'Est du Québec and Trois-Rivières contain 6 per cent of the total labour force within the axis, and it should be noted that this figure is just a little less than the figure for Hamilton. Furthermore, whereas Montréal contains one-third of the axis labour force concerned with textiles and clothing, this broad region contains only 11 per cent. But the textile and clothing industries are the primary source of employment in l'Est du Québec and Trois-Rivières. Thus, though the industry is locally dominant, it does not provide an extraordinarily large number of jobs when viewed in the context of the entire axis.

Furthermore, the textile and clothing industries are not the leading industries in the area with respect to the value of output; the leader is the pulp and paper industry, which provides employment for 17 per cent of the labour force in the area. This industry is located particularly in the city of Trois-Rivières and the towns of Cap-de-la-Madeleine, Shawinigan, and Grand'Mère. To all intents and purposes the industry is controlled by three large companies whose head offices are in Montréal.

Ottawa–Hull and Québec City

The administrative centres of Ottawa–Hull and Québec City are minor industrial metropolises located on the periphery of the East Axis Manufacturing Area. The Québec census metropolitan area, which includes Lévis and Lauzon on the south bank of the river, contains only 2.2 per cent of the axis manufacturing labour force. The primary industries are those associated with food and beverages, but shipbuilding and repair, and the pulp and paper industries are also well represented. The Ottawa–Hull metropolitan area contains about the same proportion of the axis manufacturing labour force as Québec City, but manufacturing employment in the Ottawa portion of the urban complex is increasing at a much greater rate than in Québec City. Although pulp and paper and the food and beverage industries are the dominant sources of manufacturing employment, the electrical products industry has become quite important in recent years.

THE WEST AXIS AREA

The West Axis Manufacturing Area is defined as that portion of the axis lying west of an imaginary line drawn between Oshawa and Lake Simcoe. This area contained nearly 52 per cent of the axis manufacturing labour force in 1971, and nearly two-fifths of all manufacturing employment in the country. Furthermore, employment in manufacturing in this area grew at a faster rate (3 per cent per annum) between 1961 and 1971 then anywhere else in the rest of the axis, or the country. There has, therefore, been a comparative shift of employment in this sector of industry from the eastern portion to the west, though, as usual, the word "shift" is not meant to imply that many people actually packed their suitcases and moved. The comparative shift occurred as a result of differential growth. Within the West Axis Manufacturing Area two broad sub-areas have been identified, and these are the West Lake Ontario Crescent and the zone between Kitchener and Windsor (Figure 5.4).

The West Lake Ontario Crescent

One of the more inspired regional adjectives is the description of the West Lake Ontario Crescent as the "Golden Horseshoe". It is a description that has entranced, and misled, many a Canadian student, for the image created is that of a beautiful, well-organized, and planned environment occupied by man. If the word "golden" refers to anything, it is money; for this area has the highest per capita income of any portion of the axis or of Canada. This income is derived from the tremendous concentration of manufacturing and tertiary activities in the area. The word "golden" can hardly refer to the environment, for much of it is cement, steel, and macadam, and although areas of beauty exist, there has been little regard for preservation. Within the area there is a tremendous diversity of types of manufacturing industries although there are a few areas of particular specialization.

Oshawa is the major focus of automobile manufacturing in Canada, since it contains over one-half of all persons employed in this type of activity in the country. Whitby and Bowmanville, to the immediate west and east of Oshawa, have small plants concerned with producing rubber products and tires, some of which are used in the automobile industry. The importance of Hamilton in the iron and steel industry has already been recognized. In terms of employment, the Hamilton area provides about one-third of all the jobs in those activities directly related to iron and steel smelting and casting in the country.

These areas of specialization are counterbalanced by the great diversity of manufacturing employment in the Toronto census metropolitan area. Almost every industrial group is represented (Kerr and Spelt, 1965), with food and beverages, metal fabrication, electrical products, and printing and publishing being the most important. Because of the diversity of output, many of the factories are quite small, the average firm employing about forty-four workers, and most of the production is geared toward the local and Canadian consumer markets. For example, within Toronto are produced the vast bulk of the nation's batteries, books, miscellaneous non-ferrous products, soaps and washing compounds, scientific instruments, and toys and games. Between 1961 and 1971 consumer-based manufacturing became even more concentrated in the Toronto area in response to the great comparative increase in population within this portion of southern Ontario. In fact, by 1971 this area contained very nearly one-quarter of the entire manufacturing labour force of Canada, and the rate of increase in manufacturing employment between 1961 and 1971 was greater than anywhere else in the country.

The Kitchener–Windsor area

The region between Kitchener and Windsor developed as a very important manufacturing area between 1951 and 1971, because it lies along the vital road and rail links connecting Toronto to Detroit and the American mid-west. A large number of plants within this zone are U.S. subsidiaries, and many are owned by companies in the metropolises of Detroit and Chicago (Ray, 1965). In terms of the volume of manufacturing employment, this broad area is twice as important as the Est du Québec/Trois-Rivières zone, and the rate of increase in manufacturing employment between 1961 and 1971 has been only slightly less than that for the "crescent". Though many of the towns and cities in the zone have a diverse industrial base, it can be perceived from Figure 5.4 that there are some industries that are particularly dominant. For example, the household electrical products industries provide most manufacturing jobs in London and Guelph, the machinery manufacturing industry in Brantford and Woodstock, and the automobile industry in Windsor and Chatham.

CHANGES IN MANUFACTURING EMPLOYMENT

Changes in manufacturing employment between 1961 and 1971 have been alluded to in the descriptions of the major axis manufacturing regions in the previous sections. Basically, there has been a comparative shift in manufacturing employment with respect to the axis as a whole from the East Axis to the West Axis, with a small comparative increase in the central zone between. The East Axis area experienced a comparative decrease of about 27,000 jobs, with the remaining positive shift occurring to the central zone. As the growth in manufacturing employment in the axis was only a little less than that for the nation as a whole, these shifts can be interpreted as comparative changes not only within the axis but for the country as well. Thus, the East Axis area declined with respect to the nation, while the West Axis area increased its share of manufacturing employment.

It is far too easy, however, to overestimate the shifts, and to ignore the actual absolute changes that have occurred. In both the West and East Axes there have been reasonably large increases in manufacturing employment, and the volume of these increases is very much greater than the magnitude of the comparative shifts. Shifts and increases in employment are basic influences of population growth, for people need employment to provide for their livelihood.

The location of new manufacturing plants

In terms of manufacturing employment and growth, our discussion is basically concerned with the location of increments of employment, and the conclusion is that these increments have been primarily located in the major metropolitan area. A reasonably good predictor of employment shifts is the location of new plants, which can be obtained from detailed listings produced annually in *New Manufacturing Establishments in Canada* (Statistics Canada). It should be noted that these listings ignore factory closures, or the "deaths" of plants, so it is not possible to calculate the net increase in number of factories at certain locations from this particular source. Collins (1972) has attempted to use an alternate source of information to arrive at an estimation of the net change in number of establishments at particular locations, but the imperfections in the data do not justify further use of that information. Nevertheless, the general conclusions arrived at by Collins (1972) for Ontario are useful.

The axis area received 60 per cent of all new manufacturing plants located in Canada between 1961 and 1971. In some major groups the axis received well over three-quarters of the entire set of new additions (clothing, electrical equipment), while in others (such as wood and petroleum) the concentration was not so great (Table 5.3). It should be noted that some of these major groups are combinations of those listed in Table 5.2, such as food and beverages, while others are subdivisions of some of the headings, such as metal and machine fabrication. These differences occur because of the classifications of the plants, which are listed individually in the source used. Even with these classificatory problems, it is clear that clothing, furniture, printing and publishing, and metal fabrication are the categories containing the bulk of new plants. These are also categories that usually contain the majority of plant closures, so a large proportion of these "new plants" may reflect change of ownership in a highly speculative sector of the economy. The latter observation is particularly true of the clothing industry.

Half of all the new manufacturing plants that were established within the axis between 1961 and 1971 located within the census metropolitan areas (1961 boundaries) of Montréal and Toronto (Table 5.4). The other half were distributed among almost all the other towns and cities within the axis, with no particular urban area receiving a disproportionate number. For example, Hamilton (CMA) received only 2.2 per cent and Québec City 2.0 per cent of the axis total. Furthermore, the industries tended to locate in a manner that is quite predictable from the previous general discussion of the distribution of industries within the axis. Two-thirds of all the new clothing establishments, and over half of all the new knitting mills located within Montréal (CMA). Toronto, on the other hand, received a disproportionate share of a variety of industrial groups (such as paper and allied products, printing and publishing, metal and machine fabrication), but in no category did it receive more than a half of new axis plants. Hamilton received a disproportionate share of plants concerned with primary metals and metal fabrication; Québec City a disproportionate share of plants in printing and publishing, leather, and rubber and plastics; and Ottawa a disproportionate share of plants in rubber and plastics, metal fabrication, and printing and publishing.

This overwhelming concentration of new plants in the Toronto

Table 5.3: Number of new manufacturing plants locating in the axis, 1961–71, by major group

| MAJOR GROUP | AXIS | | CANADA | | AXIS % OF CANADA |
	TOTAL	%	TOTAL	%	
Food and beverages	1075	8.8	2265	11.1	47.5
Rubber and plastics	45	.4	60	0.3	75.0
Leather	185	1.5	218	1.1	84.9
Textiles	305	2.5	412	2.0	74.0
Knitting mills	233	1.0	253	1.2	92.1
Clothing	1320	10.8	1437	7.1	91.9
Wood	858	7.0	3121	15.3	27.5
Furniture	1240	10.1	1806	8.9	68.7
Paper and allied products	108	0.9	187	0.9	57.8
Printing and publishing	1479	12.1	1987	9.8	74.4
Primary metals	157	1.3	250	1.2	62.8
Metal fabricating	1533	12.5	2453	12.1	62.5
Machine manufacturing	472	3.9	757	3.7	62.4
Transport equipment	489	4.0	1026	5.0	47.7
Electrical equipment	329	2.7	419	2.1	78.5
Non-metallics	444	3.6	930	4.6	47.7
Chemicals	474	3.9	633	3.1	74.9
Miscellaneous	1465	12.0	2068	10.2	70.8
Tobacco	8	0.1	10	0.1	80.0
Petroleum	19	0.2	46	0.2	41.3
Total	12,238		20,338		60.2

Table 5.4: The location of new manufacturing plants within the axis in selected cities by major group, 1961–71

MAJOR GROUP	MONTRÉAL	TORONTO	OTTAWA	HAMILTON	QUÉBEC CITY
Food and beverages	19.0	22.2	0.9	2.8	2.8
Rubber and plastics	22.2	20.0	6.7	0.0	6.7
Leather	21.6	24.3	0.0	2.7	8.1
Textiles	31.1	23.6	2.3	1.0	0.0
Knitting Mills	54.5	14.2	0.0	1.3	1.3
Clothing	60.4	17.2	0.2	0.2	1.0
Wood	6.8	16.7	1.7	2.1	1.5
Furniture	19.2	26.6	1.0	1.9	2.4
Paper and allied products	35.2	44.4	0.0	2.8	2.8
Printing and publishing	27.2	32.8	1.0	2.4	4.1
Primary metals	10.2	19.1	0.0	6.4	3.2
Metal fabricating	26.3	32.6	2.1	4.6	1.2
Machine manufacturing	19.9	34.5	0.4	3.2	1.1
Transport equipment	11.9	14.3	2.0	3.1	2.0
Electrical equipment	24.3	33.4	3.0	0.0	0.0
Non-metallics	14.6	9.0	0.7	2.3	2.3
Chemicals	14.6	25.5	2.1	2.1	2.1
Miscellaneous	22.0	29.2	2.0	1.2	0.9
Tobacco	12.5	12.5	0.0	0.0	0.0
Petroleum	15.8	15.8	0.0	0.0	0.0
Total	25.4	25.3	1.4	2.2	2.0

and Montréal areas exhibits little sign of diminishing in intensity, as more recent information substantiates the 1961–71 situation. Obviously, the greater diversity of types of new plants entering the Toronto area implies greater employment stability in the future as well as a wide array of job opportunities. Over one-third of all the new plants established in the Montréal area are either in the clothing or associated textile industry, and this intense specialization is not only limiting in terms of employment opportunities, but also likely to lead to cyclical unemployment.

Although most of the discussion is at the macro-level, it is important to note that the use of census metropolitan areas conceals some rather important within-urban-area shifts in new plant location and resultant job opportunities. From information contained in Field and Kerr (1968), Thibodeau (1971), and Collins (1972), it is possible to draw two important conclusions with respect to the movement and location of new plants in the Toronto and Montréal areas. First, there is an excess of "deaths" over "births" of manufacturing plants in the central cities of Toronto and Montréal. This is particularly noticeable in the city of Toronto where the number of plants declined by 23 per cent between 1961 and 1970, and employment in manufacturing decreased by a similar amount in the same period. The decline was not so great in the city of Montréal (which covers a larger area) where the number of establishments declined by 7 per cent, and employment by a similar proportion in the 1961–70 period.

These declines are offset, however, by increases beyond the central city but within the metropolitan area. Thibodeau (1971), in fact, indicates that there has been little relocation of industry beyond I le de Montréal, but there has been a centrifugal movement within the island. Collins (1972) describes the pattern of changes as being akin to a doughnut where the decline in the central city is offset by growth in the other municipalities of the metropolitan and census metropolitan area. For example, in the Borough of North York the number of manufacturing establishments increased by 36 per cent in the same period, and in Montréal Nord the number of establishments and employment more than doubled. The employment and growth, therefore, are being retained within the major metropolitan regions, but not within the central part of the cities. Montréal and Toronto are still the only real manufacturing growth poles in the axis.

TERTIARY ACTIVITIES AND THE
TOTAL LABOUR FORCE

The tertiary sector of economic activity, which, it will be recalled, includes Trade (wholesale and retail); Finance, Insurance and Real Estate; Commercial, Business, and Personal Services; and Public Administration and Defence, occupies the majority of the total axis labour force and provided the seven-tenths of all the new jobs in the axis between 1961 and 1971. Although these activities have been grouped into a single category it is wise to detail the particular locational characteristics of the different sub-groups, for without such an understanding it is impossible to comprehend the true meaning of the trends.

A large number of activities included within the tertiary sector are required by the population to serve their daily needs. These embrace a large group of activities included within the retail Trade sector, such as food stores, gasoline service stations, and drugstores; certain financial institutions; a variety of Community, Business, and Personal Service industries, such as elementary and secondary schools, churches, taverns, hairdressers, and so forth; and finally some local administrators who are included within the Public Administration and Defence industry group. These activities, and the employment they generate, are found in almost every community, whatever the size, and they exist to serve the immediate needs of the population of the community and the local rural hinterland.

Other activities are required infrequently, perhaps once or twice per month, and as a consequence the local demand generated in hamlets and villages is frequently insufficient to support tertiary activities which provide this type of service or good. Furthermore, the fact that the service or good is required infrequently means that people are prepared to spend more time (and money) in travelling longer distances to obtain this type of service or good. The activities which are required infrequently also cut across the major industry headings, for they include such activities as department stores, apparel and shoe stores in the Retail Trade sector; investment dealers in the Finance sector; doctors, dentists, shoe repair shops, and entertainment in the Community, Business, and Personal Service industries; and certain postal, planning, or public library services which are provided by the Public Administration and Defence sector.

Finally, there are a large number of activities that are required very infrequently, or that serve other tertiary activities, or that serve the entire country or individual provinces, and these are located in certain specific urban areas. These activities include many wholesale trade businesses in the Trade sector; jewellery, household furniture and appliance stores, and bookstores in the retail Trade major group; universities and colleges, hospitals, funeral homes, and so forth, which are included within the Community, Business, and Personal Service industries; and provincial and federal government legislative and civil service activites, which are included wthin the Public Administration and Defence sector. These activities are usually, though not always, located in the larger urban areas, either because size itself is attractive in that the local demand is quite large, or they may have been placed where they are by a political decision, as in the case of defence establishments.

THE DISTRIBUTION OF TERTIARY EMPLOYMENT WITHIN THE AXIS

The general arrangement of tertiary activities in urban centres that has been described has a well-founded empirical and theoretical base (Marshall, 1969; Murdie, 1965; Martin, 1970), and it leads to a discussion of the distribution of tertiary employment based upon excess provision. All urban areas, whatever their size, will have some employment in tertiary activities, but some, because they serve large hinterlands and many other urban areas as well, will have larger excesses than others. These "excesses" can be defined in a number of ways, each of which can be interpreted differently, but in this section one definition is used, and it must be noted that it follows the spirit if not the exact method developed by Martin (1970).

In order to define an "excess" there has to be a norm to which the tertiary employment in a particular urban area can be compared. The norm, in this instance, is assumed to be the average situation for Canada as a whole. In 1961 there were 162 persons employed in the tertiary activities for every 1,000 persons in the country, and in 1971, this figure had increased to 205 per thousand. This increase is, in itself, quite remarkable, for it reflects a significant increase in importance of this group of economic activities. If the country averages are accepted as norms, then it could be postulated that those urban areas with more than 162 persons per thousand in 1961, or 205 per thousand in 1971, contained an "excess" of tertiary employment. The excesses are the result of certain urban areas serving far more than the local community, and the urban areas with the greatest excesses literally depend upon an increasing demand for the services that they offer in their hinterland as well as their local community for growth.

The extent of the excess can be presented in index form by dividing the urban area tertiary employment per thousand of the local population by the average figure for the country. For example, the 1961 index for Sherbrooke is $187/162 = 1.15$; and for Cornwall it is $145/162 = 0.90$. This does not mean that Sherbrooke contained more than enough services or that Cornwall had less, for it says nothing about the variety available. The majority of the tertiary employees, for example, may be located in one particular service (such as a university). It does, however, indicate that Sherbrooke has more than the national norm of tertiary employment, and that it depends, therefore, on the provision of tertiary activities to its non-local area for part of its economic "health". Cornwall, on the other hand, has less employment in tertiary activities than would be expected according to the national norm, which can be interpreted as indicating that it is less dependent on the non-local service area for its economic "health". An alternative interpretation, from the point of view of the inhabitants of Cornwall, is that the town does not have its fair share of tertiary employment. This may be attributed to the facts that some people go to Montréal for goods and services that are in occasional demand, and certain governmental services that might be located in Cornwall are located elsewhere in eastern Ontario.

Urban areas containing "excess" tertiary employment

The indices of excess tertiary employment are listed for the fifty-five urban areas plotted in Figure 5.3 in Table 5.5. Although the size of each index is influenced by the over-bounding and under-bounding problems for municipalities, discussed in Chapter 2, the variation of the value of the index between the larger cities and towns is quite interesting. Table 5.5 contains two indices for each urban area. The first is with respect to the total employment in tertiary activities, and the second to tertiary employment less employment in public administration. The difference between the modified index (tertiary employment less employment in public administration) illustrates the importance of the public administration component, and the modified

Table 5.5: Excess tertiary employment, including and excluding public administration, for fifty-five axis cities, 1961

URBAN AREA	INCLUDING PUBLIC ADMINISTRATION	EXCLUDING PUBLIC ADMINISTRATION
Ottawa	1.73	1.12
Kingston	1.53	1.41
Pembroke	1.47	1.12
Hull	1.47	1.12
Barrie	1.44	1.22
London	1.43	1.47
Trenton	1.40	0.84
Toronto	1.39	1.49
Québec	1.34	1.24
Orillia	1.33	1.47
Cobourg	1.27	1.07
Belleville	1.25	1.19
Lévis	1.25	1.33
St. Thomas	1.25	1.37
Chatham	1.23	1.34
Niagara Falls	1.23	1.26
St-Hyacinthe	1.22	1.37
Brockville	1.21	1.32
Guelph	1.20	1.27
Joliette	1.20	1.32
Owen Sound	1.19	1.27
Sherbrooke	1.16	1.24
Peterborough	1.15	1.27
Kitchener	1.14	1.26
Montréal	1.13	1.21
Woodstock	1.13	1.25
St-Jean	1.13	0.86
Lindsay	1.08	1.15
Brampton	1.06	1.12
Brantford	1.05	1.14
Windsor	1.02	1.11
Lauzon	1.01	1.05
Trois-Rivières	1.00	1.08
Hamilton	0.99	1.08
Sarnia	0.97	1.05

Table 5.5: (continued)

URBAN AREA	INCLUDING PUBLIC ADMINISTRATION	EXCLUDING PUBLIC ADMINISTRATION
St. Catharines	0.96	1.05
Whitby	0.05	1.03
Cornwall	0.90	0.96
Victoriaville	0.89	0.99
Oshawa	0.86	0.93
St-Jérome	0.82	0.88
Ste-Thérèse	0.81	0.83
Sorel	0.81	0.86
Drummondville	0.79	0.88
Granby	0.78	0.86
Valleyfield	0.77	0.84
Welland	0.77	0.83
Shawinigan	0.76	0.70
Thetford Mines	0.76	0.83
Magog	0.70	0.78
Cap-de-la-Madeleine	0.69	0.75
Port Colborne	0.68	0.75
Grand'Mère	0.66	0.67
Asbestos	0.57	0.63
Shawinigan Sud	0.56	0.60

index discounts the effect of employment that is placed in a particular urban area as a result of some arbitrary political decision.

The difference among the indices is particularly noticeable in the cases of Ottawa, Trenton, and Pembroke. The military operations located at Trenton greatly inflate the index, and when the defence presence is removed, the city of Trenton has a tertiary employment deficit. Employment in federal government activities in Ottawa endows the city with an extraordinary excess of tertiary employment, but as this activity is, in reality, the only real reason for the existence of the city as an urban area of size, this fact is not surprising. When the public administration component is removed, Ottawa has only a small tertiary employment excess, and this is attributable to its position as a service centre for a large part of the middle axis area. Pembroke contains an unusual mixture of federal government and defence installations which, along with the lumber mills, are the *raison d'être* for the city's existence.

One of the more noticeable features of the modified list of indices is the difference in magnitude of the numbers between the Ontario portion of the axis and the Québec portion. The major regional centres of Ontario (Toronto, London, Orillia–Barrie, and Kingston) have larger excess index values than the major centres of Québec (Montréal, Québec City, Sherbrooke, Trois-Rivières, and Joliette), for the index values relating to Lévis and St-Hyacinthe are regarded as inflated due to under-bounding. The reason for this difference in general magnitude of values may well be the general proliferation of small municipalities which are scattered all over the countryside in Québec and have maintained their position as minor rural centres despite the willingness of people to visit larger, more distant towns for their weekly needs. In Ontario, by contrast, the inhabitants of many small villages tend to visit larger cities and towns for their frequently required services and goods, with the result that this employment is, in a sense, taken over by the larger centres.

A hierarchy of service centres

These trends, in effect, re-enforce the dominance of the larger centres which, because of the vast array of services and goods available for their local population, also attract customers from non-local areas. Furthermore, as the distance that people are prepared to travel to these larger centres is increasing, it is likely that the bigger urban centres will gain even more tertiary employment at the expense of the smaller towns and villages (Hodge, 1972; 1966). Thus, the hierarchy of service centres that appears to exist within the axis is likely to be intensified. In Figure 5.5 a hierarchy of service centres for the axis is demonstrated with respect to two indicators. One indicator is the "excess" tertiary employment (less public administration) and the other is total employment in tertiary activities (less public administration). The modified tertiary employment index is regarded as suggestive of the extent of the non-local area served by the centre, for the larger the "excess" tertiary employment the greater the non-local population that is served compared with the local population. The total tertiary employment (less public administration) measure is used as an indicator of the size of the centre, for generally the larger the centre the more dominant is its position in the service structure of a region.

The two indicators are used together by drawing negatively sloped lines in Figure 5.5. These lines are positioned to take into account both indicators and the difference in magnitude of the index between Ontario and Québec. Of course, hierarchies are very much unique to the eye of the beholder, so probably a more accurate description would be "levels of urban dominance". The first three levels of the hierarchy are suggested to be:

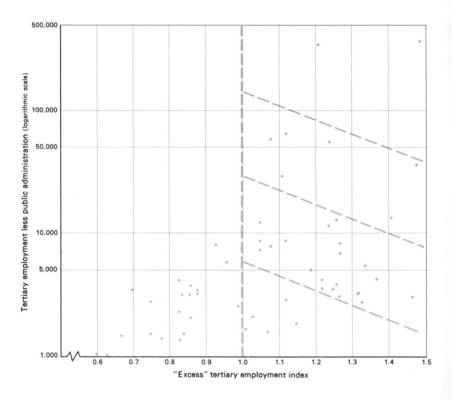

Figure 5.5: Tertiary employment and the "excess" employment index for fifty-five axis cities

Level 1   Toronto and Montréal
Level 2   Ottawa, Hamilton, Québec City, London, Windsor, and
          Kingston
Level 3   Kitchener, St. Catharines, Sherbrooke, Brantford, Hull,
          Peterborough, Trois-Rivières, Sarnia, Guelph, Chatham,
          Belleville, St-Hyacinthe, St. Thomas, Niagara Falls,
          Barrie, Orillia, Woodstock, Joliette, Brockville, Owen
          Sound, Lévis.

It should be noted that this hierarchy is suggested with respect to
the tertiary activities (less public administration) *alone*. Other influences, apart from administrative functions, that have been excluded
are the variety of services, the extent of influence of various elements
of the media, and patterns of interaction. These, taken either singly
or together, would undoubtedly modify the suggested pattern of
dominance.

CHANGES IN THE TOTAL LABOUR FORCE, 1961–71

The hierarchical arrangement of tertiary employment, and the comparative shift of manufacturing to the West Axis and major metropolitan centres, have combined to produce a fairly simple pattern of
comparative shifts in the total labour force between 1961 and 1971.
The data in Figure 5.6 relate to estimated comparative shifts of manufacturing employment by county (as defined for 1961, with a few
modifications), although nearly all of the employment is concentrated
within the major urban areas located in the counties. The intervals
are chosen to indicate above-average, average, and below-average
changes in labour force, for the comparative shift index is calculated
with respect to the 1961–71 axis labour force growth rate (3 per cent
per annum).

The above average category distinguishes those counties in which
the growth of the labour force was 2.5 per cent or more than expected.
The counties containing Hamilton, Metro Toronto, Montréal, and
Québec City are clearly distinguished. Of these, York County has the
best performance in all sectors, with a diversified manufacturing
structure, a wide array of tertiary services, and provincial as well as
local administrative duties. Montréal (Ile de Montréal and Ile Jésus)
also has a good performance, although its manufacturing structure is
more specialized, and its tertiary sector lacks the provincial administrative employment of Toronto. The Hamilton area depends rather more

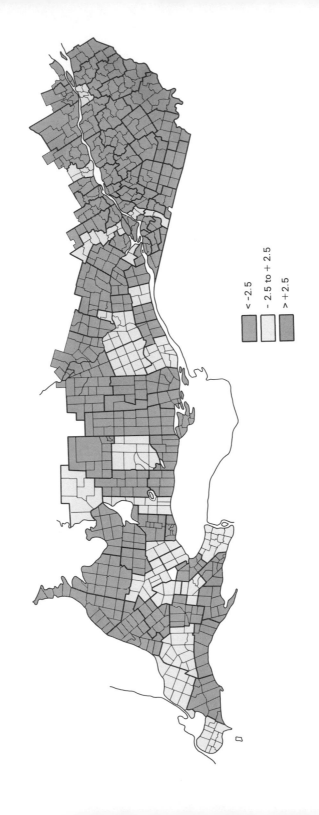

Figure 5.6: Comparative shift: total labour force, 1961–71 by census division (1971 data estimated)

< -2.5

-2.5 to +2.5

> +2.5

on manufacturing, particularly those industries related to metals, while Québec City relies basically on service employment.

The counties of average growth, that is, those experiencing a comparative growth of +2.5 per cent to −2.5 per cent between 1961 and 1971, include nearly all the remaining larger urban areas in the axis. The physical extent of average growth is overemphasized in Figure 5.6 for Ontario, because the counties are so much bigger in this portion of the axis compared with Québec. It is probably wise, therefore, to re-emphasize that in the middle portion of the axis, the increase in the labour force in this category is confined almost entirely to Ottawa–Hull and Peterborough. The counties of below-average labour force growth group around Georgian Bay, border Lake Erie, cover much of eastern Ontario and most of Québec (beyond Montréal and Québec City). Thus, despite the proliferation of federal and provincial programs in the 1960s designed to encourage the expansion of employment opportunities in slow-growth areas, the trends of the 1951–61 period (Crowley, 1971) continued through the 1961–71 decade as well. In fact, about one-half of all new jobs created in the axis between 1961 and 1971 were located in the census metropolitan areas of Toronto and Montréal.

THE ECONOMIC STRENGTH OF THE AXIS

There has been some previous mention (Chapter 1) of the concept of urban areas as surplus users. Those urban areas which can appropriate the manufacturing and tertiary activities required by society will grow at the expense of others. Though the process of growth is quite complex, it is possible to express this process simply, as follows. Let us suppose the existence of two urban areas located 100 miles apart, one large in population size, containing a diversified manufacturing base and a variety of tertiary services, and the other much smaller, containing only a few manufacturing plants and a more limited array of tertiary services. Let us also suppose that an aircraft-manufacturing company wishes to locate a new plant to build small, light, two- and four-passenger aircrafts in one of these urban areas, and it is envisaged that the plant will employ 750 people. Where will the plant be located, and what will the growth repercussions be on the two towns?

Economists who, some claim, are descended in direct line from a dubious relationship between Merlin and Guinevere, have a very clever way of avoiding difficulties by prefacing most comments with the phrase "other things being equal". Donning the conical hat, the answer to the first question is that "other things being equal" the plant will be located in the larger urban area. The "other things" that are assumed equal include the availability and price of suitable land, and the lack of any personal preference by the decision-making entrepreneur for small towns and their associated pleasures. The reasons why the large urban area will be chosen are founded on the size of the area and its pre-existing diverse manufacturing base. The entrepreneur knows that he/she will be able to subcontract locally (if he/she wishes), have repairs to machinery undertaken locally, and may even find the necessary financial services locally. Also, there will be a large domestic labour market with a variety of industrial skills, and the firm will be able to obtain pre-trained labour.

The employment impact of the plant on the large town can be discussed in "direct" and "indirect" employment terms. The direct employment impact of the new plant is 750 new jobs that are created. The indirect employment impact depends upon the number of jobs that are created as a result of work subcontracted or let to other manufacturing firms within the urban area, the money spent by the 750 employees on tertiary services within the urban area which thereby increases their employment, and the money spent by the indirectly induced labour in the other manufacturing plants and the expanded tertiary services, and the jobs as a result of the money spent by these people.

The magnitude of the indirect impact, therefore, depends upon the amount of work and money that can be retained in the urban area, and this, in turn, depends upon the variety of manufacturing firms available as well as the variety of tertiary services. It is possible for a large urban area with a variety of manufacturing firms and a wide array of tertiary services to retain a large proportion of these jobs and money for the plant would not need to make many purchases beyond the area and neither would the people. Thus, for large urban areas it is expected that the ratio between the direct and indirect employment impacts will be quite large, for example 1:3 or 1:4. The sum of the elements of the ratio gives the *multiplier*, which, in terms of employment, permits the calculation of the total employment generated by a certain increment of new jobs.

To indicate the expected value of the multiplier for small towns, let it be supposed that the aircraft company is "bribed" by some federal, provincial, or local incentive program to place the plant in the small town. The direct employment impact is, of course, 750 new jobs, even if some of the people to occupy the positions have to be imported from other areas. These people will require certain tertiary services, many of which can be provided locally, but some may have to be obtained elsewhere. The plant itself will not be able to subcontract or let many tasks to local firms because they are non-existent; neither will the demand from the new plant be sufficient to warrant any additions to the variety of local manufacturing firms. Therefore, many of the tasks will be taken to firms in other urban areas. Consequently, the indirect employment effect will be less than in the larger city for many of the indirect effects will have percolated to other urban areas, and the direct/indirect impact employment ratio will be quite small, perhaps 1:1, or even 1:0.5. Concomitantly, the multiplier will also be small.

There are several principles to be learned from this simple example that has assumed away a number of complicating matters. The first is that the *agglomerative* forces of large urban areas are quite strong, particularly with respect to labour force, capital, and other manufacturing firms. Secondly, a diverse manufacturing base encourages growth, because there are a variety of firms with which a new plant may develop business. This pre-existing manufacturing infrastructure is extremely important for new firms, because they minimize the necessity for immediate purchase of new machinery. Thirdly, the indirect employment impact, or the multiplier effect, is usually larger in the bigger urban areas. Fourthly, an investment in a small urban area may well yield a bigger indirect impact in an adjacent large urban area, while an investment in the larger urban area may well result in hardly any associated indirect impact being passed on to the smaller urban area. All these principles help to explain the great growth of the East Lake Ontario Crescent and Montréal during the 1960s.

AN INTER-REGIONAL INPUT-OUTPUT MODEL

When the situation described above is transferred to a provincial framework for Canada, it is apparent that the axis area (as defined by the provinces of Ontario and Québec) should receive disproportionately larger indirect impacts from particular investments than the rest of the country. This is because of the position of the axis as the manufacturing and, to a lesser extent, the service centre of the country. The strength of this economic domination can be estimated using an inter-regional input-output model developed by Appleton (1972) for the Agricultural Economics Research Council of Canada. The model used focuses on output multipliers, that is, the change in dollar value of output in different regions that is associated with a given change in output in a particular sector, or sectors, in a particular region, or regions. Output multipliers are not, of course, the same as employment multipliers, but it can be assumed that the employment impacts in most industrial sectors are proportional to the monetary impacts.

The regions included within the model are defined as the West, Ontario, Québec, and the Maritimes. In essence, the West is represented by the input-output table for Manitoba as developed by Cormack and Malik (1961) and subsequently updated, the Maritimes by the Atlantic provinces table (Levitt, 1969), Ontario by the tables prepared by Frank, Batrik, and Haronitis (1970), and Québec from information prepared by Matuszewski and updated in Lafort and Marshall (1972). These, along with the national input-output tables for the Canadian economy provide sufficient clues for the construction of a four region input-output model, though the representation of the West by Manitoba must be regarded as controversial.

The sectors included within the tables for each region embrace the entire array of major industrial groups as defined by the Standard Industrial Classification of Canadian Industry, with certain modifications. These major groups are listed in Table 5.6, and it is obvious that many contain a wide variety of industrial activities. For example, the transport equipment major group includes aircraft, automobile, railroad, shipbuilding, and any other types of transport equipment manufacturers. Thus, an examination of the impact of a change in output for a particular industry, such as the aircraft industry, cannot be estimated, because the change will relate to the general impact of all types of transport equipment firms combined. This point is most important for, in the ensuing discussion, the author may refer to a particular type of industry, and it must be recalled that such a referral is really artistic licence.

The rows of the input-output table contain not only the twenty-four major groups listed in Table 5.6, but a "Household" row, which is basically income to the residents of the different regions; a "Provincial and Municipal Revenue" row, which contains the value of commodity taxes plus indirect taxation and government services; an "Import" row from beyond the country; and a "Total Inputs" row. The columns contain, along with the twenty-four major groups, a "Consumer Expenditure" row as final demand; a "Provincial and Municipal Expenditures" row; an "Export" row to beyond the country; and a "Total Outputs" row. The model is, therefore, open to the world beyond Canada, and although this creates additional construction problems, it is at least realistic. The general conceptual structure of the model is presented as Figure 5.7.

Table 5.6: Sectors included in the interregional input-output model of the Canadian economy

MAJOR GROUP, DIVISIONS, OR COMBINATIONS

 1. Agriculture
 2. Forestry
 3. Fishing and Trapping
 4. Metal Mines
 5. Non-metallic Minerals
 6. Mineral Fuels (coal, oil, gas)
 7. Food, Beverages, and Tobacco
 8. Rubber, Chemicals, and Chemical Products
 9. Leather, Textiles, Knitting Mills, Clothing Industries
10. Wood, Furniture, and Fixture Industries
11. Pulp and Paper
12. Printing, Publishing, and Miscellaneous Manufacturing
13. Primary Metals
14. Metal Fabricating Industries
15. Machinery Industries
16. Transportation Equipment Industries
17. Electrical Products Industries
18. Non-metallic Mineral Products Industries
19. Petroleum and Coal Products Industries
20. Construction Industry
21. Trade (wholesale and retail)
22. Communications and Utilities
23. Finance, Insurance, and Real Estate
24. Transportation, Storage, Community, Business, and Personal Service Industries

It will be noted from Figure 5.7 that there are 11,024 possible flows between sectors and provinces in Canada, and between the provinces and the rest of the world. Significant flows, that is, flows exceeding 1 per cent of the total outputs of a particular sector for the twenty-four sectors listed in Table 5.6 plus the two final demand sectors mentioned in the previous paragraph, are indicated by a black square. There are no black squares in the import row or export column because information with respect to each sector by province is difficult to disaggregate at this level. If it were possible to include imports and exports, the entries would, of course, be found only in the matrices on the diagonal.

A detailed analysis of these black blobs is a rewarding experience for lovers of abstract art, but perhaps a few general statements would be just as useful. First, there are relatively few significant flows compared with the total number possible, and most of these are within the different provinces. Secondly, there are a number of significant interprovincial flows between Ontario and Québec, which are construed as within axis flows, and the majority of these involve manufacturing. This situation contrasts with the third observation, which is that both Ontario and Québec exhibit significant flows of manufactured goods from the axis to the West, but that the axis receives from the West mainly raw materials. A similar flow pattern occurs with the Maritimes. Finally, although there are a number of significant flows from the Maritimes to the West, there are hardly any reciprocal flows from the West to the Maritimes. There is, however, much greater reciprocity between the Maritimes and the axis. Thus, the axis is the link that forges the Maritimes and the West, and balances the flow pattern.

Some examples

The implications of the patterns of black blobs in Figure 5.6 can be presented in more concrete terms by examining the interprovincial distribution of indirect impacts that occur as a result of a $1 million increase in output in particular sectors in various provinces. The coefficients, which are used to generate these impacts, are fixed, regardless of level of output, so there are no economies of scale, and the negative of the increases will give the theoretical result of similar decreases in output. Although these assumptions are not realistic, they do not detract from the general implications of the results. The indirect impacts are presented as proportions for each region (including "foreign") in Table 5.7 along with the multipliers (internal to Canada, and internal plus external).

To illustrate the result of specialization within the axis, the impact of an increase in output in the Transport Equipment Industries in Québec and Ontario is examined first. It will be recalled that the industry is concentrated, along with metal fabrication, in the West Axis Manufacturing Area, though there are transport equipment manufacturers in the East Axis Manufacturing Zone. In each case, the majority of indirect benefits are retained by the province of loca-

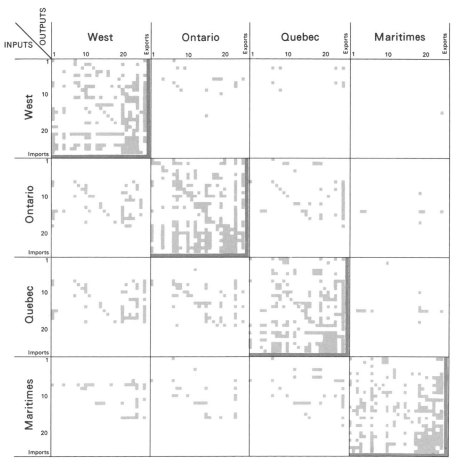

Figure 5.7: An interprovincial input-output flow table for the Canadian economy

Table 5.7: Some examples of the distribution of indirect impacts (in percentage) on changes in output in certain sectors of industry in various provinces, and the internal (Canadian) and total multiplier effect

EXAMPLE OF CHANGE IN	WEST	ONTARIO	QUÉBEC	MARITIMES	FOREIGN	MULTIPLIERS (ROUNDED) INTERNAL	TOTAL
Transport equipment industries in Québec	4.6	22.0	41.0	1.6	30.8	4.3	5.8
Transport equipment industries in Ontario	3.3	60.6	6.1	1.3	28.8	4.7	6.3
Pulp and paper in the Maritimes	2.4	8.9	5.7	67.0	15.9	6.1	7.1
Pulp and paper in Québec	4.6	18.9	48.4	2.1	25.9	4.1	5.2
Pulp and paper in Ontario	4.1	63.1	8.5	1.6	22.7	4.4	5.4
Pulp and paper in the West	68.3	10.3	2.8	0.4	18.2	6.6	8.1
Community, Business, and Personal Service industries in Ontario	3.8	66.2	5.8	1.1	23.1	5.4	6.7

tion of the direct impact, but in the Québec case these are less than half the total. The indirect impacts in the Foreign area are very large, which could be predicted from the strong links that exist between the U.S. parent companies of automobile and aircraft manufacturers. If an employment interpretation is accepted for the first row, the percentages and multipliers imply that the establishment of an auto plant employing 1,000 people in Québec will result (in time) in the generation of a further 4,758 jobs, of which 219 will be in the West, 1,046 in Ontario, 1,949 in Québec, 75 in the Maritimes, and 1,468 in Foreign parts. The multipliers and percentages also imply that a plant employing 1,000 people in Ontario would result in an additional increase of 3,180 jobs in Ontario compared with the 1,949 in Québec.

This same situation is repeated in the second example concerning the impact of an increase in output of the Pulp and Paper Industry in each of the four regions. This example is designed to demonstrate the different impacts of the same industry in the four regions, and Pulp and Paper is chosen because the industry is well represented in each. Apart from the observed repetition of events discussed in the preceding paragraph, it is important to note that a disproportionately large share of the indirect impacts that "leak out" of the direct impact provinces *always* accrue to Ontario, and secondarily to Québec. Furthermore, a much larger proportion of the indirect benefits from an increase in output in the West and the Maritimes is retained by Canada than by the axis provinces. This is particularly noticeable if a comparison is made between the Foreign impact components for the Maritimes and Québec.

The third example examines the results of a change in output in a part of the tertiary sector, and though it pertains to the Community, Business and Personal Services as a whole, the negative signs are included to indicate that a decrease in output (in, for example, the education industry) is being postulated. The example focuses on Ontario, and the results indicate that the indirect impacts are absorbed almost entirely by Ontario and Foreign parts. Furthermore, the multiplier (or negative multiplier) is quite large, indicating quite a severe impact to employment opportunities. The current provincial policy for reducing employment in elementary, and later, secondary education will, therefore, have severe repercussions on the economy of those few areas that depend upon this kind of employment for growth. It is, of course, hoped that the direct and indirect reduction of jobs attributable to these changes will be offset by similar increases in other kinds of tertiary employment.

These three examples, the general pattern of significant flows, and the dominance of the axis as the manufacturing centre of Canada, re-enforce the contention that the area is of primary importance from a national as well as a provincial point-of-view. Furthermore, as most of the manufacturing and tertiary employment is located in the major urban areas, it is evident that the axis cities control and gain a disproportionate share of the direct and indirect impacts of national economic growth. To many people these impacts are benefits, because growth is deemed desirable for business and profits. This view is, however, being questioned in a situation where the impacts seem to be abrogated by two distinct areas within the axis, for untrammelled growth is giving rise to extremely high economic and social living costs. On the other hand, areas that could well absorb the growth are finding it difficult to maintain their competitive position as centralization continues unchecked. The immediate urban task is to come to grips with these centralizing forces, and this aim can be realized only within a theory that charts the trends of Canadian society. Before this theory is described it is necessary to document the position of the axis within the interactive pattern of Canadian society, and to review the state of local government and its financial basis.

6   INTERACTION

People, land, houses, jobs, goods — in isolation they are nothing. Land is fixed in location; it can be used only by people moving to and from it. Houses are moved very rarely, and they can be occupied only if they are in a location that is useful with respect to other aspects of the environment. Many jobs are also fixed in location, but it is becoming apparent that probably equally as many can also be moved closer to people, particularly within large urban areas, and occasionally between them as well. Goods definitely have to be moved for they are invariably produced in a few discrete locations and then transported to other factories or people who use them. All these movements of people, products, and information that take place between areas of the world's surface are referred to in general terms as *spatial interaction*, and without this interaction the axis and Canada would regress to a state of economic and cultural poverty akin to that of Europe in the Dark Ages.

Just as many of Canada's social problems are really distributional problems — such as the continued concentration of wealth and income in the hands of a few people in a few urban areas — so are many of Canada's economic, cultural, and political problems related to distribution. But, in the latter case, the word distribution refers to the transportation or spread of news, ideas, and goods over physical space. Canada — and the axis — is really an essay in transport, for spatial interaction is, and has always been one of the key operating forces of our society (Berton, 1970). Although the vital need for interaction has been evident throughout the ages, the dramatic impetus of the Industrial Revolution greatly accelerated the trend toward specialization. This specialization occurs not only in the form of economic and functional separation, which is often regarded as the most important feature of industrialized economies, but spatial separation as well. The evidence suggests that this trend is continuing apace, and that, for example, people are living farther from the places where they work or shop, and also farther from their families and friends.

On the other hand, this separation has been countered by a variety of means to overcome it, such as the telephone, automobile, truck, and airplane. New technology of these kinds is designed to reduce the effect of separation, as measured by distance, by increasing the speed and capacity of carriers, and thus lowering the cost per unit distance. In recent years these technical innovations have so permitted the world to be embraced by a web of almost instant interaction that the effects of distance have, in some cases, been reduced to a minimum. If McLuhan can perceive a "global village" is it possible to discern an "axis neighbourhood" within a "Canadian hamlet"? In other, less cliché-ridden terms, is it possible to distinguish the axis, in terms of interaction, as a distinct entity within the Canadian and North American system of flows?

Flows can be defined in terms of volume and direction. Much of the ensuing discussion is concerned with analysing the determinants of volume; for the combinations of possible directions of the flows are relatively fixed, since they are based on the pattern of origins and destinations. For example, Figure 6.1 shows a hypothetical map of

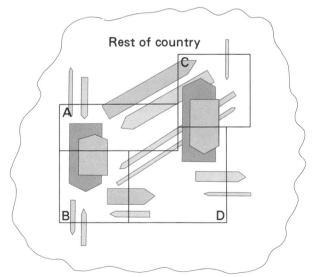

Figure 6.1: Flows between four hypothetical counties and the rest of the country

the flow of goods between four counties (A, B, C, and D) and the rest of the country. Each of these counties is both an origin and destination of flows, and the width of the arrows is proportionate to the volume of the flow involved (Table 6.1). Matrices of flows of this type, as measured by people or money, have been discussed previously with respect to migration within Canada and Québec, and the impact of inter-provincial inter-industry input-output linkages. The general conclusion of these studies has been that linkages within the axis are so much stronger than the linkages between the axis and the rest of the country that the whole area is a strong independent economic entity.

Figure 6.1 illustrates this particular concept in terms of the volume of flows between places. A cursory glance at the diagram yields the impression that the flows between A and B and between C and D are much larger than between any other sets of combinations or regions. Thus, A and B, and C and D, may be defined as so sufficiently similar and interdependent with respect to their linkages that they form two regions within the four-county area. Regions defined on the basis of flows are described as *functional regions*, and they imply a similarity based on common strengths and direction of linkages. Thus, whereas some of the discussion in the previous chapters has involved the use of flows, the analysis has not focused specifically on the flows between the origins and destinations. The discussion has, in fact, tended to focus just as much on the within area flows as on the between area flows.

Table 6.1: Volume of flows between four hypothetical counties and the rest of the country (volume in thousands)

ORIGIN	DESTINATION					
	A	B	C	D	R OF C	TOTAL
A		20	10	0	2	32
B	18		2	10	3	33
C	9	3		19	0	31
D	0	4	21		6	31
R of C	4	3	2	2		11
Total	31	30	35	31	11	138

In an urban context these between area flows become especially important if the predominant direction is toward one particular destination. A pattern of this kind is illustrated in Figure 6.2 where the volume of flows originating in each county is the same as in Figure 6.1, but the destinations are greatly different. County D is the primary focus of all flows, with B developing as a secondary focus contiguous with D. A pattern of this kind is frequently exemplified in the real world by journey-to-work movements, for employment opportunities may be more abundant in the central city, and less abundant in the suburbs at the periphery. It is to be noted from the diagram and table that not only is D the primary destination of flows from each county, but it is also the largest single source of flows spreading to the three other counties and the rest of the country. A situation of this type, in which one area is the primary destination, and also a major source of flows to all the other areas, results in a *functional nodal region*. If the node is also an urban area, then the descriptive phrase "urban-centred region" is often applied, and this term has been used in a subjective descriptive sense quite frequently in previous chapters.

Urban-centred regions are very popular in the current urban planning and local government literature. Thus, it may be appropriate at this juncture to comment on the concept, particularly with respect to the delimitation of boundaries and the indices that may be used for

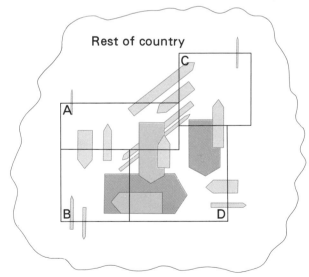

Figure 6.2: Flows between four hypothetical counties and the rest of the country, with one county being the destination

definitional purposes. It is obvious that both the definitional index and the boundary problem are interrelated, for the former is used to define the latter. As dissection of the patterns of spatial interaction in the axis proceeds, it will become apparent that the variety of actual flows which can be used to measure interaction is quite limited. At the time of writing, telephone data, road traffic flows, shipments of manufactured goods, and air traffic flows are the primary tabulated sources of information. Furthermore, these data are only available and useful for quite specific areas, and these areas may not be the real sources or the real destinations. Are the observed flows the results of demand, or are they the results of demand channelled into a system that restricts the user? For example, can it be assumed that a person on a flight from Montréal to Toronto actually wants to go to Toronto, or does he really wish to go to Oshawa? Thus the origins and destinations may well be generalizations that, like filtered light, can conceal more than they reveal.

The most amusing product of the urban-centred region concept is that it leads to a search for a boundary which has been taken as seriously by regional analysts as if it were as important as the Holy Grail itself. Parenthetically, it may also be added that the boundary of a nodal region is probably as illusory as that mystical myth of medieval religion. In most cases the boundary is really a zone, for it is impossible to determine exactly where the functional influence of a

Table 6.2: Volume of flows between four hypothetical counties and the rest of the country, with one county being the primary destination (volume in thousands)

ORIGIN	DESTINATION					
	A	B	C	D	R OF C	TOTAL
A		9	6	16	1	32
B	5		2	24	2	33
C	6	4		20	1	31
D	8	13	7		3	31
R of C	0	2	0	9		11
Total	19	28	15	69	7	138

particular node diminishes below that of another. Also, the extent of the zone depends upon the index used, and the analyst is left with the unenviable task of weighting the relative importance of different indices and comparing the definitions suggested by sets of superimposed zones. By far the best procedure is to recognize that all conceptual boundaries are highly general and emphasize that it is not so much the periphery that is of interest but the contents within. Of course, if the region is to consist of statistical units, such as census divisions or subdivisions, then the boundary is determined by the outermost boundary of the census artifacts which have been included as a result of some chosen cut-off point. This latter procedure is, in fact, used by the Ministère de l'Industrie et du Commerce (1967) in their delimitation of spheres of influence in the Province of Québec.

A CONCEPTUAL MODEL OF INTERACTION

At this juncture it may be useful to outline some principles concerning spatial interaction. By so doing, it is possible to develop a descriptive model that can be applied to particular sets of data to derive more general patterns of interaction. The descriptive model can be applied to flows within the axis, and between the axis and the rest of Canada, not to test the principles but to test whether the axis is a distinct economic and social system within the Canadian system.

DISTANCE-DECAY

A basic principle emerging from much of the work concerning flows and marketing is known as the "distance-decay" effect. This principle describes the way in which interaction tends to decline in magnitude as the distance from the origin of the flow, or the focus of the destination, increases. The actual rate of decline varies according to the particular measure that is being used, but the general form of the distance-decay curve is usually the same regardless of the indicator used. The form of the curve is usually of the logarithmic type, that is, interaction decreases at a decreasing rate proportionately with distance. A curve of this type is illustrated in Figure 6.3a, and its logarithmic equivalent in Figure 6.3b. The symbols a and b are parameters which control the position and shape of the curve, for log a is the height of the curve on the vertical axis when the logarithm distance is unity, and b is the slope of the curve. In the logarithmic case (that is, when both axes are transformed into logarithms), the slope of the curve is a measure of elasticity which indicates the incremental change in interaction with each unit change in distance. Thus, if *b* is greater than unity the indicator is distance-elastic, but if *b* is less than unity the indicator is distance-inelastic.

Variations in elasticity of this kind are indicated by the curves for migration and employment in Figure 6.4. Both curves have been derived from data tabulated by Dahms and Pearson (1969) in their

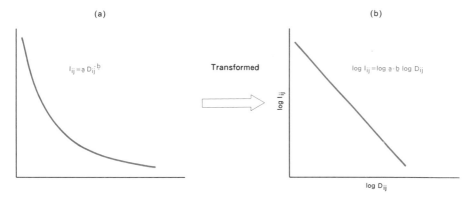

Figure 6.3: A typical distance decay curve: (a) arithmetic case; and (b) logarithmic transformation

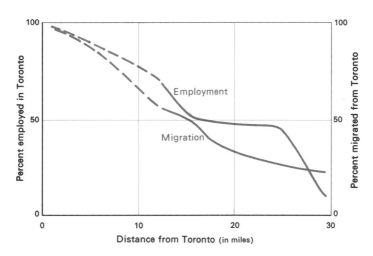

Figure 6.4: Distance decay curves for migration and employment in the Toronto region

study of the fringe area to the north of Toronto. The data on these particular graphs pertain only to the municipalities located on Highway 11 as far as, and including, Newmarket. The employment data are actually the proportions of a sample of workers in each municipality who work in Metro Toronto. Similarly, the migration data relate to the proportion of a sample of households in each municipality that have moved recently from that area. Interestingly, the employment curve seems to be more distance-elastic than the migration curve up to a distance of about twenty-five miles (which probably represents a real commuting range of around twenty miles).

Thus, the rate of decline in the distance-decay curves is influenced by the type of indicator used to measure interaction. But it is important to note that it is not distance itself that produces this decline. The decline is associated with distance because many economic and social forces are subsumed within the measure. In the first place, distance represents time because it takes time to travel the space separating the origin and destination. Secondly, distance also indicates cost because it costs money to transport people, goods, or messages over space. Furthermore, these transport costs vary according to the mode of transportation used, and the real economic cost of some of these modes may be offset by arbitrary personal preferences or politically determined freight-rate structures. For example, in the discussion of industrial location in the previous chapter, the point was made that freight rates are established for zones, and that these zones increase in width with distance from the shipping point. Thus, although transport costs increase with distance, they do so at a decreasing rate. The same applies to telephone rate structures, mail charges, airline passenger costs, and so forth. The influence of personal preference is nowhere more clearly obvious than in the overwhelming desire of most commuters to use their own automobiles rather than public transportation facilities. The automobile is regarded as a necessity for shopping and social trips, and the gross overhead costs of car ownership are undoubtedly placed disproportionately on these uses by owners who use their vehicles primarily for the journey to work.

Distance-decay between competing centres

The slope of the distance-decay curve is also related to the strength of the origin and destination to or from which the interaction is focused. This relationship is illustrated in Figure 6.5, which depicts the relative influence of the three major cities in Québec. The data for Montréal and Trois-Rivières relate to municipalities lying along a ray drawn between these two urban areas on the north side of the St. Lawrence River; the information for east of Trois-Rivières to Québec City pertains to municipalities lying along a ray drawn between these two urban areas on the south side of the river. The data can be interpreted as concerning the likelihood of a person living in a municipality between the particular cities visiting these centres to purchase a special item, and it has been derived from tabulations in Ministère de l'Industrie et du Commerce (1967). It is to be noted that these data ignore sales volume, for if this characteristic were included, the peak for Trois-Rivières would be far lower than that for Québec City, and that for Québec City would be lower than that for Montréal.

Nevertheless, it is apparent that the distance-decay curve for Trois-Rivières is far steeper than that for Québec City, and the slope of the curve for Québec City is only slightly less than that for Montréal. There is, therefore, a definite size effect on the extent of the sphere of influence of these centres as delimited by the intersections of the various distance-decay curves. The sphere of influence of Montréal extends a radius of fifty-seven miles in the direction of Trois-Rivières,

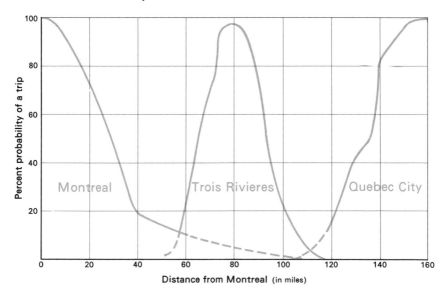

Figure 6.5: The probability of a trip to Montréal, Trois Rivières, and Québec City

and that of Québec City, fifty-one miles toward Trois-Rivières from the east. With these two urban centres likely to grow even more, it is quite likely that the sphere of influence of Trois-Rivières will contract even farther in the future. Interestingly, these break-points defined on the basis of empirical information conform quite closely to those calculated on the basis of 1966 city population data substituted into Reilly's "Law" of Retail Gravitation (sixty-three miles and fifty miles respectively). Intriguingly, Reilly's formula suggests that the break-point for retail gravitation between Québec City and Montréal is about 110 miles.

The sphere of influence of Québec City is, in fact, larger in physical extent than that of Montréal, although it is smaller in population size. This raises the interesting question of the effect of competing centres which, because of their strategic location, may offer an intervening opportunity which disrupts the normal interaction between places. It is quite obvious that Trois-Rivières is in a location which appears intervening, although its growth record does not suggest that this position is advantageous. Transport improvements (particularly the autoroutes) have so shortened the time-distance between Montréal and Québec City that the presence of this historic regional centre is now almost ignored. On the other hand, places like Sherbrooke and Drummondville have maintained their competitive position though they may soon be encompassed by the sphere of influence of Montréal. By contrast, Québec City has few competing centres within its region, so none (apart from Rivière-du-Loup) really intervenes to intercept the potential flow of business toward the provincial capital.

THE EFFECTS OF SIZE, INCOME, AND CULTURE

A second basic generalization is a rather obvious one; it states that flows of all types will tend to be greatest between the larger centres because of the magnified potential for interaction. Of course, the effect of size is modified by the distance-decay effect, although the extent of modification depends greatly on the slope of the distance-decay curve. If the slope is steep, that is, if the indicator is very distance-elastic, the effect of population size will be severely modified. On the other hand, if the slope is shallow, the effect of city size will be accentuated in contrast to the restraining influence of distance. This is quite an important observation with respect to the axis, because it implies that as the importance of the distance-decay effect decreases due to the construction of limited-access freeways and improved inter-city rail and air service, the larger cities show larger increases in interaction with other urban areas than the smaller towns or villages. Thus, it becomes evident that the larger cities, under these circumstances, not only dominate over a wider area, but also interact far more with each other and re-enforce their respective competitive strengths.

Probably the clearest way of illustrating the joint effects of population size and distance-decay is to examine the interaction that results using various hypothetical numbers. To do this, the size and distance effects must be incorporated into a general model. In Figure 6.3 the distance-decay effect is represented by an equation of the form:

$$I_{ij} = a\, D_{ij}^{-b},$$

which can be re-written $I_{ij} = a\, /\, D_{ij}^{b}$
where, I_{ij} is the estimated interaction between two urban centres i and j,

D_{ij} is the distance separating i and j;

b is the slope of the distance-decay curve; and

a is the constant or interaction when D is almost zero.

This equation can be expanded to include population as follows:

$$I_{ij} = a\, P_i^{c}\, P_j^{d}\, /\, D_{ij}^{b}$$

where P_i and P_j are the populations of cities i and j. (The exponents c and d have been included to suggest that the population figures may need to be modified for interaction estimation purposes.)

This modification is necessary because it is evident that not all people have the same potential for interaction. Rich people are more likely to travel than poor people, and young people are freer to go where they wish than those with the responsibilities of families. Furthermore, linguistic differences may be a real influence on the extent of interaction, as Mackay (1958) demonstrated in his classic study of telephone calls between Montréal and other cities in Québec and the rest of Canada. His conclusion was that cities at the same distance from Montréal had significantly greater levels of interaction with Montréal if they were located in Québec than if they were in Ontario (or the rest of Canada). Furthermore, interaction was modified by the U.S.–Canada boundary far more than the Québec–Ontario provincial boundary. This, of course, raises the serious question as to whether the modification in interaction demonstrated by

Mackay is really a provincial boundary effect or a linguistic-cultural effect which just happens to be approximated by the boundary.

The weight of evidence would have to be that the linguistic-cultural effect is extremely important. Data concerning the linguistic characteristics of travellers resident in Montréal but journeying to Toronto, Ottawa, or Québec City, and using three different modes of public transportation, has been extracted from sample survey information in CTCRB (1970) and presented in Table 6.3. As is evident from Figure 1.6, these three cities and Montréal represent three unique locations in the axis linguistic mosaic, and it could be hypothesized that, even though Montréal is located in a French-speaking province, if language is a limiting factor, trips to Toronto would be made primarily by anglophones, and those to Québec City by francophones. The nature of travellers to Ottawa should lie somewhere between the proportions for these two cities. The data in Table 6.3 indicate that this is so for three different modes of transportation. For example, in air traffic, nearly 79 per cent of the travellers to Toronto have English as their primary language and 18 per cent have French, whereas over 58 per cent of the travellers to Québec City have French as their primary language and 40 per cent have English. The figures for air traffic between Montréal and Ottawa lie in between these extremes. Furthermore, it is noticeable that most of the traffic, whatever the primary language of the travellers, is at least moderately bilingual.

A second feature of the data that is worthy of comment relates to the different linguistic preferences for the various modes of transport. Probably the most interesting element illustrating this difference is contained in the French-only row for each of the modes in the Montréal–Québec City flow. Whereas 15.7 per cent and 13.7 per cent of French-only-speaking travellers to Québec City use the bus and rail services, very few (2.3 per cent) use air transportation. This is a startling difference that can relate to a number of interlocking factors. Undoubtedly, income differentials are important, and these are, of course, a product of employment opportunities. Most air travellers are businessmen, and businessmen residing in Montréal are usually at least moderately bilingual, or English-speaking. Thus, it is not surprising that French-Canadians who speak French only tend to use the cheaper mode of transportation. Also, it could be added that the location of Montréal airport at Dorval on the west side of the city of Montréal places it in a more accessible position to the English suburbs than to the predominantly French-speaking eastern part of the island.

Distribution of linguistic characteristics for travellers resident in Montréal (percentage of total sample trips)

	MONTRÉAL-TORONTO	MONTRÉAL-OTTAWA	MONTRÉAL-QUÉBEC CITY
Air Traffic			
English only	26.26	20.91	6.92
French only	0.98	0.00	2.31
English but mod. bilingual	40.73	33.64	21.54
French but mod. bilingual	3.37	3.64	14.62
English but bilingual	11.80	10.91	11.54
French but bilingual	14.04	24.55	41.54
Other main language	2.81	6.36	1.54
Rail Traffic			
English only	26.21	22.59	4.36
French only	2.10	3.15	13.66
English but mod. bilingual	40.94	31.70	12.87
French but mod. bilingual	4.85	9.63	29.70
English but bilingual	10.36	11.21	7.72
French but bilingual	9.71	17.86	30.50
Other main language	5.83	3.85	1.19
Bus Traffic			
English only	23.08	17.33	5.19
French only	3.08	5.87	15.80
English but mod. bilingual	34.62	24.53	10.61
French but mod. bilingual	10.00	15.47	34.99
English but bilingual	6.15	9.33	6.77
French but bilingual	12.31	19.47	24.15
Other main language	10.77	8.00	2.48

Source: CTCRB (1970), p. 95.

THE INTERACTION MODEL AT WORK

The interaction model discussed in the previous section can be used to generate an index of flows between places based on distance-decay and population size effects. The parameters *a*, *b*, *c*, and *d* can be calibrated (to be discussed later) and inserted in the formula to generate the expected interaction based on these principles alone. The effect of various calibrations of parameters on the results of the model are listed in Table 6.4 for combinations of cities of 10,000 and 2,000,000 located fifty miles and 320 miles apart. The hypothetical flows that are calculated are, as is suggested, abstract numbers relating to relative volume, and can be scaled to conform to actual flow volumes by a calibration of the governer *a*. Thus, in Table 6.4, the constant *a* is set equal to unity, and the exponents are varied to indicate the different effects of distance-decay and population size.

In the first hypothesis, the exponents are set at unity, so that the size effect is represented by the actual population sizes of the cities, and the distance-decay effect is directly related to the actual physical distance. In the second hypothesis the distance exponent is set at 0.5, which implies that the distance-decay effect is actually calibrated as being proportional to the square-root of distance. This is based on the

Table 6.4: Hypothetical flows (in thousands) among pairs of cities at various distances with different model parameters

POPULATION OF CITY PAIR	50 MILES	320 MILES
Parameters $a = 1, b = 1, c = 1, d = 1$		
10,000 — 10,000	2,000	312
10,000 — 2,000,000	400,000	62,500
2,000,000 — 2,000,000	8,000,000,000	12,500,000
Parameters $a = 1, b = 0.5, c = 1, d = 1$		
10,000 — 10,000	14,144.3	5,592.8
10,000 — 2,000,000	2,828,454.2	1,118,036.7
2,000,000 — 2,000,000	565,690,849.9	223,607,345.5
Parameters $a = 1, b = 0.5, c = 0.5, d = 0.5$		
10,000 — 10,000	1.4	0.6
10,000 — 2,000,000	20.0	7.9
2,000,000 — 2,000,000	282.8	111.8

observation of many transport economists, which is that transport costs are usually linearly related to the square root of distance, that is, they increase with distance but at a decreasing rate. The result is that interaction is much greater under the second hypothesis than the first, and that the decrease with distance is much less in the second than the first. A similar modification of the size measures is postulated in the third hypothesis, with the result that interaction becomes negligible for the smallest city pair at a distance of 320 miles, and is decreased dramatically in all categories. The corollary to this conclusion is that if the general propensity to travel or interact is much greater in large wealthy cities than in poor small ones, the resultant effect on interaction is quite dramatic. Thus, if the value of b is calibrated to be 0.5, and that of c and d 2.0, the interaction between the largest city pair would be phenomenal.

Interaction between one city in the axis
and others both within and beyond

One of the more centrally isolated cities in Canada is Kingston. Furthermore, it is virtually centrally located within the axis, as it is a leisurely six-hour drive from this site of Canada's first parliament to both Windsor and Québec City. It is also located almost exactly half-way between Montréal and Toronto, and is only a two-hour drive from Ottawa. With this type of intriguing relative location it is interesting to observe the pattern of variation in interaction between Kingston and other cities within the axis, the rest of Canada, and the United States. The degree of interaction is measured by telephone calls made between businessmen and residents of the city of Kingston and other cities in North America during two five-day periods in the summer of 1970. The telephone has become such an integral part of the social and economic life of Canada that it is difficult to envisage how life could continue without it and what invention could possibly replace it. Not only was the telephone invented in Canada (within the axis, in the town of Brantford), but the per capita rate of phone calls is higher in Canada than in any other country in the world. Thus, for such a garrulous nation, the use of phone calls as a measure of interaction is both historically and numerically appropriate.

At the outset, it is interesting to compare the interaction results for Kingston with those prepared by Mackay (1958) for Montréal. Mackay's data are slightly different from data prepared for Kingston, in that Ontario is included with the rest of Canada, and the Québec data include areas outside the axis. The interaction model being assumed in Figure 6.6 is

$$I_{kj} = P_j / D_{kj}$$

where I_{kj} is the number of telephone calls between Kingston and the jth place, P_j is the population of the jth place, and D_{kj} is the distance between Kingston and the jth place. It is to be noted that this model differs from the more general interaction model discussed previously in that the population of Kingston is excluded because that value is constant for each city pair, and that the parameters a, d, and b are set equal to unity.

The Kingston data (Figure 6.6b) exhibit patterns that are, on the whole, quite different from those relating to Montréal (Figure 6.6a). Whereas the Montréal data suggest that, for any P/D value, interaction is greatest within Québec followed by the rest of Canada and the United States, the Kingston data suggest that interaction is greatest within the Ontario portion of the axis, followed by the Québec portion, the rest of Canada, and finally the United States. Thus, the Kingston results do not exhibit the same degree of provincial bias as those for Montréal, although it must be noted that the number of cities in Québec telephoned from Kingston is very few. The similarity between the interaction patterns within the two portions of the axis is emphasized by the general form of the relationships between these actual and P/D predicted values plotted in Figure 6.6c. The Ontario and Québec axis data are quite similar and the lines almost overlap. The slope of the rest of Canada curve is not as steep, and the U.S. curve is barely different from a horizontal line.

The Kingston data would, therefore, tend to suggest that even though there are differences in interaction between the two portions of the axis, the differences are not as great as those between Kingston and the rest of Canada, and certainly not as great as those between Kingston and the United States. These differences are further exemplified when the exponents b and d, and the constant a are estimated, using multiple regression procedures (Table 6:5). The distance exponent is very large because of the particular arrangement of the largest cities around Kingston which, in effect, intercept possible interaction with places more distant within the axis. In other words, Toronto, Montréal (and to a lesser extent, Ottawa) are the real boundaries of Kingston's interaction field, and places beyond

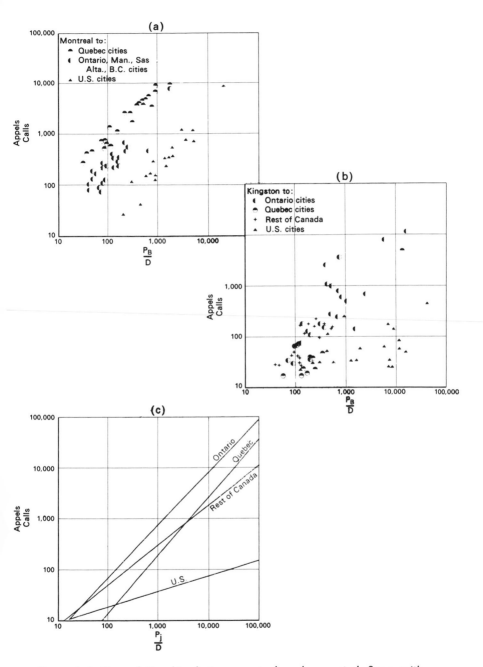

Figure 6.6: The relationship between actual and expected flows with respect to (a) Montréal; and (b) and (c) to Kingston

them appear more distant than they really are. This is a good example of a real intervening opportunity, for these large cities in effect act as an impermeable filter that blinkers Kingstonians from the area beyond. Noticeably, the parameters for the rest of Canada indicate that interaction is almost proportional to distance and population size, and in the United States population size is far less important than distance.

The Kingston data are, therefore, extremely interesting in that they suggest the existence of an interaction system which can be defined in terms of three subsystems: 1) flows within the axis; 2) flows between the axis and the rest of Canada; and 3) flows between the axis and the rest of North America. But, as these subsystems have been defined with respect to one indicator, and the flows from one city, it is well to analyse their existence further by using more cities and additional indicators. Unfortunately, the data that are available in published form concerning flows of people, products, and information, have not, by and large, been collected for the purpose of identifying systems of interaction. Rather, the data have been collected with the aim of "balancing the books", whether in terms of trade or population. Information flow data, despite their importance in the society of today and tomorrow, have rarely been collected on any formal basis. The result is that it is possible only to suggest some fragments of the structure that exist to bind the axis and the rest of the country together.

FLOWS WITHIN THE AXIS

One of the better surveys of interaction in general, and certainly the

Table 6.5: Parameters estimated for the Kingston interaction model

	a	b	d	R^2*
Axis	999.2	−2.399	0.976	80.7
Rest of Canada	3.8	−1.038	0.836	53.4
United States	257.2	−0.836	0.228	51.3

*The R^2 is a goodness-of-fit measure. If the flows predicted by the interaction model were exactly the same as those that actually occurred, the R^2 value would be 100.0 per cent. Thus, the axis data is well represented by the model in this particular case, whereas the rest of Canada and U.S. flows are less well represented.

best preliminary survey of flows within the axis, has been undertaken by Simmons (1970), using data pertaining to telephone calls, rail freight, truck flows, and airline flows. The most complete set of data is for telephone calls, and the more detailed conclusions relate to interaction as measured by this indicator. Information concerning rail-freight and truck flows is extremely fragmentary and related only to the largest cities. Furthermore, the data do not cover the entire area. Finally, the airline traffic data, though useful, relate to a network which is of too coarse a mesh to be really useful for analysing within axis flows. It is interesting to note that in a revised article concerning interaction in this same area, Simmons (1972) discards the rail and truck data, barely notes the airline information, and concentrates solely on the telephone information. Therefore, the pattern of within-axis interaction will be analysed using telephone data, supplemented by migration data in Québec. This second indicator is not used by Simmons.

FUNCTIONAL NODAL REGIONS WITHIN THE AXIS AS DEFINED BY TELEPHONE INFORMATION

The telephone information relates to the number of long-distance calls between toll centres in the axis on a typical business day in spring 1967. Personal calls are defined as those which originate in a home of one kind or another, business calls are defined as those which originate in a non-residential location. While this latter definition may be regarded as a charitable view of all non-residential calls, the assumption that employees usually refrain from making long-distance calls at the company's expense is probably quite correct, particularly among the lower echelons of business management. Long-distance calls are defined as all those between toll areas, and since these toll areas are not necessarily conterminous with urban areas this discrepancy can result in problems. For example, the toll centre pertaining to Smiths Falls (Ontario) is quite large, so many calls cover a long distance, but are not classified as such because they are within the same centre. On the other hand, on the Niagara Peninsula the toll centres are quite small, so many calls that are over a short distance appear as long-distance for they are between centres. Thus, although the ensuing discussion refers to cities, it should be remembered that these are toll centres that embrace, primarily, that particular urban area.

On this spring day, nearly 330,000 inter-city calls were recorded, or one for every thirty-three persons in the axis. Of these, 50.4 per cent occurred between twenty-five pairs of cities, and these pairs are indicated in Figure 6.7, in which the width of bars is proportionate to the total volume of calls between each pair. The general linearity of the pattern and dominance of Montréal and Toronto is remarkable, though not surprising. If the data for these twenty-five pairs of cities, separated into residential and non-residential calls, are used to calibrate the parameters *a*, *b*, *c*, and *d* of the general interaction model, the results further support the applicability of the model as a general descriptive concept (Table 6.6). In this particular instance the size of a toll centre is measured not by its population but by the number of telephones located in that centre. As the flow data are two-way, the parameters *c* and *d* cannot be interpreted meaningfully, but the exponent of distance is interestingly different in the two equations. The inference is that distance is not such a detriment to long-distance calls in the business world as it is to personal calls. This inference is quite reasonable, not only because business calls are deductible from profits as a business operating expense, but also because long-distance calls are more necessary in commerce. It is also entertaining to note that the effect of a particular pattern of cities which, it is suggested, particularly influenced the distance exponent in the Kingston case, is absent when many city pairs are used.

The general interaction model is quite applicable, therefore, to flows within the axis as measured by telephone calls. The size of centres and the distance separating them are the prime determinants of the magnitudes of the flows. Further perusal of Figure 6.7 also reveals that two metropolises dominate a wide portion of the axis and, in effect, exclude each other from their clearly prescribed territories.

Table 6.6: Parameters estimated for the general interaction model applied to telephone calls between twenty-five city pairs in the axis

TYPE OF CALL	*a*	*b*	*c*	*d*	R^2
Residential	5.50	−0.97	0.50	0.61	73.0
Business	1.01	−0.65	0.33	0.68	81.0

Source: Data obtained from Simmons (1970), p. 206; parameters calculated by the author.

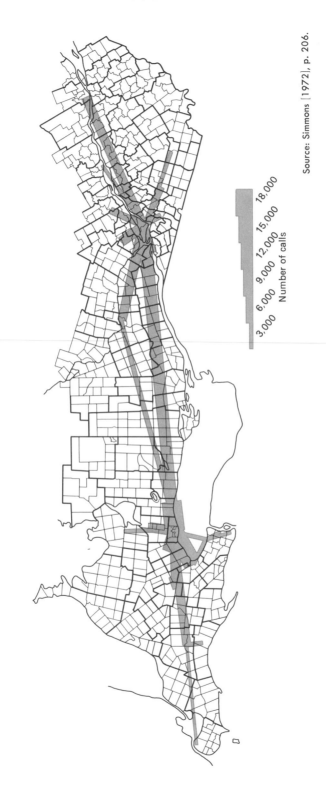

Figure 6.7: The twenty-five largest volumes of telephone call flows in the axis, 1966

Number of calls

3,000 6,000 9,000 12,000 15,000 18,000

Source: Simmons [1972], p. 206.

This is indicated quite clearly by the map of largest outflow of business messages in Figure 6.8. In this diagram of one-way largest outflow links, it is apparent that Montréal and Toronto, in effect, partition the axis between themselves into two functional nodal regions. Although London and Ottawa appear to have their own separate subregions, and to a much lesser extent Windsor, Sherbrooke, and Québec City, these in turn have their highest outflow to either Toronto or Montréal. Thus, the London subsystem is part of the

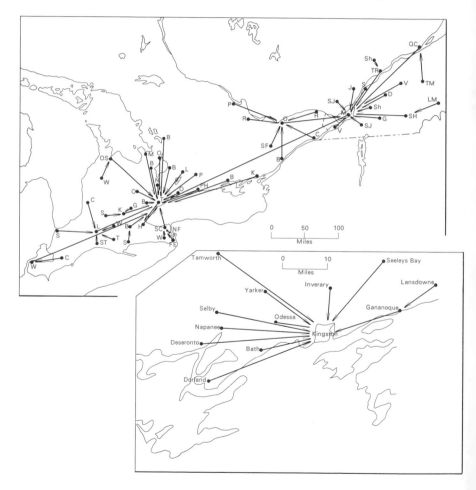

Figure 6.8: The directions of the largest outflows of business telephone calls within the axis

Source: Simmons [1972], p. 207.

Toronto region. Montréal and Toronto would be reciprocally highest linked if it were not for the proximity of Hamilton.

Hierarchies of interaction

Dominance involves hierarchies or patterns of sub-dominance, and interaction flows reveal these just as clearly as service activities. The existence of a hierarchical effect on the pattern of telephone calls within the axis is revealed partially in Figure 6.8 by the directions of largest outflow of business calls. If the details of this diagram are abstracted into an organizational structure of dominance and sub-dominance it is clear that the general spatial interaction model operates within a hierarchical structure (Figure 6.9). Toronto and Montréal are the highest order centres, dominating between them the entire axis. This dominance is exerted either directly over "regional" centres (such as Midland, Kingston, Sorel, Drummondville, and so forth), or indirectly through "major regional" centres (such as Windsor, London, Ottawa, Québec City, and so forth). The cities within these toll centres dominate, in turn, the local area, and the physical extent of this communication dominance depends upon the general pattern of settlement and proximity of centres.

As an attempt at reconstructing the way in which the "major regional" and "regional" centres dominate these smaller areas, long-distance telephone call data (business plus residential) pertaining to the Kingston area in 1970 have been added to Figure 6.9. All the towns and villages within a radius of about thirty-five to forty miles show Kingston as the largest single destination of their total long-distance calls. For example, the proportionate destinations of all long-distance calls from Gananoque to the ten most-called areas are:

Kingston	45.9 per cent
Lansdowne	10.0 per cent
Brockville	6.7 per cent
Toronto	4.3 per cent
Ottawa	3.2 per cent
Montréal	2.7 per cent
Seeley's Bay	2.6 per cent
Mallorytown	0.9 per cent
Belleville	0.9 per cent
Elgin	0.8 per cent

Although Toronto, Ottawa, and Montréal are among the top ten most-called centres from Gananoque, they are not among the top three. Therefore, for each regional centre a map of dominant flows could be prepared such as that in the inset of Figure 6.8, and these larger scale maps would define the communication field dominated by each centre.

Of course, the hierarchy continues beyond the sub-regional level. Sub-regional settlements such as Deseronto, Napanee, and Gananoque have their own, much smaller, communication fields. For example, in Lansdowne–Gananoque is the focus of the vast majority of long-distance calls, and Kingston is the second focus, with less than half the total number received by Gananoque. Thus, Kingston dominates Lansdowne via Gananoque. Unfortunately, the communication fields dominated by these sub-regional centres are difficult to define using long-distance telephone data because most of the interaction at this local scale is measured by local rather than long-distance calls. Nevertheless, the hierarchical effect is strong, and it helps to explain the way in which large metropolises dominate extensive portions of the country. They dominate by "taking over" the "major regional" or "regional" centres, rather in the same way as company mergers occur through the "taking over" of holding companies. This situation is hardly surprising; for it re-enforces one of the basic themes of this volume, which is that the urban system of the axis (and Canada) exhibits the characteristics of the economic system within which it has grown. Thus, it is hardly surprising that the inhabitants of Québec view with alarm the possible overwhelming influence of Toronto over Montréal some time in the future. This particular trend is analysed in greater detail in a later chapter.

INTERACTION WITHIN THE AXIS AS MEASURED BY MIGRATION

The second type of interaction within the axis that is being considered represents a far more tangible and permanent movement than that of long-distance phone calls. In Chapter 2, a migration probability-model was used that incorporated growth to forecast and distribute the future total population within the province of Québec. There was no real attempt made during that discussion to indicate why the migration patterns occurred as they did, so in this section it is interesting to relate the flows to the general interaction model. It must be noted at the outset that not only are the data more tangible and permanent than telephone calls, they are also different, because in this particular case

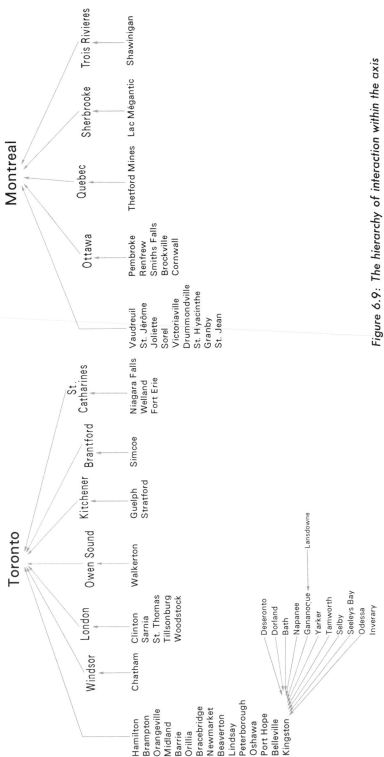

Figure 6.9: The hierarchy of interaction within the axis

the actual direction of each flow is known. Thus, it is possible to determine the parameters for the general interaction model with respect to 1) within axis Québec flows; 2) between the axis and rest of Québec flows; and 3) between the regions of the rest of Québec flows. It will be recalled that the migration data for Québec relates to nine rather large administrative regions, five of which are virtually synonymous with the axis. Thus, there are twenty within axis flows, forty between the axis and the rest of Québec flows (which can be divided into inflows and outflows), and twelve flows with the rest of Québec.

The parameters of the general interaction model as estimated from the data for the four groups of flows are presented in Table 6.7. At the outset it should be noted that the general interaction model describes the within-axis migration flows in Québec extremely well. The parameters c and d are quite close to unity indicating that the population sizes of the origin region and destination regions exert influences of comparable strength. The distance exponent is larger than that for long-distance telephone calls throughout the axis, and this is quite understandable. The telephone-call distance exponent in general reflects the structure of charges, which increase with distance but at a decreasing rate, whereas the migration distance exponent indicates that people prefer moving shorter distances to longer ones. In fact, the effect of distance is almost squared in the outflow model, and although the more populated regions in the axis tend to be the more

Table 6.7: Parameters estimated for the general interaction model, applied to fiscal migration in Québec

	LOG a	b	ORIGIN c	DESTINA-NATION d	R^2
Within axis flows	−6.61	−1.65	1.05	1.11	92.8
Outflow	6.64	−1.93	1.44	−1.57	86.3
Inflow	−0.37	−1.10		1.35	83.2
Within rest of Québec flows	11.35	−1.01			55.4

Source: Calculations undertaken with data from Robert (1972).
Note: The blanks in the table indicate that the parameters do not test as being significantly different from zero at the 0.05 confidence level using a two-tailed t test.

likely origins of migrants, they definitely find each destination region unattractive. The general interaction model for this set of flows is, in fact, modified to be $aP_i{}^c/ P_j{}^dD_{ij}{}^b$, which suggests that there is not only a strong distance-decay effect, but also a strong population-decay effect as well. The unattractive features of regions in Québec located beyond the axis is further exemplified by the parameters of the inflow model which suggests that the distance-decay effect for in-migrants is not nearly as strong as for outflows or within-axis flows, and the population size of the origin region has no real influence on the magnitude of the migration stream. In fact, the only real influence on the magnitude of inflows to the axis area in Québec from beyond the axis is the population size of the destination region, and the tendency is for the more populous regions to be disproportionately attractive. Finally, the only real influence on the magnitude of migration flows within the rest of Québec is distance.

It is apparent, therefore, that there are significant differences in migration patterns within the province of Québec with respect to the axis and non-axis areas. Flows within the axis behave in accordance with the general concepts embodied in the general interaction model, whereas those linking the axis to the rest of Québec do not. Furthermore, the model is hardly applicable at all to flows in the rest of Québec. These differences are neatly summarized in Figure 6.10, which relates the expected interaction derived from an interaction model in which a and the exponents are assumed to be unity ($EM_{ij} = P_iP_j/ D_{ij}$) and the actual migration (M_{ij}). The flows that tend to conform with the principles embodied in the general interaction model, that is, flows within the axis ($P_i{}^cP_j{}^d / D_{ij}{}^b$) and flows into the axis ($P_j{}^d/ D_{ij}{}^b$) yield general predictions for any P_iP_j/D values that are remarkably similar, whereas the outflow and rest of Québec flow predictions are radically different. Thus, the slopes of the general relationship between these actual and predicted values suggest that the Québec portion of the axis is quite distinguishable from the rest of the province in terms of interaction. It is an entity in which flows conform to general principles, and it is also an entity which greatly determines the magnitudes of flows which either originate externally or have destinations beyond the axis.

FLOWS BETWEEN THE AXIS AND THE REST OF CANADA

Long-distance telephone calls and migration data for all or part of the axis, therefore, suggest that the axis is a strong entity in which fundamental principles of interaction govern the flow of people, messages, and, by inference, goods. The migration information also suggests that those principles operate comprehensively within the axis, but that they do not operate as comprehensively in areas external to the axis in Québec. In this section, flows of manufactured goods and airline passengers are used to provide some additional evidence concerning this suggestion.

The manufactured goods data are particularly interesting because the actual flows of this type of product generally imply certain development principles. Since the industrial revolution, the wealthiest

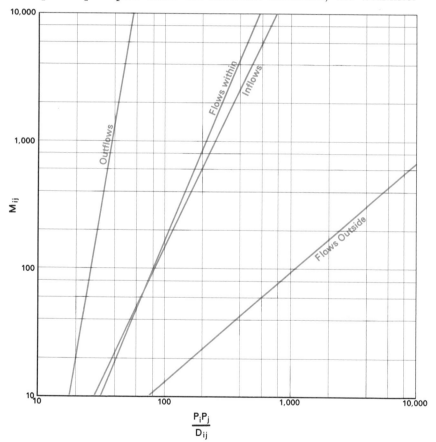

Figure 6.10: The difference between axis and non-axis migration flows in the Province of Québec

countries have generally been those that were able to export manufactured goods, while the poorest have been those exporting raw materials. The wealthy countries sought to solidify this arrangement through empires, colonies, trade preferences, and the control of capital. Similarly, within Canada, the axis dominates manufacturing production, and energy and raw materials are imported from beyond the axis to fulfil the input requirements. In return, the axis exports manufactured goods to the rest of the country, and seeks to solidify this pattern by maintaining a structure of rail freight rates that are favourable to this particular pattern. The notion of a "wealthy" axis and a "less wealthy" rest of Canada is hard to dispute in face of an average per capita income in the axis in 1971 of $2,589 compared with $2,069 in the rest of the country. The fact that this gap declined by ten percentage points between 1961 and 1971 is little solace to the average family of four living beyond the axis which is over $2,000 poorer than its axis counterpart.

THE FLOW OF MANUFACTURED GOODS

The data being used pertains to 1967, and it involves the flow of manufactured goods, measured in thousands of dollars value, between provinces. Owing to the fact that nearly all manufacturing in Ontario and Québec is located within the axis area, the flows to these two provinces really means flows to the axis. The sizes of the origins and destinations are measured by the population (in 1966) of the various provinces, and the number of interactions for Canada as a whole is ninety. These can be broken down into nine flows from Ontario plus Québec (the axis) to the other provinces, nine flows into the axis from the other provinces, and seventy-two flows between the provinces and the rest of Canada. The combining of Ontario and Québec reduces the total volume of flows being considered by almost half; for 43 per cent of all flows (by value) in Canada occur between these two provinces within the axis.

The general interaction model, and its modification with respect to axis inflows and outflows, describes the Canadian flow situation quite nicely. It is interesting to note that there are differences among the various groups of flows which distinguish the axis from the rest of Canada. The friction of distance in Canada as a whole is less than in Canada with all axis flows excluded. This fact is, in part, due to the nature of flows with respect to the axis. Outflows from the axis exhibit no distance-decay effect, whereas inflows to the axis exhibit a friction of distance similar to that for all flows within the country. The destination of axis outflows appears to be proportional to the population size of the recipient province, whereas the origin of inflows is strongly size-oriented. This is reasonable, because only the larger provinces (as measured by population) have a significant amount of manufacturing.

There is some support, therefore, for the argument that the axis has a favoured position with respect to manufacturing. This is demonstrated by the lack of any distance-decay effect with respect to outflows of manufacturing from the axis area. On the other hand, the friction of distance is quite apparent in each of the other models. Furthermore, the effect of distance on manufacturing flows in the rest of Canada outside the axis is quite severe. The axis is, therefore, a part of Canada that is in an advantaged position within the general system of manufacturing flows. The reason for this is undoubtedly related to the favourable rail freight-rate structure which has been developed over the years. This freight structure, for example, makes it cheaper to ship some manufactured goods from Toronto and Montréal to Vancouver, than from Winnipeg to Vancouver. It is a structure that, in effect, encourages the manufacturing domination of these two metropolises over the entire country.

Table 6.8: Parameters estimated for the general interaction model applied to the flow of manufactured goods between provinces in Canada in 1967

	LOG a	b	ORIGIN c	DESTINA-TION d	R^2
Within Canada flows	−7.36	−2.15	2.23	0.71	81.1
Axis outflows	−0.10	n.s.		0.99	98.9
Axis inflows	−6.22	−2.20	2.99		91.5
Within rest of Canada flows	−7.14	−2.26	2.43	0.55	77.9

Source: Calculations undertaken with data from DBS (1967).
Note: As the flows are with reference to the axis there are no parameters for outflow origins and inflow destinations; n.s. means not significantly different from zero using a two-tailed *t* test at the 0.05 confidence level.

THE FLOW OF AIRLINE PASSENGERS

The airline passenger data is interesting because they comprise the only set of flow information that is available for a number of time periods. The general pattern of trip volumes between the twenty-three dominant origins and destinations in Canada in 1971 further emphasizes the importance of the axis (Figure 6.11a). The largest flows, as would be expected, are between the major airports within the axis, and those linking the axis to the rest of the country. Also, there exists a hierarchy of flows which focuses upon Montréal and Toronto in the axis area (Figure 6.11b). This hierarchy can be defined by the pattern of largest outflows, and it suggests the existence of five major metropolitan fields, based on Vancouver, Edmonton, Winnipeg, Toronto, and Montréal, with the latter two forming a reciprocal pair to which the other metropolises are connected. In this situation, it is interesting to note that Toronto tends to dominate all of Canada indirectly, that is via the other metropolises, whereas Montréal dominates Québec and the Maritimes directly. The influence of Toronto, therefore, in terms of interaction, is more national than that of Montréal. In summary, the axis, as represented by these two large airports (at Malton and Dorval), is the locus of the largest single avenue of traffic, as well as the focus of most nationwide flows.

The unique position of the axis in this pattern of flows is emphasized in Figure 6.12, which illustrates the relationship between passenger flows (in thousands) and the general interaction model (assuming that a and the exponent equal unity). For any P_iP_j / D_{ij} value, flows between the axis and the rest of Canada are greater than flows within the rest of Canada. The ratio of the difference appears to have decreased slightly between 1961 and 1970, but even at this latter date, for any P_iP_j / D_{ij} value, flows between the axis and the rest of Canada were at least four times greater than flows within the rest of Canada. The slope of the lines indicating the relationship between the predicted values and actual values in Figure 6.12 are also interesting. The 1970 axis and the Rest of Canada line suggest that the general interaction model is not a reasonable descriptor of the flow situation, whereas the slope of the line for 1961 suggests that it is.

This change through time in the descriptive applicability of the basic principles incorporated with the model is related to the apparent lack of any discernible distance-decay effect in 1970 in flows between the axis and the Rest of Canada. This observation is based upon an

50,000	100,000	150,000	250,000	500,000

Figure 6.11: Air passenger traffic flows; (a) within Canada; and (b)
between Canada and the United States

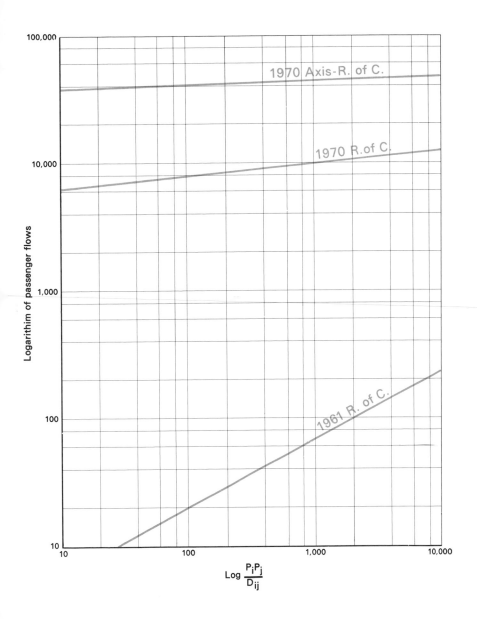

Figure 6.12: The relationship between expected and actual air passenger
flows between Canada and the United States

analysis of the parameters estimated for the general interaction model for 1961 and 1970 using total flows between city pairs (Table 6.9). The exponents c and d do not relate to directions of flow and cannot be interpreted in any way other than that they imply that the product of size is important. A perceptible but weak distance-decay effect is apparent in 1961, but absent in 1970. As far as the axis is concerned, the only important influence on traffic volume is city size, and according to Figure 6.11b, position in the hierarchy of airline passenger flows.

The changing importance of distance as an influence on traffic flow with respect to the axis can be related to increasing general wealth, changing tastes, and the concentration of economic and political power within the urban areas of the axis. Air travel is particularly responsive to these trends, for it is vital to business, commerce, and governmental administration within the country. The airplane permits face-to-face contact in any large urban area anywhere within the country in one day. The axis is the focus of this traffic; not only are the major flows directed toward it, but it also contains the largest flow between any city pair in the country. An interesting observation is that, in a country where distance has been historically so important, the distance separating large urban areas does not appear to influence the volume of traffic between them. It is, therefore, these metropolitan areas that are the forging links that tie the country to the axis market place!

Table 6.9: *Parameters estimated for the general interaction model applied to airline passenger traffic between the major cities of Canada and the axis*

	LOG a	b	c	d	R^2
Axis and the rest of Canada					
1961	−1.70	−0.36	0.75	0.53	66.6
1970	−0.20	n.s.	0.53	0.37	39.7

Source: Parameters calculated from data in "Aviation in Canada 1971 — a statistical handbook of Canadian civil aviation", Statistics Canada, 1972 (Catalogue 51-501 Occasional).

FLOWS BETWEEN THE AXIS AND
THE UNITED STATES

Having provided an array of evidence to suggest that, in terms of inter-action, the axis is a significant functioning entity within Canada that exists as a twin set of functional nodal regions, and which, in turn is the focus of the rest of the country, it is now appropriate to pose the question: is the axis also an entity that is clearly separated from the United States? The question will be examined by comparing air traffic flows between major metropolitan areas in the axis and the United States, with those for the axis to the rest of Canada.

The boundary between Canada and the United States has long been recognized as an impediment to interaction and a divider of route networks. Mackay's (1958) study, the broad results of which are presented in Figure 6.6a, suggests that on the basis of telephone calls, cities in the United States are, in effect, fifty times farther away from Montréal than is indicated by their physical distance. The Kingston telephone-call data re-enforce this observation (Figure 6.6c), as they suggest a very large differential in interaction between this medium-sized city and U.S. urban areas, compared with other Canadian cities. In fact, at a P_j/D of 10,000, calls with Ontario cities are over 1000 times greater, and with cities in the rest of Canada over 100 times greater, than the volume with U.S. urban areas.

These fragments of interaction suggest a tremendous boundary in-fluence, and with the airline-traffic data, the presence of such an important influence is re-enforced. The impact of the boundary can be determined only from 1970 airline passenger flows, and for ease of comparative interpretation the data are included within Figure 6.12. The predicted flows for 1970 have been calculated on the basis of the general interaction model (with the same parameter assumptions), and it is quite apparent that for any P_iP_j/D_{ij} value, the volume of traffic flow between the axis and the United States is a great deal lower than that between the axis and the Rest of Canada. In fact, the magnitude of the difference is very close to that suggested by the Montréal and Kingston telephone-call data. Even more important, as Mackay's data relate to the mid-1950s and the Kingston and airline-traffic data to the late 1960s, it could be inferred that the influence of the international boundary on interaction has remained fairly constant over the past two decades.

CONCLUSION

The different fragments of evidence, though occasionally abstract in presentation, together yield a series of messages that are sharp and clear. The axis is an independent functional entity within Canada, which, in terms of interaction, is differentiated from the rest of the country, and is clearly distinguishable from the United States, even at the macro-scale level. The unity of the axis is assured by the co-existence of two powerful urban nodes (Montréal and Toronto) which exert a dominating influence over the smaller functional regions within the axis area. This dominance is achieved through a hierarchical structure, and flows between each element of this structure conform closely to well-established general principles of interaction.

These two powerful urban nodes are also the focus of interaction for the country as a whole through their dominance over major metropolitan functional nodes in the other regions, and a large volume of interaction occurs despite the distance which separates these urban areas. This is demonstrated by the fact that distance in the general interaction model with respect to flows between the axis and the rest of Canada usually appears to have no influence on the volume of the flow. The reasons are manifold, but the advantageous structure of rail freight rates enjoyed by the axis with respect to the rest of Canada is undoubtedly a major factor underlying this pattern. The axis can, in effect, be viewed as the "developed" part of Canada, in which the growth of manufacturing has been encouraged by preferential freight-rate structures. For example, the cost of shipping a steel product from Hamilton to Edmonton is $2.11 per 100 pounds, whereas the cost from Hamilton to Vancouver is $1.35 per 100 pounds. Thus, the Canadian consumer in Edmonton is subsidizing the lower transport costs for steel to Vancouver in order to preserve the competitive position of Hamilton for both the domestic and export market.

The situation is even more biased with respect to the import of raw materials into the axis from the rest of the country. As an example, we may cite the famous "Rapeseed Case" in which it used to cost $0.81 per 100 pounds to ship rapeseed from Lethbridge (Alberta) to Montréal, but if it was processed into oil and meal at Lethbridge and then shipped to Montréal, the cost was $1.22 per 100 pounds. Without wishing to enter into the maniacal maze of rail freight-rate structures (which have driven more than one researcher to a psychiatrist's couch), it is difficult to understand whether this difference was meant to assure cheap domestic raw material supplies for the processing industry in Montréal, or prevent the development of the processing industry in Lethbridge. The steel and rapeseed situations are but examples of the way in which the major metropolises within the axis have achieved a position of dominance over the rest of the country, for these are only two samples of thousands of anomalies. But the repercussions of these many thousands of little preferences are immense; for over time, much of the economic wealth of the nation has been transferred to the large urban areas within the axis. Furthermore, as added icing to the economic cake, the growth of government at the federal level has also accrued primarily to an urban area within the axis, thus re-enforcing the economic strength of the area.

This dominance is likely to become even more accentuated in the future. In an earlier chapter with respect to urban growth within the axis, the colloquial question was posed: what is wrong with letting the chips fall where they may? One answer could well be: "nothing". But many people living beyond the axis would also add: "nothing, just so long as the chips are not falling on a biased table." This discussion of interaction has revealed some very definite biases which need to be discussed fully in the context of urban policy because they affect urban growth. If the current situation continues into the future, the control which the axis exerts over the economic, political, and social life of the country will be even stronger. Furthermore, this all-pervading influence will be channelled through two large metropolises, and it not hard to envisage a time when one of these will dominate the other. At that time, Canada will be very much like a European country where one city dominates the nation (London controls the United Kingdom, Paris dominates France). But Canada is not a European nation, it is a vast area with many different cultural and economic interests. Such diversity cannot survive if two metropolises are permitted to strengthen their dominant positions, because their values will then be all-pervasive.

All physical flows have to be channelled into routes of one kind or another, and it is the ordering of these flows into specific paths that gives rise to a transport network. Urban areas are located at discrete intervals along, or, more usually, at intersections in this network, so the physical layout of the channels provides the formative skeleton of the axis. In effect, it is the particular structure of the physical network in the axis that distinguishes the axis as a "corridor"; for the major urban centres are connected by a delicate sinuous pattern of routes. Ottawa's eccentric position sets it slightly apart, but it can still be regarded as part of this corridor. This corridor can be defined quite specifically in terms of air, road, rail, and water transportation.

CAPACITY AND STRUCTURE

A transport network can be defined in terms of its capacity and structure. There is always some element of the system which limits the capacity of the network, and there is always a distinct pattern that characterizes its physical structure. With respect to road networks, the number of lanes, their width, and the permissible average speed along the routes all control the capacity of the system. The maximum capacity is determined by the largest flow possible through the most constricted section of the network. Although they cannot be seen, the capacity of airline routes is also controlled by similar features, but in this case the capacity of the network is more likely to be influenced by the runway and passenger capacities of the air terminal.

AIR TRANSPORTATION

Of Canada's seven major airlines, five operate services within the axis, and two more operate long-distance flights out of Toronto and

Although both maps illustrate the corridor nature of the routes, the dominance of Montréal and Ottawa as final aircraft destinations is not so easily explained. Part of the explanation undoubtedly lies in the political nature of aircraft route negotiations, for airlines can only land their carriers in airports specified by the federal Ministry of Transport. But it also appears that whereas flights from the eastern part of the United States have both Toronto and Montréal/Ottawa as their final destinations, those from the mid-west United States, and from the western portion of the continent, turn around at Montréal or Ottawa after passing through Toronto. Under this type of flow system, the turn-around capacity of Dorval airport has to be far larger than that at Malton, although the passenger handling capability has to be about the same.

The relatively short distances of air passenger flights within the axis do lead to definite inefficiencies. Airport services, taxiing, and gaining altitude contribute greatly to flight costs, and at a stage length of only 340 miles between Montréal and Toronto, costs per mile for the types of aircraft used are quite high. In addition, faster aircraft cannot contribute greatly to efficiency from the point of view of the traveller, since the present flight time of about one hour between Montréal and Toronto is offset by the half-hour it takes to get from the downtown sections to the respective airports, and the incredible three-quarters of an hour to one hour wasted in comic Chaplinesque routines at the air terminals. The new Rapidair service between Toronto and Montréal has been quite successful in terms of passenger generation (over 1,000,000 passengers in the first year of operation), but the service is still plagued by terminal inefficiencies.

The future of air transport within the axis

The forecasts of future air travel prepared by the federal Ministry of Montréal. Most of the trip destinations of passengers using flights beginning and ending within the axis are in Toronto and Montréal, with Ottawa ranking as the third most important (Figure 7.1a). Although it is difficult to envisage what this pattern would be otherwise, it is interesting to contrast the internal axis trip destinations with those of the final destinations of aircraft entering the axis from the rest of Canada and the United States. Figure 7.1b is based on data obtained for a sharp but sunny Wednesday in January 1973, and it indicates that Montréal, followed by Ottawa, are the most frequent aircraft final destinations.

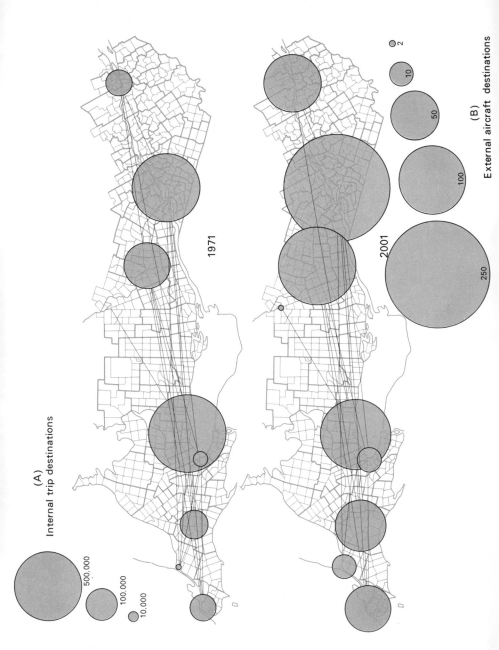

Figure 7.1: The destination of (a) internal passenger trips, 1971, and
(b) all aircraft entering the axis from the rest of Canada and
the United States, 1973

Transport, based on past trends, future population growth and propensity to travel (McPherson, 1972), suggest significant increases at the six major air hubs in the country (Figure 7.2). Although considerable reservations have been expressed about all the forecasts used in this book, these particular projections must be viewed with even more suspicion than the others. This is because the forecasts are subject not only to future population estimates, but to future costs, family structure, expected incomes, and so forth. In fact, some forecasts made in different countries as recently as five years ago have had to be deflated, and airport plans have been revised.

Probably the greatest increases are likely to occur in air freight, for at the moment cargo accounts for only about 1 per cent of the total value of air traffic. A large proportion of the expected increase is likely to accrue to Montréal and Toronto, though it is to be doubted whether the Montréal volume will be as large relative to the Toronto volume as is suggested in Figure 7.2b. The rapid growth in air freight, which will be accentuated by the increased use of large "jumbo" jets, will undoubtedly re-enforce the advantages of the two largest Canadian metropolises for the location of high value-added industries. These industries produce high-value but small, light components which can bear the cost of the higher freight rates that are incurred through air transportation.

Business trips form the bulk of all airline travel, and about 90 per cent of all airline traffic between Montréal and Toronto involves businessmen. As the length of a human life is finite, and time is the only real scarce resource, it is quite likely that inter-city business travel between Montréal and Toronto will continue to focus upon the airplane. There appears to have been a large increase in traffic flow associated with Rapidair, and if the time could be cut still further even more traffic would be stimulated. But these savings in time could be achieved only by reducing terminal congestion and impediments. The aspect of technological change that dominates the literature on short distance inter-city movements is STOL (short take-off and landing) and VTOL (vertical take-off and landing). At the present time, it is predicted that STOL will be introduced within the axis by the end of the decade, and the over one million passengers that used Rapidair in 1972–3 certainly provide a significant market on one route.

Enthusiasm varies (Pratt, 1972) concerning the value of STOL (and subsequently VTOL). While travel time may be reduced by STOL aircraft, it is not flight speed that reduces travel time (Table

7.1). Rather, STOL relies on being able to operate closer to the city centre and from a site that incorporates super-efficient passenger and baggage handling. In fact, the saving in travel time is really made at the unbelievably efficient STOL terminal. Such sites have been suggested on the waterfront areas of Toronto and Montréal at a cost of around $4.5 million each, excluding land costs. Though the runways would be quite short (2,000 feet), the costs of acquiring and/or reclaiming the necessary land would obviously be extremely high, and it is debatable whether these costs, and the additional noise and pollution factors, are justifiable given the saving in time that is involved. The same time-savings could be achieved by streamlining and extending the present Malton and Dorval terminals.

Future airports

One of the most important influences on the future of aviation in the axis is government, and this involvement takes place at many levels (MacGougan, 1972). The involvement occurs because the governments wish to make air communication more efficient, and also because airports are perceived as agents of regional development. The federal government is intricately involved because it has the authority to build and operate airports for international and interprovincial air travel, provide in-flight control, and operate regulations concerning safety and standards. Probably the most controversial aspect of this

Table 7.1: *A comparison between time consumed in travel between Toronto and Montréal using the conventional system as against a proposed STOL system (in hours)*

	STOL TURBO-PROP	CONVENTIONAL JET
Access	.25	.45
Terminal	.67	1.40
Flight	1.47	1.08
Egress	.33	.57
Total	2.72	3.50

Source: CTCRB (1970).

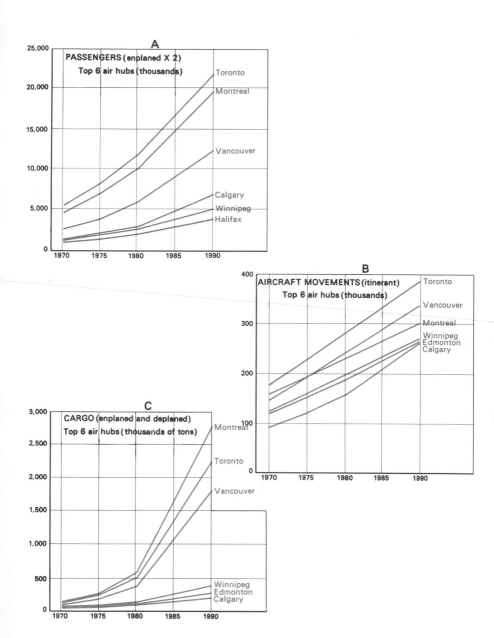

Figure 7.2: Forecasts of passengers, cargo, and aircraft movements through the six major Canadian airports

federal influence concerns the expansion of existing facilities, and the location of new airports.

Currently, at a cost of more than $400 million, a second airport is being built at Ste-Scholastique to serve the Montréal region; and a second airport is envisaged to serve Toronto from Pickering Township. Without wishing to cast aspersions on the different airport planning teams for these two areas, the case for both airports is quite marginal. The case for the second Toronto airport rests on the shortage of airplane and passenger handling facilities at Malton and the impact of noise on the surrounding residential areas. The major case for Ste-Scholastique appears to be its use as an agent for regional development north of Montréal. In both instances, the passenger and aircraft movement forecasts can be regarded as over-optimistic, with the result that the sizes considered necessary for the new airports are gargantuan.

With respect to Ste-Scholastique, it is probably wise to suggest that airports are *not*, of themselves, generators of growth. They may respond to growth forces already existing in an area, but they do not create these forces. Certainly airports, if placed in a location where they can be used, create employment, but they do not necessarily have a multiplier effect on employment growth. In fact, very few industries will select a particular location just because it has an airport, and the effects of noise may well incur a negative multiplier effect. Thus, it is probably misguided to laud the construction (at great public expense) of an airport as a stimulant of economic growth, particularly when the existing airport, with one or two additions and extensions, seems quite capable of handling reasonable present and future air traffic.

Much of the early discussion concerning the need for a second airport serving Toronto and the surrounding area centred on the noise impingement of the current facility at Malton on the adjacent residential areas lying in the flight paths. The fact that the airport was located there first, and that subsequent residential development was allowed to take place in the noise-lands of the facility, is an entertaining commentary on the nature of urban location decisions. Undoubtedly, Malton airport has experienced a tremendous increase in passenger and aircraft use, but it seems likely that the increased size of aircraft will result in a decrease in the rate of increase of aircraft landings. Furthermore, the larger aircraft tend to be quieter than the "stretched DC8"-type jet, so the noise pollution is likely to diminish slightly. As Malton has the runway and physical facilities to accommodate substantially more aircraft than use it at present, it is doubtful whether a cogent case could be made for a new airport on the basis of aircraft overloading alone.

A much better case could be made on the basis of present and projected passenger congestion, which currently exists at definite peaks. The Malton terminal has been extended, and there is room for further extension. If these, and any additional facilities could be organized efficiently (Beinhaker and Elek, 1972), there would be little need for a completely new airport. The money that is allocated for a new airport could be spent far more efficiently on improving public transport access to Malton airport and streamlining the terminal system. Unfortunately, as the province has jurisdiction over surface access, and the Ministry of Transport (which wishes to spend the money) has jurisdiction over the actual airport or new airports (MacGougan, 1972), this trade-off, which would enhance the efficiency of public transportation in the urban community, is not likely to take place. In fact, in all the planning of these two new airports (Ste-Scholastique and Pickering) there were no comprehensive assessments of the urban impact of the proposed investments.

WATER TRANSPORTATION

The Great Lakes and St. Lawrence Seaway have undoubtedly had a tremendous impact on the economy of the Windsor–Québec City axis. Even the most remote portion of the axis is no more than 150 miles from this cheaper form of bulk transportation. Although the discussion will focus on the Great Lakes–St. Lawrence waterway as a cargo-carrying facility, its use as a recreational attraction should not be ignored. A good measure of the relative importance of the different ports for cargo is the docking capacity of the various harbours (Figure 7.3). Toronto and Montréal have by far the most extensive lengths of berths, followed by Québec City and Windsor. Though many of the smaller ports are in decline, the larger ports appear to be thriving. Toronto, for example, is in the process of constructing a new outer harbour two-thirds the size of its large inner harbour.

The reason for this general pattern of decline, along with growth in the largest ports, can be attributed to changes in technology associated with the opening of the St. Lawrence Seaway. The Seaway was opened in 1959, allowing vessels of twenty-six feet draft to penetrate over 1,000 miles into the heart of the continent. Freight traffic has risen from 20,000,000 tons in 1959 to 54,000,000 tons in 1973, although the rate of increase in recent years has not been very great. One of the most significant results is that the number of lake-serving vessels built to the maximum size possible to fit the locks (730′ × 75.5′ × 26′) has increased tremendously. Unfortunately, as only the ports of Québec, Trois-Rivières, Bécancour, Sorel, Montréal, Cornwall, Prescott, Toronto, Hamilton, and Port Colborne are capable of handling vessels of this size, the others have languished.

Another technological innovation, which has now risen well above the horizon into the late morning sky is containerization, which, it is estimated, cuts total shipping costs by up to 25 per cent by reducing "idle time" spent loading and unloading. Although general cargoes are less significant on the Great Lakes as compared with bulk cargoes, the trend toward containerization has only been recognized, by the construction of new facilities, at Québec, Montréal, and Toronto. It should be noted, however, that containers may well be accelerating the obsolescence of the Seaway for it is now easier to trans-ship at Halifax and other east coast ports from large vessels to railroad flat cars, thus completely by-passing the Seaway system.

In fact, the tonnage carried over the Seaway system in 1972 reversed a decline which had been experienced in the previous year. Coal shipments from U.S. ports to Canada continued a pattern of decline evident for some time, and iron ore shipments also continued to decline, although westward movements remained fairly constant. The shipment of wheat, however, reached new records owing to strong export markets, and about 25 per cent of this trade was carried directly by ocean-going vessels. If trans-shipments from lake vessels to ocean-going vessels, or from one mode of transport to another are to take place they occur primarily at Montréal, which is the head of navigation for ocean-going, medium draft vessels (twenty-six to thirty-five feet). The balance between loadings and unloadings of vessels involved in coastal (domestic) and international trade is illustrated in Figure 7.4, which indicates that Toronto and Hamilton are primarily destinations for water-borne cargo, that Montréal is almost perfectly balanced between loading and unloading, and that Québec City is hardly involved at all with loading coastal vessels.

The future of water transport

Although there will always be a considerable volume of shipping in

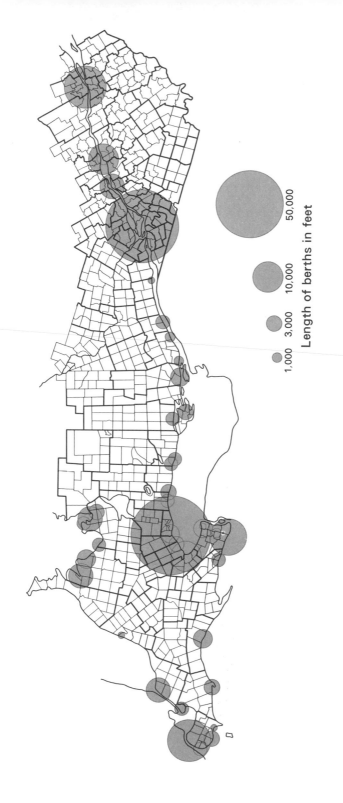

Figure 7.3: The capacity of the harbours on the Great Lakes—St. Lawrence Seaway System

Length of berths in feet

1,000   3,000   10,000   50,000

the Great Lakes–St. Lawrence Seaway system, there is little doubt that it will not be as important as once predicted. Despite the fact that a few re-enforced ships can reach Montréal and Québec throughout the year, the fact still remains that the invested capital in the Seaway lies idle for about four months every year. This has important repercussions in the financial aspects of the system; for the debt repayment is falling behind schedule. Financed jointly by Canada and the United States, it was originally planned that the construction debt would be retired in fifty years. Unfortunately, revenues have been less than expected and the debt stands at around $700 million, and it is difficult to resist comparing the size of this debt with the land bank scheme for providing homes for Canadians.

The reasons for the Seaway not being used as much as expected are many and quite complex (Carr, 1970). One basic premise upon which the project was implemented was that the impending exhaustion of the Lake Superior iron ores would result in the westward shipment of Ungava ores to the United States markets in great quantities. Although this realignment of iron ore movements has occurred to some extent, enrichment and pelletization at low cost has restored the feasibility of the Lake Superior mines, and the magnitude of the expected rise in westward traffic has not been achieved. In addition, large grain exports to the U.S.S.R. did not continue through the 1960s, and grain exports are only now beginning to boom again. A second basic premise was that the Seaway would permit the entry of a large number of ocean-going vessels directly into the Great Lakes system. Unfortunately the lock sizes and maximum drafts have not proven large enough, since the average size of ocean-going vessels is now much greater than it was twenty years ago. Thus, Montréal, Québec City, and Baie Comeau have continued as major trans-shipment points for wheat, with the lakers (shallow-draft ships built especially for the Great Lakes system) picking up backhauls of cargo at Sept-Iles.

But it must be remembered that although the Seaway has not experienced the traffic volume predicted by the planners, the entire system is an extremely viable economic alternative for low-cost, bulk goods, particularly since the true costs of the system are not passed on at present to the carriers. This viability, however, depends upon future American-Canadian relations. In fact, the story of the Seaway, so often hailed as an example of cooperation between friendly neighbours, is really a story of continuous bickering. At the moment,

Figure 7.4: The volume of loaded and unloaded cargo for coastal and
international trade in Québec City, Montréal, and Hamilton

the United States government does not allow Canadian ships to travel directly between American ports and thus compete in her domestic markets, and the Canadian government has reciprocated the ban. There are also continuous discussions concerning rates, for the American government, observing that the Seaway has not really benefited the United States as much as originally forecast, desires higher rates while the Canadian government is prepared to support lower rates and thus continue the public subsidy of the System.

Despite these arguments, the Great Lakes–St. Lawrence Seaway has had an important influence on the growth of urban areas within the axis. Waterways have always been the prime determinants of urban location within the axis, and the new improved system has contributed much to the decline of the smaller ports and growth of the few large ones. It is expected that Montréal and Toronto will continue to reap the advantages of superior facilities and huge local markets. As trans-shipment is likely to continue to be necessary, the ports at Québec City should continue to thrive, but Trois-Rivières may decline as the trans-shipment functions concentrate further downstream. This particular transport mode has, therefore, re-enforced the dominance of the largest urban areas within the axis.

RAIL TRANSPORTATION

The steel rail is the backbone of Canada, and, like any other backbone, once a nation has reached maturity it ceases to grow further. In fact, with age comes hardening, and in the Canadian case this hardening came with early maturity. Although freight traffic has experienced a slight growth during the past decade, passenger traffic has declined steadily. In fact, apart from the war years, passenger traffic has declined every year since 1920. In 1972, Canadian National Railway (CNR) freight traffic was up 7.2 per cent over 1971 and container traffic was up over one-third, whereas the number of miles travelled by passengers was down 7.8 per cent. Despite the decrease in passenger-miles, the passenger side of CNR's operation showed an increase in revenue of 3.9 per cent as a result of fare increases and the deletion of marginal services.

Passenger rail traffic within the axis

Although passenger traffic accounts for only 5.3 per cent of total CNR revenue in 1972 (CNR *Annual Report*, 1972), it continues to attract a great deal of attention. This is because the railroad would undoubtedly prefer to get out of the passenger service business, whereas the government feels obliged to attempt to maintain a level of service, even though it may be skeletal in remote areas. The conflict is heightened by the fact that the CNR is publicly owned, though acting autonomously in most areas of its operation, and is, therefore, open to pressures from the government. The Canadian Pacific Railway (CPR), on the other hand, vociferously proclaims its desire to cease passenger traffic altogether, except for its commuting services around Montréal. The Canadian Transport Commission, which hears requests for the closing of passenger services, has to assess these requests and make sure that the CPR does not leave the CNR with the unprofitable part of the business. The passenger situation is accentuated by the fact that the railroads decided many years ago that freight was more profitable and easier to handle than people, and as a consequence did little to maintain the attractiveness of their passenger services.

Figure 7.5 presents a schematic illustration of the frequency of passenger trains along CNR routes for a spring weekday in 1972. It should be noted that CPR also operates some passenger routes and that both companies are able to serve many more urban centres for freight movements. As with airline traffic, the Windsor–Toronto–Ottawa–Montréal–Québec City orientation of the population dominates the pattern of the diagram. There are minor links connecting the axis with the rest of Canada and with the United States. It is interesting that the aberrative position of Ottawa causes a major re-orientation of the flows away from a single straight line. Indeed it seems likely that if a new track is to be built for some type of advanced train, it should be built on a new track linking Toronto directly to Ottawa.

In fact, the Windsor to Québec City axis involves a very simple structure and a very simple network. The vast majority of the population and the entire area can be served by a single avenue of track connecting Windsor to Toronto, Ottawa, Montréal, and Québec City. This single avenue also connects each of these places with all the other places by the shortest route possible. The simplicity of this maximally connected axis network contrasts strongly with that required to connect completely the large cities between Chicago and the Atlantic seaboard (Figure 7.6). This simplicity could be of great advantage to interaction within the axis for it implies that a new transport system could be introduced to serve the vast bulk of the population rela-

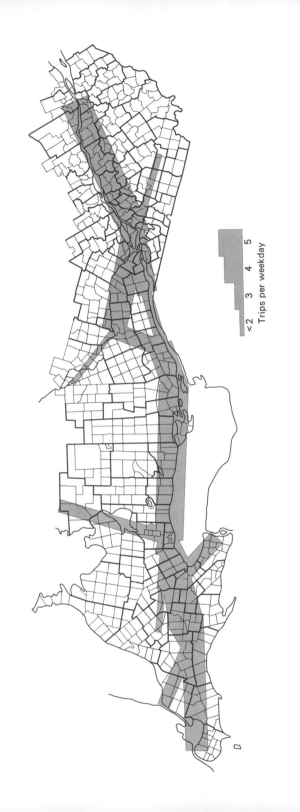

Figure 7.5: The frequency of weekday train services within the axis

Trips per weekday

<2   3   4   5

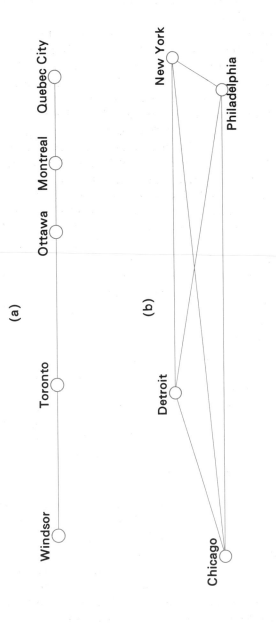

Figure 7.6: The simple maximally connected network for (a) the axis; and (b) a similar area in the United States

tively cheaply. The Montréal–Ottawa link should be built first, then the link between Ottawa and Toronto, and finally, the two extremities would be joined.

Apparently, even on perfect tracks, conventional trains are limited, by friction between the driving wheels and rails, to speeds of around 200 mph. The "Turbo" is intended to average about 90 mph on the Montréal–Toronto run, covering the 340 miles in around four hours, which compares well with the total estimated time for conventional aircraft of three hours, forty minutes. The problem is that operation at the highest speeds (200 mph) necessitates the realignment of track to eliminate curves, requires new bridges, superior signalling, and so forth, which would cost an estimate of $1.5 million per mile. In view of the magnitude of these costs, completely new systems such as tracked air-cushion vehicles, hovering above an elevated concrete track or beam, propelled by frictionless induction motors, and travelling at speeds up to 200 mph, may be quite feasible (McLaren and Myers, 1971). If speeds of this magnitude could be obtained there would be little need for STOL, or conventional air links between axis cities, and, consequently, new airports costing more than $1 billion. The repercussions on Air Canada would, however, be quite severe, as one-third of its internal revenue is generated from Montréal–Toronto traffic.

As far as the Province of Ontario is concerned, urban and interurban transportation systems appear to be an important future priority. Thus far, the improvements to the system involving rail transit have been limited to the subways running east-west and north-south in Toronto, and the GO-train system extending farther east-west along the lake front from Oakville to Pickering. Extensions either implemented or forthcoming to this system include Newmarket and Richmond Hill in the north, and Malton (and the airport), Bramalea, Brampton, and Georgetown in the west.

Running on conventional tracks, the GO-trains are clearly not as suited as rapid transit to high density applications within the core of big cities. The subway system in Montréal is being extended in conjunction with the impending 1976 Olympic Games, and a variety of new schemes are being discussed for Toronto.

The great need, as far as the axis as a whole is concerned, is to improve surface-train-type transportation between the major cities to the point where average speeds in excess of 100 mph can be maintained. This would reduce the necessity for the extensive short-haul air transportation that is currently being used, and leave the airports for the more restricted longer-haul and international traffic.

Freight transportation

Although freight provides most of the income for the railroads, it has largely been ignored in this section because it is assumed that materials will continue to be carried by this conventional means. The railroads have, of course, lost a considerable quantity of traffic to trucks, because the inauguration of the freeway system has been a tremendous boon to road haulage within the axis. But for cargoes originating in or destined for places beyond the axis the railroad is still supreme, and the rapid growth of container traffic is providing a welcome new source of business.

In fact, the growth of container traffic has been an important additional stimulus for the decentralization of freight yards from the central cities to the periphery. Though the story of the railroads in urban areas is one of almost continuous decentralization of clearing and freight yards, the container business has been of such recent and sudden development that it has accelerated this historic movement. As a result of this decentralization, the railroad companies (particularly cnr) are now concerned with relocating many of their central city facilities, and as much of this land is in effect, owned by the federal government, it can be used for urban redevelopment on a priority-use basis. In both Toronto and Montréal a large amount of lakeside land is given up to freight yards, and in both cities there are moves afoot to redevelop this land for commercial, residential, and parkland purposes. Many of the railway line rights-of-way could be used for long sinuous parklands that would provide access to open space for a large portion of the urban population. In 1972 the federal government announced plans to spend annually $10 million, rising in five years to $25 million, on relocating rail facilities in Canadian cities to their outskirts.

The general trend of these many changes that have been documented as either in progress or predicted is that the larger cities will receive the benefits, and the smaller towns will be relatively disadvantaged with respect to rail transportation. The speeding up of the passenger service would inevitably imply that the smaller centres would be by-passed, and a completely new Windsor–Toronto–Ottawa–Montréal–Québec City line would by-pass most of the smaller lakeside and river towns altogether. The concentration of external freight movements to Montréal and Toronto provides additional support for the contention that these two cities will remain the only real links between the axis and the rest of Canada and the world beyond.

ROAD TRANSPORTATION

It has been estimated that 50–85 per cent of all individual inter-city movements are made by road, of which 10–20 per cent are made by trucks. A glance at any road map reveals the extent to which the axis population relies on this means of transport, and also indicates how the population is bound to be committed to this means of travel for many decades to come. The relative volumes of traffic within the axis are illustrated in Figure 7.7, which has been compiled from a variety of reports pertaining to a period covering the late 1960s (Bérard, 1970: Ontario Department of Highways). The concentration of inter-city traffic on the major urban areas is phenomenal, and the few routes linking the axis to the outside world are also clearly distinguished.

Although the road network is the most wide-reaching of any discussed so far in this chapter, it is important to recognize that there is a variety of types and capacity of road. All four-lane roads within the axis are identified in Figure 7.8, and it is apparent that the heavily travelled routes demarcated in Figure 7.7 are these same limited-access freeways. The transportation corridor, running in almost a straight line along the length of the axis, is clearly identified by this route, with the various branch paths focusing on Toronto and Montréal. These roads have, in fact, been constructed in stages emanating from these two largest cities, and future construction will link Sarnia to London, and Ottawa to the Macdonald–Cartier Freeway. The completion of the Freeway in the late 1960s marked the beginning of a completely new era in freight and passenger transport along the entire axis. People and goods can now move with such ease and rapidity along this "strip" that it has become the prime locator and spreader of economic development from the major growth centres. It is now almost impossible for the railroad to compete against the truck for the transport of manufactured goods over a distance of less than 700 miles.

Rather than examine the entire network of paved roads *in situ*, a diagram of road density has been prepared to illustrate the varying

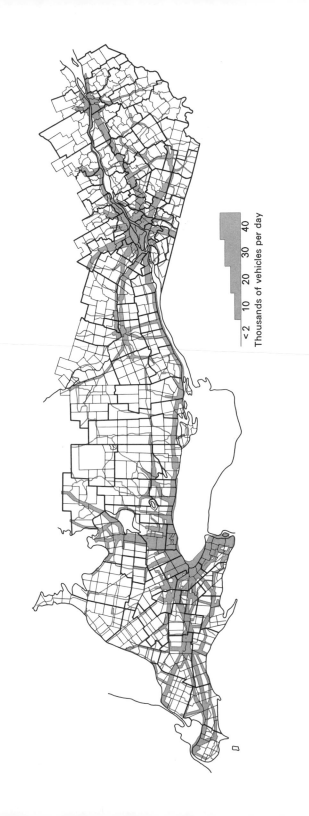

Figure 7.7: The volume of traffic on the main roads within the axis (summer average weekday traffic)

< 2   10   20   30   40

Thousands of vehicles per day

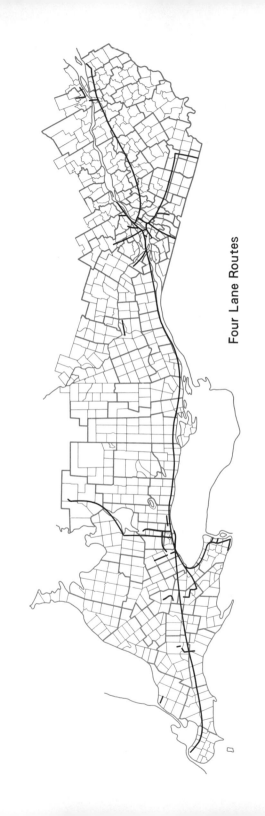

Four Lane Routes

Figure 7.8: Four-lane roads within the axis, 1971

availability of highways throughout the axis area. This diagram (Figure 7.9) is an extension of that found in Dean (1969) for Ontario, and the method used for calculating road network densities in Québec is exactly the same as that for Ontario. The array of density values is grouped into intervals ranging from "very dense" to "devoid", and the broad patterns of values are much as expected, since they tend to correspond to the population density maps. The areas of highest road network density are around the major cities, with a re-markably intensive pattern existent from Toronto through to the Niagara Peninsula. But it is significant to note that the Québec portion, while having a number of strong urban foci, does not have a hinterland density beyond Montréal similar to that found beyond Toronto and Hamilton. A large part of the central and southeastern portions of the axis are quite sparse, and the decline in density seems to occur quite rapidly with distance from the central transport cor-ridor. This corridor is distinguished almost continuously along the entire length of the axis by the lower limit of the "quite dense" category.

Bus transportation

Bus lines are in a unique position among all large public carriers as they have the most flexible route system open to them. An interesting feature of this form of travel is that the inter-city bus industry seemed to be in decline within the axis up to 1965, but since that time the gross passenger miles travelled have increased and levelled off at a higher plateau. There is now an extensive bus service covering the entire axis and embracing almost every small town and many ham-lets, but the bulk of the frequent service (Figure 7.10) follows the four-lane highways outlined in Figure 7.8 and connects the major cities and the regional centres. It is obvious that the resurrection of inter-city bus transportation is based on the greater speeds and more frequent service which is now possible on the freeways, and the availability of a large youth market arising from the post-war baby boom. The future competitiveness of the industry depends upon its retention of some of this youth market as it matures.

Truck transportation

The trucking industry has been mentioned frequently as a competitor

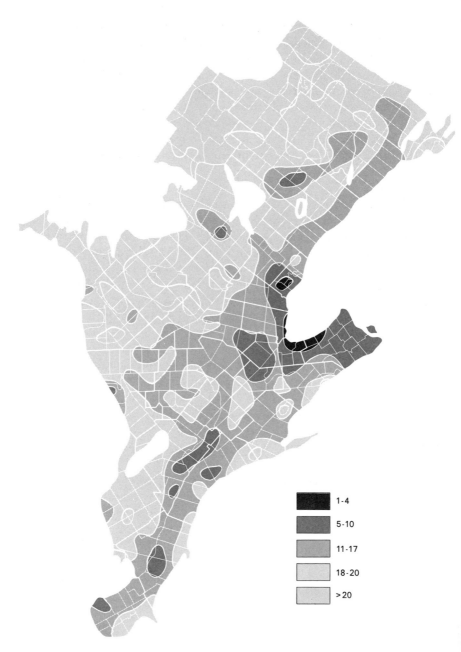

Figure 7.9: The distribution of axis road network density, late 1960s

Source: Ontario section based on Dean [1969], Plate 85.1.

Legend:
- 1-4
- 5-10
- 11-17
- 18-20
- >20

to the railroad, particularly over distances less than 700 miles. The advantage of the truck is that it offers door-to-door service, flexibility, and direct delivery. These attributes are particularly important for manufactured goods, particularly those that have a fairly high value relative to weight. Furthermore, many large firms can, in effect, purchase cheaper transport facilities by operating their own haulage business and internalizing the costs of transport. In this case a firm is, in effect, vertically integrating by providing its own distribution mechanism. These advantages would not be possible without the high-speed road network available within the axis and constructed at public expense.

The latter point is vital to remember when the free-enterprise characteristics of the industry are proclaimed as public virtues. The fact that the carriers pay road and other taxes does not detract from the fact that they are using a network built at public expense, which they themselves could not have afforded to build. This means that the trucking industry is as much subject to public control and planning as the railroad industry, which could not have been established either without government land grants and subsidies. Therefore, the freight-rate structure, regulation, and planning, of the trucking industry is as much a federal concern as the railroad industry and is recognized as such. Furthermore, in the preparation of a national transportation policy which attempts to remove the various biases that place the axis in an advantageous position *vis-à-vis* the rest of the country, and which also place the large metropolitan centres in a favoured position with respect to the smaller cities and towns, the roles of the truck and the train must be considered together.

Automobile transportation

As the most flexible and privately powerful method of personal transport yet devised, the automobile dominates travel patterns within the axis. Except, perhaps, in city centres where many automobiles can be priced out of the territory, the inhabitants of the axis can contemplate the likelihood of an even greater number of automobiles in the future than are currently in existence. In 1971, there were about 4.6 million automobiles in use by axis residents, or two cars for every five persons (men, women, and children) inhabiting the area. The number of automobiles in use increased by over 1.6 million between 1961 and 1971, which represents a rate of increase of 4.6 per cent per annum.

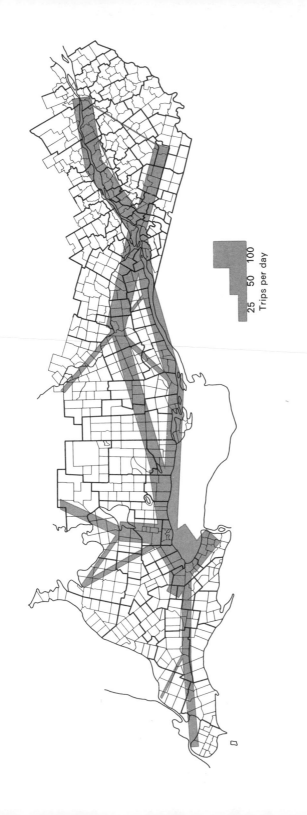

Figure 7.10: The frequency of weekday bus services between major cities within the axis

25 50 100
Trips per day

The implication is that the number of automobiles on the roads is doubling every sixteen years.

This rate of increase is in excess of the rate of increase in population in the axis during the same period. Thus, the number of automobiles is related not only to the size of the population, but to the propensity of that population to own these vehicles. A measure of this propensity is the automobile ownership ratio which can be measured as the number of persons per car. This ratio has changed from 3.3 persons per car in the axis in 1961 to 2.6 persons per car in 1971. The ratio appears to be higher in Ontario than in Québec (Figure 7.11), but the trend is for the Québec figure to approach the Ontario one as time passes. Furthermore, the overall trend is for the ratio to diminish with the passage of time. This increasing propensity to own automobiles is related not only to the increasing affluence of Canadian society, but also to the fact that they are a necessity in most urban areas where service facilities are located at some distance from each other and public transportation is inconvenient. In fact, it could be argued that the automobile is such a convenient mode of transport that it will prove hard to displace.

The question arises, therefore, as to the possibility of simply halting and perhaps reversing the trend in the ownership ratio. If the ratio for the axis only drops to 2.4 by the year 2001, the number of auto-

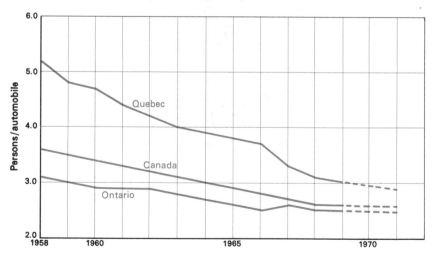

Figure 7.11: The change in automobile ownership ratios in Canada and the provinces of Ontario and Québec

mobiles owned by axis residents will be about 8,000,000, and the infrastructure, let alone fuel energy, required for this number of vehicles will demand tremendous investment in roads within urban areas as well as in automobile-serving activities. It *may* well be that the amount of capital required to provide sufficient public facilities to halt the decline in the ratio, and perhaps to raise it, will be far less than the cost of providing the necessary additional infrastructure for 8,000,000 vehicles. For example, the infrastructure required for only 7,000,000 vehicles (implying a ratio of 2.7 persons per automobile) *may* be far less than that required for 8,000,000, and the difference in capital outlay could be used to provide a more efficient and frequent public transportation service by bus in particular sections of urban areas.

COMPETITION AND COOPERATION

Throughout the preceding discussion there has been considerable mention of competition among the different modes of transport within the axis. Ironically, this is the very situation that most transport economists abhor, for the most persuasive argument is that it is cooperation among the different modes that is required, and competition within each mode. In other words competition between rail and road haulage should be replaced by cooperation, and the apparent oligopolist pricing of the road haulage firms should be replaced by true competition. The theoretical basis for the necessity for cooperation among the different modes is fairly sound, as each mode can be used most efficiently for a specific range of transport purposes.

The specificity of the uses can be couched in terms of terminal costs versus line-haul costs. The easiest way to explain the nature of these costs is to relate them to certain examples. Railways have very high terminal costs relative to their line-haul costs, because of loading, unloading, maintenance, and so forth. Conversely, road-using vehicles, such as trucks, have very low terminal costs, but relatively higher line-haul charges. The result is that the truck dominates short haul movements, and both railway and truck compete for traffic in a broad zone from about 250–700 miles, depending upon the type of freight being shipped. At a distance of less than 250 miles, within the axis and Canada, the truck is dominant, and for distances greater than 700 miles, the railway dominates. Thus, in terms of cooperation among modes, it would be wise to integrate the railway and truck into a system which would allow both to operate efficiently for the national benefit. This is particularly important for within axis flows, because nearly all inter-city freight trips within the axis are less than 700 miles in length.

This same argument can be applied to passenger transportation as well. In Figure 7.12, the theoretical frequency distribution of trip capacity by length for different modes of transport are plotted on the same graph for comparative purposes. Note that the horizontal axis calibrates a logarithmic rather than arithmetic scale. The bus covers

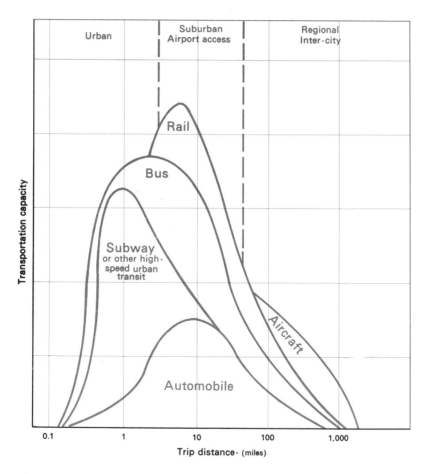

Figure 7.12: The theoretical distribution of passenger trip capacity by length of trip   Source: McLaren and Myers [1971].

the widest range of distances, followed by the automobile, rail commuter and passenger service, and subway; the aircraft is used strictly for long distances. On the basis of these distributions, it is possible to define those modes which should be integrated cooperatively into an urban transport system (subway, bus, and occasionally the automobile) for trip distances of five miles or less; those that should be involved in a "suburban" transport system involving trip distances of five to fifty miles (railroad, bus, automobile, and the subway); and an inter-city system catering for trips of fifty to 2000 miles (aircraft, rail, bus, and automobile).

PASSENGER TRAVEL BEHAVIOUR

Planning of any kind involves (or should involve) rational thought on the basis of evidence and reasonable trends. Part of the transport planning problem is that it is difficult to analyse human decision-making, and this is particularly the case in an area that is becoming as urbanized as the axis. It is for this reason that it is impossible to decide completely the modes that should be used for the different trip lengths envisaged. As an example, automobile, bus, rail, and air, are four modes of passenger transport we shall consider. An individual has to decide which mode he/she is going to use for an inter-city trip from the centre of Montréal to the centre of Toronto. For the sake of brevity, three factors are considered important by the prospective passenger and these are: cost, total time in transit, and the flexibility and convenience of the system.

Each of the various modes is ranked according to the preferences of the user, and the structure of these preferences is hypothesized to be as follows:

	Car	Bus	Train	Airplane
Cost	3	1	2	4
Time	3	4	2	1
Flexibility	1	2	3	4
Sum of ranks	7	7	7	9

The optimum choice is difficult to determine, particularly in the above case where three of the characteristics are valued equally according to the sum of the ranks. The problem is even more complex if the characteristics are valued or weighted differently. Poorer travellers may regard cost as being much more important than richer travellers, and businessmen may not consider cost important at all from their travel allowance point of view. In fact, businessmen may regard time as three to four times as important as flexibility and cost, in which case the airplane would prove to be the preferred mode of transport.

This aspect of preference and time is extremely important with respect to inter-city travel within the axis, for most of the weekday trips are for business. Time can be placed in a geographic context quite easily by assuming that a group of businessmen wish to travel from Toronto to Montréal at the lowest cost possible, with cost including travel costs as well as the value of time "lost" in the journey. This example presumes that the businessmen live at various points adjacent to entrance ramps to the 401 highway (Macdonald–Cartier Freeway), and that they have to decide, within the limits of the assumptions, whether to drive or to fly.

The cost of flying can be calculated by assessing the cost of driving to Toronto airport (at 10¢ per mile), calculating the cost of the time spent in driving (at the prevailing wage rate); finding the cost of the ticket, the time spent travelling from the airport in Montréal, and the value of the amount of time "lost" on the journey; and subtracting from this total the value of the time spent working (reading briefs, dictating letters, and so forth) on the airplane. By contrast, the cost of driving is assessed simply at 10¢ per mile from the home to Montréal, plus the cost of the working time "lost" while driving. The ctcrb (1970) report suggests that an average driving speed of sixty miles per hour from Toronto to Montréal is possible, and that a total time of flying, travelling to and from, and waiting at airports of 220 minutes is about average, with 65 minutes involved in the actual flying.

Given these times, it is quite possible to determine that businessmen who value their time at $3 per hour (the national "all worker" average rate) should fly if they live west, or within a distance of five miles east, of the airport. The various breakpoints for hourly work rates of $6, $12, are indicated in Figure 7.13. It should be noted that even in the case where time is all important, the fact that a certain amount of time has to be wasted, and the businessman can work for one hour during the flight means that the breakpoint is ninety-one miles east of the airport.

The implications of the example are quite interesting; for it indicates that the range of domination exerted by the airport increases as

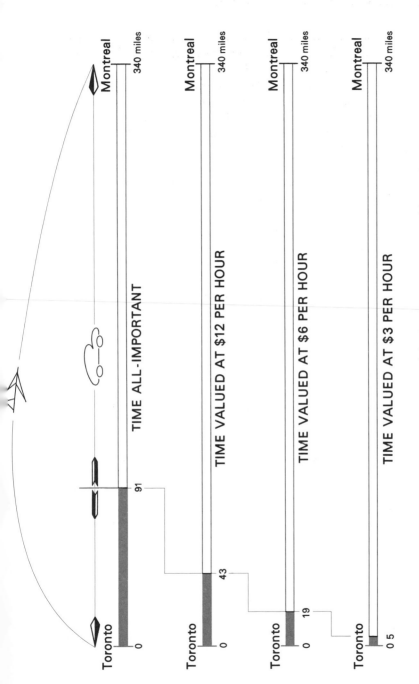

Figure 7.13: Breakpoints for travel by air or automobile between Toronto and Montréal

Toronto | Montreal
TIME ALL-IMPORTANT
0   91   340 miles

Toronto | Montreal
TIME VALUED AT $12 PER HOUR
0   43   340 miles

Toronto | Montreal
TIME VALUED AT $6 PER HOUR
0   19   340 miles

Toronto | Montreal
TIME VALUED AT $3 PER HOUR
0 5   340 miles

the value of time increases. Furthermore, if the airport terminal becomes more efficient, and the whole boarding system faster, as was originally postulated with the Rapidair service, then the range of influence of the airport would be even more extensive. But if a faster rail service or similar advanced system which could reduce the travel time were in operation, and on which the businessman could "work", then that service would be the most efficient of the three modes for the particular distances operative within the axis. It is only when one or two modes are allowed to develop services superior to others that they begin to impinge upon each other's markets. The axis is currently experiencing a situation where automobile and air transportation is impinging upon the rail market owing to the federal (and provincial) provision and maintenance of certain specific facilities (airports and freeways). The result is that air travel is frequently preferred, even though the airports experience certain peak traffic congestion which causes reverberative delays, and a colossal amount of fuel energy and capital is consumed by the desire for more cars.

INSTITUTIONAL BEHAVIOUR

The effect of institutions on the Canadian transport industry via the CTC, its forerunners, and the various provincial agencies has been immense, and is well documented in Currie (1967). The result of many of these regulations operated by these agencies has been to encourage competition between modes, rather than to foster their use in the spheres to which they are best suited. Future policy should be directed towards fostering integration or cooperation among the various modes, and to accelerate this integration where it already exists.

Probably the most outstanding example of integration among modes being fostered by a technical innovation is with containerization. In this case goods are imported and exported from the axis in containers that are moved by water, rail, and truck, and an extremely sophisticated service has been developed in a short space of time. It would, perhaps, be wise for the federal government to exert more pressure for Canadian control of the various facilities and types of companies that are involved in this new type of transportation. Canadian Pacific provides services by airplane, train, truck, and bus, so there is little reason for the CNR or some larger Crown corporation to refrain from entering the integrated transport scene. Such an integrated nationally owned service would be of vital importance to ensure efficient links between the axis and the rest of Canada, as well as overseas. Another example of cooperation, which could be developed a great deal further at the same time, is the "piggyback" service, which integrates truck and rail transport.

There is also a trend toward planned cooperation among modes within urban areas in the axis. Car parking is free at most GO-train stations, a feature which resembles the "park and ride" situation found in conjunction with the commuter rail service of many American and European cities. A short step from the "park and ride" situation is the attempted removal of the parked car altogether, either by a fixed route or "Dial-a-bus" system that focuses on the commuter station. This type of service needs to be subsidized in most urban areas, but the subsidy may be offset by the public saving involved in the removal of the "need" for a second car. A future development that cannot be ignored is the introduction of planned mixed-mode corridors within large urban areas, such as limited access expressways with rapid transit occupying the median strip.

This idea of mixed-mode corridors is being extended by planners to regional and inter-city transport systems. In a sense, of course, the axis has already had a mixed-mode system for some time, for the lake, major roads, and chief rail lines coincide in the same geographic territory. In fact, it is the juxtaposition of these different modal routes that results in the axis being a transport corridor. Future developments, however, require that this juxtaposition be more than a geographic accident, for the use of the different modes should be planned so that the weaknesses and inefficiencies of one mode are offset by another. This would involve some re-routing, renovation, and price inducements, but it is vital to the future integration of transport modes within the axis.

One of the first problems encountered by any young boy is that of the too-small hockey skates: one year's skates rarely fit the following year. This immediately raises two problems: structure and finance. The structural problem is that he cannot force his feet into the old boots, and the financial problem is that he needs some extra cash to go down to the skate-exchange to obtain a larger pair. Furthermore, some additional cash is required to maintain the larger pair and make repairs. Urban areas within the axis have similar problems arising from growth, though it could be wished that they were as simple to solve. Urban areas are collections of people who reside together within a community which has to be managed. The management of this entity requires money, and even if the urban area is relatively small and grows slowly, the amount of cash required to provide and maintain roads, sewers, local police, parks and so forth, is quite large.

It is very easy for the inhabitants of the axis to appreciate that the urban areas in which they reside require more money. It is also easy to appreciate, in these days of inflation and rapid urban growth, that the urban areas would require more money and claim to be short of the amounts considered necessary. After all, some elements of the "fiscal squeeze" are present in all homes, so it is not too difficult to extend an understanding of these problems to the urban scene. It is apparently rather more difficult to comprehend the repeated concern expressed by provincial government ministers and bureaucrats over the structure of local government (BMR, 1972). This difficulty is evidenced by the fact that any announcement and implementation of changes in local government structure usually come rather early in a government's term of office, and are invariably ignored or shelved when an election is in the offing. This is not only because it is difficult for the voting public to appreciate the need for changes in the structure of local government, but also because such changes disrupt the *status quo*, and no one dislikes the *status quo* being disrupted more than local politicians.

STRUCTURE

Laymen knowledgeable in the literature of Canadian local government (Crawford, 1954; Lajoie, 1968; Feldman and Goldrick, 1969; Tessier, 1971) will recognize that the following dissertation adds a few pages to an already voluminous and opinionated mass. This cannot be helped, for one of the basic macro-urban problems of the axis does involve the proliferation and operation of local governments serving this urban population. The British North America Act, which comes under the care and jurisdiction of the British parliament in Westminster, does not recognize or establish the municipalities as legal entities. What it does do is grant to the provincial governments the responsibility for urban areas. Thus the provincial governments can, theoretically, take away local government privileges from a municipality, but they are not likely to do so, because it is politically more difficult to rescind than to grant. They can, however, make unilateral decisions with respect to local structure and rescind certain powers where it is in the public interest to do so.

This entrenchment in the B.N.A. Act of provincial control over the municipalities is extremely important as far as the axis is concerned. Even though it has been demonstrated that the axis is a functioning entity which serves as the nucleus for the rest of the country, and is the primary generator of economic activity, its urban areas are under the jurisdiction of two provincial governments. Thus, the urban areas, which have experienced rapid growth because of their position and importance with respect to the nation as a whole, are not in the legal position of national constructs, but are subject to the whims of provincial pressures. Even though the government of a particular urban area may perceive a problem as its personal concern, in some cases (such as that of tax-exempt land) there is very little that it can do to resolve the issue unless the provincial government sees fit to deal with the problem specifically. This it is not likely to do unless the benefits can be accrued by a larger constituency.

Though most of the municipalities within the axis came into being after Confederation, quite a number had been established prior to

1867. The first municipalities were incorporated by special acts, or charters, of the legislatures, but it soon became apparent that general enacting legislation was required to provide for the erection of various types of municipal units (cities, towns, villages, townships, etc.) when they were necessary. Each of these levels of municipal units would have specific powers and responsibilities, as well as methods of obtaining and receiving revenue. The first general enacting legislation was developed in Upper Canada in 1849; it is known as the Municipal Act, or Baldwin Act, after its sponsor. Even though this Act has been much amended, it is still the basic legislation governing the operation of municipalities within the Province of Ontario, and has been copied by most of the other provinces.

In Québec the first statutory provision for municipalities was the Municipal Code, enacted in 1871; though modified periodically, it is still the founding legislation for most municipalities in the province (Ministère des Affaires Municipales, 1968–69). It makes provision for two kinds of municipalities, the county municipality and the local municipality. In essence, the county municipalities have control of all powers given them by the Municipal Code in the territories that are beyond the legal limits of the local municipalities. These territories include village, parish, and canton municipalities, all of which require certain population minimums to be formed. The services entrusted to the county and local municipalities involve road construction and maintenance, water provision, fire and police protection; to pay for these, and other services, they may levy property taxes and service charges. Far fewer municipalities – but 40 per cent of the population – are within urban areas established under the Law of Cities and Towns, which dates from 1876, and was modified considerably in 1903 and 1922. This is basically a size law, which says that local municipalities reaching a population of 2,000 can become a town, and those reaching 6,000 can become a city. The distinction between a city and town is purely academic, because both are vested with the same powers, which are of much wider scope than those vested to municipalities by the Municipal Code. Nearly all the urban areas within the axis have been established by or placed within the limits of general enacting legislation, except for Montréal, Québec City, and Toronto, which are still operated under special charters.

There are, however, certain important differences between the general enacting legislation developed in Ontario and that developed in Québec. In Ontario, there is a greater number of services and activities which are operated by special bodies rather than by the municipal councils. Activities in Ontario which are more frequently administered by special bodies are police, education, public libraries, parks, public health, conservation, and community planning. Of course, during the passage of time, the larger urban areas have drawn many of these functions to their own jurisdiction. In Québec there are also special bodies, but not nearly as many as there are in Ontario, because most of the functions they would carry out are allocated to the municipalities through the general enacting legislation.

The reasons for the creation of these special bodies are not exactly clear, but they appear to have been developed in response to ideas about municipal government that were popular in the United States during the late nineteenth century (Plunkett, 1973). The general principle was that of separation of powers in order to keep certain activities out of the political arena. For example, it was felt that education should not be a political concern over which the philosophy of a particular party would prevail. Rather, education should be apolitical, and the persons interested in education *per se* should be able to run for election without having to subscribe to a particular political philosophy, or be interested in a broad spectrum of municipal affairs. This theory was applied to a variety of services; subsequently, in Ontario a large number of special bodies in different parts of the province have developed.

The B.N.A. Act ignored the municipalities because, at that time, they were not considered important, and they were already under the jurisdiction of the legislative councils of Upper and Lower Canada. Right through to the present century, the urban areas in the axis were relatively small, clearly separated from one another, and exhibiting definite urban-rural relations rather than urban-to-urban relationships. In 1871 only 10 per cent of the population of the axis resided in municipalities of 10,000 or more people, and even by 1941, this proportion had reached only 55 per cent. But by 1971, over 82 per cent of the population of the axis lived in urban areas containing more than 10,000 people, and the demands placed upon municipal governments by the urban population had increased at an even greater rate than the rate of urbanization. With this accelerated urbanization came the realization that the municipal fragmentation that had developed was inefficient and incapable of serving the needs of the public.

NUMERICAL FRAGMENTATION

Fragmentation can be viewed in two ways: numerically and spatially. The estimated numerical extent of fragmentation at the local government level within the axis is indicated in Table 8.1. The numbers within this table must be viewed as estimates but the errors vary according to the different sources used. The counts of municipalities and school boards are regarded as reasonably accurate, since they are based on actual listings prepared by the Department of Municipal Affairs in the two provinces. The number of other special purpose bodies is quite accurate for Ontario, for it is based on estimates by Clasky (1970) for Ontario as a whole with Northern Ontario excluded. But for Québec, the number of other special purpose bodies is, quite frankly, a guess, which is subject to an error of about 200 on either side. This guess is based on counts from many different listings which do not agree, and the differences cannot be resolved by any local experts.

The sheer difficulty of obtaining completely accurate estimates of the number of local government units is itself, rather instructive. Imagine the dilemma of the educated citizen trying to find out which body is responsible for what in his/her local area! In fact, experience indicates that elected officials and local government employees themselves are frequently uncertain of the hierarchy of responsibility and range of jurisdiction of the multitude of councils and boards claiming to have an interest in an urban region. Furthermore, the estimates in Table 8.1 indicate that the number of local government units within the axis has not decreased very much between 1961 and 1972. The decreases that have occurred have been the result of the amalgamation of school boards to a county basis in Ontario, and a large number of fusions of school areas in Québec. In fact, the total reduction in number of school boards in the axis accounts for all but 120 of the total decreases in the various types of local government units in the ten-year period.

One of the more interesting features of local government units is that they seem to exist regardless of the size of the population served. This is particularly true in the case of the 1,827 municipalities that existed within the axis area in 1972. When we compare provincial figures, it appears that though the average area of a municipality in the Québec portion of the axis is quite similar to the average area in the Ontario portion, the average population served by these munici-

Table 8.1: The extent of the geographical and administrative fragmentation of local government within the axis, 1961 and 1972

	ONTARIO PORTION OF THE AXIS		QUÉBEC PORTION OF THE AXIS		AXIS AS A WHOLE	
	1961	1972	1961	1972	1961	1972
Municipalities and townships						
less than 2,000	357	376	228	234	585	610
greater than 2,000	380	324	983	893	1,363	1,217
School boards	2,772	140	1,275	780	4,047	920
Estimated other special purpose bodies	2,900	2,900	500	500	3,400	3,400
Total estimated number of locally governing bodies	6,409	3,740	2,986	2,407	9,395	6,147

palities is quite different. In the Ontario portion, the average population is very nearly 10,000, whereas in the Québec portion the average is half this figure. This difference, of course, emphasizes the more urban nature of southern Ontario as compared with southern Québec. But, these averages do not illustrate the extremely skewed distribution of population among the municipalities. Although the average population size of a municipality within the axis in 1972 is about 6,500, only one-eighth of the municipalities have a population greater than this, and, as can be discerned from Table 8.1, almost two-thirds have a population of less than 2,000. Though the need for numerous administrative structures may be accepted for the more populous parts of the axis, there is obviously a tremendous proliferation and duplication of effort in the less populated areas.

The abundance of special-body governments

Apart from the vast number of small municipalities, the aspect of Table 8.1 that staggers the mind is the incredible number of special purpose bodies. Even given the large error margin in the estimate, it is apparent that about two-thirds of all the local government bodies within the axis fall into this category. As most people are unsure of the range of activities embraced by these bodies, it is, perhaps, advisable to examine the special-body structure of one urban area. The example chosen is Metropolitan Toronto, since the structure of government within this urban area has been extremely well documented for the year 1968 (BMR, 1968). (Toronto, along with Montréal, has appeared all too frequently in this volume, but there is a relative abundance of well-researched information and published reports available pertaining to these areas in contrast to others within the axis.)

Metro Toronto is a good example for this particular sub-section, because there are very few municipal governments within its area. There are six municipal councils serving a population that is only a little less than that served by thirty municipalities on Ile-de-Montréal. These six municipalities (the City of Toronto, East York, Etobicoke, North York, Scarborough, and York) have been combined by statute of the provincial government into what is, in effect, a federation. Certain activities of importance to the metropolitan area as a whole are administered by the Metro Toronto Council, which contains representatives from each of the six municipalities. There are,

therefore, special purpose bodies that relate not only to the six municipalities, but to Metro Toronto as well.

These special-body governments have been classified by the Bureau
of Municipal Research (BMR, 1968) into six categories based on the
functional orientation of the board or commission. The classification
of each of these bodies is indicated by the appropriate symbol in
Table 8.2. In total it can be observed that in 1968 there were ninety-

*Table 8.2: Special-body governments by municipality in Metro Toronto
and its area municipalities, 1968*

Metropolitan Toronto
1. Toronto Transit Commission (E) 5
2. Canadian National Exhibition Association (E) 43
3. Metropolitan Toronto School Board* (S) 18
4. Metropolitan Toronto Separate School Board (S) 19
5. Metropolitan Toronto Retarded Children's Education Authority (S) 6
6. Metropolitan Toronto Library Board* (S) 9
7. Metropolitan Toronto and Region Conservation Authority (S) 55
8. Toronto and York Roads Commission (S) 5
9. Metropolitan Toronto Children's Aid Society (S) 35
10. Catholic Children's Aid Society of Metropolitan Toronto (S) 27
11. Metropolitan Toronto Planning Board* (R) 28
12. Courts of Revision, The Municipality of Metropolitan Toronto (R) 16
13. Metropolitan Toronto Licensing Commission (R) 3
14. Metropolitan Board of Commissioners of Police (R) 5
15. Metropolitan Toronto Housing Company Limited (M) 7
16. Civic Garden Centre Board of Management (M) 18
17. Board of Management of the O'Keefe Centre (M) 7
18. Metropolitan Toronto Industrial Commission (P) 18
19. Convention and Tourist Bureau of Metropolitan Toronto (P) 42

City of Toronto
20. Electric Commissioners (E) 3
21. Parking Authority (E) 3
22. Housing Authority (E) 5
23. City of Toronto Limited Dividend Housing Corporation (E) 5
24. Toronto Harbour Commissioners (E) 5
25. Board of Health (S) 6
26. Public Library Board* (S) 9

Table 8.2: (continued)

27. Board of Education* (S) 20
28. Planning Board* (R) 14
29. Committee of Adjustment (R) 4
30. Housing Standards Appeal Committee (R) 6
31. Historical Board (M) 17
32. Runnymede Hospital Board of Directors (M) 18
33. George Bell Arena Board of Management (M) 7
34. Ted Reeve Arena Board of Management (M) 7
35. Stanley Park Stadium Property Board of Management (M) 7
36. North Toronto Memorial Arena Board of Management (M) 7
37. University Settlement Recreation Centre Board of Management (M) 7
38. Good Neighbors Club Board of Management (M) 7
39. Redevelopment Advisory Council (A) 24

Borough of North York
20. Hydro-Electric Commission (E) 3
21. Board of Health (S) 7
22. Public Library Board* (S) 9
23. Board of Education* (S) 12
24. Planning Board* (R) 11
25. Committee of Adjustment (R) 5
26. Community Centres Board of Managers (M) 4
27. Memorial Community Hall Board of Management (M) 7

Borough of East York
20. Hydro Commission (E) 3
21. Board of Health (S) 7
22. Public Library Board* (S) 9
23. Board of Education* (S) 10
24. Planning Board* (R) 9
25. Committee of Adjustment (R) 5
26. Cedar Vale Park Board (M) 7
27. Sports Centre Board (M) 7
28. Community Centre Board (M) 7
29. Trace Manes Park Board (M) 7
30. Todmorden Mills Park Board (M) 8
31. Leaside Memorial Community Gardens Board (M) 7
32. Arts Board (A) 7
33. Historical Committee (A) 25
34. Recreation Committee (A) 25
35. East York Foundation (A) 7

36. Safety Council (A) 15
37. Parking Advisory Committee (A) 7

Borough of Scarborough
20. Public Utilities Commission (E) 3
21. Board of Health (S) 7
22. Public Library Board* (S) 9
23. Board of Education* (S) 12
24. Planning Board* (R) 9
25. Committee of Adjustment (R) 5
26. Recreation and Parks Commission (M) 9

Borough of Etobicoke
20. Hydro Commission (E) 3
21. Board of Health (S) 9
22. Public Library Board* (S) 10
23. Board of Education* (S) 12
24. Combined Roman Catholic Separate School Board (S) 5
25. Planning Board* (R) 11
26. Committee of Adjustment (R) 5
27. Community Centres Board (M) 7
28. Cemetery Board (M) 2
29. Historical Board (A) 6
30. Safety Council (A) 23

Borough of York
20. York Township Housing Company Limited (E) 7
21. Parking Authority (E) 3
22. Board of Health (S) 5
23. Public Library Board* (S) 4
24. Board of Education* (S) 10
25. Planning Board* (R) 9
26. Committee of Adjustment (R) 5
27. Community Centres Board (M) 7
28. N. McEachren Community Centre Board (M) 7
29. Historical Committee (A) 24
30. Safety Council (A) 23

---

* Indicates part of a two-tier structure

Note: Letter in parentheses indicates classification of agency. Figure following parenthesis indicates number of members of agency's policy-making body, including *ex-officio* members, and, in the case of boards of education, two separate school representatives (three on the Metro school board) who vote on secondary school matters. The number of members of some bodies, especially in the advisory category, will vary from time to time. Metro Toronto special bodies are listed by their full title, while those in area municipalities are abbreviated where no confusion thus arises.

Source: BMR (1968), pp. 10–11.

four special-body governments in the Metro Toronto area in addition to the six municipalities and federated council. Twenty-seven of these are concerned with providing *Services* (s), and are dependent upon tax revenues obtained by requisition or request from the municipal or Metro councils. In this category are the various Metro and municipal school boards, libraries, health services, and the road commission. The next most frequently occurring group are the twenty-four bodies concerned with *Management* (m). They usually involve boards managing a particular facility, such as a park, arena, hospital, cemetery, or community centre. They also obtain funds from tax revenues raised by the local or Metro council.

Probably the best known type of special-body governments are those concerned with *Regulation* (r), of which there are seventeen in the metropolitan area. These include planning, licensing, policing, tax adjustment, and housing standards, and are all dependent upon the various councils for funds. Also fairly well known are the agencies which provide a good or service in the structure of a *Business Enterprise* (e). These agencies are usually self-sufficient as they raise their revenues from user-charges levied for the good or service being offered; they can, therefore, operate fairly independently from the councils. They include public utilities such as electricity, as well as parking, and frequently they own a large amount of capital in the form of buildings and equipment, and employ a large staff.

Finally, there are two groups of bodies that are not very large consumers of tax revenue. The metropolitan area contains eleven authorities concerned with *Advising* (a) the local councils on matters concerning the arts, local history and historical buildings, and redevelopment; while the two bodies involved with *Promotion* (p) are creatures of the Metro council. In 1968, there were 1,012 board members serving on these ninety-four special bodies, and many received a salary or compensatory fee for their involvement. Some of the bodies operate a very large business, such as the Toronto Transit Commission, the Port of Toronto, the School Boards, Boards of Health, and Police Departments, and employment within some of these bodies increased at a very high rate during the 1960s. In fact, local government was one of the big growth industries during this period, and it is likely to remain so in the future.

The advantages and disadvantages
of special-body proliferation

The excellent report by the BMR (1968) on the 101 governments of

Metropolitan Toronto contains a good discussion of the problems arising from special-body proliferation. Considerations relating to public awareness, control, and efficiency are the most important. There seems little doubt that, in general, the public is simply not aware of the number of different units of local government which influence their lives. Evidence of this lack of awareness is seen in the very low voter turnout in elections for representatives to those boards that require such democratic procedures. The situation is quite serious, because the operation of the bodies then falls into the hands of those who perceive it as being of direct interest to them and their economic activity. As a result, many of the boards are dominated by financial, insurance, and real-estate interests (Lorimer, 1972), which view such representation as important for business protection as well as public relations.

This limited public awareness goes far to explain the rather poor degree of public control that is often exercised over what are, after all, public bodies. As public bodies they should be concerned primarily with the public interest, and they should ensure that this interest is served and that the avenues for interaction between the governed and the government are visible and clear. One of the methods for achieving this interaction is, theoretically, the large number of citizens who are appointed or elected to the special bodies. Unfortunately, because of the number of *ex officio* members, duplication of appointments, and duplication of business interests represented on the boards or commissions, the degree of public control is much less than it appears. The result is that the majority of the community is not represented, and furthermore, is totally ignorant of the fact that it is not represented. In fact, it would appear that the operating dictum of much of the local government is: what the public doesn't know it can't worry about.

Efficiency, as any worker knows, is a very difficult concept to measure. There are obviously certain advantages to be gained by having a specific body concerned with the provision of a particular function. But this judgement is rendered only from the point of view of the provision of the service, and not from the viewpoint of those receiving the service. In gross terms, the receiver is the urban area as a whole, and it is probably now well-understood by most students of the urban scene that an urban area is an interactive system. Thus, the actions of one special body have implications for other units of local government, and the successful execution of a particular program in one part of the city requires the cooperation of many different government units. All too often it appears that cooperation is lacking or difficult to arrange and that the individual bodies have little appreciation of the effect of their decisions on other units within the urban structure. For example, the seemingly simple extension of sewer and water lines has many ramifications: new housing developments follow, which means there will be a new concentration of young families, which means there will be a demand for new schools, which will have to be built by school boards, or buses will have to be provided to transport children to existing ones. A sewer is easy to plan for and construct, but the economic and social restructuring that results is appallingly complex. It is evident, therefore, that the excessive proliferation of special government bodies can lead to real inefficiencies from the point of view of the urban area as a whole.

GEOGRAPHIC FRAGMENTATION

The great majority of the 6,000 local government units existing within the axis relate to a geographic area, though a large number of special bodies are concerned with the operation of a particular concern, such as a building or arena. The axis can be viewed as a mosaic of small government territories, with the different units of government often superimposed across one or a number of others. Probably the most clearly defined are the more than 1,800 municipalities and townships which divide the axis into a web of independent councils and local administrations. In order to illustrate the extent of fragmentation, Figure 8.1 has been prepared, showing the number of census subdivisions within the axis in 1966; for in the vast majority of cases, these subdivisions coincide with townships, and in many instances in Québec, and in a few in Ontario, they coincide with municipalities. A large number of municipalities are also included, but a diagram indicating all the municipalities and townships would be an even more chaotic mass of blobs and lines.

In most cases the special-body governments are confined in areas of jurisdiction to the municipalities in which they are located. Thus, for example, the Board of Health in the City of Toronto has jurisdiction over matters relating to health within the city, while the Board of Health for the Borough of East York has jurisdiction over its territory. There are, however, some cases where special bodies have jurisdiction over much larger areas, and probably the best example of this is the county school board structure in the province of Ontario.

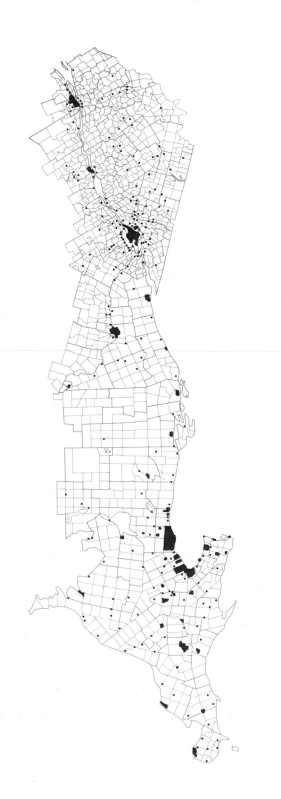

Figure 8.1: The profusion of county, township (rural municipalities and cantons), and municipal units of local government

While the decision to rationalize the 2,772 school boards that existed in 1961 into larger units was extremely sensible, it is doubtful whether the historic and antiquated counties were the most appropriate geographic level. There is still an enormous difference in the populations served by the various school boards, and a tremendous variety of interests which have to be served. It is apparent that many school boards find it difficult to cater to the large populations and variety of interests, and it is for this reason, as well as other reasons, that the most urbanized areas, such as Metro Toronto, have to work with a two-tier school board system.

Fragmentation within urban regions

The tremendous geographic complexity of the numerous municipalities in one integrated urban region is probably best exemplified by the municipal jig-saw within the urban agglomeration surrounding Québec City. The thirty-six municipalities indicated in Figure 8.2 embrace an area of about 360 square miles and contain over 400,000 people. The general pattern of growth and current locus of major employment opportunities suggest that this is a multi-nodal region; the portion of Québec City adjacent to the waterfront serves as the principal focus, and Ste-Foy and Charlesbourg on the north bank and Lévis–Lauzon and St-Romuald on the south bank form secondary poles of attraction (Lord, 1972). The growth of the urban region has followed a definite concentric pattern out of the historic core of Québec City, so that the general age distribution of the population and transportation demands follows predictable patterns. The result is that the fairly simple metropolitan economy is confounded by an incredibly complex set of municipal islands all of which have interests in common, but which attempt to tackle them (for the most part) in isolation (Quesnel-Ouellet, 1972).

The situation depicted for the Québec urban region illustrates the major problems of geographic fragmentation which exist in all the major urban regions within the axis. In these areas the municipal boundaries do not represent the life patterns of the residents of the area. The people live in one municipality, work in another, and quite probably seek their recreation in a third. Thus, the urban living space does not relate to the administrative space, and this disparity raises difficulties of taxation, policing, education, and transportation (both public and private). As the municipalities grow and run into one another the political boundaries create artificial barriers to the efficient provision of all kinds of services, not least of which are sewage and water. Also, in fragmented urban regions there are always larger, wealthier, and more populated municipalities, which seek and obtain the most attractive provincial, federal, and industrial investments, leaving the poorer municipalities to house the lower income families and the noisier and dirtier industries.

Figure 8.2: The urban agglomeration of Québec City

REDUCING FRAGMENTATION

The extensive numerical and geographic fragmentation of local government documented in the previous section is, of itself, a powerful argument for reform, but the argument becomes even more overwhelming if the changing rôle of these governments is taken into account. The traditional position of local government — enshrined within the service delivery nature of its administrative structures as well as within its supposedly apolitical stance — is that its major concern is with the operation of a physical plant. The operation of the vast majority of local government units within the axis still reflects this viewpoint, even though many local governments have gradually expanded their rôles during the last thirty years. In effect, the governmental units have been forced by the demands of society to enlarge their spheres of interest from the mere servicing, extension, and maintenance of roads, sewers, water systems, and so forth, to a range of community social and welfare services including parks, recreation facilities, youth programs, and community planning.

The decision-making concerning these additional services has, for the most part, been undertaken within the traditional "city father" administrative structure of municipal government. Because of its inherent autocratic nature, such a government structure is unable to cope realistically with its new responsibilities. To do so successfully requires a resolution of a variety of issues involving business (corporate and private) ethics, conflicting values, and community goals. These issues cannot be discussed and resolved within an autocratic apolitical structure, for they demand debate of a democratic political nature (Plunkett, 1973). Furthermore, as these issues are interactive and common to integrated urban areas which, in some cases, embrace a large number of municipalities, it is evident that the political resolution must take place within the arena of the functional urban region. The rapid growth of many urban areas during the past two decades has now made this reorganization even more imperative. The pressures created by matters such as housing shortages, escalating prices of urban land, the provision of public transportation, and the assimilation of immigrants to city life, have served to compound the difficulties of many local governments, which are now clearly out of phase with the urban socio-economic climate prevailing within the axis.

There is, therefore, a pressing need to reduce the extent of local government fragmentation. Ideally, such a restructuring should drastically reduce the number of special-body agencies or commissions, provide an adequate demand-based financial system, and raise the general level of political responsiveness. These can be regarded as the three basic criteria on which any program for reorganization is judged. But before embarking upon a review of the restructuring that is taking place within the axis, it must be noted that such reorganization, though vitally necessary "from the bottom up", is also necessary "from the top down". The urban impact of all major locational and economic decisions taken by the federal and provincial governments should be assessed within a national context. This is obvious from the mass of documentary evidence produced in the preceding chapters that emphasizes the vital importance of the urban areas within the axis to the social and economic life of the nation as a whole. For example, at the federal level, it is counter-productive for the Department of Regional Economic Expansion, the Ministry of Transport, and the Central Mortgage and Housing Corporation to make isolated decisions that affect the growth and form of urban areas. The most sensible form of organization would be for a federal Ministry to have the power to coordinate and plan (with the provinces) all matters of a federal government nature affecting a broad urban region such as the Windsor–Québec City axis.

FORMING LARGER UNITS

The case for forming larger units of local government has been well recognized for a number of years and consolidations of various kinds have occurred throughout the axis. There are two basic concerns with any consolidation procedure; one is the way in which the consolidation is to take place, the other is the re-allocation of functions performed by the government units. It is the interplay of these two concerns which distinguishes the various methods of consolidation that have taken place in the past and are being attempted in the future.

The functional allocation problem is particularly important, since it involves considerations of an economic and non-economic nature. In economic terms, there are some services that are provided more cheaply than others if they are produced on a larger scale. For example, water filtration and purification systems are much more cost-efficient if they are built with a large capacity rather than a small one. In this particular case, other than fluoridation, there are very few concerns of a non-economic nature that matter, so it would be appropriate to allow the size of plant and its service area to be determined purely on the basis of minimizing costs. On the other hand, there are other services that can be provided reasonably efficiently for smaller aggregations of people, and in which non-economic concerns are of vital importance. Examples of this type of function are recreational services (parks and skating rinks), and neighbourhood planning (as distinct from general regional planning). In these cases, even though smaller units may result in a sluggish administrative procedure, the necessity for community involvement outweighs any other consideration.

Methods of amalgamation

There are at least four different methods which have been used in the past for the consolidation of municipalities within the axis. These methods, and the legal procedures involved, are constituted under laws of the provinces of Québec and Ontario. Thus, though the discussion of the various methods of amalgamation will be presented in general terms pertaining to the entire axis, it is well to recognize that they are governed by two entirely different sets of laws. The methods of consolidation to be considered include annexation, fusions, new special bodies, and federation.

Annexation

Growing municipalities frequently run out of space for new housing, industrial land, recreational services, and so forth. One of the most common methods of acquiring needed space in all parts of the axis is annexation, and an instructive, detailed description of the procedure used in Sarnia is given by Nixon and Campbell (1971). Typically, the annexation procedure involves the absorption by a growing central city of the rural territory in the township or parish immediately adjacent to it. Though the procedures vary slightly between Québec and Ontario, an important feature in common is that the annexations have to be approved by a review body established by the provincial governments. Although annexation is usually initiated by a larger central city, it can also be initiated by a community that wishes to be annexed. The various provincial bodies which rule on the case have the power to decide not only whether the annexation should occur, but whether enough or too much land is involved.

Between 1961 and 1971 there were over 300 annexations within the axis area, of which 194 were in the Québec portion and 130 in the Ontario portion. The vast majority were annexations of a small piece of land in a township or parish to a town or city; the number of persons involved was small. But, in a few instances the area annexed was quite large (over 1,000 acres), and occasionally more than 1,000 persons were involved. The net product of a number of annexations to a particular city over a long period of time can be quite dramatic. In Table 8.3 there are details of the amount of land gained by annexation over a period of two decades for a selected sample of cities. The increases have been extremely variable, depending upon the growth rate of the individual central city and the amount of surrounding land available.

Although annexation has proved to be extremely useful, it cannot be regarded as the best mechanism for solving the problems of fragmentation within the axis. Frequently a residual territory, usually part of a township, is left behind, which may well have lost a major part of its residential assessment. This residual territory still needs to be governed, even though it is emasculated and waiting for further encroachment. Annexation by a rapidly expanding central city is, at

Table 8.3: The enlargement of selected cities within the axis, mid-1940s to mid-1960s

| MUNICIPALITY | TOTAL ACREAGE | | INCREASE IN ACREAGE |
	1945	1966	
Barrie	2,150	4,781	2,631
Brockville	1,374	6,024	4,650
Grand'Mère	2,226	2,227	1
Hamilton	10,316	31,725	21,409
Peterborough	3,568	10,326	6,758
Sherbrooke	4,516	12,921	8,405
Sorel	2,003	2,400	397
St-Hyacinthe	1,170	4,205	3,035
Stratford	2,835	3,263	428
Valleyfield	1,158	4,204	3,046
Windsor	8,251	31,584	23,333

Sources: Report of the Ontario Committee on Taxation, p. 498; *Statistiques Municipales,* various years.

best, only a stop-gap measure; within time the shortage of space problem is bound to re-emerge. In some parts of the axis further annexation is impossible: cities and towns are already adjacent to each other, with common boundaries and common problems. There is little possibility of annexation in these cases, because no large urban area really likes to be annexed by another. In fact, the resentment which frequently exists, even if it is not expressed in the public hearing preceding the annexation order, is often intense.

Fusions

Because annexations do not necessarily result in fewer local government units, a law has been passed in Québec allowing the voluntary fusion of two or more contiguous municipalities. The objective of the program, as announced in 1964, is a drastic reduction in the number of small municipalities (less than 2,000 population) through direct amalgamation. The law is basically permissive, for fusions can occur if two or more municipalities voluntarily agree to combine their territories into one unit of local government. Once an agreement has been reached, the municipalities send their request to the Ministère des Affaires Municipales, where the request is approved by ministerial decree.

In general, the program has not been terribly successful. The number of small municipalities within the axis in Québec has been reduced by less than one hundred between 1961 and 1971, and a number of these reductions occurred through annexation. The number of fusions may, however, be on the increase, as seven were ratified in 1972, and well over thirty requests were in preparation. The fusions are usually of a village with its surrounding parish (such as Ville de St-Eustache with the parish of St-Eustache), and, as such, they still produce fairly small units of local government. It appears that it takes a fair amount of encouragement for local councils voluntarily to initiate and agree to direct amalgamation.

New special-purpose bodies

The many problems arising from an excessive geographic fragmentation of local government units can be approached from two points of view. There are certain problems which, to all intents and purposes, are of more direct interest to the local units themselves. These problems invariably relate to the lack of economies of scale; they can be overcome by providing services for larger units. Thus, many municipalities wish to amalgamate for the purpose of providing certain specific services, such as sewage and waste disposal, conservation, libraries, water purification, planning, and even airports, even though they do not wish to combine their respective governments completely. To cater to this wish, the provincial governments have amended the various bodies of general enacting legislation to allow local governments to establish special-purpose bodies to serve these specific functions. This is one of the reasons why there are so many special-purpose bodies within the axis. They can be established only by intermunicipal agreement and they require the approval of the appropriate provincial government.

A second group of problems arising from excessive geographic fragmentation can be regarded as of interest more to the provincial governments than to the local governments. These are problems arising from service inequalities which cannot be condoned by governments supposedly concerned with the provinces as a whole. (It should be noted that the federal government also ought to be concerned about provincial inequalities which may occur between the two different portions of the axis.) There are certain concerns that are of direct interest to the provincial governments and various methods of improvement can be implemented only at this level. One of the most important of these concerns arises from the inequalities of service provision which result from fragmentation, particularly when these inequalities are thought to bring about social and economic disadvantages to certain sections of the population. It is for this reason that the provincial governments of both provinces have amalgamated school boards, which now serve a number of municipalities and can spread the costs over a wider and more varied tax base.

Federation

Within the axis is located the most analysed and discussed structure for the amalgamation of local governments that has been implemented on the North American continent. The establishment of Metropolitan Toronto and its large Metropolitan Planning Area has been hailed by students of local government as the most significant and positive advance in local reorganization that has occurred outside of Europe, though there have been a few dissenting voices. The most extensive review of the history and structure of the Metropolitan Toronto experience has been undertaken by Kaplan (1967, 1971), and there have been a number of studies of various parts of its operation (Fish, 1971). Fortunately, the recent implementation of a more streamlined unit of local government known as Metropolitan Winnipeg will serve to place the Metro Toronto structure in perspective (Axworthy, 1972).

Basically, Metro Toronto is a federation of six municipalities into a two-tiered system: the top tier provides services for the metropolitan area as a whole, and the bottom tier provides services of local importance. The allocation of functions is listed in Table 8.2. This table shows that planning, transportation, police, education, and certain welfare concerns are allocated to the metro level. Some of these functions operate within a two-tiered structure, with certain members of the municipal boards being appointed to the Metro-wide board. The Metro council consists of delegates from the municipal councils, and they in turn elect their chairman. Thus, the influence of the public is felt only indirectly through the municipally elected aldermen; this remoteness is one of the main objects of criticism of the Metro Toronto scheme (Garon *et al.*, 1969). The council has fairly extensive powers, particularly in planning, yet the chairman is elected by a council of delegates from the municipalities. Thus, the broad policies of the council are not subject to the form of debate which would occur if the Metro councillors and chairman were elected directly by the public.

Furthermore, there is a fairly strong case to be made for the fact that the area embraced by the Metro Toronto government is not large enough. The influence of Toronto, in terms of commuting, prices, traffic flow, and so forth, certainly extends far beyond the present Metro boundaries. This reality is recognized by the establishment of a planning region for Metro, which effectively gives it responsibility for the planning of the thirteen municipalities of the area immediately adjacent to it. Thus, they are part of the planning region without being represented on the Metro Council. Also, the tremendous dynamism of Metro Toronto has stimulated rapid growth in the surrounding municipalities, so that they now find it difficult to cope with the resulting interlocking problems. As a consequence, an even larger unit of government is required to handle broad regional needs.

NEW STRUCTURES

The compelling need for local government amalgamation and reorganization, which cannot be met by the piecemeal procedures outlined in the previous section, has resulted in a number of new structures being either proposed or partially implemented. In Ontario these new structures are in the form of regional government units, and in Québec as "communautés urbaines" and "regroupement". These different procedures are designed to serve specific purposes, they are not comparable between the two provinces, and they are at entirely different stages of development. In essence, regional government is developed far further in Ontario than in Québec, and in both cases the pace of implementation is very much related to the rhythms of provincial politics.

Regional government

The movement towards establishing a level of local government between province and municipalities has grown out of the recommendations of two major studies of municipal law and finance (the Beckett Committee, 1965, and the Smith Committee on Taxation, 1966); the movement of regional development and transportation planning toward the consideration of larger units (MTARTS, 1967); and the rapidity of growth in the Toronto Centred Region (Drueger, 1971, Found and Morley, 1972). These different forces came together in the 1968 provincial government report *Design for Development: Phase Two*, which linked the regional economic development program to the development of regional municipal government. Although the Metropolitan Toronto Council is actually the first regional level of government, the first of the new regional governments formed after the *Design for Development* statement was issued was that of Ottawa–Carleton.

As of January 1, 1973, six regional government units had been established within the Ontario portion of the axis. The impending establishment of another five has been announced, and the location and geographic extent of each of the eleven is indicated in Figure 8.3. Each of the new regions has to be established by specific legislation approved by the provincial parliament, and the arrangements contained with the various acts differ for each region. Generally, a two-tier government is established for each region, although a one-tier system is being envisaged for the City of Hamilton and Wentworth County. The municipal governments are reorganized and amalgamated to serve local needs, and a regional-level administration and council has to be formed to represent all the municipalities. This reorganization at the local municipal level has resulted, in fact, in a reduction of 50 per cent in the number of municipalities in the six regions formed by the beginning of 1973.

Apart from reorganization and amalgamation at the local level, the most important issue concerns the way in which the service and administrative functions are allocated among the three levels of government. A summary of the allocations implemented for the six regions formed prior to 1974 is indicated in Table 8.4. Although there are differences among the regions, a remarkable degree of uniformity has emerged in the short period of time that the program has been in operation. Generally, the regions are responsible for the major services, such as police, water, sewers, social services, and borrowing, whereas the municipalities deal with matters concerning · zoning, garbage collection, and parks. Provincial subsidies and grants are allocated to the regional councils on a formula basis, and the council has the responsibility for disbursement of these particular funds.

Naturally, the regional government program has received a great deal of opposition from some groups, particularly local politicians in suburban township areas who perceive that their power may be eroded as municipalities are reorganized and regional councils formed. It is noticeable, however, that the problem of indirect representation, which has been noted in Metro Toronto, has been recreated in a number of the new regions. In Ottawa–Carleton and in Muskoka, the Metro scheme has been adopted, in Niagara a combination of direct election and appointed representation from municipal councils is employed, and in the others, more direct election is used. Provincial politicians seem to be predictably loath to create new and larger local power-bases, and local politicians appear to be afraid of domination by the larger urban communities. This fear is transmitted to the local community in order to create a "grass-roots" movement opposed to any form of reorganization. In fact, a very tentative analysis of the Niagara area suggests that the introduction of regional government has resulted in a more economic provision of a greater number of local and regional services. This statement has to be regarded as very tentative because the measurement problem is immense.

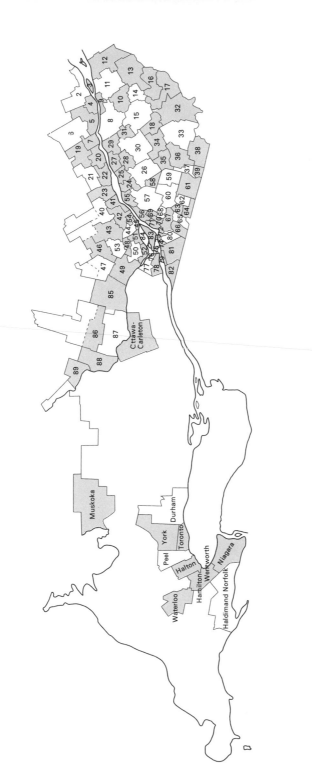

Figure 8.3: The location of new and proposed regional government units in Ontario, and Tessier's proposed regroupment in Québec

Table 8.4: Allocation of service and administrative functions between the provincial, regional, and local levels of government

FUNCTION	METRO TORONTO	OTTAWA-CARLETON	NIAGARA	YORK	MUSKOKA	WATERLOO
Borrowing	R*	R	R	R	R	R
E.M.O.	R	R	R	R	R	R
General welfare	R	R	R	R	R	R
Child welfare	R	R	R	R	R	R
Homes for the aged	R	R	R	R	R	R
Juvenile Court (costs by order)	R	R	R	R	R	R
Nursing services and day nurseries (costs)	R	S	R	R	R	R
Anatomy Act	R	S	R	R	R	R
Health Unit	L*	R	R	R	R^3	R
War veterans burial	R	L	R	R	R	R
Sanatoria for consumptives	S*	S	R	R	R	R
Homes for the retarded (costs)	R	L	S	S	S	R
Water Supply	S	R	S	S	L	S
Tax Levy	S	S	S	S	S	S
Sewage	S	S	S	S	S	S
Planning	S^1	S^2	S	S	S^2	S
Roads	S	S	S	S	S	S
Traffic	S	S	S	S	S	S
Grants to hospitals	S	S	S	S	S	S
Parking	S	S	S	S	L	S

Service						
Police	R	L	S	R	P*	R
Public transit	R	L	L	L	L	R^7
Parks	S	L	L	S	L	L
Tax collection	L	L	L	L	L	L
Gas and electricity distribution	L^2	L^2	L^2	L^2	L^2	L^2
Library	L	L	L	L	L	S^6
Recreation and community centres	L	L	L	L	L	L
Solid waste	S	L	L	L	L	S
Fire protection	L	L^5	L^5	L^5	L^5	L^5
Ambulance service	R	L	L	L	L	L
Sidewalks	L	L	L	L	L	L

* Codes: S — Shared   R — Regional   L — Local   P — Provincial

Notes:

1 Separate Boards at regional and local levels

2 Separate Boards at local level (optional for planning in Muskoka)

3 The District Municipality of Muskoka is part of the Muskoka-Parry Sound Health Unit

4 The Regional Municipality of Sudbury will be part of the Sudbury & District Health Unit

5 However, a regional fire co-ordinator is required

6 A regional function in the four-township municipality only

7 At the option of the regional council

Source: BMR (1972) and the Municipal Organization Branch (1972).

The "Communauté Urbaine"

The opposition of local groups and of some students of local government (Bédard, 1965) to a large-scale program of municipal reorganization has been recognized from the outset in the Province of Québec.
As a consequence, the provincial government decided (1970) to
adopt procedures which would not eliminate municipalities, but
would transfer a few important functions to a higher-level authority
embracing a number of contiguous local units. Following the recommendations of the LaHaye (1970) report for agglomerations containing more than 100,000 people, the formula adopted is that of the
"urban community". Thus, the areas embraced by Ile de Montréal,
the Québec agglomeration, and the large region centred on Hull
(Outaouais), have been designated as urban communities (Ministère
des Affaires Municipales, 1971). Although the program is claimed
to be one of merely transferring powers which cannot be handled
properly by the municipalities to the higher level, the policy is viewed
by the municipalities as an imposition from the provincial government. As a consequence, the program is in various stages of development in the three urban regions. In Hull, it has merely been studied,
in the Québec region, it has been studied and is in the process of
formation, and on Ile de Montréal, the urban community is in
operation.

The urban communities are designed to be governed by an assembly
representing the municipalities. This representation is proportionate
to the population size of the municipality, but the representatives are
not directly elected. They are, as in Metropolitan Toronto, appointed
indirectly from the municipal assemblies, which are directly elected.
The community is administered by a permanent body of local government civil servants, and they, in turn, are managed by a community
manager. Thus the control exercised by the urban population is, at
best, indirect, and the representatives at the urban community assembly tend to be more responsive to the needs of their own municipalities than to those of the urban community as a whole.

The functions of the urban communities, though fairly limited,
are fundamental to the operation of complex urban regions. The main
functions allocated to the urban community level are general urban
planning, police, regional transport developments, assessment, air
pollution, and sewage. All these tasks are difficult to manage and

coordinate, so it is no wonder that the 1972 and 1973 budgets of the Montréal Urban Community were attacked severely by the mayors of the suburban municipalities. The community obtains revenue on a per capita basis from the municipalities, and also receives grants from the provincial government. It can borrow as a unit and float bond issues. But even though the powers of the community are fairly clear, and its financial position is reasonably secure, it will be some time before the urban communities assume a leading managing and co-ordinating rôle in the regions they are designed to serve.

Regroupment

The report of the LaHaye Commission (1970) suggested not only the establishment of a new level of government to serve the urban agglomerations of Montréal, Québec City, and Hull, but also a provincially initiated program of municipal regroupment. As a consequence, an Act to Promote the Regroupment of Municipalities (Bill 276) was passed by the provincial Assembly in December 1971, and subsequently amended in 1972. A proposed plan of the way in which the regroupments might appear geographically is presented in the Québec portion of Figure 8.3, which is based on a report prepared for the Minister of Municipal Affairs (Tessier, 1971) at that time. This proposal would have resulted in a reduction of 60 per cent in the number of municipalities within the axis in Québec. This regrouping proposal pertains to areas within the urban communities discussed in the previous section as well as to the non-metropolitan areas beyond.

Although the Act indicates that the Minister ". . . may establish regroupment units . . . ", it appears that this power is constrained by political realities. These realities are such that very little reorganization beyond those within the urban communities of Hull and Québec City have been proposed in concrete terms for discussion. If the discussions result in an agreement suitable to the various municipalities, then they will jointly petition for regroupment. Thus, the operation of the Act really depends upon the willingness of the municipalities to regroup according to a design which is either the same or similar to that recommended by the Ministry. The general unwillingness of the municipalities to consider these proposals is resulting in very little progress.

FINANCING LOCAL GOVERNMENTS

An analysis of local government finance concerned with the source of revenues and direction of expenditures is fraught with difficulties, and these are compounded if the student wishes to examine the way in which these revenues and expenditures have changed over a period of time (Goldenburg, 1939; Plunkett, 1972). Although there is an extensive literature on the topic of Canadian municipal government and finance (Powell and Black, 1971; BMR, 1973) as well as many different sources of information, such as the Statistics Canada municipal finance series (Series 68-204 and 68-207), the biennial reports of the Canadian Tax Foundation (1971), and various provincial financial reports, the gaps in the information relating to quality of service, number offered, sources of finance for public commissions, and so forth, make a detailed analysis beyond the scope of this volume. Thus, the purpose of this section is to indicate the way in which excessive fragmentation and finance are intermingled, and to sketch the basic problems that face the fiscal management of local government units within the axis.

REVENUES AND EXPENDITURES

Probably one of the most important aspects of local government finance that needs to be clearly understood is that the sources of revenue for the local units are quite different from those of the provincial and federal levels. This is indicated in Table 8.5, which details the proportion of total revenue received by the three levels of government from six different sources in 1969. In that year, the total revenue received by the local government units within the axis was about $4 billion ($4,000. m.), the amount received by the two provinces was $7.5 billion, and the federal government received $14.5 billion. The table suggests the existence of a trickle-down effect, with transfers from the federal to the provincial levels, and from the provincial to the local levels. The basic source of revenue at the federal level is income taxes from individuals, although corporation taxes are included in this heading to simplify the table. "Other" taxes include import and export duties, sales taxes, and so forth.

Sources of revenue

The basic point concerning federal revenues is that they are derived

Table 8.5: A comparison of the sources of revenue for the federal, provincial, and local government levels (the figures are proportions of the total revenue received by each level), 1969

LEVEL OF GOVERNMENT	INCOME TAX (INDIVIDUAL AND CORPORATION)	PROPERTY TAX	TRANSFER FROM PROVINCIAL	TRANSFER FROM FEDERAL	OTHER
Federal	58.0	0.7			41.3
Provincial					
Ontario	27.2			16.8	56.0
Québec	31.6			22.0	46.4
Local					
Ontario		44.0	39.2	1.8	15.0
Québec		38.5	43.0	.6	17.9

Source: Statistics Canada, 68–204, 68–207, 68–211.

from taxes that can be considered either proportional or progressive. Most of the "other" taxes are proportional, that is, they are a flat percentage charge on the price of the product or service. Thus, in an inflationary situation, the amount of revenue received increases at the same rate as the rate of inflation. Income taxes are progressive, since the rate of taxation is theoretically greater for the larger incomes than for the smaller incomes. In an inflationary situation, where incomes may rise faster than it is possible to readjust the tax structure, the amount of revenue received from this source class may increase at a rate greater than the rate of inflation, and governments may well find their coffers bulging and their budgets badly predicted. As a consequence, it is not incorrect to suggest that the federal government controls the major sources of revenue, and at times of inflation, these sources can yield embarrassingly large amounts.

The provincial governments obtain their revenue from three main sources. Proportionately rather more is derived from income taxes in Québec than in Ontario, whereas Ontario receives a greater amount from "other" taxes than Québec does. In fact, the "other" taxes provide slightly more than one-half of the revenue in Ontario, and a little less than one-half in Québec. These rather large amounts are obtained primarily from sales taxes, and secondarily from licensing, excise duties, and so forth. A substantial portion of the revenue in both provinces is gained from federal transfers which are chiefly of the conditional variety. These monies are provided for federal-provincial cost-sharing programs, or are earmarked for specific purposes, such as education and social services. It is interesting to note just how large the importance of federal transfers have become, and also that the grab-bag of "other" taxes has assumed an unduly prominent rôle in revenue raising.

The local governments also have three sources of revenue, but these are quite different from those employed at the provincial or federal level. The bulk of the revenue is obtained from property taxes and provincial transfers, and smaller amounts from "other" sources. The revenue included in "other" sources is obtained from licences and permits, hotel taxes, and special levies. The amounts transferred from the provincial governments to the municipalities rose sharply during the 1960–71 period, and has continued to increase at the same rate in the early 1970s. On average, throughout the axis, the amounts received by local governments from provincial transfers rose by nearly 450 per cent in the ten-year period, and a vast proportion (90 per cent) of these grants are conditional. Furthermore, most of the grant money is for one purpose — education — with transportation and communications and welfare receiving much smaller subsidies by comparison. The conditional grant system serves only to compound the fiscal dilemma of local governments, as they are forced to distort their local priorities to take advantage of the conditional grant and cost-sharing schemes offered by the provincial governments.

The property tax

The vast proportion of the money that can be raised by municipalities is obtained through the property tax. The proportion of direct revenue obtained by this means by municipalities within the axis varies from a low of 65 per cent to a high of 85 per cent, and in the nineteenth and early twentieth centuries the property tax was a reasonable source of local operating money. As far as taxes in general are concerned, it combines the twin virtues of ease of assessment and collection; and in an agricultural era when the wealth of an individual could be measured by the amount of property he or she owned, and the variety and quality of services demanded was quite limited, it was also a socially acceptable form of taxation. Unfortunately, the property tax has become quite regressive, for the lower incomes now tend to pay proportionately far more of their income for this tax than the higher income families do. In fact, a study of Guelph cited in the 1972 Ontario Budget statement indicates that whereas families with a gross income of $5,500 per annum or less pay 5 per cent or *more* of their income in property taxes, families with a gross income of $15,000 or more pay 3 per cent or *less* of their income in property taxes. Obviously this situation is socially inequitable and it is recognized as unacceptable.

The use of property for raising local taxes is also recognized as spatially inequitable. With urban growth, it has become apparent that various social and income groups tend to locate in specific parts of an urban region. These specific parts may also be discrete local municipalities, with the result that some municipalities may have a much more favourable tax base than others. The end product of this type of fragmentation is a variety in quality of municipal services, and therefore opportunities, which are socially unjustifiable as the urban region is an interdependent economic entity. The classic examples of this type of spatial inequality in North America are the wealthy suburban communities surrounding an older central city where most of the suburbanites are employed. Spatial inequalities of this type have been recognized and partially circumvented by the creation of larger school districts throughout the axis, and they are also recognized as being the prime reason for the formation of regional governments and urban communities.

But although larger regions may be formed, the property tax is still an unacceptable method for raising local revenue. At the outset, it is doubtful whether any tinkering with the mill rate, methods of assessment, or mix of properties concerned, will ever eliminate its regressivity. Furthermore, it is not as responsive to the vagaries of inflation as income taxes or proportionate taxes are. In fact, it is quite unresponsive and it is not only incapable of raising the amounts required by municipalities, but it cannot keep up with expenditures rising as a result of inflation. It is for this reason that the municipalities have become so dependent upon provincial transfers and subsidies and are likely to become even more dependent upon this source in the future. It is apparent that the municipalities really require a source of revenue which is non-regressive, provides the amount of money necessary to fulfill the expanding local needs, is inflation independent, and is also independent of provincial or federal control. The latter point is extremely important when the range of local expenditures is considered.

Expenditures

The gross level of expenditures at any one time is equal to the amount raised as revenue plus the amount raised from borrowing. Borrowing has to occur to facilitate periodic capital construction, and of course this borrowing has to be paid for with interest. One of the disadvantages of excessive fragmentation is that municipalities are often too small to borrow at the most favourable rates, and it is noticeable that one of the first functions transferred to the regional level is borrowing, for the larger units permit the debt to be spread over a much wider base.

The range of administrative, service, and social activities undertaken by municipalities within the axis is immense. An illustration of the types of activities and expenditures undertaken by a middle-sized municipality within Canada (and within the axis) is as follows (Plunkett, 1972, pp. 85–86):

General Government
  Legislation
  Administration
  Other miscellaneous governmental activities
Protection to Persons and Property
  Police
  Fire
  Street lighting
  Protective inspection
  Traffic lights and signs
  Other security-oriented activities
Public Works
  Road and sidewalk maintenance
  Snow and ice removal
  Parking operations
  General maintenance
Sanitation and Waste Removal
  Garbage collection and disposal
  Sewage: collection, treatment, and disposal
  Street cleaning
Health
  Local Board of Health
Social Welfare
  Welfare assistance programs
  Grants to local volunteer agencies
Education
  Payment of property tax levy raised on behalf of school boards
Recreation and Community Services
  Parks
  Recreation programs
  Public libraries
  Other facilities — museums, cemeteries, and so forth.
Debt Charges
  General
  Local improvement
  Interest on temporary borrowing
Utilities and Other Enterprises
  Expenditures to cover short-term debts
Contributions to Capital and Loan Fund
Joint or Special Expenditures
  Payments to regional, metropolitan, or community governments
  Payments for services operated jointly with other municipalities

Miscellaneous
  Discount on taxes
  Industrial promotion
  Tourist promotion
  Other odd things

Even though many of these activities and expenditures are supplemented by fiscal transfers from the provincial governments, it is important to note just how many of these activities are vitally important for normal day-to-day living.

It is difficult to obtain a clear picture of the way in which the expenditures are distributed among each of the individual items in the above list, or the way in which the magnitude of the disbursements has changed over the 1960–70 period. Table 8.6 contains details relating to the proportionate distribution of municipal expenditures in 1970, and the rate of change between 1960 and 1970 in each of these categories. The most important point to note regarding this table is that it is doubtful whether the categories are comparable over the years, and over the provinces. This is not surprising given the time period, the number of municipalities involved in the two provinces, each of which has its own minor peculiar budget allocation system, and the governmental structure. Nevertheless, it is noticeable that the rate of increase in municipal expenditures in Québec is slightly higher than it is in Ontario, and that this difference is related to the great increases in expenditures on sanitation and waterworks and education. Education incurs the vast majority of all local expenditures; public works in both provinces consume about one-tenth. The costs of social welfare and public health are now being borne primarily by the provincial and federal governments, and the combination of ceilings on education expenditures and the current low birth rates has reduced the rate of increase in this category.

AMELIORATING THE FISCAL DILEMMA

Nevertheless, the pressures on local government purses are increasing every day, particularly with respect to public transportation, neighbourhood preservation, and social and community services. These pressures, and the continuing large disbursements for education, require a substantial revision of the fiscal base of local government. Ideally, this revision should be directed towards providing a financial structure which is responsive to inflation, is equitable both geographically and among income groups, and permits a higher degree of local autonomy over decisions about priorities. Application of these criteria to the proposals presented by MacKay (1973) yields some interesting observations, particularly if the proposals are discussed in descending order of likelihood of implementation.

Increasing grants

Probably the most likely procedure for ameliorating the fiscal dilemma is to increase provincial government grants. These grants have been increasing in magnitude at a high rate during the past fifteen years. Unfortunately, most of them have been conditional, and may have had a determining effect on municipal priorities. This situation is acceptable when the benefits extend beyond the municipal boundary involved and therefore involve province-wide matters, but it is not acceptable if the grants are designed to impose actions on the municipalities. It would be more desirable for the provinces to increase not only conditional grants, but unconditional grants as well, particularly in situations where significant inter-municipality inequalities occur. The formula for such decision-making might be rather cumbersome, however, and in the long run the procedure will not lead to a basic solution because it does not ensure an adequate and expanding financial base.

Transfer municipal responsibilities

The second proposal is to transfer certain responsibilities, currently partially funded by direct taxes raised by the municipalities, to the provincial governments. This proposal is predicated upon the fact that there are a number of activities, financed in whole or in part by the municipalities, which yield benefits to the provinces as a whole and are, therefore, really of provincial concern. The argument is particularly applicable to education, which is currently financed in part by taxes on property collected by the municipalities and transferred to the school boards, and partly by direct grants and subsidies from the provincial governments. If education were to become the financial responsibility of the provincial governments, a large proportion of the money currently collected as property taxes would be released for other purposes.

There are a number of arguments which reduce the effectiveness of this procedure as a general solution. First, the municipalities are still left with a regressive tax base which is not immediately responsive to rising fiscal requirements in times of inflation. Second, obvious acceptance of the premise that matters providing provincial benefits should be financed and operated by the provincial governments might well be extended to the federal level as well. If the allocation of functions between the provincial and federal governments were reorganized according to premises of this type, the whole hornet's nest raised by the constitutional conferences of the 1960s would be reopened. It would, of course, be sensible to recognize that all large urban areas, and the axis as a macro-urban region, are of vital importance to the nation and therefore require some federal influence, but sensibility is a difficult virtue to sustain in a constitutional conference.

Provide new tax money for municipalities

If it is recognized that the current tax powers are inequitable, regressive, and incapable of providing sufficient revenue, then the best procedure might well be to introduce a new tax. As sales taxes are, in general, regressive, probably the best form of new tax would be a municipal income tax, of which the simplest would be a fixed proportion of the total income tax payable by the inhabitants of a municipality. The inequalities which may result, owing to some municipalities being wealthier than others, could well be evened out by calculating the total on the basis of a regional or community local government unit. The amount of money received would then depend on the gross structure of incomes in the area and on the rate of inflation. Introduction of a progressive tax of this type would also permit the abolition of the property tax, or a tremendous reduction in its importance as a source of local finance.

CONCLUSION

The problems of structure and finance in local government within the axis are immense but not insoluble. The issues can be resolved but they require time and patience; for many of the problems are wrapped in time and bound by constitutional constraints. Since the axis leads the nation in extent of urbanization and economic integration, it is vital that the problems of local government be tackled

Table 8.6: The proportionate distribution of general municipal expenditures in 1970, and the relative rates of increase in each category 1960–70, for municipalities in Ontario and Québec

CATEGORY	ONTARIO		QUÉBEC	
	1970	CHANGE	1970	CHANGE
General government services	2.8	1.92	4.6	3.20
Protection to persons and property	7.7	2.70	5.9	3.14
Public works	12.3	3.49	9.3	4.47
Sanitation and water works	7.5	7.35	7.6	22.41
Health	1.4	3.29	.3	1.04
Social welfare	5.0	3.94	.2	.95
Recreation and community services	3.4	3.89	2.7	6.68
Education	51.8	6.61	59.4	10.51
Other (debt, enterprises, etc.)	7.4	1.75	9.9	3.07
Total		4.26		6.41

resolutely in this area. It has been demonstrated that these problems are of vital concern to the welfare of the individual as well as the provincial and federal governments. The conclusion, therefore, has to be that local government reorganization and municipal fiscal reform is of interest to all three levels of government because each, with varying degrees of emphasis, can assist in and benefit from the changes that must occur.

Although population forecasting is difficult, future demands and future patterns have to be estimated if there is to be any logical basis for establishing policies which affect the future. At any arbitrary cross-section in time, the futurist is faced with only a poor understanding of the present, less understanding of the past, and virtually none of the future. The farther any crystal-ball gazer attempts to see into the future, the greater the uncertainty, for the relevance of and confidence in present and past known processes declines. Thus, the problem of forecasting future socio-economic trends is formidable, but as with most difficult problems, too important to ignore. Forecasts of population size, composition, and regional distribution are basic elements in any rational planning scheme, for even the crudest forms of population projection tell us something about the future and provide a basis for contingency planning.

Naturally, for planning purposes, the forecasting exercise must always be subservient to the more central issue of regulation. If the most desirable outcome for any area can be specified, the problem can be resolved as one of determining the best means to achieve this desirable end. However, before attempting to influence future patterns of development it is useful to gain some knowledge about the amount of regulation that may be required. There is little to be gained from implementing restrictive and undoubtedly costly planning proposals if the free workings of the present socio-economic system, as represented by past trends, are likely to bring about the same end. Thus, the first task of forecasting is to predict the future as accurately as possible on the basis of all cumulated information available based on the past and the present. The second task is to indicate the most likely future based on predicted demographic trends. The third task is to evaluate the various alternatives in the light of policy manipulations that may help to achieve the most acceptable future.

There are two major dimensions to the forecasting problem: temporal and spatial. The temporal problems relate to the more philosophical questions of projecting past distributions and causal mechanisms. There is, however, a strong conservatism in the way that such a basic factor as the distribution of population changes over time; for the present distribution of economic, social, and administrative activities exerts a powerful influence on future development. Furthermore, the dynamics of the urban system traditionally takes the form of incremental changes to existing clusters rather than of such radical shifts as urban abandonment or new-town formation. Thus, even though the rate of change may vary from epoch to epoch, year to year, and place to place, the processes of population change in a developed economy tend to be smooth and continuous with predictable underlying regularities. The spatial dimension to the forecasting problem can be simply stated: the forecast error is inversely related (in some way) to the size of the study area. Large regions have, in general, more stable and predictable growth profiles than small areas do, because small units are more likely to experience extreme fluctuations. The larger areas, in effect, even out the fluctuating growth patterns which may emerge within small sub-units. The wide variation in forecasts available for municipalities is well-illustrated in the projections compiled by Bourne, Harper, and Thackray (1972).

Unfortunately, for most planning purposes large areas are not particularly useful, since the distribution of population within an area is of greater interest than the absolute magnitude of the population. For example, a population forecast of 19.1 million people residing in the axis in the year 2001 is of some interest, but the ramifications of its distribution are extremely important in planning the allocation of resources and infrastructure. At a lower level of aggregation, the distribution of that population among the various sub-areas within the axis is useful, but the distribution of that population among census subdivisions located in these sub-areas is much more useful, because at this level of aggregation the population increments can be directly related to the urban areas that comprise or are within these census units. Most of the population-forecasting techniques currently in use are either incapable of, or are poorly adapted to, providing detailed spatial forecasts (Bannister, 1973; Carey, 1972). The work described in this chapter utilizes one of the few available spatial forecasting techniques, and it is based on the method of cascading averaging and differencing, a technique patterned on recent advances in a statistical procedure known as spectral analysis (Curry and Bannister, 1974). This technique is used to project the population of all census divisions (and aggregations) within the axis to the year 2001; these projections can then be compared with the most likely estimates discussed in Chapter 2.

THE DISTRIBUTION OF POPULATION IN THE YEAR 2001 BASED ON LONG-TERM TRENDS

The method of cascading averaging and differencing tries to take into account a number of observations made in Chapter 2 concerning population growth within the axis. Intra-regional variations in urban growth rates are largely a result of migratory movements rather than a real variation in rates of natural growth. But small area migration data are so poor that we need to develop a forecasting and allocational method capable of operating without *direct* inputs of migration data. The fluctuations noticeable in small area data, however, should be tempered by the growth profile of the larger area of which it is a part.

The forecasting mechanism used is capable of predicting the spatial distribution of population for a large set of small areas, in this case census subdivisions (and aggregations). Ideally, the growth of population in any census subdivision is affected by the past variations in the rates of change of population in the area, and the maximum population that can be supported in that area. As the maximum population that can be supported in any area changes with time and is extremely difficult to estimate, the method has to incorporate this particular concept along with the data concerning changes in the past. Basically, this involves designing a procedure capable of establishing and predicting non-linear growth trends, of incorporating spill-over effects among census subdivisions which arise when the maximum density limits are reached within one area, and of isolating relatively stable historic and spatial processes to use as a basis for predicting the future. Used in this way, numerical forecasting appears to be more of an art than a science.

At the outset it would appear that a scheme that relates census subdivision growth patterns to wider regional changes is likely to provide a more stable basis for projection. But the scheme must also take into account migration trends as reflected by past patterns of competitive performance among wide regions and among the smaller census subdivisions which comprise them. In other words, the concern is not only the growth pattern of large regions, but also the pattern of differentiation within the regions. High rates of increase in one census subdivision can occur, in large part, only at the expense of others, and basic patterns of growth rates reflect these competitive processes. Thus, the interest centres on whether each census subdivision increased more or less than the average for its near neighbours; and whether each larger region increased more or less than the average for its neighbouring regions at the same hierarchical scale level.

These actual differences at a given point in time must be compared with the way in which the differences have changed over time at the various census subdivisions and broader regional-scale levels. The time series of these spatial growth differences provides the data for predictions based on the concepts of relative competitive advantage at hierarchical-scale levels. Of course, the task of calculating this time series of differences is onerous, but with the aid of the computer, the task is quickly accomplished. The mechanics of the operation are described in a hypothetical example in the following section.

AN EXAMPLE OF CASCADING AVERAGING AND DIFFERENCING

The first step is to collect all the data for each census subdivision at each time period. Then, each population map is subtracted from the map following to yield a series of maps, each of which shows the absolute increments between successive censuses. This procedure structures the forecast to follow past growth patterns, and thus consider the growth record of regions. The third step is the most complicated as it involves the process of calculating averages and differences through the method of cascaded averaging and differencing.

Consider Figure 9.1a, which depicts an idealized map of sixteen regularly spaced census subdivisions with an intercensal growth figure in each cell. Divide the map into sets of first-order regions by grouping townships into sets of, for example, fours, as in Figure 9.1b. Calculate the mean change in each first order region. The results of these particular calculations are placed in circles in Figure 9.1b. Then calculate the difference between each township and the lowest order mean for that set by subtracting the mean value from the individual township value. The results of this operation are depicted in parentheses in Figure 9.1c.

The process is then continued in the same way to group, average, and difference, at higher levels. For example, in Figure 9.1d the map is aggregated into sets of second order regions by grouping the first order regions into sets of, for example, four. The mean change can then be calculated for the second order regions (placed in the centre of Figure 9.1e in a circle) and from this the differences with respect to the first order regions are determined. These differences are placed in parentheses in Figure 9.1e. The process of grouping, averaging, and differencing can then be continued to higher order levels, the ultimate stage being the point at which no further aggregations can occur.

In this particular example the ultimate stage is reached rather quickly with a map mean of 8, because there can be no grouping beyond the second order regions. The results of the first and second order averaging and differencing can then be placed together on the same map (Figure 9.1f), and it can be shown that the series of differences associated with each census subdivision and its higher order regions, taken together with the map mean, is equivalent to the original census subdivision value. For example, the north-west corner value can be restructured as

$$8 - 6 + 0 = 2$$

and the south-east corner value is

$$8 + 3 + 3 = 14$$

Thus, working with the differences is equivalent to working with the

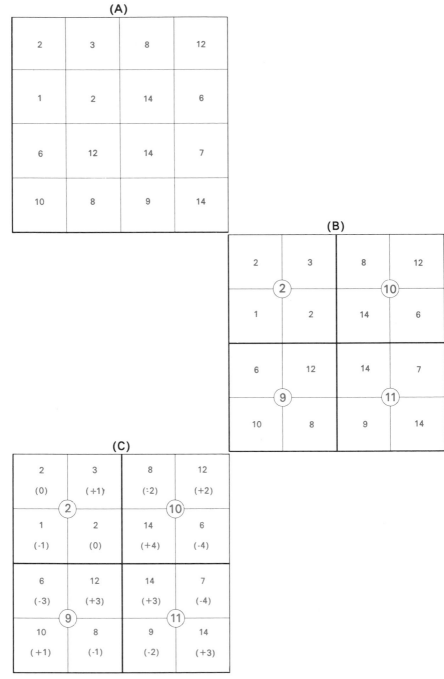

Figure 9.1: Example of cascading averaging and differencing

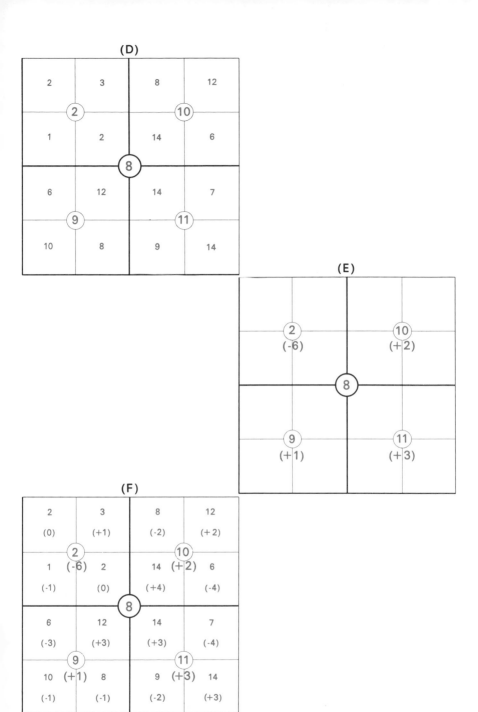

original township values, except that the differences trace out competitive advantages.

A set of data having been developed, the fourth task is to choose a specific forecasting technique which will take this information into account and project future space differentials and associated distributions. To cut a long story short — it is detailed explicitly in Bannister (1974) — the conclusion from a number of experiments is that a multiple regression equation based on two types of increments would be most appropriate. The first set of increments are calculated in the same way as in the example described previously. That is, maps of increments (which can be positive and negative) are calculated on the basis of two successive time periods. Thus, if there are ten time periods, there can be nine maps of increments or changes. The second set of increments are based on these maps of changes, for they are calculated by subtracting from one change map the map of changes for the time interval immediately preceding. There are, therefore, with ten time periods, eight possible maps of changes of changes, and they represent an acceleration or rate of change factor.

The two sets of maps of increments can then be used to generate a cascading set of averages and differences for a number of levels of aggregation. In the example discussed previously there were two levels of aggregation, but some experimentation suggested that in reality six would be a more useful number of scale levels. The forecast model then takes the form

$$P_{t+1} = P_t + b_1G_1 + b_2G_2 + \cdots + b_6G_6 + b_7A_1 + b_8A_2 + \cdots + b_{12}A_6$$

where $b_1, \cdots, b_{12}$ identify the coefficients to be estimated, and, $G_1, \cdots, G_6$ are the six differences constituting the decomposed profile of the population for each census subdivision; and $A_1, \cdots, A_6$ are the six differences constituting the decomposed profile of change for each subdivision.

Unfortunately, to estimate twelve coefficients by the regression method would require a longer time series than is available. Thus, a fifth task is to find the minimum combination of coefficients providing the best predictions. This is determined from an experiment which attempted to forecast the 1961 and 1971 known population values from varying combinations of time-space coefficients in southern Ontario (Curry and Bannister, 1974). The results suggested that four coefficients could be used to forecast the population of each census subdivision. The assumption that these coefficients are also appropriate for predicting the situation in the year 2001 is, of course, open to debate.

THE UNCONSTRAINED FORECAST

The unconstrained forecasts, containing, as they do, the very high growth rates experienced during the past three decades, predict totals for the axis in the year 2001 greatly in excess of those estimated in Chapter 2. The details for the Ontario and Québec portions of the axis are listed in Table 9.1, and the information suggests a further concentration of the axis population over the next three decades in the western portion. Whereas in 1971 about 57.8 per cent of the axis population was located in the Ontario portion, by the year 2001 over 63.5 per cent will be in the western area. This continued comparative shift to Ontario, which is certainly substantiated by demographic and economic trends, is also implied by the forecasts in Chapter 2. In that chapter, it will be recalled that the "most likely" population projections were based on 1966–71 population growth rates and 1955–61 migration patterns. The results of the Chapter 2 forecasts suggest that by the year 2001 nearly 64 per cent of the population of the axis will be located in the Ontario portion. Thus, even though the totals projected are very different, the gross spatial variations implied are fairly consistent.

The spatial variations in growth, at the census subdivision level of aggregation, are detailed in Figure 9.2. In this map, three growth categories are delimited using the same two conceptual benchmarks

Table 9.1: *Unconstrained forecast population for the axis, and the Ontario and Québec portions, in the years 1981, 1991, and 2001 (in thousands)*

	1971	1981	1991	2001
Ontario portion	6,889	9,117	12,739	17,023
percentage	57.8	60.1	62.5	63.5
Québec portion	5,029	6,046	7,647	9,788
percentage	42.2	39.9	37.5	36.5
Axis	11,918	15,163	20,386	26,811

as those in Figure 2.2. These benchmarks, it will be recalled, are a growth rate of zero, which distinguishes an absolute increase from an absolute decrease, and the predicted growth rate of population in the axis as a whole. In this case, the expected rate of increase based on the unconstrained forecasts is very nearly 2.3 per cent per annum, which is similar to the 1961–66 growth rate. On the basis of these two benchmarks, the census subdivisions are grouped into those expected to decline, those expected to exhibit increases at a rate less than the axis average, and those expected to grow faster than the average for the axis. The unconstrained forecasts result in few areas of absolute decline, and these are located primarily in the "Shield" and "Appalachian" portion of the axis. There are also large areas of decline in the rural zone between Montréal and Québec City. Slow growth occurs in most areas, and rapid growth is found around or in most of the major metropolitan centres.

Given the basis of the 2001 unconstrained forecasts it is not surprising that the distribution of urban densities which results represents little more than an expansion from the 1971 pattern. Census subdivisions that can be classified as either urban or semi-urban in terms of population densities, extend for almost the whole distance between Windsor and Québec City (Figure 9.3). The existence of continuous urbanization is emphasized by the map in Figure 9.4a, in which those census subdivisions that can be described as "urban" are mapped separately. A sinuous strip of urban development through south-western Ontario, along the Lake Ontario shore and the St. Lawrence River, is almost complete by the year 2001 to Québec City. The only extensive non-urbanized areas are in eastern Ontario, the area between Georgian Bay and Lake Huron, and the zone between Trois-Rivières and Québec City.

This increase can be expressed quantitatively and placed in perspective by a comparison with the situation in 1971 (Figure 9.4b). In Chapter 2 it was indicated that the total area of the census subdivisions that can be classified as urban in 1971 is 11,072 square miles. If all the axis urban population in 1971 were located in these census subdivisions the population density would be almost 900 persons per square mile. The unconstrained forecasts for the year 2001 yield census subdivisions comprising 20,110 square miles which can be classified as urban. Assuming that 90 per cent of the axis population of that date will be living in urban regions in these census subdivisions, the average urban population density will have risen to 1,060 persons per square mile. This is a reasonably high average

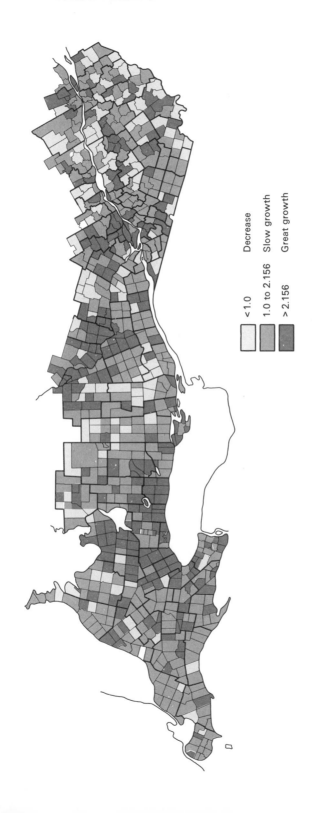

Figure 9.2: Population growth in the axis, 1971–2001: unconstrained forecasts for the year 2001

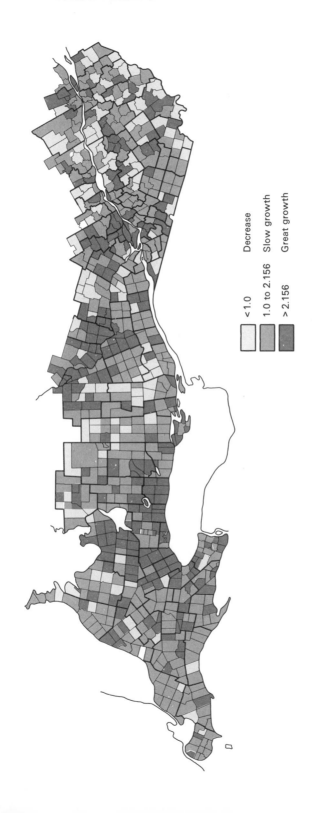

Decrease

Slow growth

Great growth

<1.0

1.0 to 2.156

> 2.156

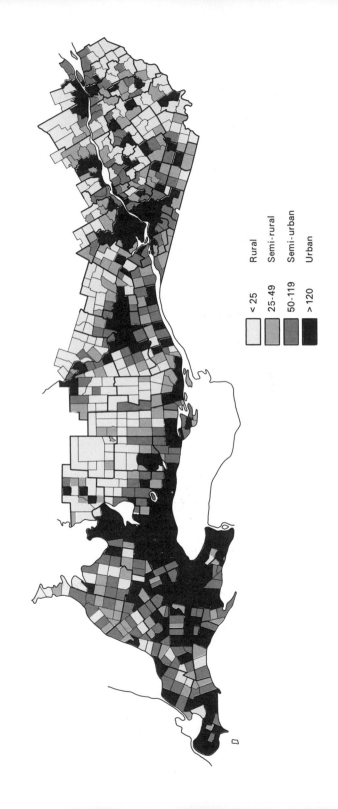

Key: <25 Rural, 25-49 Semi-rural, 50-119 Semi-urban, >120 Urban

Figure 9.3: Axis population densities in the year 2001: unconstrained forecasts

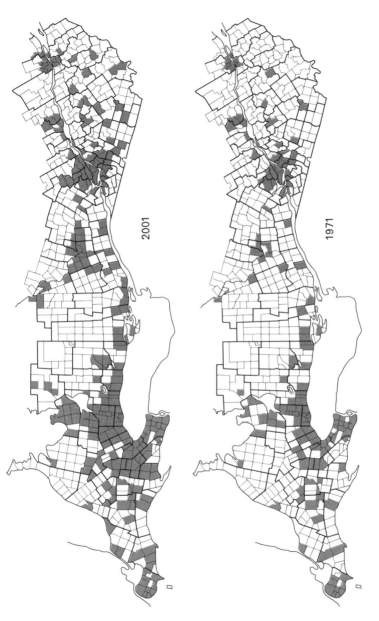

2001

1971

Figure 9.4: Census subdivisions defined as urban by (a) the 2001 unconstrained forecasts compared with (b) the 1971 situation

urban figure for a very large area, which would contain both urban and non-urban uses, and certainly substantiates the plea for more careful urban land management and planned rural-to-urban land conversion.

Expressed in terms of the predicted urban area actually being used for direct urban purposes, the unconstrained forecasts are even more impressive. It will be recalled that the amount of urban land actually being used for urban purposes in 1971 is estimated to be 2,146 square miles, and that this amount has been achieved incrementally over a period of more than 300 years of continuous European settlement. If 90 per cent of the axis population of 1971 resides in urban areas, application of the trend land absorption rate (186 acres per increment of 1000 people) suggests that over 4,100 square miles of new urban land will be required by the year 2001, and that almost 2,200 square miles of new urban land will be required if new residential construction is added at the Blumenfeld "preferred" urban densities (100 acres per 1000-people increment). Thus, the unconstrained forecasts indicate that even with land being consumed at the preferred rate, the amount of land required will double the extent of the urbanized area in thirty years, while the trend figure suggests that the total area of urban land may triple in the same period.

THE CONSTRAINED FORECAST

The unconstrained forecasts, which produce estimates based on past trends at the census subdivision level, obviously yield totals for the axis which do not conform with the "most likely" estimates cited in Chapter 2. These "most likely" estimates, which are based on 1966–71 growth rates and 1955–61 interprovincial migration patterns, yield a total predicted population in the axis in the year 2001 of 19,119,317, of which 89.2 per cent will be located in urban areas. The total population figure, therefore, has not been derived by projecting on the basis of cascading differences and summing the individual census subdivision totals, but has been derived from growth and migration patterns relating to very large areas. This total predicted axis population has, in turn, been allocated to large sub-areas within the axis, and used to project new urban land requirements (Table 3.4). The task of this section is to try to disaggregate the "most likely" sub-area population total to the census subdivision level, so that the picture of population densities in the year 2001 is comparable with that of 1971 for the "most likely" forecasts.

The disaggregation can be obtained using a variety of techniques, but in this particular case a more useful method can be derived from the cascading averaging and differencing procedure described previously. Basically, since the method uses averages for successive levels of aggregation, the procedure can be utilized by substituting the sub-area allocations described above at the appropriate level for the year 2001, and then limiting the distributive mechanism to these sub-area totals. The distributions can be achieved by using the information on past trends that are subsumed within the four parameters of the multiple regression model that was developed to predict populations at the census subdivision level in the unconstrained forecast. The result is a set of forecasts of population at the census subdivision level which reflect variations in past census subdivision growth rates, but in which the totals do not exceed the sub-area "most likely" totals.

These variations yield a map of comparative growth to the year 2001 (Figure 9.5) that is much more emphatic than the one produced from the unconstrained data (Figure 9.2). The benchmarks for the map are selected by exactly the same procedure used for Figure 9.2. The areas of decreasing population are, unlike the situation depicted in Figure 9.2, reasonably extensive. Declining populations are predicted for much of eastern Ontario, and nearly all rural areas in the Province of Québec beyond the major metropolitan areas. The areas of great comparative growth, which, in this case, experience a growth rate of greater than 1.7 per cent per annum, are confined to the major metropolitan regions, particularly an extensive zone between Toronto and Kitchener. In general, the more extensive and continuous areas of growth are expected to be located in the western one-third of the axis.

The pattern of urbanization that results is not too dissimilar to the one exhibited by the unconstrained forecasts. Urban densities are found in an almost continuous strip between Windsor and Hamilton and along the Lake Ontario shore and the north bank of the St. Lawrence River (Figure 9.6). This pattern is emphasized in Figure 9.7, in which the census subdivisions that contain population densities greater than the urban density threshold are identified. The constrained forecasts for the year 2001 yield census subdivisions comprising 16,960 square miles, which can be classified as urban; if all the "urban" population at that date resides in these census subdivisions, the average population density would be a little over 1,000 persons per square mile. Thus, even though the area of census subdivisions urbanized by the year 2001 are less for the constrained

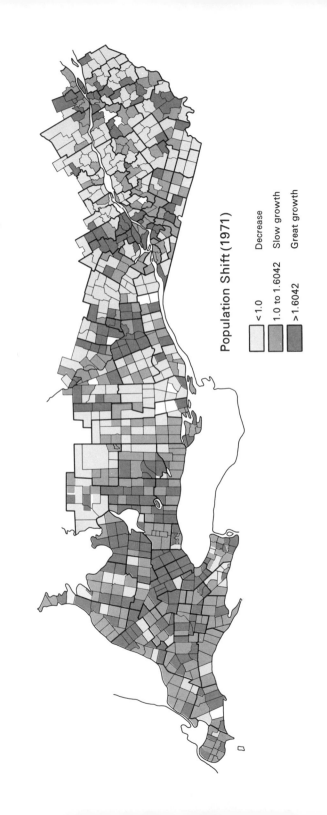

Population Shift (1971)

□ <1.0	Decrease
▨ 1.0 to 1.6042	Slow growth
▧ >1.6042	Great growth

Figure 9.5: Population growth in the axis, 1971–2001: constrained forecasts for the year 2001

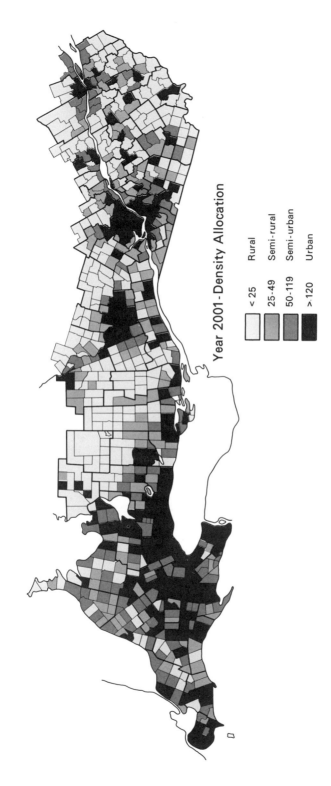

Year 2001 - Density Allocation

< 25	Rural
25-49	Semi-rural
50-119	Semi-urban
>120	Urban

Figure 9.6: Axis population densities in the year 2001: constrained forecasts

forecasts than for the unconstrained forecasts, the average density of the population residing within them is about the same.

The requirements for new urban land that will result from this rate of growth are depicted in Table 3.4. The trend figures result in an estimate of 2,117 square miles needed by the year 2001, whereas the preferred land consumption rate results in an increase of 1,124 square miles. Since it is evident that the preferred rate results in a 50 per cent increase in land directly in urban use over a period of thirty years, even this increase must be viewed with some alarm. The urban intrusion effects of such an expansion of urban population and urban land will be even more dramatic, and may well extend over the entire area defined as urban, semi-urban, and semi-rural in Figure 9.6. The question of urban intrusion effect is, however, a difficult and separate concern, and more evidence is required before a density of twenty-five persons per square mile can be inferred as the lower limit of such indirect urban impacts on the environment.

THE INFLUENCE OF MONTREAL AND TORONTO ON THE DISTRIBUTION OF POPULATION IN THE YEAR 2001

In the previous section it was noted that whereas in 1971 less than 58 per cent of the axis population was located in the Ontario portion, almost 64 per cent will be located in this area by the year 2001. Furthermore, the trends suggest that the vast bulk of this population will be located in the western one-third of the axis, particularly within sixty miles of Metro Toronto. But the mere factual detailing of what has happened and what is likely to happen, based on data and forecasts prepared with very limited assumptions, does not explain why these trends have developed. The cascading procedure and the forecasts based on migration trends and 1966–71 growth rates, both assume that past trends will continue into the future. In other words, the two forecasts incorporate the premise that the forces that have made Toronto and Montréal so dominant in the past will continue unabated to favour both urban areas. When examining these forces it is important to differentiate between those that are common to many urban areas, and those that are particular to Montréal and Toronto and that distinguish them as primate cities with their respective spheres of influence.

From the fairly well-developed body of literature relating to the distinguishing functions of primary metropolitan centres (Jefferson, 1939; Linsky, 1965; Hall, 1963) it is possible to define three basic groups which can be used to describe past changes and as indicators of future trends. Probably the most important distinguishing characteristics of a primate city in the western world is its function as the financial centre of the country in which it is located. The financial community appears to require physical proximity to its component parts to operate efficiently, and, it is suspected, to promote common policies. It is important, however, to recognize that the word "finance" covers a variety of activities, two of which need to be distinguished. The first is the rôle of the financial community as the operator of a market in which large volumes of money can be purchased or sold. This money is controlled by the banks; the distribution of assets between the banks, the location of their head offices, and the structure of their decision-making mechanism, all combine to determine the geographic location of money power.

The second aspect of the financial community that should be considered is its rôle as a market for ownership. This is, of course, interrelated with the money market, but it can be regarded as separate from it in operation. There is little doubt that one of the most important innovations that made possible the industrial revolution was the development of limited liability, and the extended ownership of firms through the sale of shares. As this system extended it soon became clear that the shares themselves had a value that depended upon the current and expected profit performance of the firm to which they related. Consequently, a formal market mechanism was required for the orderly sale and purchase of the shares, and in time these markets grew and amalgamated into "stock" markets. Stock markets are obviously very highly specialized service activities; for both buyers and sellers require maximum customer access for the most advantageous marketing of the shares. It is not unexpected, therefore, that the largest urban areas have become the focuses for these activities. Indicators of the strength of this particular group of activities are the value and volume of turnover at the various stock exchanges.

If an urban area is a financial centre, it is quite likely that other activities will tend to locate in the general vicinity because of their requirements for periodic loans, or so that they can be in a position to respond quickly to major business changes, such as those involving interest rates, bank policies, personnel movements, and so forth. Examples of activities of this type are the headquarters of major companies, defined as those in which decisions are made that affect subsidiary offices and plants located elsewhere in Canada. A second activity that also warrants some attention is information processing; this type of activity has fairly large capital demands, and requires access to the largest markets and highly skilled labour.

A third major group of activities that tend to be primate-city oriented are those concerned with the media and entertainment. The chief metropolis of any country contains the major entertainment and cultural facilities, is the location of nationally distributed newspapers and the centre of the advertising industry, and is the locus of the major hotels. Trends in some of these industries are rather difficult to calibrate in a Canadian context, but a few of the items can be used as indicators for the group as a whole. A recurring theme throughout this volume has been the perceived excessive dominance of the major metropolises over the cultural life of the country, for it would appear that the media and entertainment industries are overly concerned with metropolitan problems and values.

THE FINANCIAL COMMUNITY

The financial community is difficult to investigate, because much of the data is regarded as non-disclosable, and many of the comments regarding trends obtained in interviews are prefaced by confidential disclaimers. But, as the general tenor and direction of these "behind closed doors" statements are supported by the weight of the evidence, most of the observations can be regarded as tenable.

The banks

The Canadian banking system is highly centralized, since branch banking is permissible across the entire country. As a consequence, there are very few banks, and the largest of them have extensive branch-banking operations. The very nature of the structure, therefore, leads to a highly centralized decision-making system, though the "official" policy of most of the banks is claimed to be one of encouraging decentralization in decision making. Before Confederation, the Bank of Montreal dominated the rather small financial community of the country. In 1871 Montréal had twice the population of Toronto, and the bank epitomized the power that this city exerted over the fledgeling nation. But the businessmen of Toronto had also begun the development of their own financial community. The Imperial Bank of Canada, which was founded in 1855, began an intensive rivalry with the Bank of Montreal, though its rôle was primarily regional in these early years.

As the country grew and other banks were established, the banking industry continued to locate in Montréal and Toronto. Today, there are nine banks and the head offices of all but the Bank of British Columbia are located in one or the other of these two metropolises (Table 9.2). Although no one bank controls the industry, the fact that they are located in either of these two cities and share common interests means that they can exert near monopolistic control over the financial system of the country. By 1970 this control had become fairly evenly distributed between Montréal and Toronto, with Montréal controlling about 51 per cent of the bank assets of the country, and Toronto a little less than 49 per cent.

This almost fifty:fifty split in total assets between the two metropolises represents a significant shift in the division of money strength, for prior to the 1960s Montréal was clearly dominant. Table 9.3, which is based on information contained in two different sources (Kerr and Spelt, 1965; Neufeld, 1972), indicates that the total strength of the Toronto-based banks has risen continuously since the turn of the century. This growth has occurred partially at the expense of Montréal, but also as a result of the retention of assets in the country rather than their transfer to other banking centres, such as New York and London.

Apart from bank assets there are two other indicators of the changing relative importance of the two metropolises that can be regarded as useful predictors of future financial trends. Since 1924 the cheque clearing house serving the Toronto area has passed a greater dollar volume than the one serving the Montréal region. In 1924 the Montréal cheque clearing house passed 27.62 per cent of the Canadian total, while the Toronto clearing house passed 28.2 per cent. By 1971 these percentages had changed radically: the Toronto clearing house accounted for 43 per cent of the Canadian total, and Montréal a little less than 24 per cent. This increase in importance of the Toronto clearing house, now the most important in Canada, has been fairly steady over the last fifty years. It can be attributed to a number of factors, of which two are quite important. First, the general wealth of the Toronto area is much greater than that of Montréal. In 1971 the average personal disposable in-

Table 9.2: The relative size of Canada's nine chartered banks, and the location of their head offices

BANK	PROPORTION OF TOTAL ASSETS		OCTOBER 31, 1970 ASSETS $ MILLION	HEAD OFFICE LOCATION
	1960	1970		
Royal Bank of Canada	25.1	25.1	11,369	Montréal
Canadian Imperial Bank of Commerce	24.3	22.7	11,051	Toronto
Bank of Montreal	20.7	19.5	8,730	Montréal
Bank of Nova Scotia	11.8	13.6	6,369	Toronto
Toronto-Dominion Bank	10.8	12.0	5,423	Toronto
Banque Canadienne Nationale	4.6	4.3	1,908	Montréal
Banque Provinciale du Canada	2.2	2.2	193	Montréal
Mercantile Bank of Canada	0.5	0.6	121	Toronto (U.S.-owned)
Bank of British Columbia	0.5	0.6	121	Vancouver

Sources: Neufeld (1972), p. 100; The Financial Post, April 1971

come in the Toronto metropolitan region was about $2,870 per year, whereas the average in Montréal (Ile de Montréal) was about $2,650. This difference is reflected in the per capita retail sales figure for the two metropolitan regions: the figure for Montréal is about 15 per cent less than the figure for Toronto (Dagenais, 1969, p. 35). Thus the total income and the total volume of business is significantly greater in Toronto than in Montréal, resulting in a significantly greater volume of cheque transactions in Toronto.

But this does not explain the total magnitude of the difference between the two centres, or the rate of growth of the difference. Further explanations must lie in movements that have resulted in Toronto becoming the primary focus of activity in the financial community. This development is, perhaps, best seen in the changes that have occurred in the stock markets in Canada over the past 100 years, for a few cheques of large dollar value can account for many cheques each consisting of small amounts.

The stock exchanges

Prior to 1900 most stocks pertaining to companies operating in Canada were listed on exchanges operating in London or New York. After the turn of the century this situation changed, because improvements in communications made it possible for Canadian exchanges to be linked with the more abundant London and New York money markets. For example, a direct link between the New York and Toronto Stock Exchanges was established by ticker tape in 1881, and transatlantic cables were operating in 1886. At the beginning

Table 9.3: The division of bank assets between Montréal and Toronto, expressed in percentages of the Canadian total, 1890–1970

YEAR	MONTRÉAL	TORONTO
1890	44.5	28.3
1906	43.7	38.7
1920	52.0	40.0
1932	58.5	41.5
1960	52.6	46.9
1970	51.1	48.3

Sources: 1890–1932: Kerr and Spelt (1965), p. 87; 1960 and 1970: Neufeld (1972), p. 99.

of the present century Montréal had the largest Canadian stock exchange, and as a result, most of Canadian industry was controlled from this metropolis.

Although there are many kinds of stock — "blue chip", industrials, utilities, "high growth", and just plain bad ones — for the purpose of this discussion it is enough to make two classifications. These are "mining stocks" and "non-mining" stocks. The latter include all industrials, utilities, transport, and trust company stocks; the former include those specifically concerned with mining and exploration for minerals of different kinds, but not oil. The reasons for this distinction may appear fragmentary at the moment, but it will become evident that, in a Canadian context, this differentiation is most appropriate. It may be observed at that outset, however, that, taken as a group, mining stocks are far more risky than most of those in the non-mining sector. This is because the only real value asset of a mining company is the mineral that it has found and is mining. A company that as yet has produced nothing, but hopes to find something, is a highly speculative company in which to invest.

In the early years of the present century most of the stocks listed on exchanges in Montréal were of a non-mining nature. However, in 1903 large deposits of silver were found in Cobalt; in 1911 gold was discovered in Porcupine; and in 1912 gold was discovered in Kirkland Lake. These discoveries, and many others, required financing to support the numerous mining companies that were formed. The more conservative Montréal exchanges were reluctant to list the shares of these highly speculative companies, so they sought acceptance in Toronto. In 1895 two small mining exchanges were established and these soon merged (1898) to form the Standard Stock and Mining Exchange (Kerr, 1968). Incidentally, this exchange merged with the Toronto Stock Exchange in 1934. The significance of the concentration of the mining-stock business in Toronto was that it enabled the city's financial interests to gain control of the rich Canadian Shield hinterland. As a result, Montréal played a small part in the dynamic growth of Canadian mineral resources.

Nevertheless, Montréal remained dominant in the higher value security business up until the Great Depression. Even though the volume of shares flowing through the Toronto exchanges exceeded that of Montréal, the value of the shares traded in Montréal was much higher. In fact, in 1925 nearly 86 per cent of the total value of Canadian transactions passed through the Montréal exchanges, but by 1933, Toronto's share of transactions in high-value securities on the market exceeded Montréal's. The Toronto market had been enhanced by an increase in the price of gold in the early 1930s, while the Depression ruined many of the businesses listed on the Montréal exchanges. Thus, the Depression hit the Montréal exchanges much harder than those in Toronto, and the formation of the united Toronto Stock Exchange solidified this competitive advantage.

The position of Toronto improved even more after 1945 when the Canadian manufacturing boom of the Second World War continued into the post-war period. Associated with this boom was a tremendous increase in mining activity on the Canadian Shield, partly to provide raw materials for the expanding manufacturing sector, but also for export. The result of these twin increases in activity was tremendous activity and growth in the market for stocks, and most of this increase in activity took place on the Toronto Stock Exchange; for it was this exchange that had proven more stable during the pre-war period. Furthermore, the dominance of Toronto in mining stocks gave an added strength and variety to securities activities in this city. Consequently, by 1971, about 69 per cent of the total dollar value of securities traded in Canada was handled by the Toronto Stock Exchange, and 23 per cent by the Montréal Stock exchanges.

It would appear, therefore, that Toronto now dominates the securities business in Canada, and has a strong claim to being the leading centre of finance in the nation. Undoubtedly, much of the increase in banking activity is attributable to the great overall increase in activities of a financial nature in this city. There are, however, signs of increasing financial activities in other Canadian centres. The merging of the Canadian and Montréal Stock Exchanges in Montréal should provide some impetus to securities activities in the city. Furthermore, the relative stability and strength of the economic situation in Québec during the past two or three years should support a strengthening in activities in this area. One cannot escape the impression, however, that the Montréal financial community is now regionally oriented, whereas the Toronto community is nationally oriented. Certainly, the contrasting proportion of activities in both cities would support this contention. In interviews, many persons in the Montréal financial community speak of "French money", which remains in Montréal, and "English money" which is invested through Toronto and many Montréal brokers indicate that they receive instructions from Toronto.

The two proportions cited above indicate that 92 per cent of the total dollar value of securities traded in Canada in 1971 passed through the Toronto and Montréal stock exchanges. The residual trading took place in exchanges in Vancouver, Calgary, and Winnipeg. Of these three exchanges, Vancouver is by far the largest, since it trades an immense volume of shares in any year, though their individual average value is rather low. The rise of the Vancouver exchange took place almost entirely during the 1960s, and it appears to be associated with the growth of the oil and gas industry in the west. Although much of the investment activity in western oil occurred through Toronto, a significant proportion of the more speculative oil and mining investments were financed through the Vancouver Stock Exchange. The result has been a boom in the Vancouver financial community and the establishment of that city as the regional capital for much of the west.

THE LOCATION OF THE HEADQUARTERS OF MAJOR COMPANIES

One of the more entertaining features of newspapers, magazine articles, and business folk lore in general during the late 1960s and early 1970s has been the contention that the headquarters of major companies are fleeing from Montréal to Toronto. It could be argued, of course, that the hierarchical nature of the socio-economic system in which the Canadian urban system operates is bound to lead to the development of a primate city. This is, in fact, one of the implications of the rank-size concept, which seems to be tenable for most western countries, as well as for provinces within Canada (Berry and Horton, 1970, pp. 64–92; Davies, 1972). This concept suggests that an integrated system of cities will tend toward a rank-size distribution of populations.

Probably the clearest definition of the rank-size concept has been presented by Zipf (1949), who states that the population of the rth ranked city equals the population of the largest city (P_1) divided by its rank (r) raised to some exponent (b). This can be expressed in equation form as $P_r = P_1/r^b$. The exponent b indicates the rate at which the population of the towns decrease in size according to rank. Although this rank-size concept may appear to be in semantic conflict with Jefferson's (1939) primate city concept, it is not really irreconcilable as far as the axis is concerned. The implications of both concepts are that one urban area would, in time, become larger and dominate over the others; how much larger and how much "primate" does not really matter. At the moment it would appear that Canada is blessed with two highest-ranked metropolises, although there are signs that in the future one alone may rank ahead of the others.

If this situation does develop, the location and movement of head offices may well be crucial, because office employment is, as has been indicated in Chapter 6, a large generator of growth. It is difficult, however, to establish a comparable time-series of information for all firms and all head offices. As a consequence, a number of examples have been selected in the hope that, in total, they will suggest the same trend. These examples concern the location of designated "key" companies, and the location of some specific groups of activities, such as chartered accountants, and computing and information companies.

"Key" companies

One of the more accessible sources of information concerning head offices is found in the newspaper *The Financial Post*. This paper publishes annually a listing of companies that it regards as "key" to the Canadian economy in that particular year. This number seems to vary from year to year; for example, it was higher in 1966 than in 1972 (Table 9.4). This source not only indicates which companies are important, but also lists their addresses. The listing does not, however, distinguish the companies in terms of size and ranking of economic importance.

Nevertheless, the information is quite interesting as it does suggest a definite trend. The proportion of head offices found in Montréal and Toronto appears to have increased between 1961 and 1972. The slight decline in 1966 cannot really be regarded as a significant difference, given the data errors and nature of the sample involved. The gross increase in major metropolitan concentration, however, is evident with respect to only one of these metropolitan areas. The concentration of "key" companies in Toronto appears to have increased substantially between 1961 and 1972, so that by 1972 the head offices of one-third of all the companies concerned appear to be located in Toronto. The reasons for this concentration are manifold, and have been alluded to several times throughout this volume. It would be appropriate in this section, however, to refer to the prob-

Table 9.4: The location of the head offices of "key" Canadian companies

YEAR	TORONTO		MONTRÉAL		TOTAL IN CANADA	MONTRÉAL AND TORONTO AS A PERCENTAGE OF CANADA'S TOTAL
	NUMBER	%	NUMBER	%		
1961	652	30.2	349	16.1	2,162	46.3
1966	754	29.9	400	15.9	2,520	45.8
1972	797	33.3	355	14.8	2,395	48.1

lems of raising money for short-term loans, which are faced by companies whose head offices are not located in Toronto or Montréal. In particular, it appears that if an entrepreneur requires a large loan (about $1 million) he/she can obtain the money far more easily by flying to Toronto or Montréal and visiting the head office of the bank concerned, than by negotiating through an intermediary regional bank.

The number of head offices located in Montréal appears to have remained fairly stable between 1961 and 1972, but its share of the total number has decreased; this decrease was most apparent during the 1966–72 period. There is a tendency to relate substantial changes of this type to the recent political instability in Québec. For example, Bourne and MacKinnon (1972, p.x) write:

> A final consideration must be recognized in treating urban development in Ontario and Québec, the impact of recent political and social instability in Québec. Isolationism in any form, in any major region, will most certainly have a dampening effect on the growth of the urban system, effects which will be most pronounced in the isolated region itself.

The trends involving some redistribution of major functions between Montréal and Toronto, however, have been in effect for some time. More importantly, those activities that attract, or foster, other activities, tend to exhibit decisions that harmonize with the patterns displayed by these trends.

The location of specific groups of activities

One group which tends to locate near other financial institutions are chartered accountants. In 1963 there were 2,130 chartered accountants in Canada, and of these 39 per cent had offices in either Montréal or Toronto. Of the Montréal and Toronto total, 64 per cent were located in Montréal. By 1966 these proportions had changed substantially. At this date, 44 per cent of the 2,300 chartered accountants in Canada were located in either Montréal or Toronto, but the Montréal total was barely changed from 1963. The increase, in fact, went to Toronto, which by 1966 had very nearly one-half of the Montréal–Toronto total. This is a good example of the kind of change that had occurred prior to the political and social unrest referred to by Bourne and MacKinnon (1972).

One of the more rapidly growing modern industries in the world concerns computer equipment hardware. The rate of technological advance in computing equipment over the past two decades has been phenomenal, and the introduction of the new information processing systems that these facilities have made possible has been equally rapid. In fact, the past few years have witnessed a "cybernetic" revolution in Canadian life that will be as far-reaching as the industrial revolution was. The industrial revolution involved the substitution of mechanical power for man's physical tasks. The cybernetic revolution involves the substitution of machines for many of man's mental information and sorting tasks. It can be suggested, therefore, that the new companies producing computing equipment of different kinds will undoubtedly locate where they feel the future market will be the most promising and the chances of obtaining capital the greatest.

Nearly all of the large computer companies operating in Canada are non-Canadian owned. Although this can be regarded as a source of concern, the facts of the matter are that the capital requirements, development costs, and marketing requirements of the computer industry enhance the competitive position of the large supranational companies. It is extremely difficult for small companies to develop in this type of competitive situation, for the array of services and inducements offered by the large companies is simply overwhelming. In 1972 twelve large foreign-owned companies supplied nearly all the Canadian market, and of these the leading five — IBM, Digital Equipment Company, Burroughs, Honeywell, and Univac — controlled 85 per cent of the market. The head offices and chief manufacturing assembly plants of four of these five are located in Metro Toronto, and those of one (DEC) are located in Ottawa. Of the twelve leading companies, nine are based in the Metro Toronto area, one in Ottawa, one in Hull, and only one (Hewlett-Packard) in Montréal.

This same concentration in one metropolis is exhibited by the location pattern of the twelve leading Canadian-owned companies. Most of these "Canadian"-owned companies are really subsidiaries of large foreign-owned conglomerates, such as Litton Industries and Control Data Corporation, but they are listed as separate companies with their own Board of Directors within Canada. Furthermore, most of the companies do not build computing systems within Canada, but act as suppliers or servicers. Eight of the twelve list Metro Toronto as the location of their head offices, while two list Ottawa, and two Montréal.

Thus, the evidence concerning the location of chartered accountants yields some interesting observations which conform with the trends described previously. As far as the more established financial activities are concerned, Toronto is now definitely equal to Montréal and in some instances, superior. In the future, Montréal will find it difficult to maintain its position. The newer, more vital electronic industries, as represented by computer companies, appear to be much more concentrated in their location pattern. It is interesting to note that the head offices of all the twenty-four computer companies analysed are located within the axis, and that 70 per cent of them are in Toronto. Ottawa and Montréal share equally those situated beyond the Metro Toronto area. This preference for Toronto, of course, emphasizes the strong links which this type of industry has with those activities involving administration, evaluation, data storing, collating, classifying, and scientific calculations.

ENTERTAINMENT AND OTHER SERVICE ACTIVITIES

One of the more important attributes of large metropolitan centres is the entertainment facilities found within them. These range from facilities involving the arts (such as drama schools, art galleries, and so forth), to music (symphonies, ballet, opera), sports, exhibitions, night clubs, and other tourist attractions. They are difficult to evaluate quantitatively, and they require a considerable degree of personal judgement concerning their importance as additives to the image of the city.

Perhaps a good summary indicator of the attractiveness of a metropolis as a tourist, business, cultural, and entertainment centre is its rank in the world of "conventions". Large national and international groups invariably choose to meet in cities where abundant entertainment, sleeping, and eating facilities are available for the conventioneers (and their families or camp followers), and where the media is on hand to give them some national, and occasionally international coverage. Contrary to expectation, there were in 1971 more recognized convention hotels (and motels) listed for Toronto than for Montréal, and the number of rooms available in these hotels was greater in Toronto than Montréal. This is contrary to expectations because Montréal is traditionally regarded as the "convention" centre of Canada. Certainly, in 1961 Montréal had a greater number of rooms for transients than Toronto. The change that appears to have occurred is probably related to the entrenchment of Toronto as the business centre of Canada.

It could, therefore, be expected that Toronto might re-enforce this apparent position of slight leadership in the convention facility business. But recent signs indicate that Montréal is undergoing a new phase of hotel and entertainment construction as a result of the impending Olympic games. Whether this development will result in the re-establishment of Montréal as the convention centre of Canada, or will simply lead to an overcapacity for two or three years in the latter half of the 1970s, remains to be seen. The weight of the evidence suggests that the latter situation may be the case.

CONCLUSION

The macro-urban picture of the axis in the year 2001 can, therefore, be envisaged with a reasonable degree of confidence. The "most likely" total population of the axis will be a little more than nineteen million. The urban densities envisaged in Figures 9.6 and 9.7 represent most clearly the macro-pattern of urbanism that will develop. The broad pattern of changes suggested by the "most likely" projection suggests a further concentration of population around the two major metropolises in the area, with the western one-third of the axis growing much faster than the eastern one-third. This prediction has been examined in terms of both the attractive power of Montréal and Toronto, and the competition between the two cities. In fact, the competition between Montréal and Toronto has been an interesting theme running through much of the recent literature concerning these two cities — best exemplified perhaps by the works of Kerr (1968) and Dagenais (1969).

Both Kerr and Dagenais contend that both share, and will share, primate metropolitan functions fairly equally. But evidence from the various projections as well as the economic trends concerning certain particular "high-order" functions of the two metropolises lead to the provocative conclusion that the urban system will be structured around Toronto as the primary node. Taken further, the next highest ranked metropolises will, by the year 2001, probably be Montréal and Van-

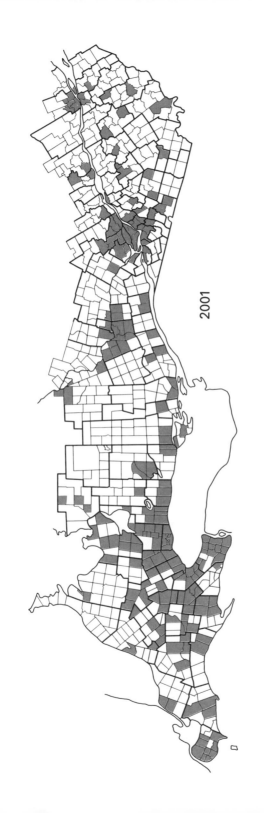

2001

Figure 9.7: Census subdivisions with "urban" population densities in the year 2001: constrained forecasts

couver; with Montréal serving the regional needs of the Province of Québec and part of the Maritimes, and Vancouver serving much of the west.

It should be realized, however, that in this context the word metropolis pertains not only to the service and business functions contained within the city involved, but to the whole range of activities found within a large area of continuous urbanization for which it is the direct focus. In the first chapter, the conceptual limits of such a broad area were defined, and the 1971 population of each determined. It will be recalled (Table 1.2) that in 1971, the total populations residing within forty miles of Toronto and within forty miles of Montréal were almost equal. By the year 2001 this will not be the case. The "most likely" forecast indicates that well over one-third of the axis population will be found within forty miles of Toronto, and somewhat less than one-quarter within forty miles of Montréal by the year 2001 (Table 9.5). In fact, the whole population of Canada will be relatively more concentrated within these limits in the year 2001 (34 per cent) than in 1971 (30 per cent). The dominance of these two metropolises, particularly Toronto, will be greatly enhanced. One of the major tasks confronting urban planners, therefore, is the management of these different urban growth patterns; even with the constrained forecasts and planned minimum densities, the amount of new urban land and housing required will be immense.

One question which may be raised with respect to these shifts concerns the reasons for the predictions with respect to the Toronto region. The social, economic, and administrative trends upon which these predictions are based have been made abundantly clear. But the more metaphysical question concerns why they should have occurred this way. Perhaps much of the answer lies in some observations concerning Montréal and Toronto postulated by Dagenais (1969). He suggests that whereas Montréal is the product of naturally advantageous physical and relative location, Toronto is a product of human will power stronger than geographical determinism. Referring to the early days of settlement in Upper Canada, he suggests that Toronto was actually founded because of Governor Simcoe's obstinacy and exaggerated fears of invasion. Ever since this time, the chief characteristic of the city has been its dependence on entrepreneurship and determinacy to control a larger and larger hinterland. These characteristics are encouraged and rewarded in the type of socioeconomic system that has existed, and, as a consequence, definite

Table 9.5: The expected concentration of population (in thousands) in 2001 within the axis, around four major cities, compared with 1971

CITY	1971		2001 "MOST LIKELY"		AREA	
	POPULATION	%	POPULATION	%	SQUARE MILES	%
Montréal (40 miles)	3,173	26.6	4,558	23.8	4,342.5	6.4
Toronto (40 miles)	3,397	28.5	6,645	34.8	2,345.1	3.5
Ottawa (15 miles)	573	4.8	1,018	5.3	487.1	0.7
Québec City (15 miles)	484	4.1	713	3.7	473.1	0.7
Total	7,627	64.0	12,934	67.6	7,647.8	11.3
Axis	11,918		19,119		67,569.0	

patterns of urban dominance and sub-dominance have developed. It is not surprising, therefore, that the end product of this development will be an urban system which conforms to a primate, rank-ordered, hierarchical pattern.

10   SUMMARY AND CONCLUSION

The main purpose of this study has been to describe the Windsor to Québec City urban axis, to analyse some major changes that have occurred between 1961 and 1971, and to take a brief look into the future. This study has involved a structure that is macro, or large-area oriented, and basically man-oriented. The chapters therefore follow a sequence that emphasizes this orientation. Chapter 1 defines the axis, describes briefly its physical structure and historical settlement, and then indicates its importance in economic terms to Canada. The second chapter describes the distribution of population within the axis, discusses the various components of urban growth and how these changed over the 1961–71 decade, and then uses these concepts to project a future "most likely" population for the axis using a simple model. People consume land, and so the third chapter is devoted to an estimation of the amounts of land consumed for various urban and non-urban purposes, changes in urban land consumption rates, major problems in the transference of land to urban uses, and urban land requirements for the year 2001, for fairly large sub-areas. Probably the most sensitive and evident manifestation of a person's occupance of urban space is the house or dwelling unit in which he/she resides. Consequently, in Chapter 4 there is a discussion of changes in the demand for and supply of housing in major metropolitan areas within the axis, as well as construction trends that may well have significant importance in the future.

People consume land, live in houses, and require jobs; for employment is the only real means of distributing income. Therefore, Chapter 5 is devoted to an economic survey of the axis, with particular attention to the major sources and locations of employment, and changes that occurred between 1961 and 1971. The economic strength of the axis is then placed in perspective with the rest of the country by means of an inter-regional input-output model. The complex process of interaction implied by this model is then analysed in greater detail in Chapters 6 and 7. No person, municipality, metropolis, province, or country can exist in isolation, so interaction in all its forms is necessary for existence and development. In Chapter 6, various concepts of interaction are used to investigate the structure of flows not only within the axis, but between it and the rest of Canada, and the United States. In Chapter 7 the actual mechanisms facilitating flows within the axis are described, and a few future route developments discussed.

The places in which the urban population resides, and which are linked together by a complex pattern of routes, have to be managed and administered. Unfortunately, there are many thousands of types and kinds of local governments, many of which have over-lapping spatial jurisdictions, and in Chapter 8 the nature of this complex political fragmentation, and its equally complex financial basis are outlined. Certain procedures aimed at rationalizing the fragmentation problem and ameliorating the fiscal dilemma are described, and those that have been implemented are discussed in greater detail. Finally, in Chapter 9 a method for projecting the spatial distribution of population in the axis is presented, and its implications evaluated. This method is then used to allocate the "most likely" forecasts (described in Chapter 2) to census subdivisions. The forecasts suggest an increased concentration of population around the two major metropolises, particularly Toronto, and some economic forces leading to primacy situations of this kind are discussed.

It has proved necessary to detail the basic outline of the monograph because the essential pieces of information are contained within this structure. The plan of the chapters does not, of itself, lead to any cohesive theory concerning future urban developments within the axis, but some of the information can be used to place the changes within the context of the theory of post-industrialism. It may be useful at this juncture, therefore, to summarize briefly the major substantive contributions of each chapter, recognizing, of course, that matters considered substantive by one individual may be considered trivial by 'others! Following this, the concept of post-industrialism and its relevance to future macro-urban developments will be explained.

SUMMARY

1. THE FORM OF THE AXIS

1) The Windsor to Québec City axis as defined has the shape of a rectangle 650–750 miles long and 100–150 miles wide, and contains an area of 67,576 square miles. The boundaries of the axis are shown in Fig. 1.1.

2) In 1971, it is estimated that 11,917,655 people reside within the axis area. 92.2 per cent of this total resides in census subdivisions containing an average population density greater than fifty persons per square mile. Furthermore, 55.1 per cent of this population resides within forty miles of Montréal or forty miles of Toronto.

3) Physiographically, the axis contains two broad lowland areas (Interlake Ontario and the St. Lawrence Lowland) comprising nearly 60 per cent of the axis land surface, and two much eroded upland areas (the Shield and Appalachian Québec). Settlement has been very much influenced by the pattern of physical features.

4) Climatically, southwestern Ontario is far more favourable for agriculture (and settlement) than the rest of the axis.

5) The current pattern of urbanism also reflects the historical settlement of the area by the French, English, and United Empire Loyalist colonizers.

6) The principal regional centres within the axis are Québec City, Trois-Rivières, Sherbrooke, Montréal, Ottawa–Hull, Kingston, Peterborough, Oshawa, Toronto, Hamilton, Kitchener, St. Catharines, London, and Windsor. The spheres of influence of these centres, when aggregated, comprise the axis.

7) The population of Canada is becoming more concentrated in the axis area. 53.1 per cent of the country's population was located in the axis in 1961, and 55.3 per cent in 1971. The population of the axis is also more wealthy than the rest of the country, having a per capita income in 1971 of $2,589 compared with $2,069 in the rest of the country. However, this wealth difference decreased substantially between 1961 and 1971.

8) About 72 per cent of the employment in manufacturing in Canada was located in the axis in 1970, though there has been a slight decrease in this concentration between 1961 and 1970.

Furthermore, although only 13.0 per cent of the country's farmland is located in the axis, the farms in the area received 38.7 per cent of the total cash receipts of all farms in Canada in 1971.

9) Linguistically and culturally, the axis consists of two distinct entities. 52 per cent of the axis population claims English as its mother tongue in 1971, and 79 per cent of this population resides in Ontario; 36 per cent is French, and 78 per cent of this population resides in Québec. There are other large minorities, however, which have exhibited tremendous increases in population between 1961 and 1971. In particular, Italians, residing primarily in Toronto and Montréal, in 1971 comprised nearly 4 per cent of the axis population, and now outnumber French-Canadians in the Ontario portion of the axis.

10) Compared with other elongated urban agglomerations in the rest of the world, the Windsor to Québec City urban axis is very long, but has a far lower average population density per linear mile. Thus, problems existing in these other areas should not be thought to exist in the axis, nor should programs necessary in extremely dense areas be used throughout the axis. But the axis is just as important to Canada as the other elongated urban agglomerations in the rest of the world are to their respective countries, and it is for this reason that urban developments that occur in this area have national repercussions.

2. GROWTH, EXPANSION AND CONVERGENCE

1) The population of the axis grew at a faster rate (2.0 per cent per annum) between 1961 and 1971 than Canada did as a whole (1.7 per cent per annum). There were, however, two distinct growth periods. The 1961 to 1966 period was an extension of the rapid population growth era which followed World War II, and in this five-year period the axis population increased at a rate of 2.3 per cent per annum. During the last five year period, the axis population has grown at a rate of 1.7 per cent per annum. Problems arising as a result of rapid population growth may well, therefore, be minimal in the future.

2) This decline in growth rate of the population is attributed to a great decrease in the birth rate, particularly in Québec, and a decrease in the number of immigrants entering the axis from

beyond Canada, during the last half of the 1960s.

3) The rate of population growth between 1961 and 1971 in the Ontario portion of the axis (2.3 per cent) exceeds that in Québec (1.7 per cent). This considerable difference can be related to higher birth rates and a greater volume of immigration in Ontario than in Québec.

4) But growth rates in those parts of the axis defined as urban are about the same, and very high (about 2.5 per cent per annum). Average growth rates in semi-urban areas are much less, and in rural areas there have been absolute decreases in population.

5) The areas of great population growth (greater than 2.0 per cent per annum) are confined almost entirely to the suburban areas of four urban regions around Toronto, Montréal, Ottawa–Hull, and Québec City. A comparative shift analysis indicates that there has been a relative convergence of population to these areas over the 1961–71 period.

6) An interprovincial migration model suggests that in a situation of zero population growth the population of Canada would become even more concentrated in the axis.

7) A forecast model based on 1956–61 interprovincial migration patterns and 1966–71 regional growth rates indicates that the "most likely" population in Canada in the year 2001 is 32.933 million, and for the axis is 19.119 million. These figures are comparable with, though slightly less than, those forecast by others.

8) Migration patterns within the axis suggest an increasing concentration of population around the major metropolitan centres. With a decrease in the rate of natural increase, and net immigration from beyond the country, migration to urban areas is likely to be the major source of urban population growth in the future.

3. THE USE OF THE LAND

1) It is estimated that 2,146.2 square miles, or 3.2 per cent of the axis surface is occupied by continuous urban uses. About 52.4 per cent of the land surface is within the boundaries of census farms.

2) Figure 3.1 provides a cartographic representation of the propor-

tion of land in each of the 730 axis census subdivisions that is defined as urban. Urban land use is particularly heavy in the general area between Whitby and the Niagara Peninsula, in the Montréal region, and around the other major urban areas listed previously.

3) While land is transferred from rural to urban uses at the periphery of urban areas, this zone is the place least likely to be within the jurisdiction of one single municipal planning authority.

4) Urban land consumption rates (the amount of urban land actually used at a particular date expressed as a ratio of the urban population at that date) are lower for large urban areas than for smaller towns or cities. Furthermore, there appears to be no difference in land consumption rates for cities in the same size class in Ontario and Québec.

5) The average macro-urban land consumption rate for the axis as a whole in 1971 is estimated to be 139 acres per thousand people. The trend in urban land consumption rates is such that land is being consumed for urban purposes at an increasing rate, and that by the year 2001 the consumption figure may well be 160 acres per thousand people, if the trend continues. This implies an average land absorption rate (amount of new land absorbed by each additional person in an urban area) of 0.186 acres per person throughout the thirty-year period.

6) The trend in land consumption and absorption rates is excessive as it reflects densities that are too low to sustain adequate urban services and infrastructure. A maximum average land absorption rate for the thirty-year period of 0.100 acres per person would be much preferable.

7) The area occupied by farms declined by 4,148 square miles in the 1966–71 period. This decrease occurred primarily as a result of farm abandonment, afforestation, and the transfer of land to recreational purposes. A rough-and-ready estimate leads to the suggestion that about 6.4 per cent of this land was transferred to urban uses.

8) The one area where urban encroachment on prime agricultural land is of serious consequence is in the Niagara Peninsula. In this area, between 1951 and 1966, about 430 acres per year were lost as a result of direct urban expansion, sprawl, and speculation. The "solution" to this unique problem is to regard

the Niagara fruit belt as a national resource like the national and provincial parks.

9) Apart from the 266 square miles which are estimated to have been transferred from agricultural to urban use in the 1966–71 period, 252 square miles have probably been consumed by indirect urban intrusion effects. One component of urban intrusion is land speculation. Land speculation companies own large tracts of land around the major metropolitan areas, and in the Toronto sub-area, prices for agricultural land are now so high that it is difficult to believe that the entire area is not held for speculative purposes.

10) The estimated "most likely" axis population coupled with the trend average land absorption rate (0.186 acres per person) yields an estimated requirement of 2,115 square miles of new urban land by the year 2001. The preferred land absorption rate (0.100 acres per person) yields an increment of 1,124 square miles. Most of this land will be required at the fringe of the Toronto and Montréal metropolises.

11) It would be possible to control future urban land prices by purchasing a proportion of future urban land requirements and holding the land in a land bank. If the year 2001 is set as the target date, and a number of other assumptions are accepted, it would be possible to purchase 50 per cent of all urban land required in the axis to the year 2001 for about $1.12 billion (at 1971 prices). This figure could be reduced by lowering the land bank proportion (for example, down to 20 per cent) and reducing the target date (for example, 1991). In the latter case the money required to establish the bank would be about $282 million, but as the purpose is to control the land market, 20 per cent may be far too low, although 1991 may be a reasonable target date.

4. HOUSING

1) The advantages of home-owning over renting are not great. There are, however, certain equity advantages if a period of continuous inflation can be envisaged.

2) In the aggregate, the demand for housing is determined by the number of existing household units, and the rate of formation of new households. Between 1961 and 1971 the total number

of household units in the axis increased at a rate of 3.2 per cent per annum. Since this definition of a household unit is predicated upon the conterminous existence of a dwelling unit, it is estimated that a significant proportion of this increase may have been derived from "undoubling" of families living in the same dwelling unit.

3) A larger proportion of new dwelling units was constructed in the 1960s than in any other decade, because of the general maturing of the population. It is estimated that about 160,000 additional dwelling units were required simply to cater to the increased number of people who entered the family formation stage. The greater number of immigrants from outside Canada probably generated an increased demand for housing of about 6.7 per cent.

4) A life-cycle model of housing demand is perhaps the most satisfactory basis for analysing and developing policies relevant to future housing requirements.

5) In the first ten years of a family's existence, renting is less expensive than purchasing. Hypothetical figures indicate that the mortgage, interest, and property tax payments can consume nearly one-quarter of a family's total ten-year income, whereas renting similar space would consume only one-sixth.

6) Demographic trends indicate an increasingly high rate of new family formation during the 1970s, but by the year 2001 a large proportion of the population will be in a period of late adulthood or approaching retirement. The result could be a surplus of twenty-to-thirty-year-old single family homes (given that new housing will continue to be built).

7) In 1971, 56.3 per cent of all occupied dwelling units in Canada were located within the axis. In terms of type of house, the axis contained 47.7 per cent of all single detached homes in Canada, 72.9 per cent of all single attached units, 74.8 per cent of all row houses, 67.9 per cent of all apartment units, and only 13.2 per cent of all mobile homes.

8) Almost one-half of all dwelling units within the axis are of the single family variety.

9) The total number of dwelling units in the axis increased by 923,000 between 1961 and 1971. The bulk of this increase came in the form of apartment units (52 per cent) and single detached residences (38 per cent).

10) The most noticeable feature during the 1960s was a tremendous increase in the number of apartment units, most of them in high-rise buildings, 42 per cent of all apartment units in existence in the axis in 1971 were constructed during the 1960s. This construction occurred primarily in the largest urban areas. This apartment boom can be construed as being on the one hand demand-based, and on the other hand the result of the prohibitive costs of more preferred forms of housing.

11) Three-quarters of the total increase in number of occupied dwelling units in the 1961–71 period were located within the census metropolitan areas of Hamilton, Kitchener, London, Montréal, Ottawa–Hull, Québec City, Toronto, and Windsor. Each of these urban areas has experienced a decrease in density of occupancy between 1961 and 1971.

12) On the basis of the trends for decreases in dwelling unit occupancy density, and other assumptions, it is possible to forecast that the number of dwelling units in the axis will increase from 3.399 million in 1971 to 5.685 million in 2001. The increase could be achieved easily within the limits of the preferred population densities discussed in Chapter 3.

13) The cost of a single family detached home increased most between 1961 and 1971 in Windsor and Toronto, and least in Montréal and Québec City. This increase reflects escalations in building costs, land prices, and mortgage rates. At least 28 per cent of the difference in house prices between Montréal and Toronto is related to the costs of serviced lots.

14) Although general housing standards improved between 1961 and 1971, the inner parts of the large axis cities contained a disproportionately large share of lower quality dwelling units.

5. THE ECONOMIC STRUCTURE OF THE AREA

1) The axis labour force increased from 3.554 million in 1961 to 4.781 million in 1971 — a growth rate of 3.0 per cent per annum. In 1971, Agriculture and the other primary industries occupied 5 per cent of the axis labour force, Manufacturing 27.8 per cent, and Construction, Transportation, Trade, Administration, and the Service industries, 67.2 per cent. Employment increased fastest in the Service industries.

2) The chief distinguishing feature of the axis is its concentration

in manufacturing, even though the 1961–71 rate of growth of employment in this sector of industry in the axis has been slightly less than that in the rest of Canada.

3) Agriculture occupies only 4.5 per cent of the axis labour force. The more productive areas of agriculture are around Montréal, in the Eastern Townships, southwestern Ontario, and the Niagara Peninsula. Dairy and general mixed farming are most important, but there are areas of specialties, such as fruit farming on the Niagara Peninsula, and tobacco in Norfolk county.

4) Over one-third of all manufacturing jobs are found in the area between Oshawa and Niagara Falls, and a further one-quarter are located in the Montréal region.

5) Since 1911, not only has manufacturing become more concentrated within the axis, but specialization between Ontario and Québec has occurred. Textiles and clothing are produced in the Montréal region, and automobiles and steel in Ontario.

6) Two major manufacturing regions can be distinguished: the East Axis Manufacturing Area, and the West Axis Area. Within the East Axis Area, Montréal, l'Est du Québec and Trois-Rivières, and Ottawa–Hull and Québec City are the principal regions. Within the West Axis Area, the West Lake Ontario Crescent, and the Kitchener–Windsor area are of primary importance.

7) Although both regions increased their total employment in manufacturing between 1961 and 1971, there has been a comparative shift to the west, and a comparative decrease in the east.

8) The axis area received 60 per cent of all new manufacturing plants located in the country between 1961 and 1971. The vast majority of these plants located in either Montréal or Toronto. Over one-third of all the new plants located in the Montréal area are in either the clothing or the associated textile industry, whereas there is a greater diversity of types of new plants in the Toronto area. There has been some decentralization of plants from the inner city.

9) The tertiary sector of activity (Trade, Finance, Services, Public Administration) provided 70 per cent of all the new jobs created in the axis between 1961 and 1971. Tertiary employment appears to be a particularly important activity in Ottawa,

Kingston, Pembroke, Hull, Barrie, London, Trenton, Toronto, Québec, Orillia, Cobourg, Belleville, Lévis, and St. Thomas.

10) On the basis of total tertiary employment, and "excess" tertiary employment (less public administration), it is possible to define a hierarchy of service centres in the axis. The first two levels of this hierarchy are:

Level 1: Toronto and Montréal

Level 2: Ottawa, Hamilton, Québec City,

London, Windsor, Kingston

11) The counties containing Hamilton, Metro Toronto, Montréal, Sherbrooke, and Québec City appear to have grown much faster than expected in total employment between 1961 and 1971.

12) The results of several experiments involving an inter-provincial input-output model re-enforce the contention that the area is of primary importance from a national as well as from a provincial point of view.

6. INTERACTION

1) This chapter involves the use of a general model of interaction to discern whether the axis can be considered a distinct entity within the Canadian and North American system of flows. Interaction appears to be influenced by the costs of distance, size, income, and culture.

2) Telephone flow data indicate that Montréal and Toronto dominate a wide portion of the axis and, in effect, exclude each other from their clearly prescribed territories. A hierarchy of interaction that focuses on these two metropolises can be distinguished.

3) Migration data suggest that the Québec portion of the axis is quite distinguishable from the rest of the province in terms of interaction.

4) Application of a general model of interaction to the flow of manufactured goods between the axis and the rest of Canada provides some support for the argument that the axis is in a favoured position with respect to manufacturing.

5) The flow pattern of airline travellers for the country suggests the existence of five major metropolitan fields, based in Vancouver, Edmonton, Winnipeg, Toronto, and Montréal. The latter two form a reciprocal pair to which the other metropolises are connected. Toronto dominates all of Canada indirectly,

whereas Montréal dominates Québec and the Maritimes directly. It appears that the friction of distance has weakened between 1961 and 1971.

6) International air traffic data indicate a strong negative effect of the Canada–U.S. boundary or interaction.

7) The axis is an independent functional entity within Canada that, in terms of interaction, is differentiated from the rest of the country, and is clearly distinguishable from the United States, even at the micro-level. Two powerful urban nodes exert a dominating influence over the smaller functional regions within the axis area.

7. CHANNELS OF INTERACTION

1) The physical location of the different transport routes within the axis is concentrated in an east-west path. This provides the axis with one of its most distinguishing characteristics and gives it the appearance of a corridor.

2) The leading air terminals are in Toronto (Malton), Montréal (Dorval), and Ottawa. The primary destinations of passengers are Toronto and Montréal.

3) The largest volume of traffic flow in the axis and in Canada is between Montréal and Toronto. In fact, one-third of Air Canada's total internally generated revenue is derived from this one route. It is not all clear that STOL will offer any great advantages over the current Rapidair system between these two cities.

4) The main ports on the Great Lakes–St. Lawrence River provide a focus for an extremely important water transport system. Toronto, Montréal, Québec City, and Windsor have the most extensive lengths of berths of all axis ports.

5) Freight traffic on the St. Lawrence Seaway has risen from 20,000,000 tons in 1959 to 54,000,000 tons in 1973. The rate of increase in recent years has not been very great, and the predicted traffic volumes have not been realized. Nevertheless, the Seaway is an extremely viable artery for bulk goods, though this viability depends upon the continuance of low rates.

6) Rail passenger traffic in Canada has declined continuously since 1920 (except for the war years), but freight traffic increased in 1972 over 1971. The vast majority of the population in the axis could be served by an avenue of track connecting

Windsor to Toronto, Ottawa, Montréal, and Québec City. If such a track, capable of using high speed vehicles (200 mph maximum), were built, there would be no need for STOL.

7) The rapid growth of container traffic has revitalized the freight-carrying rôle of the rail system, and at the same time accelerated the decentralization of freight yards to the periphery of the major metropolises. Most freight movements focus upon Montréal and Toronto.

8) A map of road network density (Figure 7.9) indicates that the most intensive pattern existing is from Toronto to the Niagara Peninsula. There does not appear to be the same level of intensity in Québec as in Ontario, beyond the Montréal region. The map of road network density defines the axis corridor quite clearly.

9) The axis appears to have witnessed a lengthy period of competition rather than cooperation among transport modes, and cooperation rather than competition within modes. Probably the most recent reversal of this trend can be seen in the development of container service: it is forcing cooperation between rail and road haulage.

8. STRUCTURE AND FINANCE

1) The provincial governments have jurisdiction over local governments within their areas. Most local governments have been established under the provisions of general enacting legislation that was established during a period when the axis had an agrarian-based economy. An essential difference between Ontario and Québec is that the municipalities have a wider array of powers in the latter than in the former. There are, as a result, more "special bodies" in Ontario.

2) It is estimated that there has been a considerable reduction in the number of local government units in the axis between 1961 and 1972. In 1961 there were probably about 9,395 local government units, and in 1972 about 6,147. This reduction was achieved primarily by an amalgamation of school boards in both provinces.

3) The average size of municipalities is rather small (6,500 people). One-eighth of all the municipalities have a population greater than 6,500, and two-thirds have a population less than 2,000.

4) About two-thirds of all local government units are "special bodies" of one kind or another. These special bodies embrace services, management, regulation, enterprises, and a few have advisory and promotion roles. The proliferation of "special bodies" may well impede cooperation.

5) In forming larger units there are two considerations. One involves the method of amalgamation, and the other the allocation of the functions to the new administrative areas. The following methods of amalgamation have been used: annexation, fusions, new "special bodies", and federation. New structures are also being implemented, such as regional government, urban "communities", and regroupments.

6) The basic sources of funds for local governments are the property tax and transfers from the provincial treasuries. The property tax is regressive, spatially inequitable, and not responsive to inflation. Provincial transfers are usually provided for special projects or services, and are thus subject to provincial policies which may not coincide with local needs.

7) Most local government funds are consumed by education and public works.

8) There are several methods which can be used for ameliorating the local government fiscal dilemma. Of these, increasing grants, transferring some municipal responsibilities to the provincial level, and providing new sources of tax money, are considered.

9. THE AXIS IN 2001 AD

1) This chapter is concerned with the articulation of a technique that takes into account the spatial and temporal problems associated with forecasting. It then focuses upon a discussion of some of the trends underlying the major predicted outcome.

2) A set of unconstrained forecasts, based on past time-space trends at the census subdivision level, results in a forecast of 26.811 million people in the axis in the year 2001. This projection, however, is considered to be a gross overestimate.

3) The "most likely" forecast for the axis (19.119 million by the year 2001), detailed in Chapter 2, is used to develop a set of constrained population forecasts for census subdivisions. These are constrained by the sub-area forecasts detailed in Table 3.4.

The parameters of the model used to obtain the unconstrained forecasts are used to allocate these estimates.

4) The "most likely" forecast indicates that there will be a comparative shift of population to the Ontario portion of the axis, which, by the year 2001, will contain nearly 64 per cent of the axis population as compared with 58 per cent in 1971. A continuous sinuous strip of census subdivisions exceeding the urban density threshold exists between Windsor and Québec City by the end of the century. The greatest growth zone will be in the general area between Toronto and Kitchener. Average urban densities in "urban" census subdivisions will be a little over 1,000 persons per square mile.

5) The greater comparative growth of the Toronto area over that of Montréal, which is forecast by the unconstrained and constrained models, is related to the greater growth of high-order metropolitan functions in Toronto.

6) The head offices of eight of the nine banks in the country are located in either Montréal or Toronto. The distribution of bank assets is now split almost evenly between these two metropolises, whereas prior to 1930 Montréal clearly dominated. The Toronto Cheque Clearing House now passes a far greater dollar volume per year than does the Montréal-based one.

7) The Toronto Stock Exchange is now the foremost exchange in the country. In 1971, 69 per cent of the total dollar value of securities traded in Canada was handled by the Toronto Stock Exchange, and 23 per cent by the Montréal exchanges.

8) Montréal and Toronto are gaining an increasing proportion of "key" Canadian companies, but Toronto's share is increasing and Montréal's decreasing. These two cities share equally in other service facilities, such as chartered accountants, while Toronto tends to dominate in the computer field.

9) The comparative shifts to the western portion of the axis, predicted in the constrained and unconstrained forecasts, are supported by trends in the location of the financial, business, and other service industries. In the year 2001, about 35 per cent of the axis population will be located within forty miles of Toronto, and about 24 per cent within forty miles of Montréal. These proportions are substantially different from the 1971 situation in which both areas were of similar population size. The conclusion is that by the year 2001, the Canadian urban

system will be structured around Toronto as the primary node, with Montréal serving the regional needs of Québec and part of the Maritimes, and Vancouver serving much of the West.

ONWARD TO THE POST-INDUSTRIAL URBAN LIFE

Many of the elements of change that have been detailed, described, and forecast in this study can be placed within the broader context of general socio-economic mutation. Much has been written concerning the transformation of society to an era of "post-industrialism" (Webber, 1968; Webber and Webber, 1967; Hirschhorn, 1972a), so it is probably wise to attempt, in this concluding section, to relate the macro-urban developments in the axis to this broad concept. In order to avoid a lengthy philosophical discussion, the concept of "post-industrialism" will be described briefly together with some of the signals that identify the stage of the axis in this development. Following this, there will be an attempt to relate some of the implications of the concept to future macro-urban trends, and to identify one or two regulatory innovations that could be applied to modify these trends if such modifications are considered appropriate.

THE CONCEPT OF POST-INDUSTRIALISM

The changes that have taken place in the general socio-economic structure of society over the last 200 years have occurred at bewildering speed. In some places these changes have been superimposed on a landscape already well developed in the pre-change era, but in other places they have occurred on a landscape barely developed and susceptible to quite rapid readjustments. The axis contains some elements of the former, such as the Chaudière Valley, which exhibits a landscape that has responded quickly to change and innovation. The primary change that has occurred is the transformation of society from a rural agrarian state to one of urbanism and manufacturing (Lepine, 1972). The adjective "industrial", therefore, in this context relates narrowly to manufacturing, and is not used in its more general and broadest sense to refer to any form of work, whether it be agricultural, manufacturing, or of a tertiary nature.

One of the most important indicators of a move from an agrarian society to an industrial (that is, manufacturing) state is a shift in the composition of occupations. In 1911, almost 39 per cent of the country's work force was employed in primary activities (agriculture, mining, forestry, trapping, etc.), whereas in 1961 less than 14 per cent was so employed (McInnis, 1973). On the other hand, about 17 per cent of the work force was employed in the manufacturing industries in 1911 as compared with 23 per cent in 1961. The shift to post-industrialism is also marked by similar changes, but in this case it involves a decline in the proportion involved in manufacturing industries, along with a continued decline of those involved in agriculture. The 1961–71 period is critical in this respect, for the proportion of the country's employment in manufacturing industries appears to have declined from almost 23 per cent to a little less than 22 per cent. This decrease has been accompanied by a continuous increase in the proportion employed in the tertiary activities. In 1911, this was about 44 per cent, in 1961 it exceeded 63 per cent, and by 1971, it had reached 68 per cent.

There are two interesting features of this shift that deserve comment. The first is that while the Canadian pattern of change is similar to that of other industrial nations it is not the same. The United States, for example, exhibits a far more accentuated shift from primary employment to manufacturing and then to tertiary activities. In fact, Canada, rather like Australia, is transforming far more directly from a primary employment nation to a post-industrial society, having flirted briefly with employment in industrialism along its transitional path. The second feature of the shift is that it has been accompanied by tremendous increases in output, and, therefore, productivity (per worker and per unit of capital) in the primary and manufacturing sectors. Greater productivity has been achieved by specialization and tremendous capital investment, which, in turn, makes the work more automated and less "human".

The second feature deserves slightly more comment as it gives rise to a second indicator of the shift to post-industrialism. The great increases in productivity in the primary and manufacturing sectors have resulted in quite large increases in profits and real income. The changes in productivity in the tertiary sector are not as apparent, and are difficult to measure. These increases in productivity have resulted in a decrease in the amount of labour required for a given level of output of primary and manufactured goods. The trend in efficiency is such that it is probably possible for Canada to produce most of its material needs at the present time with less than one-half of its work force employed. By the end of the century, it is conceivable that less than 10 per cent of the labour force could produce most of the country's material requirements! But, man has other requirements besides material needs, and these are provided by the vast array of activities subsumed within the tertiary rubric. But the delivery systems for the production of tertiary services does not appear to be as economically efficient as that for primary and manufactured goods, and, as a consequence, it can be argued that the economic efficiency of these two sectors in effect "pay for" the less economically efficient tertiary sector.

A simple model can be envisaged to illustrate this contention. Automobile workers note their tremendous increases in productivity and submit a claim for wage rate increases accordingly. Such claims are reasonable, because the increases in economic productivity per worker will support the increases. Other workers in the primary and manufacturing sector also submit claims for wage rate increases, and their claims also are reasonable in the light of productivity increases. Workers in some tertiary activity (such as filing clerks) perceive wages increasing in other areas, and also request increases, even though there may not have been any great increase in their productivity. Such increases could be supported as long as the output productivity of other sectors continues to increase. During the past few decades the tremendous economic efficiency of the primary and manufacturing sector have, in fact, helped to support the parallel increase in incomes required by persons working in the tertiary sector. Unfortunately, with a greater and greater proportion of the work force employed in the tertiary sector, increases in productivity in the other two have to be even greater, and an indicator that this is not occurring is inflation (Hirschhorn, 1972b).

Inflation is, of course, related to many different causes, but in this particular discussion it is argued that inflation is bound to occur in the transition to the post-industrial society until the delivery system for tertiary services is made more efficient. There are, currently, many attempts underway to try to achieve this goal, the most obvious being in the fields of education and medical care, where costs have spiralled over the past decade. Education costs seem to be under reasonable control (as a result of demographic trends rather than anything else), whereas medical costs are still increasing at an inordinate rate as the demand continues to increase within an inefficient delivery system. It should, however, be realized that in a money-economy efficiency is measured economically, not socially. It may, for example, be impossible to measure accurately the "efficiency" of a child-care worker.

There are, however, indicators of stress other than inflation which signal this transitionary period to the post-industrial age. One of the more interesting of these concerns the nature and role of work. Remuneration for work and the proceeds from investments have become the socially accepted mechanism for income distribution. The necessity for income-generating jobs led, in the late nineteenth and early twentieth centuries, to the concept of work "dignifying" man, and this concept was extended in trade union philosophy to the notion that man had a "right" to work. Fortunately, although the efficiency of production in the primary and manufacturing sectors has resulted in a decline in the real need for labour in these activities, there has been an expansion of employment opportunities in the tertiary sector because many of the service wants of society are still far from satisfied (Webber, 1968). There are real signs, however, that the tertiary sector cannot absorb more labour, implying that if the prevailing notions of work continue there will be persistent labour surpluses in the post-industrial society. But as jobs are still required to obtain income, it is evident that employment will have to be "rationed-out", and this can be achieved by combinations of procedures involving shorter working weeks, longer vacations, earlier retirements, periodic leaves for retraining and further education, and so forth.

THE WINDSOR TO QUEBEC CITY AXIS IN A POST-INDUSTRIAL AGE

The axis is the only part of Canada that has really experienced most of the elements of an industrial society as well as an agrarian situation. As a consequence, the transition to post-industrialism is most marked in this area where the trends for concentration, resulting from large-scale production and the need for numerous inter-firm inter-linkages, are re-enforced in a post-industrial era. It should be noted that the concentrations referred to relate to large urban regions, and do not imply increasing densities of concentration. Some of the forces arising from post-industrialism which compound these macro-urban concentrating trends need to be identified, since their separate analysis can lead to interesting views concerning urban policy.

In the first place, it is evident that a large component of the service needs of the population are people-dependent in a locational sense. It is, for example, impossible to envisage the establishment of a large shopping centre of the size of Galeries d'Anjou or Yorkdale anywhere else other than within the suburban fringes of the largest metropolises. The employment created by these people-dependent services is, therefore, very restricted in its location. Thus if the service needs of this type multiply then the employment so generated will be confined in its location to the larger urban areas. Furthermore, the concept of service provision as "entertainment" accompanied by imposed accessibility results in the hinterland of the facility being extended into the rural areas which, in turn, lose some of their local service functions as a result of competition. Thus, the concentration of population in the larger urban regions will result in a further concentration of employment opportunities arising from the growth of locationally people-dependent services.

There are, however, a number of activities which, though people-serving, cannot be regarded as locationally people-dependent in the same way as retailing activities can. Perhaps the best examples of activities of this type involve post-secondary education and public administration. Universities, community colleges, CEGEP's and other institutions of higher learning sprouted and bloomed like orchids in the axis during the 1960s, nurtured by the public purse, and fostered by nefarious educational policies. In a number of cases, the institutions have been placed or encouraged to grow in middle-sized towns and cities, and in these situations they have invariably been either the primary, or the only source of growth. In effect, they can be regarded not only as contributions to the post-secondary educational scene, but also as important countervailing forces to the pervading trend toward concentration. The cessation of further post-secondary expansion at the present time virtually eliminates this activity as a dispersive force. For example, it is estimated that about 90 per cent of the growth in employment in Kingston between 1961 and 1971 was related either directly or indirectly to the expansion of the post-secondary institutions in that city (Yeates, 1973).

Federal and provincial levels of public administration can exist in locations quite isolated from the majority of the population being served. The location of the federal bureaucracy in Ottawa is a vivid example of the way in which administrative services can be used to disperse forces leading to growth. Unfortunately, Queen Victoria and her advisers seem to have been the last to have recognized the value of public administration as an employment-creating agent in a slow growth area, for since that time federal and provincial governmental activities have remained within the urban areas in which they were first located. As a consequence, the multiplier effects resulting from growth in employment in these two levels of public administration have accrued in large part to the urban regions in which they are located. One of the principal reasons why the growth of the Toronto region in the future is predicted to exceed that of Montréal is that all these growth forces are concentrated in Toronto, whereas the Québec provincial public administration component is established elsewhere.

Another important feature of post-industrial society, which adds yet another concentrating force, is the different nature of the employment market. The great increase in the female participation rate in the labour force has been noted in Chapter 5. Declining birth rates, changing life styles, day care, higher general levels of education and aspirations, family financial pressures arising from inflation, and so forth, have all contributed to this trend. In the future, it can be expected that in a majority of families both partners will desire some form of full-time or part-time non-home employment. This is an extremely positive stimulant to concentration, for the probability of two persons being able to obtain satisfactory employment is far greater in a large urban area than in a small city or town. The location of the family, consequently, will be determined by the perception of joint employment opportunities, rather than opportunities for one of the partners.

The overall conclusion, therefore, is that the transition of Canadian society to a post-industrial era adds yet another array of forces fostering the concentration of the population into macro-urban regions. This concentration will occur as a result of migration, so there will be parts of the axis, and Canada, that will suffer net losses of population. Past experience suggests that the rate of growth in the major metropolises, particularly in general areas around Toronto, will exceed the capabilities of the housing and urban land assembly delivery systems to provide dwelling units at reasonable prices. Furthermore, the spread of the population over a large amorphous macro-urban region compounds the transportation inefficiencies that have already arisen in the suburban fringe of large North American cities. The Toronto Centred Region Plan (Government of Ontario, 1970; 1971), though fragmentary, recognizes this impending situation, and proposes spatial limits to growth, as well as alternative growth centres. But shifts in growth patterns can occur only by transferring growth-generating forces, and this has proven extremely difficult to accomplish. Past attempts at decentralization have focused on the manufacturing industry, but these programs have generally proven expensive and limited in their job-creating potential.

If it is the clearly stated policy of the provincial governments to control the growth of the major metropolises in the axis, and the evidence in this study suggests that it should be, then it should be recognized that the only real possibility for growth transference in a post-industrial age lies in focusing on those tertiary activities which are not locationally people-dependent. For example, in the case of the axis, it could be specifically recommended that the Ontario provincial government define certain cities well beyond the Toronto region as new growth centres, and decentralize some public administration activities accordingly. Another example, this time relating to the entire axis, is that both provincial governments should relocate most of the post-secondary education facilities to alternative designated growth centres. There are, of course, other examples, but these two convey the nature of the teeth required to implement such a policy. Decentralization requires, of course, extensive land acquisitions in the designated growth centres, as well as the remodelling of these centres. Considerable financing would be necessary, as well as harmonization with the general development of the entire country; for the axis is the key to the nation.

REFERENCES

ANDERSON, I.B. *Internal Migration in Canada, 1921 to 1961.* Staff Study No. 13. Ottawa: Economic Council of Canada, 1966.

APPLETON, P. *An Economic Framework for Regional Policy Analysis.* Ottawa: Agricultural Economics Research Council of Canada, 1972.

AXWORTHY, L. (ed.) *The Future City.* Winnipeg: The Institute of Urban Studies, 1972a.

——. *The Politics of Innovation.* Winnipeg: The Institute of Urban Studies, 1972b.

——. "Modes of Change in the Ontario Economy." Unpublished Doctoral thesis, Department of Geography, University of Toronto, 1974.

BANNISTER, G. "Forecasting the Spatial Distribution of Population in the Windsor to Quebec City Urban Axis: A Brief Review of Some Existing Techniques and an Alternative Approach." Report prepared for the Ministry of State for Urban Affairs, Ottawa, 1973 (mimeo).

BARLOW, J.F. "Windsor, A Suburb or a Satellite of Detroit?" Unpublished B.A. thesis. Department of Geography, University of Windsor, 1967.

BATRIK, S.M. "The Input-Output Structure of the Niagara Region," *Ontario Economic Review,* 10 (1972), pp. 5–39.

BÉDARD, R.J. *La Bataille des Annexions.* Montréal: La Patrie, 1965.

BEINBAKER, P., and ELEK, A. "Passenger Terminal Planning and Design," in R.M. Soberman (ed.), *Readings in Airport Planning.* Toronto: University of Toronto, CUCS and the Department of Civil Engineering, 1972, pp. 323–409.

BÉLANGER, M. "Le Québec rural," in F. Grenier (ed.), *Québec.* Toronto: University of Toronto Press, 1972.

BÉLANGER, M., *et al.* "Le complexe périmétropolitain montréalais: une analyse de l'évolution des populations totales," *La Revue de Géographie de Montréal,* 26 (1972), pp. 241–50.

BÉRARD, M. "Le réseau routier du québec: un essai de classification fonctionnelle." Unpublished M.A. thesis, Université Laval, Québec, 1970.

BERRY, B.J.L. and HORTON, F.E. *Geographic Perspectives on Urban Systems*. Engelwood Cliffs, N.J.: Prentice-Hall, 1970.

BERTON, P. *The Last Spike*. Toronto: McClelland and Stewart, 1970.

BIAYS, P. "Southern Quebec," in J. Warkentin (ed.), *Canada: A Geographical Interpretation*. Toronto: Methuen, 1968, pp. 281–333.

BLUMENFELD, H. *The Modern Metropolis*, Cambridge, Mass.: M.I.T. Press, 1967, p. 175.

BOUCHER, P. "Modifications sectorielles des limites territoriales des municipalités de la province de québec, du 1er juin 1961 au 1er janvier 1968." Microfilm thesis, l'Institut de Géographie de l'Université Laval, Québec, 1969.

BOURNE, L.S. "Market, Location and Site Selection in Apartment Construction," *Canadian Geographer*, Vol. XII, No. 4 (1968), pp. 211–26.

———. "Apartment Location and the Housing Market," in L. Bourne (ed.), *Internal Structure of the City*. Toronto: Oxford University Press, 1971.

BOURNE, L.S., and MACKINNON, R.D. (eds.). *Urban Systems Development in Central Canada*. Research Paper No. 9, Toronto: University of Toronto, Department of Geography, 1972.

BOURNE, L.S., HARPER, P.D., and THACKRAY, D. *Population Projections for Ontario and Quebec Cities 1971–2001*. Toronto: University of Toronto, CUCS, 1972.

BRITTON, J.N.H. "Economic Structure of Ontario–Quebec Cities: An Occupational Analysis," in L. S. Bourne, and R. D. MacKinnon (eds.), *Urban Systems Development in Central Canada*. Research Paper No. 9. Toronto: University of Toronto, Department of Geography, 1972.

BROWN, T.M. *Canadian Economic Growth*, Ottawa: Queen's Printer, 1965.

Bureau of Municipal Research (BMR). "The 101 Governments of Metro Toronto," *Civic Affairs*, October Issue, Toronto, 1968.

———. "Reorganizing Local Government: A Brief Look at Four Provinces," *Civic Affairs*, Spring Issue, Toronto, 1972.

———. "Property Taxation and Land Development," *Civic Affairs*, Summer Issue, Toronto, 1973.

CAMU, P., et al. *Economic Geography of Canada*. Toronto: Macmillan, 1964.

Canadian Transport Commission Research Branch (CTCRB). *Inter-City Passenger Transport Study*. Ottawa: Queen's Printer, 1970.

CAREY, G.W., et al. *Urbanization, Water Pollution, and Public Policy*. New Brunswick, N.J.: Centre for Urban Policy Research, 1972.

CAROL, H. "Development Regions in Southern Ontario Based on City Centred Regions," *Ontario Geography*, 4 (1969), pp. 13–29.

References 363

———. "The City Centred Region and Regional Development in Southern Ontario," in R. R. Krueger and R. C. Bryfogle (eds.), *Urban Problems: A Canadian Reader*. Toronto: Holt, Rinehart and Winston, 1971, pp. 311–18.

CARR, D.W. *The Seaway in Canada's Transportation: An Economic Analysis, Vol. I, Final Report*. D. Wm. Carr and Associates, Ltd., 1970.

CAZALIS, P. "The Physical Geography of the Province of Quebec," *Annuaire du Québec*, Québec City: Editeur Officiel du Québec, 1962, pp. 1–15.

CHUDLEIGH, E.L. *Alternatives for the Ontario Tender Fruit Industry*. Toronto: Ministry of Agriculture and Food, 1972.

CLASKY, S.J. "Background to the Development of Regional Government in Ontario." Paper delivered to the conference on regional government, University of Windsor, February 14, 1970.

CLIBBON, P.B., and HAMELIN, L. "Landforms," in J. Warkentin (ed.), *Canada: A Geographical Interpretation*. Toronto: Methuen, 1968, pp. 57–77.

COLLINS, L. *Industrial Migration in Ontario: Forecasting Aspects of Industrial Activity Through Markov Chain Analysis*. Ottawa: Queen's Printer, 1972.

COOPER, C. *The House of Symbol of Self*. Working Paper No. 120. Institute of Urban and Regional Development, University of California, 1971.

CRAWFORD, K. *Canadian Municipal Government*. Toronto: University of Toronto Press, 1954.

CRERAR, A.D. "The Loss of Farmland in the Growth of the Metropolitan Regions of Canada," *Resources for Tomorrow: Conference Background Papers*. Ottawa: Queen's Printer, 1962.

CROWLEY, R. "Labour Force Growth and Specialization in Canadian Cities." Working Paper A–71–1. Ottawa: Ministry of State for Urban Affairs, 1971.

CURRY,L. and BANNISTER, G. "Forecasting Township Populations of Ontario from Time-Space Covariances," in L. S. Bourne, *et al.* (eds.), *Urban Futures for Central Canada*. Toronto: University of Toronto Press, 1974.

DAGENAIS, P. "La métropole du Canada: Montréal ou Toronto," *La Revue de Géographie de Montréal*, Vol. 23, No. 1 (1969), pp. 27–38.

DAHMS, F.A., and PEARSON, N. *A Study of the Fringe Area North of Metropolitan Toronto*. Guelph: University of Guelph, Central Ontario Regional Development Council, 1969.

DAVIES, J.B. "Behaviour of the Ontario-Quebec Urban System by Size Distribution," in L.S. Bourne, and R.D. MacKinnon (eds.), *Urban*

Systems Development in Central Canada. Toronto: University of Toronto Press, 1972.

DEAN, W.G. (ed.). *Economic Atlas of Ontario.* Toronto: University of Toronto Press, 1969.

DE'ATH, C. "Anthropology on the Town: Urban Anthropologists and Urban Planning in Canada." Occasional Paper No. 3. Division of Environmental Sciences, Waterloo: University of Waterloo, 1972.

DENNIS, M., and S. FISH. *Programs in Search of a Policy.* Toronto: Hakkert, 1972.

Department of Highways. *Niagara Peninsula Planning Study.* Ontario: Department of Transport and Communications, 1964.

DERKOWSKI, A. *Residential Land Development in Ontario.* Toronto: Urban Development Institute, 1972.

DILL, H.W. JR., and OTTE, R.C. *Urbanization of Land in the Northeastern United States.* Washington, D.C.: USDA, ERS-485, 1971.

DONENCICH, T.A., and KRAFT, G. *Free Transit.* Lexington, Mass.: Charles River Associates Research Study, 1970.

DOUCET, M.J. *Trends in Metropolitan Land Use and Land Consumption: Metropolitan Toronto, 1963–1968.* Research Paper No. 35. Toronto: University of Toronto, CUCS, 1970.

Economic Council of Canada. *Annual Report.* Ottawa: Queen's Printer, 1969.

EDWARDS, A.M., and WIBBERLEY, G.P. *An Agricultural Land Budget for Britain, 1965–2000.* Studies in Rural Land Use, No. 10. Ashford, England: Wye College, 1971.

FARRAR, F.A. "Migration and Economic Opportunity in Canada, 1921–1951." Unpublished Ph.D. dissertation, Department of Economics, University of Pennsylvania, 1962.

FEHERDY, Y. *Etat global de l'occupation du sol de Montréal.* Montréal: Service d'Urbanisme, 1971.

FELDMAN, L.D., and GOLDRICK, M.D. (eds.). *Politics and Government of Urban Canada: Selected Readings.* Toronto: Methuen, 1969.

FIELD, N.C., and KERR, D.P. *Geographical Aspects of Industrial Growth in the Metropolitan Toronto Region.* Toronto: Regional Development Branch, Department of Treasury and Economics, 1968.

FISH, S. *Parties to Change.* Toronto: Bureau of Municipal Research, 1971.

FOUND, W.C., and MORLEY, C.D. *A Conceptual Approach to Rural Land-Use Transportation Modelling in the Toronto Region.* Downsview, Ont.: York University Transport Centre, 1972.

FRANK, R.H., BATRIK, S.M., and HARONITIS, D. "The Input-Output Structure of the Ontario Economy," *Ontario Economic Review,* 8 (1970), pp. 3–33.

GAD, G. *A Review of Methodological Problems in Estimating Urban*

Expansion. Research Paper No. 25. Toronto: University of Toronto, CUCS, 1970.

GAGNON, J. *Vocation économique de la Rive-Sud de Montréal.* Québec: Ministère des Affaires Municipales, 1969.

GARON, L., HÉBERT, G., and POUSSARD, F. *Etude comparative des organismes métropolitains.* Québec: Ministère des Affaires Municipales, 1969.

GENTILCORE, R.L. "Settlement," in R.L. Gentilcore, *Ontario.* Toronto: University of Toronto Press, 1972.

Geography Section. *Areas of Census Divisions, Subdivisions and Enumeration Areas.* Preliminary Report. Ottawa: Statistics Canada, 1971.

GERTLER, L.O. *The Niagara Escarpment Study Fruit Belt Report.* Toronto: Queen's Printer, 1968.

GIBSON, S. "Land Banking: Investment in the Future," *Civic Affairs,* 1 (1973), Toronto: Bureau of Municipal Research.

GILMOUR, J.M., and MURRICANE, K. "Structural Divergence in Canada's Manufacturing Belt," *The Canadian Geographer,* 17 (1973), pp. 1–18.

GIRARD, J. *Géographie de l'industrie manufacturière du Québec.* 2 vols. Québec: Ministère de l'Industrie et du Commerce, 1970.

GOLANT, S.M. *The Residential Location and Spatial Behaviour of the Elderly: A Canadian Example.* Research Paper No. 134. Chicago: University of Chicago, Department of Geography, 1972.

GOLANT, S., and BOURNE, L.S. *Growth Characteristics of the Ontario-Québec Urban System.* Research Paper No. 4. Toronto: University of Toronto, CUCS, 1968.

GOLDENBERG, H.C. *Municipal Finance in Canada: A Study Prepared for the Royal Commission on Dominion-Provincial Relations.* Ottawa: Queen's Printer, 1939.

GORACZ, A. *Housing Requirements to 1981.* Ottawa: Central Mortgage and Housing Corporation, 1969.

GOTTMAN, J. *Megalopolis: The Urbanized Northeastern Seaboard of the United States.* New York: The Twentieth Century Fund Inc., 1961.

Government of Ontario. *Design for Development: The Toronto Centred Region.* Toronto: Queen's Printer, 1970.

———. *Design for Development: A Status Report on the Toronto-Centred Region.* Toronto: Queen's Printer, 1971.

GRAY, E., HEMINGWAY, S., and HOFFMAN, D. *Planning for Agriculture in Southern Ontario.* Report No. 7. Guelph: Ontario ARDA, 1972.

GREGOIRE, G. (ed.), *Région Sud: Atlas.* Montreal: Université du Québec, C.R.U.R. - I.N.R.S., 1972.

HALL, P. *London 2000.* London: Faber & Faber, 1963.

HARRIS, R.C. *The Seigneurial System in Early Canada: A Geographical*

Study. Madison: University of Wisconsin Press, 1966.

HELLEYER, P. *Report on the Task Force on Housing and Urban Development*. Ottawa: Queen's Printer, 1969.

HILL, F. *Spatio-Temporal Trends in Population Density: Toronto: 1932–66*. Research Paper No. 35. Toronto: University of Toronto, CUCS, 1970.

———. *Migration in the Toronto-Central Region*. Research Paper No. 48. Toronto: University of Toronto, CUCS, 1971.

HIND-SMITH, J. "The Impact of Urban Growth on Agricultural Land: A Pilot Study," *Resources for Tomorrow: Conference Background Papers, Supplementary Volume*. Ottawa: Queen's Printer, 1962, pp. 155–79.

HIRSCHHORN, L. "Two Essays on the Transition to Post-Industrialism." Working Paper No. 170. Berkeley: University of California, Institute of Urban and Regional Development, 1972a.

———. "Taxation, Inflation and the Transition to Post-Industrialism." Working Paper No. 169. Berkeley: University of California, Institute of Urban and Regional Development, 1972b.

HODGE, G. "Do Villages Grow? Some Perspectives and Predictions," *Rural Sociology*, 31 (1966), pp. 183–96.

———. "The Emergence of the Urban Field," in L. Bourne, and R. MacKinnon, *Urban Systems Development in Central Canada*. Research Paper No. 9. Toronto: University of Toronto, Department of Geography, 1972.

HOWARD, J.F. "The Impact of Urbanization on the Prime Agricultural Lands of Southern Ontario." M.A. research report, Department of Geography, University of Waterloo, Waterloo, 1972.

HUDAC. *Home Ownership Versus Rental Study*. Toronto: HUDAC, 1971.

HUGHES, D.R. "Migration of Young Adults from Frontenac County, Ontario." Unpublished Masters thesis, Department of Geography, University of Western Ontario, London, 1971.

ILLINGS, W.M. *Population, Family Household, and Labour Force Growth to 1980*. Staff Study No. 19. Ottawa: Economic Council of Canada, 1967.

JACOB, A.L. "Interaction in Urban Systems: A Canadian Illustration." Unpublished M.A. research paper, Department of Geography, University of Toronto, Toronto, 1971.

JEFFERSON, M. "The Law of the Primate City," *Geographical Review*, 29 (1939), pp. 226–32.

JONES, F.E. "Some Social Consequences of Immigration for Canada," in R. Blishen, *et al.*, *Canadian Society: Sociological Perspectives*. Toronto: Macmillan, 1971, pp. 427–32.

KALBACH, W.E. *The Impact of Immigration on Canada's Population*. Ottawa: Statistics Canada, 1970.

KAPLAN, H. *Urban Political Systems: A Functional Analysis of Metro*

Toronto. New York: Columbia University Press, 1967.

——. "Metropolitan Government," in R.R. Krueger and R.C. Bryfogle (eds.), *Urban Problems: A Canadian Reader.* Toronto: Holt, Rinehart and Winston, 1971.

KERR, D. "The Spatial Organization of the Iron and Steel Industry in Canada," in R.L. Gentilcore (ed.), *Canada's Changing Geography.* Toronto: Prentice-Hall, 1967, pp. 139–48.

——. "Metropolitan Dominance in Canada," in J. Warkentin (ed.), *Canada: A Geographical Interpretation.* Toronto: Methuen (1968), pp. 531–56.

KERR, D., and SPELT, J. *The Changing Face of Toronto.* Ottawa: Queen's Printer, 1965.

KIRKLAND, J.S. *Demographic Aspects of Housing Demand to 1986.* Ottawa: Central Mortgage and Housing, 1971.

——. *Patterns of Housing Quality in Selected Canadian Cities.* Ottawa: Central Mortgage and Housing, 1972.

KRUEGER, R.R. "Changing Land-Use Patterns in the Niagara Fruit Belt," *Transactions of the Royal Canadian Institute,* Vol. 32, No. 2 (1959).

——. "Changing Land-Use Patterns in the Niagara Fruit Belt." Waterloo: University of Waterloo, Department of Geography, 1968.

——. "Regional Planning and Regional Government in Ontario," in R.R. Krueger and R.C. Bryfogle (eds.), *Urban Problems: A Canadian Reader.* Toronto: Holt, Rinehart and Winston, 1971.

LA HAYE, J.C. *Rapport de la Commission provinciale d'urbanisme.* Québec: Editeur du Québec, 1968.

——. *Report of the Quebec Provincial Commission on Town Planning.* Québec: Editeur du Québec, 1970.

LAJOIE, A. *Les structures administratives régionales: déconcentration et décentralisation au Québec.* Montréal: Presses de l'Université de Montréal, 1968.

LAMONDE, P. (ed.). *Région Sud: Population et Emploi, 1951-1986.* Montréal: Université du Québec, C.R.U.R.-I.N.R.S., 1972.

LANGMAN, R.C. *Patterns of Settlement in Southern Ontario.* Toronto: McClelland and Stewart, 1971.

LATHAM, J., and YEATES, M. "Population Density Growth in Metropolitan Toronto," *Geographical Analysis,* 2 (1970), pp. 177–85.

LEFORT, J., and MARSHALL, R. *Le tableau économique du Québec, 1966.* Québec City: Division de la Recherche, Bureau de la Statistique du Québec, 1972.

LEPINE, Y. "Intégration d'une communauté rurale de la banlieue maraichère de Montréal à la société urbaine post-industrielle." Unpublished M.A. thesis, Institut de Géographie, Université Laval, Québec, 1972.

LEVITT, K. "A Macro Economic Analysis of the Structure of the Economy of the Atlantic Provinces, 1960." Paper presented to the Canadian Economics Association, York University, 1969.

LINSKY, A.S. "Some Generalizations Concerning Primate Cities," *Annals of the Association of American Geographers,* 55 (1965), pp. 506–11.

LITHWICK, H. "Housing: In a Search for Crisis," in Sayegh, K.S. (ed.), *Canadian Housing: A Reader.* Waterloo: University of Waterloo, 1969.

———. *Urban Canada: Problems and Prospects.* Ottawa: Queen's Printer, 1970.

LITHWICK, N.H., and PAQUET, G. (eds.), *Urban Studies: A Canadian Perspective.* Toronto: Methuen, 1968.

LORD, A. *Etude sur la restructuration municipale de l'Agglomération urbaine de Québec.* Québec: Ministère des Affaires Municipales, 1972.

LORIMER, J. *A Citizen's Guide to City Politics.* Toronto: James, Lewis and Samuel, 1972.

MACGOUGAN, G.R. "Airport Financing in Canada," in R.M. Soberman (ed.), *Readings in Airport Planning.* Toronto: University of Toronto, CUCS and the Department of Civil Engineering, 1972, pp. 441–73.

MACKAY, I.A. "Towards a Solution of the Fiscal Dilemma," *Urban Focus,* Vol. 1, No. 4 (1973), pp. 2–3.

MACKINNON, R.D., and HODGSON, M.J. "Transportation Network Models for the Southern Ontario and Quebec System of Cities," in L.S. Bourne and R.D. MacKinnon (eds.), *Urban Systems Development in Central Canada.* Research Paper No. 9. Toronto: University of Toronto, Department of Geography, 1972.

MACLAREN, W.S., and MYERS, B.B. *Guided Ground Transportation Study,* Ottawa: Ministry of Transport, Transportation Development Agency, 1971.

MAHER, C.A., and BOURNE, L.S. *Land Use Structure and City Size: An Ontario Example.* Research Paper No. 10. Toronto: University of Toronto, CUCS, 1969.

MANGAZOL, C. "Manufacturing Industry in Montréal," in L. Beauregard (ed.), *Montreal: Field Guide.* Montreal: Les Presses de l'Université de Montréal, 1972, pp. 125–35.

MARSHALL, J.U. *The Location of Service Towns.* Research Publication No. 3. Toronto: University of Toronto, Department of Geography, 1969.

———. "The Urban Network," in R.L. Gentilcore (ed.), *Ontario.* Toronto: University of Toronto Press, 1972.

MARSHALL, R. *Le système de comptabilité économique du Québec: quelques résultats.* Québec: Division de la Recherche, Bureau de la Statistique du Québec, 1969.

MARTIN, L.R.G. *The Toronto II Airport Study: Land Ownership and*

Market Anaylsis. Waterloo: School of Urban and Regional Planning, University of Waterloo, 1972.

MARTIN, M.F. *Analyse de la structure urbaine de la province de Québec, dans les activités économiques tertiaires.* Quebec: Office de Planification et de Développement du Québec, 1970.

MCDONALD, G.T. "Ontario Agriculture in an Urbanizing Economy, 1951–1966," in L.S. Bourne, and R.D. MacKinnon, *Urban Systems Development in Central Canada.* Research Paper No. 9. Toronto: University of Toronto, Department of Geography, 1972.

MCINNIS, R.M. "Long Run Trends in Industrial Structure of the Canadian Work Force: Regional Differentials, 1911–1961." Mimeographed paper. March, 1973.

MCLAUGHLIN, B. "Present and Future Demands for Land as Influenced by Urbanization." Paper delivered to the Land-Use Conference of the Ontario Soil and Crop Improvement Association, December 12–13, 1972.

MCPHERSON, J.C. "Forecasting, Route Structure, and Scheduling," in R.M. Soberman (ed.), *Readings in Airport Planning.* Toronto: University of Toronto, CUCS, and the Department of Civil Engineering, 1972, pp. 29–47.

Metropolitan Toronto and Region Transportation Study. *Growth and Travel, Past and Present.* Toronto: Queen's Printer, 1966.

———. *Choices for a Growing Region.* Toronto: Queen's Printer, 1967.

MICHELSON, W. *Man and His Urban Environment,* Reading, Mass.: Addison-Wesley, 1970.

Ministère des Affaires Municipales. "L'évolution du gouvernement municipal au Québec," *Annuaire du Québec,* Québec: Editeur Officiel du Québec, 1968–69, pp. 163–68.

———. "La Communauté Urbaine: Une Formule d'Organisation et de Gestion des Agglomérations," *Annuaire du Québec,* Québec: Editeur Officiel du Québec, 1971, pp. 1–40.

———. *Tableux synthèses.* Québec: Ministère des Affaires Municipales, 1972.

Ministère de l'Industrie et du Commerce. *Atlas du Québec: l'agriculture.* Québec: Editeur Officiel du Québec, 1966.

———. *Les Poles d'Attraction et leurs Zones d'Influence.* Québec: Ministère de l'Industrie et du Commerce, 1967; réédition, 1971.

Ministry of Transport. *An Evaluation of Urban Transport Efficiency in Canada.* Ottawa: Queen's Printer, 1971.

Municipal Organization Branch. *Comparative Analysis of Regional Government Legislation in Ontario.* Toronto: Ministry of Treasury, Economics, and Intergovernmental Affairs, 1972.

MURDIE, R. "Cultural Differences in Consumer Travel," *Economic Geography*, 41 (1965), pp. 211–33.

NEUFELD, E.P. *The Financial System of Canada*. Toronto: Macmillan, 1972.

NEWLING, B.E. "The Spatial Variation of Urban Population Densities," *The Geographical Review*, 59 (1969), pp. 242–52.

NIEDERCORN, J.H., and HEARLE, E.F.R. "Recent Land-Use Trends in 48 Large American Cities," *Land Economics*, 60 (1964), pp. 105–09.

NIXON, G.P., and CAMPBELL, M.A. *Four Cities: Studies in Urban and Regional Planning*. Toronto: McClelland and Stewart, 1971.

OEPPEN, J. "Spatial Competition: A Simulation Approach." Unpublished M.A. thesis, Department of Geography, Queen's University, Kingston, 1973.

Ontario Department of Municipal Affairs. *Urban Land Use in Ontario: Areas and Intensities*. Toronto: Department of Municipal Affairs, Community Planning Branch, 1969.

——. *1972 Municipal Directory*. Toronto: Queen's Printer, 1972.

PERRON, J. *Représentation graphique de la répartition des industries de la région de Québec*. Québec: l'Institut de Géographie de l'Université Laval, 1971.

PLUNKETT, T.J. *The Financial Structure and Decision-Making Process of Canadian Municipal Government*. Ottawa: Central Mortgage and Housing Corporation, 1972.

——. "Urban Canada, Regional Reform, and the Municipal Managerial Dilemma." Paper presented to the 67th annual conference of the Municipal Finance Officers Association, United States and Canada, at Kansas City, Missouri, June 5, 1973.

POLESE, M. (ed.). *Région Sud: système urbain*. Montréal: Université du Québec, C.R.U.R.-I.N.R.S., 1972.

PORTER, J. *The Vertical Mosaic*. Toronto: University of Toronto Press, 1965

POWELL, M., and BLACK, A. *Municipal Government and Finance: An Annotated Bibliography*. Ottawa: Policy Planning Division, CMHC, 1971.

PRATT, D.H. "STOL Air Transport Systems in Canada," in R.M. Soberman (ed.), *Readings in Airport Planning*, Toronto: University of Toronto, CUCS and the Department of Civil Engineering, 1972, pp. 411–39.

PUXLEY, E. *Poverty in Montreal*. Montreal: Dawson College Press, 1971.

QUESNEL-OUELLET, L. "Changement dans les structures municipales: Etude de la Région de Québec." Paper presented to the annual meeting of the Canadian Political Science Association, Montreal, June 3, 1972.

RACINE, J.B. "The Genesis of a Metropolis," in L. Beauregard (ed.), *Montreal: Field Guide*. Montreal: Les Presses de l'Université de Montréal, 1972, pp. 107–15.

RAVENEAU, J., OTTMAN, L., and GAGNON, Y. "L'utilisation du sol des agglomérations urbaines du Québec de plus de 4,000 habitants en 1971, essai de typologie." Paper presented to the Canadian Association of Geographers, Thunder Bay, 1973.

RAY, D.M. *Market Potential and Economic Shadow.* Research Paper No. 101. Chicago: Department of Geography, University of Chicago, 1965.

———. *Dimensions of Canadian Regionalism.* Geographical Paper No. 49. Ottawa: Department of Energy, Mines and Resources, 1971.

REEDS, L.G. "Agricultural Regions of Southern Ontario, 1880 and 1951," in R.L. Gentilcore (ed.), *Canada's Changing Geography.* Toronto: Prentice Hall, 1967, pp. 84–91.

REID, F.L. "The Supply of Immigrants to Canadian Cities: 1921–1961." Unpublished Master's thesis, Department of Economics, Queen's University, Kingston, 1973.

RICHMOND, A.H. *Immigrants and Ethnic Groups in Metropolitan Toronto.* Toronto: Institute for Behavioural Research, York University, 1967.

ROBERT, B. "Problèmes de comptabilisation des flux migratoires: aperçu méthodologique préliminaire," *Statistiques,* 1 (1971), Québec: Bureau de la Statistique du Québec.

———. "Eléments pour l'étude des déplacements géographiques de la Population Québecoise." *Annuaire du Québec,* Québec: Editeur Officiel du Québec, 1972, pp. 152–67.

———. *Evolutions démographiques régionales et migrations intérieures de population: province de Québec; 1941–1966.* Québec: Bureau de la Statistique du Québec, 1973.

ROGERS, A., and MILLER, R. "Estimating a Matrix Population Growth Operator from Distributional Time Series," *Annals of the Association of American Geographers,* 57 (1967),751–56.

RUSSWURM, L.H. *The Development of an Urban Corridor System: Toronto to Stratford Area, 1941–1966.* Toronto: Queen's Printer, 1970.

———. "Urban Fringe and Urban Shadow," in R.R. Krueger, and R.C. Bryfogle (eds.), *Urban Problems: A Canadian Reader.* Toronto: Holt, Rinehart and Winston, 1971, pp. 104–21.

SAYEGH, K.S. (ed.). *Canadian Housing: A Reader.* Waterloo: University of Waterloo, 1972.

Service d'Urbanisme. *La vague d'expansion métropolitaine.* Technical Bulletin No. 1. Montréal: Service d'Urbanisme, 1964a.

———. *Centre-Ville.* Technical Bulletin No. 3. Montreal: Service d'Urbanisme, 1964b.

———. *Urbanisation.* Technical Bulletin No. 5, Third Edition. Montreal: Service d'Urbanisme, 1969.

SIMMONS, J.W. *Patterns of Interaction Within Ontario and Quebec.*

Research Paper No. 41. Toronto: Centre for Urban and Community Studies, 1970.

———. *Net Migration Within Metropolitan Toronto.* Research Paper No. 44. Toronto: University of Toronto, cucs, 1971.

———. "Interaction Among the Cities of Ontario and Quebec," in L. Bourne, and R.D. MacKinnon (eds.), *Urban Systems Development in Central Canada.* Research Paper No. 9. Toronto: University of Toronto, Department of Geography, 1972.

spelt, j. *Urban Development in South-Central Ontario.* Toronto: McClelland and Stewart, 1955 (reprinted 1972).

———. "Southern Ontario," in J. Warkentin (ed.), *Canada: A Geographical Interpretation.* Toronto: Methuen, 1968, pp. 334–95.

spurr, p. "Land and Urban Policy." Unpublished cmhc Research Paper. Ottawa, 1971.

stone, l.o. *Urban Development in Canada.* Ottawa: Queen's Printer, 1968.

———. *Migration in Canada.* Ottawa: Statistics Canada, 1969.

Systems Research Group (srg). *Canada 2000: Population Projections.* Toronto: srg, 1970.

tessier, m. *Proposition de réforme des structures municipales I, II.* Québec: Editeur Officiel du Québec, 1971.

thibodeau, j.c. (ed.) *Région Sud: L'agriculture.* Montréal: Université du Québec, c.r.u.r.-i.n.r.s., 1972.

thibodeau, j.c. *Implantation manufacturière dans la région de Montréal: mouvement centrifuge ou centripède?* Montréal: Les Presses de l'Université du Québec, 1971.

thoman, r.s., and yeates, m. *Delimitation of Development Regions in Canada: With Special Attention to the Georgian Bay Vicinity.* Ottawa: Area Development Agency, Department of Industry, 1966.

tremblay, m.a., and anderson, w.j. (eds.). *Rural Canada in Transition.* Publication No. 6. Ottawa: Agricultural Economic Research Council, 1966.

trotier, l. *Répartition de la population du Québec en 1961.* Québec: Conseil d'Orientation Economique du Québec, 1966.

watts, f.b. "Climate, Vegetation and Soil," in J. Warkentin (ed.), *Canada: A Geographical Interpretation.* Toronto: Methuen, 1968, pp. 78–111.

webber, m. "Planning in an Environment of Change, Part i: Beyond the Industrial Age," *The Town Planning Review,* 39 (1968), pp. 179–95.

webber, m., and c.c. webber. "Culture, Territoriality and the Elastic

Mile," in H. Eldrige and Wentworth, *Taming Megalopolis, Vol. I.* New York: Doubleday, 1967, pp. 35–53.

WEIR, T.R. "The People," in J. Warkentin (ed.), *Canada: A Geographical Interpretation.* Toronto: Methuen, 1968, pp. 137–86.

WHEBELL, C.F.J. "Corridors: A Theory of Urban Systems," *Annals of the Association of American Geographers,* 59 (1969), pp. 1–26.

———. *Spatial Variation in Net Migration Parameters in Ontario.* Toronto: Regional Development Branch, Department of Treasury and Economics, 1971.

WILSON, C. "The Climate of the Province of Quebec." Unpublished Ph.D. thesis. Québec, Université Laval, Institut de Géographie, 1972.

WOLFE, R.I. "Economic Development," in J. Warkentin (ed.), *Canada: A Geographical Interpretation.* Toronto: Methuen, 1968, pp. 187–230.

WOLFORTH, J., and LEIGH, R. *Urban Prospects.* Toronto: McClelland and Stewart, 1971.

WOODYARD, M. *Components of the In-Migration Stream in Central Canada.* Research Paper No. 57. Toronto: University of Toronto, CUCS, 1972.

YEATES, M. "The Congruence Between Housing Space, Social Space, and the Community Space, and Some Experiments Concerning its Implications," *Environment and Planning,* 4 (1972), pp. 395–414.

———. Growth in the Kingston Urban Region in the Immediate Past, and Prospects for Growth in the Future," *The Queen's Geographer,* 1 (1973), pp. 1–6.

———. *An Introduction to Quantitative Analysis in Human Geography.* New York: McGraw-Hill, 1974.

YEATES, M., and GARNER, B.J. *The North American City.* New York: Harper and Row, 1971.

ZIPF, G.K. *Human Behavior and the Principle of Least Effort.* Reading, Mass.: Addison-Wesley, 1949.

APPENDIX A CENSUS SUBDIVISIONS AND AGGREGATES

Québec (0)

C.D.	Sub.	Sub. incl.	Name
1			*Argenteuil*
	1	1	Arundel
			Barkmere
		6	Huberdeau
	2	2	Chatham
			Brownsburg
			Carillon
			Lachute
	3	3	Gore
		8	Mille-Iles
	4	4	Grenville
			Grenville
			Calumet
	5	5	Harrington
	7	7	Lac-des-Seize-Iles
		9	Montcalm
		14	Wentworth
		15	Wentworth N.
	10	10	Morin Heights
		11	St-Adolphe-d'Howard
	12	12	St-André E.
3			*Arthabaska*
	1	1	Chénier
		15	St-Rémi-de-Tingwick
		20	Tingwick
		21	Trois Lacs
	2	2	Chester E.
		3	Chester N.
		4	Chester O.
			Chesterville
	5	5	Maddington
		13	St-Louis-de-Blandford
	7	7	Ste-Anne-du-Sault
			Daveluyville
		16	St-Rosaire
	8	8	St-Christophe-d'Arthabaska
			Arthabaska

C.D.	Sub.	Sub. incl.	Name
		22	Warwick
			Warwick
	9	6	St-Albert-de-Warwick
		9	Ste-Clothilde-de-Horton
			Ste-Clothilde
	10	10	Ste-Elisabeth-de-Warwick
		12	St-Jacques-de-Horton
		17	Ste-Séraphine
	11	11	St-Eusèbe-de-Stanfold
			Princeville
		14	St-Norbert-d'Arthabaska
	18	18	St-Valère
		19	Ste-Victoire-d'Arthabaska
			Victoriaville
4			*Bagot*
	1	1	St-André-d'Acton
			Acton Vale
		2	Ste-Christine
		12	St-Théodore-d'Acton
	2	3	St-Dominique
		9	St-Pie
			St-Pie
		10	Ste-Rosalie
			Ste-Rosalie
	3	6	St-Hugues
			St-Hugues
		11	St-Simon
	4	5	Ste-Hélène
			Ste-Hélène-de-Bagot
		8	St-Nazaire-d'Acton
	5	4	St-Ephrem-d'Upton
			Upton
		7	St-Liboire
			St-Liboire
5			*Beauce*
	1	1	Aubert-Gallion
			St-Georges O.
		10	St-Benoît Labre
			Lac Poulin
		18	St-Georges E.
			St-Georges

C.D.	Sub.	Sub. incl.	Name
		20	St-Jean-de-la-Lande
	2	2	East Broughton
			East Broughton Station
		5	Sacré-Coeur-de-Jésus
		28	St-Pierre-de-Broughton
	3	3	L'Enfant Jésus
			Vallée-Jonction
		7	Saints-Anges
		24	Ste-Marie
			Ste-Marie
	4	4	Notre-Dame-de-la-Providence
		15	St-François-de-Beauce
			Beauceville E.
		16	St-François O.
			Beauceville
	6	11	Ste-Clotilde
		14	St-Ephrem-de-Beauce
			St-Ephrem-de-Tring
	8	8	St-Alfred
		33	St-Victor-de-Tring
			St-Victor
	9	9	Ste-Aurélie
		34	St-Zacharie
			St-Zacharie
	12	12	St-Côme-de-Kennebec
			Linière
		27	St-Philibert-de-Beauce
		29	St-René
	13	13	St-Elzéar-de-Beauce
			St-Elzéar
	17	17	St-Frédéric
			Tring-Jonction
		21	St-Joseph-de-Beauce
			St-Joseph
		22	St-Joseph-des-Erables
		23	St-Jules
	19	19	St-Honoré
		25	St-Martin
		35	Shenley
	32	32	St-Théophile-de-la-Beauce
			St-Théophile

C.D.	Sub.	Sub. incl.	Name
6			*Beauharnois*
	1	1	Grande-Ile
			Salaberry-de-Valleyfield
		2	Ste-Cécile
		6	St-Timothée
			St-Timothée
			Melocheville
	3	3	St-Etienne-de-Beauharnois
			Beauharnois
			Maple Grove
	4	4	St-Louis-de-Gonzague
		5	St-Stanislas-de-Kostka
7			*Bellechasse*
	1	1	Honfleur
		10	Sts-Gervais-et-Protais
	2	2	La Durantaye
		16	St-Raphaël
			St-Raphaël
		18	St-Vallier
			St-Vallier
	3	3	Notre-Dame-Auxiliatrice-de-Buckland
		15	St-Philémon
	4	4	St-Cajétan-d'Armagh
			Armagh
	5	5	St-Camille-de-Lellis
	6	6	St-Charles-Boromé
			St-Charles
		8	St-Etienne-de-Beaumont
		13	St-Michel
	12	12	St-Magloire-de-Bellechasse
		17	Ste-Sabine
	7	7	St-Damien-de-Buckland
		11	St-Lazare
		14	St-Nérée
8			*Berthier*
	1	1	Lanoraie-d'Autray
		3	St-Antoine-de-Lavaltrie
			Lavaltrie
		12	St-Joseph-de-Lanoraie

C.D.	Sub.	Sub. incl.	Name
	2	2	La Visitation-Ste-Vierge-de-L'Isle
		10	Ste-Geneviève-de-Berthier
			Berthierville
		11	St-Ignace-de-Loyola
	4	4	St-Barthélémi
		6	St-Cuthbert
		15	St-Viateur
	5	5	St-Charles-de-Mandeville
		7	St-Damien
	9	9	St-Gabriel-de-Brandon
			St-Gabriel
		14	St-Norbert
10			*Brome*
	1	1	Austin
			Eastman
		2	Adamsville
			E. Farnham
		3	Bolton E.
		7	St-Etienne-de-Bolton
	4	4	Bolton O.
	5	5	Brome
			Bromont
			Foster
			Knowlton
	6	6	Potton
	8	8	Sutton
			Abercorn
			Sutton
11			*Chambly*
	1	1	St-Basile-le-Grand
		3	Chambly
			Carignan
	2	2	Boucherville
	4	4	Jacques-Cartier
			Laflèche
			Longueuil
			St-Lambert
			Greenfield Park
			Le Moyne

C.D.	Sub.	Sub. incl.	Name
			Préville
			St-Bruno-de-Montarville
			St-Hubert
12			*Champlain*
	2	2	La-Visitation-de-Champlain
			Champlain
		6	St-François-Xavier-de-Batiscan
		7	Ste-Geneviève-de-Batiscan
		12	St-Luc
	3	3	Notre-Dame-du-Mont-Carmel
			Shawinigan S.
	3	21	St-Théophile
			Grand'Mère
			St-Georges
	4	4	St-Adelphe
		20	Ste-Thècle
			Ste-Thècle
		22	St-Timothée
		23	St-Tite
			St-Tite
	5	5	Ste-Anne-de-la-Pérade
			La Pérade
		16	St-Prosper
	10	10	St-Joseph-de-Mékinac
	8	8	Grandes-Piles
		9	St-Jean-des-Piles
	11	11	St-Louis-de-France
		13	Ste-Marthe-du-Cap
			Cap-de-la-Madeleine
		14	St-Maurice
	15	15	St-Narcisse
		18	St-Séverin
		19	St-Stanislas
			St-Stanislas
	17	17	St-Roch-de-Mékinac
15			*Châteauguay*
	2	1	St-Antoine-Abbé N.E.
		2	Ste-Clotilde
		3	St-Jean Chrysostôme
			St-Chrysostôme

C.D.	Sub.	Sub. incl.	Name
	4	4	St-Malachie-d'Ormstown
			Ormstown
	5	5	Ste-Martine
		6	St-Paul-de-Châteauguay
		8	St. Urbain-Premier
		9	Très Saint-Sacrement
			Howick
	7	7	Mercier
		10	Châteauguay
			Châteauguay-Centre
			Léry
17			*Compton*
	2	2	St-Malo
		18	St-Isidore-d'Auckland
	3	3	Bury
	4	4	Clifton E.
		13	Martinville
		16	Ste-Edwidge-de-Clifton
	5	5	Compton
			Compton
		6	Compton Station
			Waterville
	7	7	Ditton
			La Patrie
		9	Emberton
	8	8	Eaton
			Cookshire
			Sawyerville
		20	Westbury
			East Angus
	10	10	Hampden
			Scotstown
		12	Lingwick
	17	11	Hereford
		19	St-Venant-de-Hereford
	15	15	Newport
18			*Deux-Montagnes*
	1	1	L'Annonciation N.
			Oka-sur-le-Lac

C.D.	Sub.	Sub. incl.	Name
		2	Oka
		12	St-Placide
			St-Placide
	6	6	St-Colomban
	13	3	Ste-Scholastique
	7	7	St-Eustache
			St-Eustache
		9	St-Joseph-du-Lac
			Pointe-Calumet
		10	Ste-Marthe-sur-le-Lac
		14	Deux-Montagnes
19			*Dorchester*
	1	1	Louis-Joliette
		2	St-Anselme
			St-Anselme
		5	Ste-Claire
		9	Ste-Hénédine
		17	Ste-Marguerite
	3	3	St-Benjamin
		20	St-Odilon-de-Cranbourne
	4	4	St-Bernard
			St-Bernard
		10	St-Isidore
			St-Isidore
	4	18	St-Maxime
		24	Taschereau-Fortier
	7	7	St-Edouard-de-Frampton
		16	St-Malachie
	8	8	Ste-Germaine-du-Lac-Etchemin
			Lac Etchemin
	6	6	St-Cyprien
		12	Ste-Justine
	13	13	St-Léon-de-Standon
		15	St-Luc
		19	St-Nazaire-de-Dorchester
	14	14	St-Louis-de-Gonzague
		21	St-Prosper
		22	Ste-Rose-de-Watford

C.D.	Sub.	Sub. incl.	Name
20			*Drummond*
	1	1	Drummondville
			Drummondville S.
		3	Grantham O.
		13	St-Majorique-de-Grantham
		14	St-Nicephore
		16	Wendover & Simpson
			St-Cyrille
	7	7	Lefebvre
		17	Wickham
			Wickham
	4	4	Kingsey
		5	Kingsey Falls
			Kingsey Falls
		12	St-Lucien
	2	2	Durham S.
			Durham S.
	2	6	L'Avenir
			L'Avenir
		15	Ulverton
	9	9	St-Edmond-de-Grantham
		10	St-Eugène
		11	St-Germain-de-Grantham
			St-Germain-de-Grantham
	8	8	Notre-Dame-du-Bon-Conseil
			Notre-Dame-du-Bon-Conseil
21			*Frontenac*
	1	1	Audet
		5	Gayhurst S. E.
		12	Risborough & Marlow
			St-Ludger
	2	2	Courcelles
		6	Lambton
		15	St-Evariste-de-Forsyth
			La Guadeloupe
	3	3	Frontenac
			Lac-Mégantic (1/3)
		9	Nantes
			Lac-Mégantic (1/3)

C.D.	Sub.	Sub. incl.	Name
		14	Ste-Cécile-de-Whitton
			Lac-Mégantic (1/3)
	4	4	Lac-Drolet
		17	St-Hilaire-de-Dorset
		21	St-Sébastien
			St-Sébastien
	7	7	Marston
		8	Milan
		11	Piopolis
	7	22	Val-Racine·
	10	10	Notre-Dame-des-Bois
		13	St-Augustin-de-Woburn
	18	18	St-Méthode-de-Frontenac
		19	St-Romain
	20	16	St-Gédéon
			St-Gédéon
		20	St-Robert-Bellarmin
	24	24	Winslow S.
25			*Gatineau*
	2	2	Aylwin
	8	8	Denholm
	9	9	Eardley
	11	11	Hincks
	14	12	Touraine
		13	Hull O.
		14	Lucerne
			Aylmer
			Deschèsnes
	15	15	Low
	17	17	Masham N.
		21	Ste-Cécile-de-Masham
	24	24	Wakefield
			Wakefield
		25	Wakefield E.
26			*Hull*
	1	1	Perkins
	2	2	Templeton E.
			Templeton

C.D.	Sub.	Sub. incl.	Name
		3	Templeton E., Partie Est
	2	4	Templeton O.
			Gatineau
			Pointe-Gatineau
		5	Hull
27			*Huntingdon*
	1	1	Dundee
		8	St-Anicet
		9	Ste-Barbe
			Réserve Indienne
	2	2	Elgin
		4	Godmanchester
			Huntingdon (1/2)
		7	Hinchinbrook
			Huntingdon (1/2)
	3	3	Franklin
		5	Havelock
	6	6	Hemmingford
			Hemmingford
28			*Iberville*
	1	4	St-Athanase
			Iberville
		5	Ste-Brigide-d'Iberville
		6	St-Grégoire-le-Grand
			St-Grégoire
	2	1	Henryville
			Henryville
		2	St-Alexandre
			St-Alexandre
		3	Ste-Anne-de-Sabrevois
		7	St-Sébastien
29			*Joliette*
	1	3	Notre-Dame-des-Prairies
		4	Sacré-Coeur-de-Jésus
			Crabtree
		8	St-Charles-Borromée
			Joliette
		17	St-Paul
			St-Pierre

C.D.	Sub.	Sub. incl.	Name
		18	St-Thomas
	3	6	St-Ambroise-de-Kildare
		15	Ste-Marcelline-de-Kildare
		16	Ste-Mélanie
	2	2	Notre-Dame-de-Lourdes
		9	St-Cléophas
		11	Ste-Elisabeth
		13	St-Félix-de-Valois
			St-Félix-de-Valois
	4	5	St-Alphonse-de-Rodriguez
		7	Ste-Béatrix
	5	12	Ste-Emélie-de-l'Energie
		14	St-Jean-de-Matha
	10	10	St.-Côme
34			*Laprairie*
	1	1	Notre-Dame
		9	Laprairie
			Brossard
	2	5	St-Jacques-le-Mineur
		6	St-Mathieu
		7	St-Philippe
			Candiac
	3	2	Ste-Catherine-d'Alexandrie
		3	St-Constant
			Delson
		4	St-Isidore
		8	Réserve Indienne
35			*L'Assomption*
	1	1	L'Assomption
			L'Assomption
		3	St-Charles-de-Lachenaie
			Charlemagne
		8	St-Paul L'Ermite
		11	St-Sulpice
		12	Repentigny
	2	2	L'Epiphanie
			L'Epiphanie
		4	St-Gérard-Magella
		5	Mascouche

C.D.	Sub.	Sub. incl.	Name
		9	St-Roch-de-l'Achigan
	3	6	La Plaine
		7	St-Lin
			Laurentides
		10	St-Roch O.
36			*Lévis*
	1	1	Rivière-Boyer
		5	St-Henri-de-Lauzon
			St-Henri
	2	2	St-David-de-l'Aube-Rivière
		4	Ste-Hélène-de-Breakeyville
		6	St-Jean-Chrysostôme
		12	St-Romuald-d'Etchemin
			Charny
	2	14	Lévis
	3	3	St-Etienne
		10	St-Nicolas
			St-Rédempteur
		11	Bernières
	7	7	St-Joseph-de-la-Pointe-de-Lévy
			Lauzon
		9	St-Louis-de-Pintendre
	8	8	St-Lambert-de-Lauzon
38			*Lotbinière*
	1	1	Notre-Dame-du-Sacré-Coeur-d'Issoudun
		6	Ste-Croix
			Ste-Croix
		9	St-Flavien
			St-Flavien
			Laurier-Station
	2	2	St-Agapit-de-Beaurivage
			St-Agapitville
		4	St-Antoine-de-Tilly
		5	St-Apollinaire
			Francoeur
	3	3	Ste-Agathe
			Ste-Agathe
		11	St-Gilles
		16	St-Octave-de-Dosquet
	7	7	St-Edouard-de-Lotbinière

C.D.	Sub.	Sub. incl.	Name
		8	Ste-Emmélie
			Leclercville
		14	St-Louis-de-Lotbinière
			Lotbinière
	10	10	Ste-Françoise
		12	St-Jacques-de-Parisville
			Deschaillons
			Deschaillons-sur-St. Laurent
		18	Ste-Philomène-de-Fortierville
			Fortierville
	15	15	St-Narcisse-de-Beaurivage
		17	St-Patrice-de-Beaurivage
			St-Patrice-de-Beaurivage
		19	St-Sylvestre
			St-Sylvestre
	21	13	St-Janvier-de-Joly
		20	Val-Alain
		21	Villeroy
39			*Maskinongé*
	1	1	Hunterstown
		3	Ste-Angèle
		10	St-Léon-le-Grand
		11	St-Paulin
			St-Paulin
	2	2	St-Alexis
	4	4	St-Antoine-de-la-Rivière-du-Loup
			Louiseville
		8	St-Joseph-de-Maskinongé
			Maskinongé
	5	5	St-Didace
		6	St-Edouard
		9	St-Justin
		12	Ste-Ursule
	7	7	St-Ignace-du-Lac
42			*Mégantic*
	1	1	Halifax N.
		2	Halifax S.
			Bernierville
		3	Halifax S.-O.

C.D.	Sub.	Sub. incl.	Name
		20	St-Pierre-Baptiste
		21	Ste-Sophie
	4	4	Inverness
			Inverness
		9	Nelson
	5	5	Ireland
		6	Ireland N.
		12	Rivière-Blanche
		18	St-Joseph-de-Coleraine
			Black Lake
	7	7	Leeds
		8	Leeds E.
		16	St-Jacques-de-Leeds
		17	St-Jean-de-Brébeuf
	10	10	Notre-Dame-de-Lourdes
		11	Plessisville
			Plessisville
		19	Ste-Julie
			Laurierville
	13	13	Sacré-Coeur-de-Marie, S.
			Ste-Anne-du-Lac
		15	St-Antoine-de-Pontbriand
			Robertsonville
		22	Thetford S.
			Thetford Mines
	14	14	Ste-Anastasie-de-Nelson
			Lyster
43			*Missisquoi*
	1	11	St-Thomas
		14	Venise-en-Québec
		7	St-Georges-de-Clarenceville
			Clarenceville
	2	2	Dunham
			Dunham
			Cowansville
	4	3	Rainville
			Farnham
		4	Notre-Dame-de-Stanbridge
		8	St-Ignace-de-Stanbridge
		10	Ste-Sabine

C.D.	Sub.	Sub. incl.	Name
	3	1	Bedford
			Bedford
		5	St-Armand E. (Frelighsburg)
			Frelighsburg
		6	St-Armand O.
			Philipsburg
		9	St-Pierre-de-Véronne à Pike River
		12	Stanbridge
		13	Stanbridge Station
44			*Montcalm*
	1	8	St-Alexis
			St-Alexis
		9	St-Calixte
		12	St-Jacques
			St-Jacques
		13	Ste-Julienne
		15	Ste-Marie-Salomée
	2	6	Rawdon
			Rawdon
	2	10	St-Donat
		14	St-Liguori
	3	1	Chertsey
		2	Lac-Paré
		16	Entrelacs
	4	7	Val-des-Lacs
		11	St-Esprit
	5	5	Notre-Dame-de-la-Merci
45			*Montmagny*
	1	1	Berthier
		10	St-François-de-Sales-de-la -Rivière S.
		13	St-Pierre-de-la-Rivière S.
		14	Montmagny
	2	2	Cap-St-Ignace
	3	3	Lac-Frontière
		9	St-Fabien-de-Panet
		11	St-Juste-de-Bretenières
		12	Ste-Lucie-de-Beauregard
	4	4	Montminy
		7	Ste-Apolline-de-Patton

C.D.	Sub.	Sub. incl.	Name
	5	5	Notre-Dame-du-Rosaire
		8	Ste-Euphémie-sur-Rivière S.
	6	6	St-Antoine-de-l'Isle-aux-Grues
46			*Montmorency No. 1*
	1	1	Château-Richer
		3	Ste-Anne-de-Beaupré
			Ste-Anne-de-Beaupré
			Beaupré
	5	5	St-Féréol-les-Neiges
		6	St-Joachim
		7	Ste-Tite-des-Caps
	2	2	L'Ange-Gardien
			St-Jean-de-Boischatel
		4	Ste-Brigitte-de-Laval
47			*Montmorency No. 2*
	1	1	Ste-Famille
		2	St-François
		3	St-Jean
	4	4	St-Laurent
		5	St-Pierre
			Beaulieu
49			*Ile de Montréal et Ile Jésus*
	1		Lasalle, Lachine, St-Laurent, Pierrefonds, Roxboro, Dollard-des-Ormeaux, Ste-Geneviève, Pointe Claire, Kirkland, Beaconsfield, Baie-d'Urfé, Dorval, Ste-Anne-de-Bellevue, Senneville, Ile-Dorval, St-Raphaël-de-l'Ile-Bizard
	2		Montréal, Mont-Royal, Outremont, Westmount, Côte-St-Luc, Montréal O., Hampstead, Verdun, Ville St-Pierre, St-Jean-de-Dieu
	3		Montréal N., Montréal E., Anjou, St-Léonard, Pointe-aux-Trembles, St-Michel,
	4		Laval
50			*Napierville*
	1	3	St-Michel

C.D.	Sub.	Sub. incl.	Name
		5	St-Rémi
			St-Rémi
	2	1	St-Cyprien
			Napierville
		2	St-Edouard
		4	St-Patrice-de-Sherrington
51			*Nicolet*
	1	1	Bécancour
	2	2	Grand-St-Esprit
		4	Nicolet S.
		13	St-Jean-Baptiste-de-Nicolet
			Nicolet
		17	Ste-Monique
			Ste-Monique
	3	3	Lemieux
		16	Ste-Marie-de-Blandford
			Ste-Marie
		23	St-Sylvère
			St-Sylvère
	6	6	Ste-Brigitte-des-Saults
		15	St-Léonard
			St-Léonard-d'Aston
		18	Ste-Perpétue
	7	7	Ste-Cécile-de-Lévrard
		14	St-Joseph-de-Blandford
			Manseau
		19	St-Pierre-les-Becquets
			Les Becquets
	7	22	Ste-Sophie-de-Lévrard
	10	8	St-Célestin
			Annaville
		10	Ste-Eulalie
		20	St-Raphaël S.
			Aston Jonction
		21	St-Samuel
		24	St-Wenceslas
			St-Wenceslas
52			*Papineau*
	1	1	Amherst

C.D.	Sub.	Sub. incl.	Name
		9	Lac-des-Plages
	2	2	Bowman
		27	Val-des-Bois
	3	3	Buckingham
		4	Buckingham O.
	5	5	Buckingham S.-E.
			Buckingham
			Masson
		10	L'Ange-Gardien
			Angers
	6	6	Lac-Simon
			Chénéville
		15	Montpellier
		23	Ripon
			Ripon
		28	Vinoy
	7	7	Duhamel
	8	8	Fassett
		17	Notre-Dame-du-Bon-Secours N.
			Montebello
	11	11	Lochaber
			Thurso
		12	Lochaber N.
		13	Lochaber O.
		14	Mayo
	16	16	Mulgrave & Derry
	18	18	Notre-Dame-de-la-Paix
		19	Plaisance
		24	St-André-Avellin
			St-André-Avellin
		25	Ste-Angélique
			Papineauville
	20	20	Ponsonby
	21	21	Notre-Dame-de-la-Salette
	22	22	Portland O.
	26	26	Suffolk & Addington
		29	Namur
53			*Pontiac*
	1	1	Aldfield
	2	2	Alleyn & Cawood

C.D.	Sub.	Sub. incl.	Name
	3	3	Bristol
	4	4	Chichester
	5	5	Clarendon
			Shawville
	7	7	Grand-Calumet
	8	8	Ile-aux-Alumettes E.
	9	9	Ile-des-Alumettes
			Chapeau
	10	10	Leslie, Clapham, & Huddersfield
	11	11	Litchfield
			Bryson
			Campbell's Bay
			Portage-du-Fort
	12	12	Mansfield & Pontefract
			Fort-Coulonge
	13	13	Onslow
	14	14	Onslow S.
			Quyon
	17	17	Thorne
	18	18	Waltham & Bryson
54			*Portneuf*
	1	1	Cap-Santé
		3	Notre-Dame-de-Portneuf
			Portneuf
		9	St-Basile
			St-Basile S.
	2	2	Les-Ecureuils
		5	Pointe-aux-Trembles
			Neuville
		8	St-Augustin-de-Desmaures
		15	Ste-Jeanne-de-Pont-Rouge
			Pont-Rouge
	4	4	Notre-Dame-des-Anges-de-Montauban
			Montauban
		19	St-Rémi
	6	6	Rivière-à-Pierre
	7	7	St-Alban
			St-Alban
		13	Ste-Christine

C.D.	Sub.	Sub. incl.	Name
	10	10	St-Casimir
			St-Casimir
		20	St-Thuribe
		21	St-Ubald
			St-Ubald
	11	11	Ste-Catherine
			Lac-St-Joseph
			Fossambault-sur-le-Lac
		22	Shannon
	12	12	St-Charles-des-Grondines
			St-Casimir E.
			St-Charles-des-Grondines
		14	St-Gilbert
		16	St-Joseph-de-Deschambault
			Deschambault
			St-Marc-des-Carrières
	17	17	St-Léonard-de-Portneuf
		18	St-Raymond
			St-Raymond
			Lac-Sergent
55			*Québec*
	1	1	Beauport O.
			Villeneuve
		15	Ste-Thérèse-de-Lisieux
		21	Courville
		22	Montmorency
	2	2	Charlesbourg E.
		3	Charlesbourg O.
		5	Lac-St-Charles
			St-Emile
		7	Notre-Dame-des-Laurentides
	2	18	Charlesbourg
		23	Orsainville
	4	4	Lac-Edouard
	6	6	Ste-Foy
		8	Ancienne-Lorette
			Loretteville
		10	St-Félix-du-Cap-Rouge
		14	St-Michel-Archange
		17	Québec

C.D.	Sub.	Sub. incl.	Name
		19	Giffard
		20	Sillery
		24	Vanier
	9	9	St-Dunstan-du-Lac-Beauport
	11	11	St-Gabriel-de-Valcartier
		13	Bélair
			Val-St-Michel
	12	12	St-Gabriel O.
	16	16	Stoneham & Tewkesbury
			Lac-Delage
56			*Richelieu*
	1	2	Ste-Anne-de-Sorel
			Sorel
		6	St-Pierre-de-Sorel
			St-Joseph-de-Sorel
			Tracy
	2	5	St-Ours
			St-Ours
		8	St-Roch-de-Richelieu
	3	1	St-Aimé
			Massueville
	3	3	St-Louis
		4	St-Marcel
	4	9	Ste-Victoire-de-Sorel
		7	St-Robert
57			*Richmond*
	1	11	Stoke
	2	2	Brompton
			Bromptonville
		3	Brompton Gore
		5	Melbourne
			Kingsbury
			Melbourne
		7	St-Denis-de-Brompton
		8	St-François-Xavier-de-Brompton
			St-Grégoire-de-Greenlay
	4	4	Cleveland
			Richmond

C.D.	Sub.	Sub. incl.	Name
		10	Shipton
			Asbestos
			Danville
	6	6	St-Claude
		9	St-Georges-de-Windsor
			St-Georges-de-Windsor
		12	Windsor
			Windsor
59			*Rouville*
	1	1	Mont-St-Hilaire
		3	Otterburn Park
		7	St-Jean-Baptiste
		10	St-Michel-de-Rougemont
			Rougemont
	2	2	Notre-Dame-du-Bon-Secours
			Richelieu
		5	Ste-Angèle-de-Monnoir
		8	Ste-Marie-de-Monnoir
			Marieville
		9	St-Mathias
	3	4	St-Ange-Gardien
			Ange-Gardien
		6	St-Césaire
			St-Césaire
		11	St-Paul-d'Abbotsford
61			*Shefford*
	1	1	Valcourt
			Valcourt
		2	Maricourt
		3	Béthanie
		5	Racine
	4	4	Granby
			Granby
		7	St-Alphonse
	8	8	Ste-Anne-de-la-Rochelle
			Lawrenceville
		14	Bonsecours
		15	Stukely S.
			Stukely S.

C.D.	Sub.	Sub. incl.	Name
	6	6	Roxton
			Roxton Falls
		11	Ste-Pudentienne
			Ste-Pudentienne
	9	9	Ste-Cécile-de-Milton
		12	St-Valérien-de-Milton
	10	10	St-Joachim-de-Shefford
		13	Shefford
			Waterloo
			Warden
62			*Sherbrooke*
	1	1	Ascot
			Lennoxville
		2	Ascot Corner
		3	Ascot N.
		8	Sherbrooke
	2	4	Orford
		5	Rock Forest
			Deauville
		7	St-Elie-d'Orford
63			*Soulanges*
	1	1	Ste-Claire-d'Assise
			Rivière-Beaudette
		5	St-Polycarpe
			St-Polycarpe
		6	St-Télesphore
		7	St-Zotique
			Coteau Landing
			La-Station-du-Coteau
	2	2	St-Clet
			St-Clet
		3	St-Ignace-du-Coteau-du-Lac
			Coteau-du-Lac
		4	St-Joseph-de-Soulanges
			Pointe-des-Cascades
			Les Cèdres
64			*Stanstead*
	2	1	Barford

C.D.	Sub.	Sub. incl.	Name
		2	Barnston
			Coaticook
		9	St-Herménégilde
			St-Herménégilde
		10	St-Mathieu-de-Dixville
			Dixville
	3	3	Barnston O.
		7	Ogden
			Beebe Plain
			Stanstead Plain
		11	Stanstead
		12	Stanstead E.
			Rock Island
	4	4	Hatley
			North Hatley
		5	Hatley O.
			Hatley
		6	Magog
			Magog
			Omerville
		8	Ste-Catherine-de-Hatley
			Ayer's Cliff
65			*St. Hyacinthe*
	1	1	Douville
		3	Notre-Dame-de-St-Hyacinthe
			La Providence
		9	St-Hyacinthe-Confesseur
			St-Joseph
		12	St-Thomas-d'Aquin
			St-Hyacinthe
	2	7	St-Damase
			St-Damase
		11	Ste-Marie-Madeleine
			Ste-Madeleine
	3	2	La Présentation
		6	St-Charles
			St-Charles-sur-Richelieu
		8	St-Denis
			St-Denis
	4	4	St-Barnabé

C.D.	Sub.	Sub. incl.	Name
		5	St-Bernard S.
		10	St-Jude
66			*St-Jean*
	1	1	Lacadie
		5	St-Jean-l'Evangéliste
		6	St-Luc
	2	2	Notre-Dame-du-Mont-Carmel
			Lacolle
		3	St-Bernard-de-Lacolle
		4	St-Blaise
		7	St-Paul-de-l'Ile-aux-Noix
		8	St-Valentin
67			*St-Maurice*
	1	1	Charette
		7	St-Elie
	2	2	La Visitation-de-la-Pointe-du-Lac
		3	Pointe-du-Lac
		15	Trois-Rivières
			Trois-Rivières O.
	4	4	Ste-Anne-d'Yamachiche
			Yamachiche
		5	St-Barnabé
		13	St-Sévère
	6	6	St-Boniface-de-Shawinigan
			Shawinigan
			Baie-de-Shawinigan
		10	St-Gérard-des-Laurentides
		11	St-Mathieu
	8	8	St-Etienne-des-Grès
71			*Terrebonne*
	1	25	Blainville
			Ste-Thérèse
			Lorraine
		26	Ste-Thérèse O.
		28	Rosemère
	2	21	St-Louis-de-Terrebonne
			Terrebonne
			Bois-des-Filion
	3	12	Ste-Anne-des-Plaines

C.D.	Sub.	Sub. incl.	Name
		24	Ste-Sophie
			New Glasgow
	4	13	St-Antoine-des-Laurentides
			St-Antoine
		18	Bellefeuille
			Lafontaine
			St-Jérôme
	6	9	Ste-Adèle
		22	Ste-Marguerite-du-Lac-Masson
			Estérel
	6	27	Val-Morin
			Val-David
	5	6	Lesage
			Shawbridge
		8	Piedmond
		11	Ste-Anne-des-Lacs
			Prévost
		15	St-Hippolyte
		19	Mont-Rolland
		23	St-Sauveur
			St-Sauveur-des-Monts
			Mont-Gabriel
	7	2	Ste-Lucie
		5	Lantier
	8	3	Ivry-sur-le-Lac
		10	Ste-Agathe
			Ste-Agathe-des-Monts
			Ste-Agathe S.
		14	St-Faustin
			Lac-Carré
	9	1	Brébeuf
		4	Lac-Supérieur
		7	Mont-Tremblant
		20	St-Jovite
			St-Jovite
72			*Vaudreuil*
	1	1	Notre-Dame-de-l'Ile-Perrot
			Ile-Perrot
			Pointe-du-Moulin
			Pincourt

C.D.	Sub.	Sub. incl.	Name
	2	3	St-Lazare
		7	Terrasse-Vaudreuil
			Vaudreuil, Dorion, Ile-Cadieux,
			Hudson, Vaudreuil-sur-le-Lac
	3	2	Ste-Justine-de-Newton
		4	Ste-Madeleine-de-Rigaud
			Rigaud
			Pointe-Fortune
		5	Ste-Marthe
			Ste-Marthe
		8	Très-Saint-Rédempteur
73			*Verchères*
	1	2	St-Amable
		3	Ste-Anne-de-Varennes
			Varennes
		7	Ste-Julie
		9	St-Mathieu-de-Beloeil
			Beloeil
			McMasterville
	2	6	St-François-Xavier-de-Verchères
			Verchères
		8	St-Marc
		10	Ste-Théodosie-Calixa-Lavallée
	3	1	Contrecoeur
			Contrecoeur
		4	St-Antoine-de-Padoue
		5	St-Antoine-sur-Richelieu
74			*Wolfe*
	1	1	Disraëli
			Disraëli
		4	Garthby
			Beaulac
	1	14	Ste-Praxède
		15	Stratford
	2·	2	Dudswell
			Bishopton
			Marbleton
	3	3	Fontainebleau
		11	St-Joseph-de-Ham-Sud

C.D.	Sub.	Sub. incl.	Name
		16	Weedon
			St-Gérard
			Weedon-Centre
	5	5	Ham N.
		6	Notre-Dame-de-Lourdes-de-Ham
		7	St-Adrien
		13	Sts-Martyrs-Canadiens
	8	8	St-Camille
		17	Wotton
			Wottonville
	9	9	St-Fortunat
		10	St-Jacques-le-Majeur-de-Wolfestown
		12	St-Julien
75			*Yamaska*
	1	1	La Visitation-de-la-B.-Vierge-Marie
		6	St-Elphège
		10	St-Joachim-de-Courval
		15	St-Zéphirin-de-Courval
	3	2	Notre-Dame-de-Pierreville
		3	St-Antoine-de-la-Baie-du-Febvre
			Baieville
		11	St-Joseph de la B. du F.
		14	St-Joseph-de-la-Baie-du-Febvre
			Pierreville
	4	4	St-Bonaventure
		5	St-David
		9	St-Guillaume
			St-Guillaume
		13	St-Pie-de-Guire
	7	7	St-François-du-Lac
			St-François-du-Lac
		8	St-Gérard-Majella
		12	St-Michel-d'Yamaska
			Yamaska
			Yamaska E.

Ontario (1)

C.D.	Sub.	Name
2		*Brant*
	1	Brantford
		Brantford
	2	Burford
	3	Dumfries South
		Paris
	4	Oakland
	5	Onondaga
	6	Tuscarora Indian Reserve
3		*Bruce*
	1	Albemarle
	2	Amabel
		Indian Reserve
		Wiarton
		Hepworth
	3	Arran
		Tara
	4	Brant
		Walkerton
	5	Bruce
		Tiverton
	6	Carrick
		Mildmay
	7	Culross
		Teeswater
	8	Eastnor
		Lion's Head
	9	Elderslie
		Paisley
		Chesley
	10	Greenock
	11	Huron
		Ripley
	12	Kincardine
		Kincardine
	13	Kinloss
		Lucknow
	14	Lindsay
	15	St. Edmunds

C.D.	Sub.	Name
	16	Saugeen
		Port Elgin
		Southampton
4		*Ottawa-Carleton*
	1	Fitzroy
	2	Gloucester
	3	Goulbourn
		Richmond
		Stittsville
	4	Gower, North
	5	Huntley
	6	March
	7	Marlborough
	8	Nepean
	9	Osgoode
	10	Torbolton
	11	Ottawa
		Rockliffe Park
		Vanier
		Eastview
6		*Dufferin*
	1	Amaranth
		Shelburne
	2	Garafraxa, East
		Orangeville (1/2)
	3	Luther, East
		Grand Valley
	4	Melancthon
	5	Mono
		Orangeville (1/2)
	6	Mulmur
7		*Dundas*
	1	Matilda
		Iroquois
	2	Mountain
	3	Williamsburgh
		Morrisburg
	4	Winchester
		Chesterville
		Winchester

C.D.	Sub.	Name
8		*Durham*
	1	Cartwright
	2	Cavan
		Millbrook
	3	Clarke
		Newcastle
	4	Darlington
		Bowmanville
	5	Hope
		Port Hope
	6	Manvers
9		*Elgin*
	1	Aldborough
		Rodney
		West Lorne
	2	Bayham
		Port Burwell
		Vienna
	3	Dorchester South
		Belmont
	4	Dunwich
		Dutton
	5	Malahide
		Aylmer
		Springfield
	6	Southwold
		Port Stanley
	7	Yarmouth
		St. Thomas
10		*Essex*
	1	Anderdon
		Amherstburg
	2	Colchester North
		Essex (2/3)
	3	Colchester South
		Harrow
	4	Gosfield North
	5	Gosfield South
		Kingsville

C.D.	Sub.	Name
	6	Maidstone
		Essex (1/3)
		St. Clair Beach
	7	Malden
	8	Mersea
		Leamington
	9	Pelee
	10	Rochester
		Belle River
	11	Windsor
		Sandwich South
		Sandwich West
		Tecumseh
	14	Tilbury North
		Tilbury
	15	Tilbury West
11		*Frontenac*
	1	Barrie
	2	Bedford
	3	Clarendon & Miller
	4	Hinchinbrooke
	5	Howe Island
	6	Kennebec
	7	Kingston
		Kingston
	8	Loughborough
	9	Olden
	10	Oso
	11	Palmerston & N. & S. Canonto
	12	Pittsburgh
	13	Portland
	14	Storrington
	15	Wolfe Island
12		*Glengarry*
	1	Charlottenburgh
		Lancaster
	2	Kenyon
		Alexandria (1/5)
		Maxville
	3	Lancaster
	4	Lochiel
		Alexandria (4/5)

C.D.	Sub.	Name
13		*Grenville*
	1	Augusta
		Prescott
	2	Edwardsburgh
		Cardinal
	3	Gower South
	4	Oxford-on-Rideau
		Kemptville
	5	Wolford
		Merrickville
14		*Grey*
	1	Artemisia
		Flesherton
		Markdale
	2	Bentinck
		Hanover
		Durham
	3	Collingwood
		Thornbury
	4	Derby
		Owen Sound (1/3)
	5	Egremont
	6	Euphrasia
	7	Glenelg
	8	Holland
		Chatsworth
	9	Keppel
		Shallow Lake
	10	Normandy
		Neustadt
	11	Osprey
	12	Proton
		Dundalk
	13	St. Vincent
		Meaford
	14	Sarawak
		Owen Sound (1/3)
	15	Sullivan
	16	Sydenham
		Owen Sound (1/3)

C.D.	Sub.	Name
15		*Haldimand*
	1	Canborough
	2	Cayuga, North
		Cayuga
	3	Cayuga, South
	4	Dunn
	5	Moulton
		Dunnville
	6	Oneida
		Caledonia
		Indian Reserve
		Hagersville
	7	Rainham
	8	Seneca
	9	Sherbrooke
	10	Walpole
		Jarvis
16		*Haliburton*
	1	Anson, Hindon & Minden
	2	Bicroft I.D.
	3	Cardiff
	4	Dysart, etc.
	5	Glamorgan
	6	Lutterworth
	7	Monmouth
	8	Sherborne, etc.
	9	Snowdon
	10	Stanhope
17		*Halton*
	1	Esquesing
		Acton
		Georgetown
	2	Nassagaweya
	3	Oakville
		Milton
	4	Burlington
18		*Hastings*
	1	Bangor, McLure & Wicklow
	2	Carlow
	3	Dungannon

C.D.	Sub.	Name
	4	Elzevir & Grimsthorpe
	5	Faraday
		Bancroft
	6	Herschel
	7	Hungerford
		Tweed
	8	Huntingdon
	9	Limerick
	10	Madoc
		Madoc
	11	Marmora & Lake
		Marmora
		Deloro
	12	Mayo
	13	Monteagle
	14	Rawdon
		Stirling (1/2)
	15	Sydney
		Stirling (1/2)
		Frankford
		Trenton
	16	Thurlow
		Belleville
	17	Tudor & Cashell
	18	Tyendinaga
		Deseronto
	19	Indian Reserve
		Wollaston
19		*Huron*
	1	Ashfield
	2	Colborne
	3	Goderich
		Goderich
		Clinton (1/2)
	4	Grey
		Brussels (2/3)
	5	Hay
		Hensall
		Zurich
	6	Howick

C.D.	Sub.	Name
	7	Hullett
		Clinton (1/2)
	8	McKillop
		Seaforth (1/2)
	9	Morris
		Brussels (1/3)
		Blyth
	10	Stanley
		Bayfield
	11	Stephen
		Exeter (1/3)
	12	Tuckersmith
		Seaforth (1/2)
	13	Turnberry
		Wingham
	14	Usborne
		Exeter (2/3)
	15	Wawanosh, East
	16	Wawanosh, West
21		*Kent*
	1	Camden
		Dresden
		Thamesville
	2	Chatham
		Wallaceburg
		Chatham (1/4)
	3	Dover
		Chatham (1/4)
		Indian Reserve
	4	Harwich
		Chatham (1/4)
		Bleinheim
		Erieau
		Erie Beach
	5	Howard
		Ridgetown
	6	Orford
		Highgate
	7	Raleigh
		Chatham (1/4)
	8	Romney
		Wheatley

C.D.	Sub.	Name
	9	Tilbury East
		Tilbury
	10	Zone
		Bothwell
22		*Lambton*
	1	Bosanquet
		Arkona
		Grand Bend
		Thetford
	2	Brooke
		Alvinston
	3	Dawn
	4	Enniskillen
		Petrolia
		Oil Springs
	5	Euphemia
	6	Moore
		Courtright
	7	Plympton
		Wyoming
		Forest (1/2)
	8	Sarnia
		Sarnia
		Point Edward
	9	Sombra
	10	Warwick
		Watford
		Forest (1/2)
	11	Indian Reserve
23		*Lanark*
	1	Bathurst
	2	Beckwith
		Carleton Place (3/4)
	3	Burgess, North
	4	Dalhousie & North Sherbrooke
	5	Darling
	6	Drummond
		Perth
	7	Elmsley, North
		Smiths Falls
	8	Lanark
		Lanark

C.D.	Sub.	Name
	9	Lavant
	10	Montague
	11	Pakenham
	12	Ramsay
		Almonte
		Carleton Place (1/4)
	13	Sherbrooke, South
24		*Leeds*
	1	Bastard & South Burgess
	2	Crosby, North
		Westport
	3	Crosby, South
		Newboro
	4	Elizabethtown
		Brockville
	5	Elmsley, South
	6	Escott, Front of
	7	Kitley
	8	Leeds & Lansdowne, Front of
		Gananoque
	9	Leeds & Lansdowne, Rear of
	10	Yonge, Front of
	11	Yonge & Escott, Rear of
		Athens
25		*Lennox and Addington*
	1	Adolphustown
	2	Amherst Island
	3	Camden East
		Newburgh
	4	Denbigh, Abinger & Ashby
	5	Ernestown
		Bath
	6	Fredericksburgh, North
		Napanee (1/4)
	7	Fredericksburgh, South
	8	Kaladar, Angelsea & Effingham
	9	Richmond
		Napanee (3/4)
	10	Sheffield

C.D.	Sub.	Name
26		*Toronto Metropolitan Area*
	1	Etobicoke
		Mimico
		New Toronto
		Long Branch
	2	Scarborough
	3	York
	4	York, East
		Leaside
	5	York, North
		Weston
	6	Toronto
		Swansea
		Forest Hill
28		*Middlesex*
	1	Adelaide
		Strathroy (2/3)
	2	Biddulph
		Lucan
	3	Caradoc
		Strathroy (1/3)
		Indian Reserve
	4	Delaware
	5	Dorchester, North
	6	Ekfrid
		Glencoe (2/3)
	7	Lobo
	8	London
		London (1/2)
	9	McGillivray
	10	Metcalfe
	11	Mosa
		Glencoe (1/3)
		Newbury
		Wardsville
	12	Nissouri, West
	13	Westminster
		London (1/2)
	14	Williams, East
		Ailsa Craig

C.D.	Sub.	Name
	15	Williams, West
		Park Hill
29		*Muskoka*
	1	Huntsville
		Chaffey
		Stisted
		Stevenson
		Port Sydney
		Brunel
	2	Muskoka Lakes
		Cardwell
		Watt
		Windermere
	2	Port Carling
		Monk
		Bala
		Medora & Wood
	3	Bracebridge
		Macaulay
		Draper
		Oakley
	4	Gravenhurst
		Muskoka
		Morrison
		Ryde
	5	Lake of Bays
		Ridout
		McLean
		Franklin
		Sinclair
	6	Georgian Bay
		Freeman
		Gibson
		Baxter
		Indian Reserve
31		*Norfolk*
	1	Charlotteville
	2	Houghton
	3	Middleton
		Delhi (1/2)

C.D.	Sub.	Name
	4	Townsend
		Waterford
		Simcoe (1/4)
	5	Walsingham, North
	6	Walsingham, South
		Port Rowan
	7	Windham
		Delhi (1/2)
		Simcoe (1/4)
	8	Woodhouse
		Port Dover
		Simcoe (1/2)
32		*Northumberland*
	1	Alnwick
		Indian Reserve
	2	Brighton
		Brighton
	3	Cramahe
		Colborne
	4	Haldimand
	5	Hamilton
		Cobourg
	6	Monagham, South
	7	Murray
	8	Percy
		Hastings
	9	Seymour
		Campbellford
33		*Ontario*
	1	Brock
		Cannington
	2	Mara
	3	Pickering
		Ajax
		Pickering
	4	Rama
	5	Reach
		Port Perry
	6	Scott
	7	Scugog
		Indian Reserve

C.D.	Sub.	Name
	8	Thorah
		Beaverton
	9	Uxbridge
		Uxbridge
	10	Whitby
		Whitby
	11	Whitby, East
		Oshawa
34		*Oxford*
	1	Blandford
		Woodstock (1/3)
	2	Bleinheim
	3	Dereham
		Tillsonburg
	4	Nissouri, East
	5	Norwich, North
		Norwich
	6	Norwich, South
	7	Oxford, East
		Woodstock (1/3)
	8	Oxford, North
		Beachville
		Ingersoll (1/2)
	9	Oxford, West
		Ingersoll (1/2)
		Woodstock (1/3)
	10	Zorra, East
		Tavistock
	11	Zorra, West
		Embro
36		*Peel*
	1	Albion
		Bolton
		Caledon East (1/2)
	2	Caledon
		Caledon East (1/2)
	3	Chinguacousy
		Brampton
	4	Mississauga
		Port Credit
		Streetsville

C.D.	Sub.	Name
	5	Toronto Gore
37		*Perth*
	1	Blanshard
		St. Mary's
	2	Downie
		Stratford (2/5)
	3	Easthope, North
		Stratford (1/5)
	4	Easthope, South
		Stratford (1/5)
		Tavistock
	5	Ellice
		Stratford (1/5)
	6	Elma
		Listowel (1/2)
	7	Fullarton
		Mitchell (1/2)
	8	Hibbert
	9	Logan
		Mitchell (1/2)
	10	Mornington
		Milverton
	11	Wallace
		Listowel (1/2)
38		*Peterborough*
	1	Asphodel
		Norwood
	2	Belmont & Methuen
		Havelock
	3	Burleigh & Anstruther
	4	Chandos
	5	Douro
		Lakefield (1/2)
	6	Dummer
	7	Ennismore
	8	Galway & Cavendish
	9	Harvey
	10	Monaghan, North
		Peterborough (1/2)
	11	Otonabee
		Peterborough (1/2)
		Indian Reserve

C.D.	Sub.	Name
	12	Smith
		Lakefield (1/2)
39		*Prescott*
	1	Alfred
		Alfred
	2	Caledonia
	3	Hawkesbury, East
	4	Hawkesbury, West
		Hawkesbury
		Vankleek Hill
	5	Longueuil
		L'Orignal
	6	Plantagenet, North
		Plantagenet
	7	Plantagenet, South
		St-Isidore-de-Prescott
40		*Prince Edward*
	1	Ameliasburg
	2	Athol
	3	Hallowell
		Picton
		Bloomfield
		Wellington (1/2)
	4	Hillier
		Wellington (1/2)
	5	Marysburgh, North
	6	Marysburgh, South
	7	Sophiasburgh
42		*Renfrew*
	1	Admaston
	2	Algona, North
	3	Algona, South
		Indian Reserve
	4	Alice & Fraser
	5	Bagot & Blythfield
	6	Bromley
	7	Brougham
	8	Brudenell & Lyndoch
	9	Grattan
		Eganville (1/2)

C.D.	Sub.	Name
	10	Griffith & Matawatchan
	11	Hagarty & Richards
		Killaloe Station
	13	Horton
		Renfrew
	14	McNab
		Arnprior
		Braeside
	15	Pembroke
		Pembroke
	16	Petawawa
		Petawawa
	17	Radcliffe
	18	Raglan
	20	Ross
		Cobden
	21	Sebastopol
	22	Sherwood, Jones & Burns
		Barry's Bay
	23	Stafford
	24	Westmeath
		Beachburg
	25	Wilberforce
		Eganville (1/2)
43		*Russell*
	1	Cambridge
		Casselman
	2	Clarence
		Rockland
	3	Cumberland
	4	Russell
44		*Simcoe*
	1	Adjala
	2	Essa
		Alliston (1/2)
	3	Flos
		Elmvale
		Wasaga Beach (1/2)
	4	Gwillimbury, West
		Bradford

C.D.	*Sub.*	*Name*
	5	Innisfil
		Cookstown
		Barrie (1/4)
	6	Matchedash
	7	Medonte
		Coldwater
	8	Nottawasaga
		Collingwood
		Stayner
		Creemore
	9	Orillia
		Orillia
	10	Oro
	11	Sunnidale
		Wasaga Beach (1/2)
	12	Tay
		Midland
		Penetanguishene (2/3)
		Port McNicoll
		Victoria Harbour
	13	Tecumseh
		Beeton
		Tottenham
		Alliston (1/2)
	14	Tiny
		Penetanguishene (1/3)
		Indian Reserve
	15	Tosorontio
	16	Vespra
		Barrie (3/4)
45		*Stormont*
	1	Cornwall
		Cornwall
		Indian Reserve
	2	Finch
		Finch
	3	Osnabruck
	4	Roxborough
49		*Victoria*
	1	Bexley
	2	Carden

C.D.	Sub.	Name
	3	Dalton
	4	Eldon
		Woodville
	5	Emily
		Omemee
	6	Fenelon
		Fenelon Falls
		Sturgeon Point
	7	Laxton, Digby & Longford
	8	Mariposa
	9	Ops
		Lindsay
	10	Somerville
	11	Verulam
		Bobcaygeon
50		*Waterloo*
	1	Dumfries North
		Galt
		Ayr
	2	Waterloo
		Kitchener
		Waterloo
		Hespeler
		Preston
		Bridgeport
	3	Wellesley
		Wellesley
	4	Wilmot
		New Hamburg
	5	Woolwich
		Elmira
51		*Niagara*
	1	Fort Erie
		Bertie
		Crystal Beach
	2	Welland
		Crowland (1/2)
	3	Port Colborne
		Humberstone
	4	Pelham
		Fonthill

C.D.	Sub.	Name
	5	Niagara Falls
		Crowland (1/2)
		Willoughby
		Chippawa
	6	Thorold
		Thorold
	7	Wainfleet
	8	Lincoln West
		South Grimsby
		Caistor
		Gainsborough
	9	Lincoln
		Clinton
		Beamsville
		Louth (2/3)
	10	Grimsby
		North Grimsby
	11	St. Catharines
		Louth (1/3)
	12	Niagara-on-the-Lake
		Niagara
52		*Wellington*
	1	Arthur
		Mount Forest
	2	Eramosa
	3	Erin
		Erin
	4	Garafraxa, West
	5	Guelph
		Guelph
	6	Luther, West
		Arthur
	7	Maryborough
		Drayton (1/2)
	8	Minto
		Harriston
		Clifford
		Palmerston
	9	Nichol
		Fergus
		Elora

C.D.	Sub.	Name
	10	Peel
		Drayton (1/2)
	11	Pilkington
	12	Puslinch
53		*Wentworth*
	1	Ancaster
	2	Beverly
	3	Binbrook
	4	Flamborough, East
		Waterdown
	5	Flamborough, West
		Dundas
	6	Glanford
	7	Saltfleet
		Stoney Creek
	8	Hamilton
		Burlington
54		*York*
	1	Georgina
		Indian Reserve
		Sutton
		Gwillimbury, North
	2	King
	3	Gwillimbury, East
		Newmarket (1/4)
	4	Whitchurch-Stouffville
		Whitchurch
	5	Newmarket (3/4)
	6	Aurora
	7	Richmond Hill
	8	Markham
		Markham
	9	Vaughan
		Woodbridge

APPENDIX B   CENSUS SUBDIVISIONS
BASE MAP

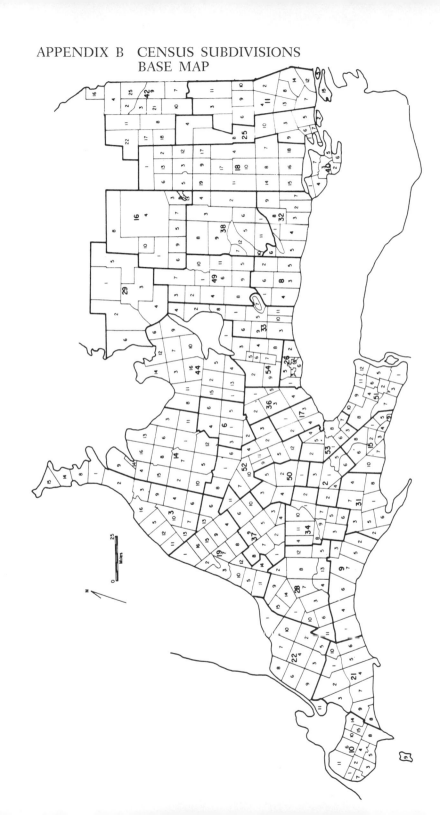

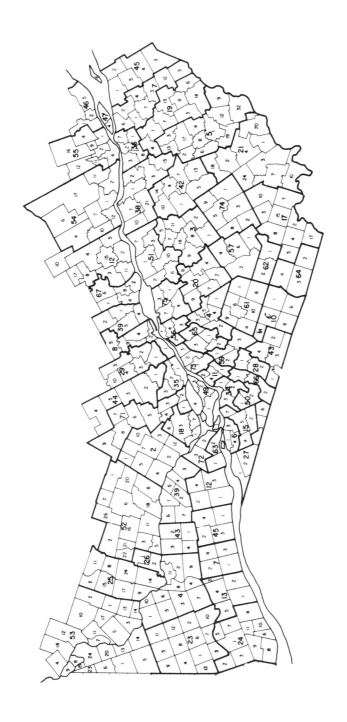

APPENDIX C URBANIZATION
ESTIMATION PROJECT

PURPOSE: To estimate the amount of urbanized area in the Windsor–Québec City Axis in the zones defined by the study.

DATA: Ontario—Minister of Treasury, Economics and Intergovernmental Affairs: Regional Development Branch Land-Use Maps (scale: 1 inch to 4 miles).

Maps included were: Lake Ontario Region, Toronto Region, Georgian Bay Region, Niagara Region, Eastern Ontario Region, Lake Erie Region, St. Clair Region, Mid-Western Region (8).

Québec—Canada Land Inventory (scale: 1:250,000).

Maps included were: 31J, 31G, 31I, 31H, 31P, 21M, 21L, 21E. The area also included 31K, and 31F but there were no land-use maps for these areas.

Air photos were used as source data and Ontario maps have been ground checked.

ACTUAL PROCEDURE:

1. Nine students were hired. With one exception they were geography students with no direct cartographic experience, but enough geographic background to understand the purposes and methods to be used.

2. Definition of urban land-use.

Ontario: Relevant land-use areas are divided into:

Pink—residential, including cottages

Dark red—commercial and industrial

Light green—agriculture, private open space, golf courses, and other rural land uses

Dark green—Public open space-parts, playing fields, county forests, etc.

Brown—extractive industry (surface mining)

Spotted green—large institutional holdings, Indian reserves

Grey—built-up area (on base map)

The definition of urban land-use includes all *pink* and *dark red* areas. When a pink area obviously referred to cottages this was noted. All dark red areas were included without discretion even when an area was an isolated patch removed from any urban centre. *Dark green* areas are also included if they are contiguous or within urban areas so long as they do not inflate the figures. For instance, if a conservation area adjoined a city but was ten times its size, it was not included. *Spotted green* is counted when it obviously refers to institutions such as hospitals. Urbanized portions of Indian reserves are coloured pink. Any *brown* or *light green* totally within an urbanized centre was included; otherwise it was not. All *grey* was counted as were airports, although a guess as to their size had to be made.

Québec: The relevant land-use areas were divided into B and O which were subsequently coloured red and green respectively.

B (built-up area) includes: all compact settlements, built-up portions of cities, towns, and villages, including any non-agricultural open space which forms an integral part of the urban agglomeration, and isolated units separated from compact settlements which were used for indus trial, commercial, and associated urban purposes (these include mine buildings, garbage dumps, saw mills, but do not include farm buildings or anything smaller than 6.4 acres).

O (outdoor recreation) includes: cottages and beach areas, parks, historical sites, golf courses, ski slopes, summer camps.

All B was counted except in a few instances where large army camps were totally labelled B but for this project should not have been.

All O was included.

3. Boundary location.
Ontario: The land-use maps were covered with plastic vellum upon which the zone boundaries were marked. These were fairly easy to locate since most of the boundaries are indicated on the land-use maps.

Québec: The zones were outlined on separate vellum overlays using Army survey maps as base guides. Census maps and the zone manual were used to locate the boundaries. However, the boundaries are not located as accurately as would be liked because there was considerable difficulty in deciding precise locations since there was insufficient information.

4. Calculations.
Ontario:
a) Using transparencies of graph paper, the number of squares of urbanized land was found for each subdivision. (It was 10 to an inch of graph paper).
b) The number of squares that were urban and the number of these that were obviously cottages were recorded on worksheets. Considerable care was taken to ensure that all patches were counted.
c) These results were then transformed into square miles. (This was done by multiplying the number of squares by .16. That is, since 1 inch equals 4 miles, therefore, 1 square inch equals 16 square miles and since there are 100 squares on the graph paper to 1 square inch there is .16 square miles to the square of graph paper). All the above informa-

tion was recorded on summary sheets for each division.

d) The same procedure was used to estimate the total area in each subdivision.

e) The number of towns mentioned on the land-use maps but not bearing any land-use colouring was found for each subdivision.

f) The above information was recorded in the data book.

Québec.

a) Same as a) above

b) Separate totals for red and green, and red only were calculated as for b) above.

c) Same as c) above; however, transformation factor was .1557. (That is at a scale of 1:250,000, 1 inch equals 3.9457 miles, therefore 1 square inch equals 15.57 square miles and since there are 100 squares of graph paper in 1 square inch, there is .1557 square miles in one square of graph paper).

d) Not done because of unreliability of boundaries.

e) and f) Same as above.

5. Procedures used for checking calculations.

Ontario.

a) The number of squares for each incidence of urban land-use was recorded separately. This figure was then checked against a count of the separate occurrences to ensure all were included. Some students also used a system of ticks to ensure everything was counted.

b) Each of the land-use maps were spot-checked. That is, three or four zones were chosen as a representative sample and were re-calculated. If there was more than 5 per cent disagreement with the original calculations, more zones were checked. This procedure acted as a verification of calculations and of the quality of work done by the students. When the final figures were tallied they were given a visual check. That is, each subdivision was looked at to see if the figures seemed reasonable. In this way, both the calculations and the recording of figures were checked to ensure there was not a mix-up.

c) One final check was made on border towns, since many places in Ontario straddle the boundaries between two or more zones. The manual was used to determine the subdivision of areas of the municipalities to townships.

d) A check of the conversion from squares of graph paper to square miles was made by totalling, for a division, the number of squares and the number of square miles in each subdivision. If the former, times .16, did not equal the latter, then the conversions were re-checked individually to find the error.

Québec.
a) Same as a) above
b) Same as b) above
c) Since there was a considerable difficulty in locating boundaries, a check was made to ensure that each occurrence of urbanization was located in the right zone. Therefore, the amount of urbanization is correctly estimated, but using the boundaries to estimate total area would have had little value.
d) Same as d) above.

DERIVATION OF RESULTS:

Ontario. The final figures were divided into Maximum and Minimum. The Maximum including all areas counted and the Minimum excluding areas that were thought to be cottages.

Québec. Also two figures stated MAX, and MIN. The MIN figure includes only the red-coloured areas (built-up). The MAX figures have three components: the red areas, the green areas (outdoor recreation), and a correction factor. This correction factor was considered necessary because a large number of towns in Québec had no urbanization stated for them on the land-use maps. In practice there seems to be no urbanized area smaller than one square of graph paper. Thus it was decided to say that the average size of those unaccounted towns would be 1/3 of a square or .0514 square miles. The correction factor was found by multiplying .0514 times the number of towns in this category (found in step 4.e) and then added in to the MAX figure.

One division was not covered by land-use maps and its figure had to be derived separately. Pontiac's (53) figures are derived by listing all towns by subdivisions as on the Army survey map. The areas were recorded for those places listed in the 1971 census manual, and they formed the MIN figure. For all other places, the correction factor was used and this was added to form the MAX figure. Thus, no recreation is included in the MAX figure.

RECORDING OF RESULTS:

Ontario. In its data book there is the following information:
Col. 1—Number of graph paper squares in whole subdivisions
Col. 2—Number of graph paper squares of total urbanized area
Col. 3—Number of graph paper squares of total minus cottages
Col. 4—Area of subdivision in square miles, calculated by Col. 1 x .16
Col. 5—Area of subdivision recorded on density printout
Col. 6—Square miles of urbanized area Col. 2 x .16 forms MAX
Col. 7—Square miles of urbanized area minus cottages Col. 3 x .16 forms MIN
Col. 8—Number of towns without any corresponding urbanized land-use markings.

Québec

Col. 2—Number of graph paper squares of red and green

Col. 3—Number of graph paper squares of red only

Col. 4—Total area of subdivision listed in density printout

Col. 6—Square miles of red and green areas calculated from Col. 2 x .1557

Col. 7—Square miles of red only calculated from Col. 3 x .1557

Col. 8a—Correction factor found by multiplying 8b x .0514

Col. 8b—Number of towns without any corresponding urbanized land-use markings

Col. 9—MAX calculated by adding Col. 7 and Col. 8a

Col. 10—MIN repetition of Col. 6

Totals for each division are also recorded (except Ontario Col. 8 and Québec Cols. 4 and 7).

CODING OF RESULTS:

For Ontario Cols. 6 and 7, MAX and MIN respectively were coded to fill from 61-65 and 66-70 on data cards as two fields of 5.2, right-justified, no decimal typed.

For Québec Cols. 9 and 10 were used in the same manner.

Coding was verified.

Punching was verified.

EVALUATION OF PROJECT METHOD:

1. There are three main possible types of error.

a) Source data:

Unavoidable—comes from the fact that the land-use maps themselves may be wrong. In the case of Québec the necessary generalization probably results in an *underestimation* of urbanized land, when counting red areas only. Including green would then overestimate since o areas had a wide definition. Underestimation of red probably is a result of generalizing land-use from air photos and since urban land-use is so minor, it is bound to lose out.

b) Subjectivity in what to include or not include as urbanized:

Avoidable but necessary—in Ontario when is a park urban-used or not? Where are the airport boundaries? Is a blotch pink or brown (colouring on some maps is almost indistinguishable)? What is a cottage area?

c) Mechanical:

Hopefully minimized by the checking procedure.

EVALUATION OF RESULTS:

The most reliable figures are the MAX for Ontario and the MIN for Québec since these required little subjectivity. However, they are not measuring the same information and are therefore not comparable.

For the best continuity and comparability between the two provinces the MIN figures for Ontario and Québec should be used. However, this must include a rider that Québec's MIN is probably an underestimation and Ontario's MIN is more accurate.

The prime concern of this study is a minority land-use, and it seems reasonable to state that some of the urbanization in Québec would have been swallowed up by the cartographic generalizing. This is especially evident when in Ontario areas as small as 1/10 of a graph paper square are mentioned but in Québec nothing smaller than one whole square is outlined.

By definition the two MAX's are reasonably comparable but Québec's MAX has a wider definition because of those phenomena included under outdoor recreation. In this case the figures for Québec are probably overestimated.

In summary, the figures derived seem to be better than any others seen so far since they are directly tied to where urbanization actually is and not to where politically defined limits of a population centre are located. The estimates found here are probably more accurate for Ontario than for Québec.